second
edition

INTRODUCTION
TO
CRIMINOLOGY

Vernon Fox
Florida State University

PRENTICE-HALL, INC., Englewood Cliffs, N.J. 07632

Library of Congress Cataloging in Publication Data

Fox, Vernon Brittain,
  Introduction to criminology.

  Bibliography: p.
  Includes index.
  1. Crime and criminals. 2. Criminal justice,
administration of. 3. Criminal psychology. I. Title.
HV6025.F67-1985   364   84-3314
ISBN   0-13-479940-2

Editorial/production supervision and
  interior design: **Esther S. Koehn**
Cover design: **Lundgren Graphics Ltd.**
Manufacturing buyer: **Ed O'Dougherty**

© 1985, 1976 by Prentice-Hall, Inc., Englewood Cliffs, New Jersey 07632

*All rights reserved. No part of this book
may be reproduced, in any form
or by any means, without permission
in writing from the publisher.*

Printed in the United States of America

10 9 8 7 6 5 4 3

ISBN 0-13-479940-2   01

Prentice-Hall International, Inc., *London*
Prentice-Hall of Australia Pty. Limited, *Sydney*
Editora Prentice-Hall do Brasil, Ltda., *Rio de Janeiro*
Prentice-Hall Canada Inc., *Toronto*
Prentice-Hall of India Private Limited, *New Delhi*
Prentice-Hall of Japan, Inc., *Tokyo*
Prentice-Hall of Southeast Asia Pte. Ltd., *Singapore*
Whitehall Books Limited, *Wellington, New Zealand*

Dedicated To My Family

CONTENTS

eight

PSYCHOLOGICAL APPROACHES   *141*

nine

PSYCHIATRIC APPROACHES   *167*

ten

GANGS, GROUPS, AND ROLES   *203*

eleven

CULTURAL AND ANTHROPOLOGICAL APPROACHES   *227*

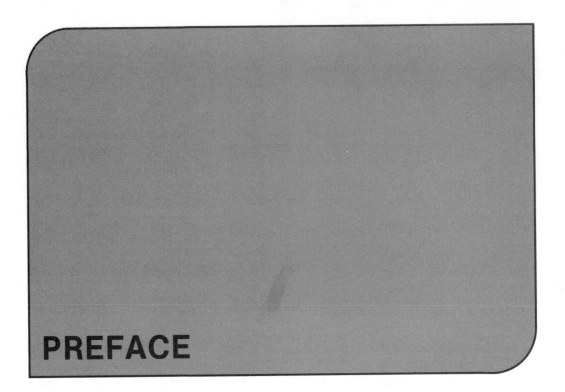

PREFACE

The purpose of this book is to provide a broad viewpoint of criminal behavior and the justice system: to help practitioners make use of theory and to help scholars translate theory into practice, thereby giving greater meaning to the entire criminal justice system.

Too frequently there has been some lack of communication between theorists and practitioners in the criminal justice system. Many practitioners view theory as rhetoric drastically divergent from reality, as is humorously indicated in this excerpt from a speech by candidate George Smathers in his successful attempt in 1950 to unseat Florida's Senator Claude Pepper:

> Are you aware that the candidate is known all over Washington as a shameless extrovert? Not only that, but this man is reliably reported to have practiced nepotism with his sister-in-law, and he has a sister who was once a thespian in wicked New York. He matriculated with co-eds at the University, and it is an established fact that before his marriage, he habitually practiced celibacy. [*Newsweek*, July 11, 1955]

On the other hand, some academicians contend that practice without research-based theory is quackery. Many theorists who have worked out explanations for criminal and delinquent behavior view with some contempt those practitioners who "work by the manual," and "don't really know what they are doing." Either extreme viewpoint is unfortunate for effectiveness in the criminal justice system because, in reality, both theory and practice are needed, and they can be mutually supportive for the benefit of the criminal justice system.

Human behavior is a unitary phenomenon that cannot really be separated into categories like sociology, psychology, biology, economics, and other disciplines. Such separation is a convenience to bring the mass of available information into proportions that can be manipulated by man. The approaches to human behavior are based in the natural sciences that include chemistry and biology and the social sciences that include sociology and anthropology. Psychology, a most important science in understanding human behavior, is having difficulty in deciding whether it is a social or behavioral science or a "hard" natural science. The arts of medicine, psychiatry, social work, education, and other therapeutic and casework approaches use the basic sciences while formulating treatment or people-changing approaches to behavior. Philosophy and religion were the first to evolve the ethical systems on which law and criminal justice are based. All these disciplines are necessary for the understanding of human behavior, including criminal behavior. The attempt to understand human behavior from a single viewpoint reminds us of the five blind men describing the elephant—each is "right" as far as he goes, but his failure to accept other viewpoints leaves his view of human behavior incredibly limited.

The spectre of an academic criminologist lost in a maximum-custody prison or major police department is just as ludicrous as that of a prison warden, correctional officer, or police chief lost in a seminar on criminological theory. The interdependence of theory and practice is vital; they are both part of the same field. Theory without practice is just as sterile as practice without theory. Good theory emerges from successful practice; a good practitioner in the criminal justice system needs to know good theory to give his or her work meaning.

The last *Summa Theologica* has been written. In the thirteenth century, Thomas Aquinas recorded the sum total of human knowledge in his time. Knowledge had probably doubled by the eighteenth century when the Industrial Revolution transformed the economic and social system. It has doubled and redoubled many times since, with parabolic acceleration by the last half of the twentieth century. Consequently, it is no longer possible to presume to be able to acquire, retain, and synthesize all knowledge into a single theory of human behavior. This is why intelligent scholars from varying backgrounds develop different theories of behavior, including criminal behavior, that are divergent to the point of being dichotomously opposed in some instances. Some study rats in mazes and base their understanding on punishment and reward; others are concerned with values and guilt feelings and base their understandings on subconscious motivation; some view humans as an easily programmed computer; some see the value of telepathy and the spirits; others focus on the "here-and-now" responsibilities of people; and the dry-witted poet debunks them all.

Appreciation goes to all the scholars whose theoretical contributions are summarized in this book. More specific appreciation is expressed to the wonderful people who contributed to the preparation of the manuscript, particularly Mary Harris and Carolyne Richardson. Without their help, this book could not have been completed.

Many diverse and complementary viewpoints and approaches to the understanding of criminal behavior and the justice system are presented within this book. It is hoped that neither practitioners nor theorists will reject any of them summarily and without exhausting their potential, but that they will accept them as contributions to understanding of complex social phenomena. People of good will can live with honest differences in a reasonable way for the benefit of all society.

VERNON FOX
Florida State University

one

INTRODUCTION TO CRIMINOLOGY

Crime is a by-product of civilization. When Dr. Pangloss was shipwrecked on the coast of Portugal, as discussed in the famous book by de Beaumont and de Tocqueville, *On the Penitentiary System in the United States*, published in 1833, he inferred that he was in a civilized country because he saw men in chains and, further, that when there is no crime, a community cannot be far advanced in civilization. In 1910, Winston Churchill told the House of Commons:

> The mood and temper of the public with regard to the treatment of crime and criminals is one of the most unfailing tests of the civilization of any country. [Quoted in Barnes and Teeters, 1959, p. 50]

In discussing the history of law, Seagle (1945, p. 245) has indicated that no advanced country is without a "stupendous amount of criminality." Durkheim (1959, p. 65) has said that crime is a natural phenomenon of society and is an integral part of all societies.

Homicide, theft, and other offenses occur in primitive society, but the reaction to these acts is by the victim or his or her family. With the advance of civilization comes a system of justice based on religion or law that places the responsibility for sanctions against commission of "crime" on society's system of criminal justice. The victim no longer "takes the law into his own hands."

To understand crime, it is necessary to acquire an overview of human behavior itself as well as of the forces that hold human society in shape. The concept of criminal behavior came after some particular human behaviors were labeled as deviant and officially adjudged to be criminal. The forces that have traditionally held human society together have been those of religion and law; in combination, these have become the base of the criminal justice system. The academic disciplines and professions concerned with criminal behavior are psychology, psychiatry, social work, and education. The academic disciplines and professions concerned with the justice system are sociology, anthropology, economics, political science, religion, and the law. All of these fields make significant contributions to the understanding of criminal behavior and the justice system, and their contributions must be acknowledged in order to understand the task-oriented discipline and field of endeavor known as *criminology*.

Many social scientists have thought for a long time that crime is a normal function of society. For example, Tannenbaum wrote (Barnes and Teeters, 1st ed., 1943, Foreword), "Crime is eternal—as eternal as society. . . . The more complex society becomes, the more difficult it is for the individual and the more frequent the human failures. Multiplication of laws and of sanctions for their observance merely increases the evil."

Florita (1953) has also indicated that crime, like sin, is normal in society and that it is man-made sanctions and laws that are abnormal. Durkheim (1900; also reported in Lunden, 1958) argued similarly as early as the 1890s. Bonger (1916) has said that modern societies structure themselves so that a constant proportion of the population comes into conflict with law enforcement.

The thesis that all societies have a "saturation point" in crime was advanced by Ferri (Grupp 1968) and several other early social scientists, who discussed "the law of criminal saturation" (de Quiros, 1911, pp. 11-21; also Barnes and Teeters, 1959). When the saturation point is reached, crime becomes a political issue; controversy arises between law and order and relaxation through "decriminalization" of laws in some areas. Examples from the 1960s and 1970s include concern about legalization of marijuana and some other drugs, prostitution, excessive use of alcohol, homosexuality between consenting adults, and some forms of gambling. On the other hand, when there is a gap between the crime rate and the saturation point, there is margin for tightening up the criminal laws. (For example, see Barron, 1964, and Menninger, 1968.)

The concept of normalcy of crime in society is supported by its prominence in literature, drama, motion pictures, and television. The pressure of group norms in the forms of law and sanctions encroaches on the freedom of the individual to behave regardless of society because the individual has to fit into the socially defined roles to be "free" and to be effective in society. This conflict generates ambiguous reactions in many conforming individuals who may reach their own saturation point and think, "To hell with what the neighbors think!" This makes crime and violence in the arts and the media forms of vicarious escape. A law-abiding citizen, for example, sometimes has difficulty in deciding who was the "good guy" and who was the "bad guy"—Robin Hood or the sheriff! Victor Hugo's *Les Misérables* depicts an escaped convict, Jean Valjean, who is followed for years by the dedicated Constable Javert. The escaped convict is eventually caught, but the story ends with Constable Javert's guilt-motivated suicide for what he has done. At St. Joseph, Missouri, there is a museum and monument dedicated to the memory of Jesse James; many residents in that area tell visitors that "this is Jesse James country."

Crime and violence are a part of modern civilized culture. Although primitive man had violence, he had no "crime" as it is known in the modern civilized world. Crime and violence lie at the fringe areas of organized society, defining the limits of conforming behavior, identifying behavior that is not to be tolerated as well as the areas of stress. As society becomes more populous and complex, social controls must be stronger, and consequently crime rates will rise. Crime is a normal phenomenon when the behavioral relationships between the individual and society are defined by the criminal law.

Crime is an index of social pathology. If a series of blank maps of a city were used to plot the incidence of crime, the incidence of welfare recipients, health problems, unemployment, and other indices of social breakdown, the configurations would be similar. Crime, then, is only one index, if a most visible one, of social breakdown. Therefore, crime is not a unitary phenomenon but one of many, and other factors must also be considered in the study of crime. Crime has the function of indicating the limits of social control over individual behavior. The interrelationships between individuals are harmonious in a smoothly functioning society, but crime and violence appear when society is disorganized, floundering, and beset with social and economic problems. Any reduction of crime must be based on a broad social and economic approach that will enhance the ability of the social order to serve the economic, social, and emotional needs of the individuals who make up that society. Any understanding of crime must be based on an understanding of human behavior, of the development of society, and of the evolvement of a criminal justice system that provides control of "deviant" behavior.

THE EMERGENCE OF HUMANS

The earth is estimated to have been created or established in some way about 4½ billion years ago. The first primordial seas appeared about 4 billion years ago, and the first life, single-celled algae and bacteria, appeared in the water about 3½ billion years ago, apparently in the equatorial regions of Africa and India. The first shell-bearing invertebrate animals developed about 600 million years ago, and small amphibians ventured onto land about 400 million years ago. Reptiles and insects appeared a little over 300 million years ago. The age of dinosaurs was between 200 and 100 million years ago, during which time birds and mammals appeared. The earliest primates developed about 70 million years ago, and monkeys and apes evolved about 40 million years ago. The oldest primate with humanlike traits, *Ramapithecus*, evolved about 10 million years ago in Africa and India. (For a more detailed description, see Wendt, 1972, and the series entitled *The Emergence of Man*.) *Australopithecus*, the closest primate ancestor to humans, appeared in Africa about 5 million years ago. The oldest tool fashioned by manlike primates has been found in Africa and is estimated to be 2 million years old. *Homo erectus*, probably the first true man depending upon the definition, emerged in Africa and the East Indies about 1,300,000 years ago and migrated to all the Old World tropical areas around 900,000 years ago. Then he migrated to the temperate zones and learned to control and use fire. About 400,000 years ago, he began making artificial shelters from branches. Humans somewhat in their present form evolved about 240,000 years ago; before then, their predecessors were animals in the wild, who did not communicate with language, nor did they have values from which laws later emerged.

The Neanderthals, emerging in Europe about 100,000 years ago and remaining until the late Ice Age between 20,000 and 30,000 years ago, are generally credited with developing the beginnings of "human" behavior, which means that they began to interact symbolically with language and other symbols in social situations. The values and value systems that ultimately developed became, much later, philosophies and ethics and laws. (See *The Emergence of Man* series, particularly George Constable's *The Neanderthals* (1973), p. 7.) That spoken language was developed in the Neanderthal period is inferred from the fact that increasingly sophisticated tools could have been made only by people who could transmit information. Simultaneously, the development of values depended upon the development of language. Early humans used words as symbols without a past or future, subsequently complicated by the introduction of plurals, then generalized concepts that eventually developed into sophisticated spoken language. (Referred to as levels of abstraction by semanticists, the progression may go from cow to cows to cattle to cattle market to the market to the economy to ideology and then to philosophy and theology. It is at the introduction of the market that values creep into abstract thinking, and they can be well systematized by the time the progression reaches philosophy and theology, from which modern law emerges.)

The Neanderthals buried their dead in ritualistic ceremony as early as 60,000 B.C., according to evidence found at Shanidar Cave in the rugged Zagros Mountains of Northern Iraq. This is interpreted as the beginning of religious rites and belief in the afterlife. These funerals, according to archeologists, indicated that humans were becoming keenly aware of some essential quality of human life, whether spirit or soul, that continued to exist after death somewhere and in some form. Compassion for others was obvious among the Neanderthals; their concern for the aged and handicapped is suggested also by remains at Shanidar. Thus the beginning of literally "human" behavior is based on the development of spoken language of an elementary sort and the consequent emergence of values and value systems.

Cro-Magnon man emerged between 30,000 and 20,000 B.C. and is considered to be the immediate predecessor of modern man. The disappearance of the Neanderthals was due either to annihilation by the more intelligent and skilled Cro-Magnon man or the extreme climate of the Ice Age. Superbly painted caves, oil lamps, belief in existence in afterlife as shown by funeral rites, and tool-making were characteristic of Cro-Magnon man, who could communicate by speech. His loosely fitted clothing appeared around 10,000 B.C. with the invention of the bone needle. He invented the bow and arrow in Europe around 10,000 B.C., domesticated the sheep and dog around 8500 B.C., and soon after developed the beginnings of agriculture. The first city, called Jericho, was established between 9000 and 8000 B.C. Agriculture is considered to have been the reason for the development of cities. Man gradually progressed from a pastoral economy to an agricultural economy and from a subsistence to a market economy between 8000 and 2000 B.C. It was at this point that permanent settlements and land control and ownership became important. Although this represented a gradual development, the ancient world had become an agricultural, market society with cities by 2000 B.C.[1] Wars in the modern sense developed at this time. The wheel was invented in Sumer about 3500 B.C. and increased the potential of technology for man. By this time, his value system had produced the very rudimentary ancient Sumerian Code, the beginnings of the criminal law system. In about 1750 B.C. came the Code

---

[1]Ethiopia had the world's longest-surviving dynasty. Deposed in 1974, Emperor Haile Selassie I, Lion of Judah, King of Kings, was the 225th active successor of the dynasty established by King Solomon and the Queen of Sheba 3,000 years ago. See Ernest Kay, *Dictionary of International Biography* (London: Dictionary of International Biography Co., 1967), p. lv.

of Hammurabi in Babylon, then the Law of Moses about 1215 B.C., and the Twelve Tables or the Greco-Roman Codes in 451–450 B.C.

It is interesting to note that drinking probably began around 4000 B.C., when grapes were cultivated in Mesopotamia and the Transcaucasion region of the Near East. Wine lists from around 1000 B.C. have been discovered in Egypt.

Writing by pictures began in Sumer between 4000 and 3500 B.C.; writing with symbols began around 3000 B.C., although there has been some evidence of written communication as early as 6000 B.C. The earliest languages that used the past, future, and subjunctive tenses were the so-called classical languages, Hebrew, Greek, and Latin. The earliest monuments with Hebrew inscriptions were in the ninth or tenth century B.C., having written on them a mixture of several Semitic languages. Egyptian documents from the sixteenth century B.C. have revealed Semitic words. Inscriptions in Greek engraved on stones found in Greece date back to the eighth century B.C., and they became numerous in the fifth and later centuries. Latin dates from 600 B.C., though some of the preceding languages date back to the Etruscan invasion of Italy in the eighth century B.C. Evidence is that sophisticated civilization has been developing for only a few thousand years.

The society of humans has developed by their talking about what they do and what happens to them. Language and religion are basic to organized society. Society is based on kinship and tribal ties; and religion provided the first political unity beyond that provided by family and kinship ties. In fact, religion formed the base of social control until the eighteenth century, when the criminal law developed as it is now known.

Abraham had led the Semites from Ur and arrived in Canaan about 1730 B.C. Moses led them from their slavery in Egypt about 1220 B.C., eventually settling them again in Canaan (now Israel), and developed Judaism through the Law of Moses given him by God on Mount Sinai about 1215 B.C. Judaism became the first major monotheistic religion, although Egypt had had a monotheistic sun-god for ten years after 1367 B.C. Hinduism developed slowly from about 1500 B.C. from a combination of the Aryans and the people they conquered, and the prose writing called the Brahmanas appeared around 800–600 B.C. Zoroaster founded his religion in the late seventh and early sixth centuries B.C. by reforming the religion of the ancient Iranians that had begun around 1500 B.C. Buddhism was begun by Gautama Buddha in the sixth century B.C. as an offshoot of Hinduism; it has become the major religion in Asia. Christianity began as a sect of Judaism at the time of Christ, but in 325 A.D. it became a separate religion at the Council of Nicaea, where the relationship of Christ to God was at issue and was settled in favor of Christ's divinity by a close vote. Consequently, the Christian religion became independent of Judaism. Islam was founded by Muhammed (570–632 A.D.) in 622 A.D. and tended to include the peoples who had lost at the Council of Nicaea. Islam, meaning "surrender to God's will," is the predominant religion in the Middle East. All these major religions and some other, minor ones developed at a time when human society was looking for a vehicle of social control. That vehicle was found in religion.

EARLY ATTEMPTS TO UNDERSTAND HUMAN BEHAVIOR

Early attempts to understand human behavior involved mysticism, magic, and the supernatural. In fact, Zoroaster was considered to be the world's first magician. There are still many people today who are concerned with fortune-telling, magic, voodoo, and mysticism. Zolar's *Encyclopedia of Ancient and Forbidden Knowledge,* is still widely read. Numerology goes back to India. Divination in ancient Egypt, oracles in Greece, Druid seers, the saints, witches, curses, astrologers, and other elements of the occult have remained until modern times (Glass, 1969). The meaning of dreams was significant long before Freud (Selchrist, 1968). Learning in the ancient sense is also still present in the thinking of many people, such as in the theory of "mental dynamics" (Finley, 1966). Extrasensory perception (ESP) is an old idea that is enjoying much current study; it is based on the idea of a sense beyond those understood by the social and behavioral sciences, one of "psychic power" enabling people to communicate with unseen and unheard people and other sources (Rhine, 1961). The concept of astrology, which was popular between 3500 B.C. and about 1610 A.D., is still popular in some quarters in modern society (L. Goodman, 1968). Ancient superstition lingers on today.

Astrology has been important in the behavior of humans since its origin in Mesopotamia, probably around 3000 B.C., when people were searching for causes of deviant behavior, their fortunes, and their destiny in signs of the zodiac. The word *zodiac* is a corruption of the Greek for "little animals." It refers to the twelve patterns made by orbiting planets as they move in a common plane in a zone of the heavens in which lie the paths of the sun and the moon, permitting the observer on earth to view them in relation to the background of constellations of fixed stars also rotating by season of the year. Many people in the past 5,000 years have cursed the signs or "thanked their lucky stars," depending upon their fortunes. The Mesopotamians had acquired some knowledge of the zodiacal belt by the fifth century B.C., and the practice of divination by the stars was introduced to the Greeks in the third century B.C. The Greeks developed astrology into a vast, complex, and apparently scientific system, which remained a dominant influence on religion, philosophy, and science for 2,000 years. The welfare of the king and the country was considered dependent upon the signs of the zodiac. In the second century B.C., astrology became personal through the casting of individual horoscopes, the first textbook on this subject having appeared in Ptolemaic Egypt about a century before Christ. Thomas Aquinas and Dante accepted astrology in the thirteenth century. Johannes Kepler (1571–1630), the astronomer who used the newly invented telescope to perform pioneer work in learning the motions of the planets, also prepared astrological almanacs and drew up horoscopes for the emperor and other high dignitaries. Astrology seemed logical to him because of his faith in God and the order of the universe, which gave meaning to the relationship between humans, the universe, and God. This made astrology a natural corollary to astronomy. Astrology, however, was dependent upon a geocentric world. When Kepler discovered that the earth was not the center of the universe, he stopped casting horoscopes. The general progress of science and scholarship had reduced astrology to an exploded superstition by the end of the eighteenth century, leaving it only as a rather popular pastime and superstition for many people.

It was this patterning of the planets in relation to sun and earth that provided the basis for early mathematics. Ancient man determined that these patterns and the season recycled every 360 days. Subsequently, there were several corrections; the ancient church calendar was based on 365¼ days, and 235 lunations were equal to 19 solar years. This was corrected to the present calendar of 364¼ days in 1582 by Pope Gregory XIII. In the meantime, the ancient Egyptian mathematical system was developed on base 60—the circle has 360 degrees, and there are 60 seconds in a minute and 60 minutes in an hour. This sexagesimal place-value system was gradually replaced by the present decimal system, beginning with the algebra of al-Khwarizmi of Baghdad in the ninth century B.C. and consummated in Western Europe in the seventeenth century A.D. in a consistent decimal system developed by Francois Vieta (1540–1603) and Simon Stevin (1548–1620). A binary, or base 2, system is now being introduced because of the on-off system of computers. In summary, mathematics and many other phases of human thought and behavior were influenced by the interpretations of ancient man regarding the movements of the planets.

Intelligent man developed anxieties and concerns that his predecessors did not. Learning from the past and concern for the future resulted in working out some ground rules, customs or norms that became patterns of behavior expected within the social formation. Concerns about supernatural causes of everyday phenomena gave rise to primitive religious rites and efforts to find supernatural interpretations.

The witch doctor or medicine man or shaman became the interpreter of supernatural happenings and, consequently, became the "law" or the shaper of conforming behavior. Anyone who deviated from this interpretation was considered to possess supernatural demons; persons who violated the norms of a tribe were possessed of the demons or full of the devil. (Now we say someone is "full of hell.") The witch doctor called on supernatural good spirits. He also performed more immediate remedies, such as putting on grotesque masks and dancing around the deviant victim of the demons to frighten the demons away, to drive away the evil spirits, and to "scare the hell" out of him. Another approach was to concoct a nauseous potion made up of saliva, fingernails, feces, pimple pus, urine, nose-pickings, hair, and other obnoxious items and make the patient eat it, thereby making his or her body intolerable for the demons. Trephining was the grinding of a hole in the person's skull with a sharp stone in order to let the demons out. The most recent incidents involving demonology in significant proportions were the witchcraft trials at Salem, Massachusetts, in 1692. Although there were some lesser witchcraft trials after 1692, they had been eliminated from the United States by 1800.

On occasion among primitive man, a sacrifice to the gods was made of a baby, a young virgin, a son, or other person in order to keep the tribe on good terms with the gods and spirits. In fact, Abraham was going to obey God's command to sacrifice his only son, Isaac (Genesis 22: 1), but he was released from the command at the last moment (Genesis 22: 12). It was not long after, in ancient Middle East civilization, that sacrifice of the "fatted calf" and other animals was substituted for human sacrifice. In a behavioral system made up of expected norms, anxieties and concerns about the future, and supernatural forces, feelings of guilt, and pangs of conscience, together with the means of their atonement through sacrifice and other rituals and demonstrations of remorse, were introduced into human behavior. While all animals respond to immediate and tangible danger, only humans worry about the future and develop guilt and anxiety about the past.

The early Ionian philosophers and pre-Socratic Greeks believed that there was order in the universe and that it was governed by regularities or laws. These functions of nature, including human behavior, resulted from the proportions of *humors*, or biles, in nature, which comprised all elements of human behavior. The elements that made up all matter, including humans, were air, fire, water, and earth. Dependent upon the proportions within the person of each of these elements, people were airy or windy, fiery, watery or wishy-washy, or earthy.

Hippocrates (460–377 B.C.), considered by many to be the first "physician" in the modern sense and whose Hippocratic oath is today taken by new physicians, considered the health of persons to be dependent upon the proper mixture of fundamental humors—blood, black bile, yellow bile, and phlegm. Persons for whom blood dominated were of a sanguine or cheerful disposition. Black bile produced a melancholic and depressed person. Too much yellow bile caused a choleric or hot-tempered disposition. An overabundance of phlegm resulted in a lazy (phlegmatic) person.

Plato (428/7–348/7 B.C.) turned to generalized philosophical concepts. The individual's soul had three elements: reason, desire, and spirit, the spirit being the agent used by reason to overcome passion. The lower part of the irrational soul was located in the body below the diaphragm, while the better part was above the diaphragm, located in the heart and in mental faculties. This established the principle of localization of functions that reached its full consideration in phrenology in the early nineteenth century. The relation between the mind and soul in relationship to the body posed problems because body needs must harmonize with the soul. Plato viewed human behavior as the mixture of these in the balance of elements and of philosophical concerns.

The concept of "mind" and "body" as separate entities has been a problem in understanding human behavior that dates back to early philosophy. Religious thinkers have emphasized the former, while scientists have emphasized the latter. Behaviorism in modern experimental psychology holds that anything that cannot be defined, observed, and measured is "mentalistic" and subjective. Subjective data, of course, pertain to personal experience bound by past and present awareness and interpretation. Objective data, or the "veridical domain," refers to data that can be observed and are available to everybody. Experimental psychologists and many social scientists are concerned only with objective data, while many clinicians, including clinical psychologists, psychiatrists, psychoanalysts, and psychiatric social workers, are concerned with personal awareness and perception, past experience, and the perspective of the patient. This difference in viewpoint on the part of different social and behavioral scientists has led to interesting debate and conflict in attempting to understand human behavior, including criminal behavior.

Hippocrates and Galen held to the theory of the humors but added a concept of vital spirit that brings life to all parts of the body, including the soul. The idea of animal spirits remained in the scholarly interpretations of human behavior until the eighteenth century and really formed the basis of the biological interpretations of behavior that emerged in the nineteenth century with Darwin, Lamarck, Lombroso, and others. The idea of humors did not end until the nineteenth century, and even then Van Heller spoke of the traditional four temperaments and Broussais theorized six temperaments.

The rise of the great religions brought new explanations of human behavior. A basic dilemma had to be resolved: Evil exists in the world. If God is omniscient and evil *still* exists, then God must not be omnipotent. On the other hand, if God is omnipotent and evil *still* exists in the world, then God is not omniscient, in that He does not know what is going on. Further, if God is both omnipotent and omniscient and evil *still* exists in the world, then God is evil. The work of the early scholastics in developing theological systems was designed to resolve this dilemma. St. Augustine, the Bishop of Hippo (354–430), in *The City of God* emphasized the will, indicating that primeval man willed to disobey God and, as a result, all men were evil and corrupt by nature. This raised serious questions about the existence and the nature of free will. Men could not be saved by their own intelligence or actions, but only by the will of God, who might infuse certain individuals with the knowledge and goodness that meant salvation in heaven. The evil nature of man in terms of slavery to bodily pleasures, such as sex, made necessary the social institutions, such as Church and state, to control man and to keep him from deviating. Thomas Aquinas (1225–74) tried to reconcile faith and reason and reestablish the Aristotelian notion that body and soul are merely different aspects of the same person. He held that man is endowed with appetites or motivations that work together in a complementary way toward the perfection of each person. Because it is natural to do good, when a man fails to follow his reason, an unnatural act or a sin results which upsets the natural order that God has instituted. An interesting diagram of the social hierarchy as seen by the Elizabethans is as follows (Spencer, 1949, p. 12):

God	pure actuality
Angels	pure intellect
Man	reason
Animals	sense
Plants	growth
Stones	being

Humans are in a critical position, being neither material nor heavenly but participating in both areas. Gelli (1498–1563) said that "man is made of two natures, one corporeal and terrestrial, the other divine and celestial: in the one he resembles beasts, in the other those immaterial substances which turn the heavens" (Spencer, 1949, pp. 11–12).

René Descartes (1596–1650) thought that natural laws governed not only events external to man but also events occurring within him, so free will becomes more important than divine law in criminal causation. This Cartesian dichotomy was based on the thesis that the powers of reason and will were divine gifts that set human beings apart from other forms of life. Consequently, humans are responsible for their acts.

Thomas Hobbes (1588–1679) was the first thinker to suggest that all phenomena were subject to scientific laws, including human behavior. The reason that humans will one course of action over another is hedonistic in that they are seeking pleasure and avoiding pain, but people differ in physical constitutions and in experience. John Locke (1632–1704) emphasized the appreciation of ideas and agreed with Hobbes that man chooses courses of action to seek pleasure and avoid pain. The approaches of everyone seeking pleasure and avoiding pain will result in conflict, so a strong state and a criminal justice system become important to control the expression of passions and the illegal acquisition of wealth. Rousseau wrote in his *Emile,* published in 1892, that civilization changes the growing child from a natural person into a social person compelled to oppose nature or our social institutions (p. 5).

It was at the height of belief in the idea that man could reason and choose alternative courses of action that Cesare Beccaria published in 1764 his *Essay on Crimes and Punishments,* in which his primary contention was that man was hedonistic, could choose his course by free will, and crimes previously delineated in the statutes, rather than being adjudicated by arbitration or judicial decision, would better control deviant behavior. Hedonistic man, who avoids pain and seeks pleasure, could read the law and decide whether or not he wanted to commit a crime. At that time, there was no criminal law as it is now known. Judgments had been made on the merits of each case as in a civil action. The result of Beccaria's ideas was a codification of the criminal laws in England and some parts of Europe by which the seriousness of a crime was evaluated and a penalty assessed accordingly. The criminal law as it is now known developed between about 1770 and 1812.

Physiognomy and related approaches to explaining behavior emerged in the late eighteenth century. Lavater (1741–1801) emphasized sense perception, saying that human behavior resulted from the animal, moral, and intellectual natures of man. To assess personality, "we have to read the physiognomy, so to speak, of grain to see if it is growing blighted or not—and use common sense and experience." That included evil eyes, honesty in looks, unhealthy countenance, insidious smile, and other factors (Lavater, 1789, p. 27). Franz Joseph Gall (1758–1828) reinterpreted Lavater's work and listed twenty-seven basic traits or propensities. Gall (1835, vol. 1, pp. 156–60) indicated that the fundamental attributes of man are innate, as in animals, and are represented in the brain.

Later, localization of brain function that resulted in the skull to fit the well-developed and underdeveloped "organs" of the brain gave a method of assessing personality by reading the "bumps." Although Gall's new system of phrenology was widely studied and used in the first half of the nineteenth century, it was dropped rapidly in the last half. The "scientific" basis of phrenology had been questioned. It is interesting to note that August Comte (1798–1857), a social philosopher sometimes called the father of sociology, was a follower of Gall's phrenology theory, but Comte emphasized the organization of behavior and denied the relevance of *mechanisms* of basic phenomena, such as irritability and sensibility. Other phases of physiognomy became popular about the same time, such as palmistry (chiromancy or palm reading) and metoposcopy—reading the lines on the forehead.

Interest in biology was concurrent with the development of physiognomy. The word *biology* was introduced by G. R. Treviranus in 1837 in his text *Biologie oder die Philosophie der lebenden Natur* and was popularized by J. B. de Lamarck. The work of Lamarck and Darwin brought biology to the forefront in explanation of behavior. Behavior became the function of structure. In this context, Cesare Lombroso (1836–1909) became the originator of the constitutional approach to criminal causation with the thesis that the typical criminal can be identified by certain definite physical characteristics. (For further detail, see chapter 2 on the positive school of criminology.) While representing the last of the "prescientific" approaches to behavior, Lombroso was the first who attempted to apply scientific methods to understanding criminal behavior. His primary contribution was the attempt to make the study of crime objective and scientific.

It was not until the nineteenth century that most of the ancient thinking perpetuated through the Middle Ages concerning behavior was changed. Theology and philosophy provided much of the serious thought concerning human behavior into the nineteenth century. Astrology lasted as a serious study until around 1650. Demonology lasted at least until the witchcraft trials at Salem in 1692, though it was considered seriously in courts until 1800 and remains intact in some sects today. The notion of animal spirits and humors as determinants of temperament lasted into the nineteenth century. It was the rise of biology as a science in the nineteenth century that replaced these types of theories and focused on the physiological construction of man. It was the rise of economics as a social science in that century that replaced ancient beliefs and traditions concerning human behavior with ideas of social classes, class struggles, and other social factors. Modern psychological and psychiatric approaches had their beginnings in philosophy and in the new science of biology. Modern sociological and cultural theories had their beginnings in the new social science of economics. Both biology and economics exerted a major influence on the thinking of man concerning human behavior and social problems, including criminal behavior.

FREE WILL

The question as to how much free will humans really enjoy remains debatable. If behavior is caused, then it is difficult to support the concept of free will. Many theologians and philosophers insist that humans can choose alternative courses of action on the basis of free choice. Many social scientists hold that alternative choices are made on the basis of previous experience, preferences previously developed, and beliefs and values previously learned—consequently, behavior can be predicted. People tend to shop for the same things in supermarkets and tend to order similar meals from the menu in their favorite restaurants. When national television networks can predict the outcome of a national presidential election within a fraction of 1 percent when the polls on the West Coast are not yet closed, it appears to be obvious that their sampling techniques and what they have learned about the behavior of the voting public supports the contention that behavior can be predicted.

The issue is of importance to the criminologist and the student of criminal behavior because it makes a difference in treatment programs. For example, if behavior is determined by free will and free choice, then correctional programs within the criminal justice system should employ inspirational-repressive and moral reeducation techniques supporting the thesis that "crime does not pay." On the other hand, if behavior is caused rather than chosen, sociological, psychological, anthropological, psychiatric, and other approaches dealing with social and emotional factors become appropriate.

Some of the confusion about free will as opposed to determinism or caused behavior arises from oversimplifications and, probably, misconceptions about the *positions* of theologians and social scientists (Higgins, 1959, p. 1785). Pope Pius XII has said that while "unconscious instinctual drives" may exercise pressure on an activity, they do not necessarily compel it and should not be considered a force completely escaping from the control of the conscience and the soul. On the other hand, R. P. Knight, a psychiatrist, indicates that determinism does not mean that factors of the past necessarily cause a neurotic course in individuals for the rest of their lives, but that their total makeup and reactions are determined by all forces, early and late, external and internal, past and present, which have played and are playing upon him. Apparently, theologians recognize that causation does exist but consider it not necessarily governing over the conscience, while psychiatrists consider religious experience to be part of all the forces that produce the personality.

JUSTICE

The concept of justice was developed in ancient Greece along with the concept of democracy in the fifth century B.C. It had its origins in the ideas of vengeance of primitive and ancient man and in the Old Testament. The concept was to protect the weak from the strong, to keep the strong from using a wrong as license to overreact in return. Solon has been given credit for the introduction of justice into Western civilization. Draco had developed the first comprehensive code in Athens about 621 B.C., but it was unduly harsh. Solon (c. 640–560 B.C.) modulated Draco's codification, except for the laws against homicide, and contributed much toward the concept of justice in ancient Greece. Plato held that justice was a rational principle at the root of moral distinctions that converge in each individual to make a rational society. A rational society was one in which the principle of justice had power as well as manifest authority. The early Stoics in the second century B.C. made kinship their source of justice; everybody else was "on his own." The serious study of "politics" or political science began with Machiavelli in 1513.

Justice is basically the protection of the weak from the strong and the mitigation of strength with wisdom. Justice involves the infusion of morality into law. While law is generally aimed at the preservation of the *status quo*, whether the ancient feudal system, the Church, the monarchy, the state, or an economic system, it changes slowly in the direction of morality, wisdom, and the protection of the weak from the strong. Justice was originally based on the need of the individual for protection. By the seventeenth century, the concept of natural rights had been enunciated, along with government at the consent of the governed, by St. Thomas Aquinas, Thomas Hobbes, John Locke, Jeremy Bentham, and others. The concept of "equal and unalienable rights" culminated in the Universal Declaration of Human Rights adopted by the General Assembly of the United Nations meeting in Paris on December 10, 1948. The Magna Carta in 1215 and the Statutes of Westminster passed during the reign of Edward I provided that all persons should be treated alike before the law and served to infuse the concept of justice into English law.

The historical development of "justice" has been slow and unsteady. Socrates thought that justice was the awarding to each that which was due him, but Plato indicated that justice was from the power structure in the interests of the stronger; this idea was repeated by Machiavelli, Hobbes, Spinoza, Marx, and Kalsem, as well as Justice Oliver Wendell Holmes. Justice is "meted out," "served," "satisfied," or society is "paid," which threatens the whiplash of retribution. It purports to mean in a democracy a sense of fair dealing, the resource and remedy of the exploited, and the protection of the weak from the strong. As a concept, "justice" irritates some lawmakers and some scientists because situations do not call for it. An operation for cancer has no relationship to justice; nor does the act of a man who cannot suppress his impulse to assault somebody (Menninger, 1966, pp. 11, 17.) Something that has to be controlled exists as a matter of public safety, health, and welfare, but "justice" is beside the point—an arbitrary concept. The series of *Great Ideas* published by Encyclopedia Britannica in 1952 cites over a thousand references to various definitions of "justice," ending with the thought that the term may be more inspirational, moralistic, and rhetorical than scientifically useful (vol. I, pp. 859–78). Apparently, the best or the least objectionable definition of justice remains that of the ancient Greeks as democracy emerged—the mitigation of strength with wisdom.

CRIME IN AMERICA

Modern society is the culmination of centuries of social interaction, attempts to understand individual and collective behavior, and efforts to find adequate means of social control. This social control began with the family and kinship ties, ethical systems and religious controls, and eventually the criminal law and criminal justice system of the modern state. In modern society, crime is defined by legislative action or governmental decree, law enforcement agencies identify suspected offenders, the courts convict those legally guilty, and correctional systems attempt to rehabilitate offenders or keep them. The nature and extent of crime in modern America provides some index as to where the social problems lie in this society and the number of people involved.

Several types of crime appear in American society. These types can be divided into (1) conventional or street crime, (2) organized crime, (3) white-collar or "thumb-on-the-scales" sharp business practices, sometimes called suite crime, (4) professional crime other than organized crime that may include some street crime but through which individual persons or partners may earn their livings, and (5) political crime, such as treason or violation of the Selective Service Act. It is conventional or street crime that receives most attention from the criminal justice system.

Specialized types of deviant and criminal behavior have appeared on occasion in American society. Hijacking passenger airlines was popular in the late 1960s and early 1970s, resulting in tight security, including the searching of passengers, in American airports. Kidnappings for high ransom have occurred occasionally—for example, in February 1974 the kidnapping of Patricia Hearst by the Symbionese Liberation Army and the kidnapping of Editor Murphy of the *Atlanta Constitution* by the "American Revolutionary Army," which turned out to be one couple.

Massacres have caused the public to react with abhorrence on occasion. At the My Lai massacre in Vietnam on March 16, 1968, probably more than 120 persons died; Lt. William Calley was subsequently found guilty of the murder of at least 22 of the Vietnamese civilians, a conviction subsequently reversed in 1974 and the reversal upheld in 1975. One of the most vicious massacres in America was at Lawrence, Kansas, on August 21, 1863, when William Clarke Quantrill's pro-Confederate guerrilla band killed 150 men and boys whose hands were tied behind their backs and whose wives and daughters were made to watch. Mass murders or a series of individual murders have also contributed to the history of crime. Howard Unruh killed thirteen people in Camden, New Jersey, in September 1949. William Cook completely wiped out two five-person families in December 1950 and January 1951. Charles Starkweather, accompanied by his girl friend, killed one man in December 1957 and seven people in January and February 1958. Richard Speck killed eight nurses in Chicago in July 1966. Charles Manson and three female members of his "family" killed seven people in August 1969. In May 1971, farm labor contractor Juan V. Corona was arrested in Yuba City, California, for killing seventeen itinerant workers; twenty-five bodies were found before the investigation was over. In August 1973, seventeen-year-old E. W. Hensley was arrested in Houston for killing a thirty-six-year-old friend, the arrest leading to the discovery of twenty-seven bodies.

Theodore Robert Bundy killed two young women in the Chi Omega sorority house at Florida State University in Tallahassee, beat two others, and beat another young woman in her nearby apartment in the early morning hours of January 15, 1978. On February 8, twelve-year-old Kimberly Leach was kidnapped in Lake City, Florida, and was found murdered about 20 miles away near Live Oak, her body decomposed. This murder was also attributed to Bundy. Prior to the Florida murders, the FBI had placed Bundy, originally from Tacoma, Washington, and subsequently a student at the University of Utah Law School, on its Top Ten Most Wanted List for questioning in thirty-six sex murders of young women, mostly in the West. He had been convicted of a violent kidnapping of Carole DeRoach in Salt Lake City but had escaped and was about to be tried for the murder of a vacationing Michigan nurse in Aspen, Colorado, when he again escaped from the local jail. His trial for the murder of the two Chi Omega sorority members was transferred from Tallahassee to Miami and received national and international publicity (Winn and Merrill, 1980; Rule, 1980; and Larsen, 1980). Some law enforcement officers have mentioned privately that the number of killings they wanted to question him about would almost double the thirty-six officially listed by the FBI. He had made his way in many places, including Florida, in stolen automobiles, under assumed names, and with stolen credit cards. He was diagnosed by Dr. Emanuel Tanay, a psychiatrist from Detroit, as a "psychopath" on May 21, 1979. He had previously been diagnosed a "sexual psychopath" by Dr. Richard A. Jarvis of Seattle, Washington.

In December 1978, twenty-nine badly decomposed bodies were found in the home of John Wayne Gacy, a friendly and sociable contractor who lived in northwest Chicago. He was later charged with thirty-three sex slayings. In the search for bodies, his $80,000 house was demolished. The killings took place between 1972 and December 1978.

Jack the Ripper was a legendary criminal who terrorized London in the 1880s, but he was never found. He was believed to be a doctor— no longer practicing—and a religious fanatic who thought that the only way "bad" women could enter Paradise was by killing them. One woman believed to have been a victim of Jack the Ripper was Elizabeth Stride, who was butchered on Berner Street on September 30, 1888, found by a man driving a buggy into the courtyard just thirty seconds after she died. She had been slain under the window of a socialist club where twenty to thirty men had heard nothing. Logan (1928) describes Jack the Ripper as he was profiled by Scotland Yard:

> (1) a man, with some surgical experience, who knew both England and America well; (2) that he had suffered from a disease that must be nameless here, contracted in the neighborhood of the murders; (3) that this had affected his brain and had caused him to "declare war" on the special class from which he chose his victims; (4) that the mutilations were the result of a blood-lust and a desire to wreak his hatred even on the lifeless bodies of unfortunates; (5) that he had a secret lair or hiding-place in the district at which he was able to remove all signs of his fearful deeds; and (6) that there were those in London who more than suspected his proclivities, but were too timid to denounce him (pp. 29–30).

Several persons had been suspected, but none was ever detained. The identity of Jack the Ripper died with him.

Certainly, all these people were more dangerous than some that have been more widely publicized. For example, Richard Loeb and Nathan Leopold killed only one teenaged boy, Bobby Franks, but the perpetrators and the victim had come from prominent families in Chicago. Many factors govern public concern and crime statistics, but both are large components in the making of public policy regarding criminal justice.

The extent of crime in America can be estimated from the *Uniform Crime Reports* published annually by the Federal Bureau of Investigation. The FBI warns against using these statistics to compare communities, states, or jurisdictions because the reporting is voluntary, except in a few states with mandatory reporting laws, and there are many uncontrolled variables that enter into the reported statistics (*Crime in the United States–1980.*) Judgment and close examination of all factors pressing on the final statistics must precede any conclusions or policy decisions based upon them. Nevertheless, these statistics constitute the best crime information ever available on a national scale, although Sweden, a small nation, may have more accurate statistics. Even so, some scholars have almost dismissed crime statistics as a waste of time and others have suggested that they are close to being worthless and may cause more harm than good if public policy is based on them (Rudoff, 1971). Some have charged that crime statistics have been artificially reduced, particularly the 1971 figures, in order to make the president's crime program look good and to obtain a share of the Law Enforcement Assistance Administration's grant funds (*Justice,* June–July, 1972). Accounting for all the doubts, the crime statistics published by the FBI concerning crime in America still appear to be the best information available, and the FBI and its advisors are trying to improve their validity and reliability. At least, they can be used as an approximation of official cases that come into the criminal justice system. Most criminologists and representatives of the reporting office of the FBI (*Uniform Crime Reports*) and the victimization studies of the National Science Foundation (*National Crime Surveys*) indicate that the crime rates are relatively stable from year to year, with the differences being in reporting, public policy, efficiency of law enforcement agencies, attitudes of the citizenry (including fear of crime), and other, similar factors.

The estimated number of major crimes (Index Crimes) reported by law enforcement agencies through the FBI in 1980 was 13,295,400 offenses, listed as follows:

TABLE 1-1.
Breakdown of Major Crimes, 1980

CRIME	NUMBER	RATE PER 100,000 INHABITANTS
Murder	23,040	10.2
Forcible rape	82,090	36.4
Robbery	548,810	243.5
Aggravated assault	654,960	290.6
Burglary	3,759,200	1,668.2
Larceny—theft	7,112,700	3,156.3
Motor vehicle theft	1,114,700	494.6
Arson	115,059	50.7

Crime in the United States—1980: Uniform Crime Reports (Washington, D.C.: Federal Bureau of Investigation, released September 10, 1981), p. 38.

The number of misdemeanors generally ranges between 90 and 93 percent of the total crime rate.

In police jurisdictions covering a population of 208,194,225, there were 2,338,600 arrests for major, or Index, crimes in 1980 and, 8,669,800 arrests for lesser offenses *(Crime in the United States—1980,* p. 190.)

This writer compared the proportion of major offenses in the State Prison of Southern Michigan at Jackson on the basis of old records for 1875, 1900, 1925, and 1950 and found the proportions to be stable over that period. One difference was that horses were stolen in 1875 and automobiles were stolen in 1950, but the proportion of people stealing the prevailing mode of transportation was similar.

It is noted that property offenses predominate in the statistics on major offenses, and drugs and alcohol tend to predominate in the lesser offenses. Yet public concern is greatest in crimes of violence. Violent crimes, including armed robbery, constitute about 13 percent of the total. Homicide alone amounts to about .33 percent, or about a third of one percent. Yet the violent crimes and homicides have been the primary public concerns in the area of crime. People are afraid of murderers and assaulters, but they are just angry about burglars and thieves.

While the Ten Most Wanted program was formalized by the FBI in 1950, records are available prior to that date. The ten most wanted offenders by the FBI in the last fifty years might provide an index of the areas of greatest public concern. In chronological order, they were (Lee, 1972):

1. Gerald Chapman (1890–1926)
2. George "Dutch" Anderson (?–1926)
3. Arthur Barry (dates uncertain–major activities in the 1920s)
4. Richard Loeb (1907–36) and Nathan Leopold (1906–71)
5. Bruno Richard Hauptmann (1899–1936)
6. John Dillinger (1903–1934)
7. Arizona Clark "Ma" Barker (1872–1935)
8. George Metesky, "The Mad Bomber" (b. 1903, was in a New York State Hospital for the criminally insane but is now free)
9. William G. Heirens (b. 1929, at time of writing, in Illinois prison)
10. James Earl Ray (b. 1928, at time of writing, in Tennessee prison)

Chapman, Anderson, and Barry were thieves, but Chapman and Anderson were accused also of killing policemen in their last days. The rest were considered to be dangerous people who killed others.

Gerald Chapman and George "Dutch" Anderson were partners. They robbed a post office truck, department store, and other places, with specialization also in jewel theft. Chapman may have been a common thief, but he had been a cellmate of Avin Dahl von Teller from Denmark, who was later known as George "Dutch" Anderson, and under his tutelage, Chapman became an aristocratic, dignified-appearing swindler, con man, and embezzler. In spite of his gentlemanly appearance, however, he has also been described as a pathological robber and killer. He was executed in Connecticut for murder in 1926. Anderson killed a policeman in Muskegon, Michigan, around the same time, but the policeman also killed Anderson.

Arthur Barry posed as Dr. Arthur J. Gibson, rode in a big red Cadillac limousine with a chauffeur, and made his living stealing jewels. When he found a prestigious residence protected by a detective agency, he posed as an agent for the agency, inspected the alarm system while he disconnected it, and pinpointed the police stations and patrol beats. If there were vicious watchdogs guarding the residence he was going to enter, Barry fed them chicken sandwiches or brought along a bitch in heat. He read *The Jeweler's Pocket Guide* daily so his fences could not swindle him and talked to victims that might be present in a soft bedside manner. He was known as the Prince of Thieves. Although he served time in prison once and there were some mysterious disappearances of others thought to have been caused by him, including New York State Supreme Court Justice Joseph E. Crater, Barry probably lived out his life in New Jersey as a free man.

Nathan Leopold and Richard Loeb were sons of wealthy Chicago businessmen and students at the University of Chicago. Leopold wanted abnormal sex and Loeb wanted to commit perfect crimes; they signed a pact in which they agreed to participate in both and then carefully planned the killing of fourteen-year-old Bobby Franks, a distant relative of Loeb, as "the crime of the century" in May 1924. They were defended by counsel Clarence Darrow, who managed to avoid the death penalty, but they were sentenced to life for murder and ninety-nine years for kidnapping after having been found guilty on July 21, 1924. Loeb was murdered by a fellow inmate, James Day, in January 1936. Leopold was paroled March 13, 1958 and died of heart failure on August 30, 1971, in Puerto Rico. Highly intelligent, Loeb and Leopold had been caught in a complementary neurotic interaction pattern in which each had reinforced the deviant behavior of the other.

Bruno Richard Hauptmann was a German-born carpenter from the Bronx, who on March 1, 1932, kidnapped the baby son of an American hero, Charles A. Lindbergh, leaving a note demanding $50,000 ransom. The child was subsequently found dead; and $14,000 was found buried in Hauptmann's garage. He was executed on April 2, 1936, in New Jersey.

John Herbert Dillinger was primarily a bank robber, but he had a long record of other felonies, including escapes and attempted escapes from several Indiana penal institutions. He was one of the most dangerous of the depression-era criminals and gang leaders in the Midwest, killing a total of ten men and wounding seven while robbing banks, primarily, with almost as much firepower as the military of that day possessed. He engineered a massive prison break from Indiana State Penitentiary at Michigan City on September 26, 1933, and ten armed prisoners escaped. Dillinger was killed by FBI agents led by Melvin Purvis after he was led by a "lady in red," Anna Sage, into ambush outside the Biograph Theater in Chicago on July 27, 1934 (Toland, 1963).

Ma Barker was considered by FBI Director J. Edgar Hoover to have been the most vicious, dangerous, and resourceful criminal the country had produced. She was responsible for bank robberies, a spectacular $200,000 kidnapping during the Great Depression, and several murders. Born near Springfield, Missouri, in 1872, she married George Barker, a sharecropping farmer. She gave birth to four sons, the notorious Barker brothers, Herman, Lloyd, Arthur, and Fred. She planned several bank robberies in the mid-1920s and ran a hideout in Tulsa, Oklahoma, for escaped convicts and bank robbers. The Barkers won some protection at the local level by contributing heavily to political campaigns of the power structure of several cities, including St. Paul, Minnesota; Kansas City, Kansas; Hot Springs, Arkansas; and Joplin, Missouri (Lee, 1972). In the early 1930s, after Arthur (or Doc) and Freddie were released from prison, Ma planned holdups of federal payrolls, post offices, and banks. Ma Barker and her son Freddie were killed in a gun battle with FBI men in a remote resort on Lake Weir, Florida, on January 16, 1935. She had never been arrested for any crime during her lifetime, remaining behind the scene and sending out her sons and other criminals to perform the crimes. Ma Barker justified her criminal activities by claiming they were to avenge the imprisonment of three of her sons and the killing of the fourth one (though police said this had been suicide).

George Metesky, known as the Mad Bomber, terrorized New York City in the early 1950s with bombs that crippled at least eight people, but there were no fatalities. He had planted dud bombs in 1940–41 and sent insulting notes to Consolidated Edison. In 1951, he began again with live bombs planted in Radio City Music Hall, Grand Central Station, and several theaters, followed by more notes to Consolidated Edison. With the assistance of Dr. Ralph Banay, a psychiatrist who developed a profile of the bomber with available information, the Consolidated Edison files were searched and George Metesky was found to have suffered an injury in their employ in 1931, which he claimed led to the development of his tuberculosis. He was committed to a New York State Hospital but is now free.

William Heirens burglarized apartments and killed three women and a six-year-old girl, Suzanne Degnan, in Chicago between June 1945 and January 1946. After killing Suzanne Degnan, he wrote in lipstick on the wall of the bathroom, "Please catch me before I kill more." This case is mentioned in chapter 9, Psychiatric Approaches, to illustrate problems of the severe neurotic, supported by reference to the psychiatric report presented just before Heirens's trial. His basic problems were seen as involving the restricting demands of a dominant, middle-class mother that resulted in his inability to relate to women. In fact, when he tried to date women, it was a traumatic situation for him. In one instance, he tried to kiss a woman and became ill and vomited. His burglaries and killing of females were related to the psychosexual problem. Now in the Illinois State Penitentiary, Heirens was the first inmate to earn a bachelor's degree from nearby Lewis University while inside the walls. He is serving a life sentence.

James Earl Ray assassinated Dr. Martin Luther King in Memphis, Tennessee, on April 4, 1968. Prior to that, Ray had been a small-time hold-up man, specializing in robbing gas stations and stores. He was considered to be inept and, typically, dropped his wallet during one robbery. That led to his arrest and conviction. He had served time in Illinois and Missouri and, in fact, had escaped from the Missouri State Penitentiary on April 23, 1967, and was still a fugitive when he killed King. Because of public opinion and the political ramifications of killing a well-known civil rights leader at the height of the civil rights movement, Ray catapulted to the top of the Ten Most Wanted list immediately. Ray went from Canada to England on May 6, 1968, using an alias. Obviously in possession of adequate funds, he moved from hotel to hotel in London, but he was arrested by London police on June 8 and was extradited to the United States. There has been strong suspicion that Ray may have been hired by another person or persons to assassinate Martin Luther King, but no direct evidence has been produced. On advice of counsel, Percy Foreman of Houston, Ray pleaded guilty on March 11, 1969, and was sentenced to ninety-nine years in the Tennessee State Penitentiary. The plea was apparently an attempt to avoid the death penalty.

CONCLUSIONS

It is apparent that crime is a by-product of civilization. The earliest social control was in family and kinship ties. Religion was the first political force that could command loyalty beyond the family, and it became central to social control throughout the development of civilization. Law became central to social control in the eighteenth century. Primitive men had no crime but developed customs that delineated the norms of behavior. Later, ancient man had no crime as it is known today but viewed interpersonal wrongs as being against society. The evolvement of English parliamentary law in the thirteenth and fourteenth centuries provided better procedural definitions. The maturation of law between 1650 and 1820 included the criminal law, which has been central to the concerns of criminal justice for two centuries. Crime is now defined legislatively according to the values of the people. Crime, then, is a sociopolitical event. The problem of the criminologist has become one of defining a sociopolitical event in terms of human behavior and social theory.

Questions

1. Explain how crime is a by-product of civilization and is considered by many social sciences to be a normal function of society.

2. What is the thesis of a saturation point in crime, sometimes referred to as a "law of criminal saturation"?

3. How did human *behavior* as distinguished from that of humanlike primates emerge?

4. Summarize the early attempts to understand human behavior.

5. Can the dilemma between free will and caused behavior be resolved? Why or why not?

6. Trace the development of the concept of justice.

7. What types of crime appear in American society?

8. What is a Crime Index offense?

9. Approximately how many major or Crime Index offenses are reported annually?

10. How can crime be described as a sociopolitical event?

two

EMERGENCE OF CRIMINOLOGY

Criminology as a field of study and human endeavor emerged along with the criminal law in the eighteenth century. The modern concept of crime developed between the Middle Ages and the end of the eighteenth century. The Latin word *crimen* from which *crime* is derived means an "accusation," a tort, or a wrong done by one individual against another. The formalizing of this concept into "crime" probably had its early beginnings in the formalization of court procedure at the Assize of Clarendon called by Henry II in 1166 A.D. when the jury system was structured essentially as it remains today, the sheriff was recognized as an officer of the law, the construction of jails was approved, and the beginnings of classification of crimes as felonies and misdemeanors appeared. In 1215, King John under compulsion from his barons issued the Magna Carta as a symbol of a general movement toward civil and constitutional rights.

The Westminster period (1285-1500) refers to the effects of the Statutes of Westminster first passed in 1275 during the reign of Edward I; these statutes held that all persons "shall be treated alike before the law." The second Statute of Westminster, passed in 1285, remodeled the institutions of justice and established a bailiff or nightwatch. The office of justice of the peace was instituted in 1316, local government was inaugurated in 1370, and courts of the Star Chamber or *ex parte* (only the state present—no defense counsel) proceedings were instituted in 1487 to try offenders against the state. Parliamentary government began in England in the fourteenth and fifteenth centuries, when legislation was introduced to secure the social order. Making war against the king, serfs leaving the soil in search of work, the keeping of dogs by persons not owning property were all outlawed. Murder at this time resulted in short sentences or fines, though imprisonment was not generally used as punishment. During the sixteenth and seventeenth centuries as a result of the consolidation of Church and state, treason and heresy became capital crimes as did swearing, adultery, and witchcraft. During the eighteenth and nineteenth centuries, piracy, forgery, and banking offenses became crimes. In the meantime, punishments had become harsh, representing vengeance rather than justice.

Criminology was the composite result of the thinking and endeavors of many people. Contributions to the understanding of individual behavior and deviation and the structuring of the social order came from the Church fathers, who espoused the divine right of kings as precursors of the social order. On the other hand, the philosophers and social contract writers of the day embraced the idea that reason and free will of man produced government at the consent of the governed. Probably the greatest single catalyst in this conflict was Cesare Beccaria (1738-1794), whose famous *Essay on Crimes and Punishments* in 1764 focused attention on the problem of crime and the courts and resulted directly in the codification of English criminal law by 1800, as well as that of other countries in Europe.

Criminology emerged with Beccaria's *Essay,* and since that time, many scholars have contributed to the field of criminology with interpretations of criminal behavior, techniques of detection and apprehension of offenders, due process and the law, and methods of treatment of offenders.

UNDERSTANDING CRIMINAL BEHAVIOR

Understanding criminal behavior is complex. Crime is a sociopolitical event rather than a clinical condition. Crime is defined in the law as behavior sufficiently deviant to damage society and to merit, therefore, legal action and the intervention of society into the lives of citizens who so deviate. It is not a clinical or medical condition that can be diagnosed and specifically treated. Consequently, there have been many approaches to the problem of crime from many different viewpoints with varying degrees of compatibility and agreement.

Many criminologists hold that criminology is a science. Elmer Johnson, (1964, p. 7), who was a prison administrator in North Carolina and now teaches university courses in criminology at Southern Illinois

University, was talking about this when he wrote that criminology has two interdependent branches, science and practice. The science part is manned by academic and research scholars, while the field of practice is frequently administered by political appointees and many people from heterogeneous backgrounds at varying levels of competence. The difficulty in the past has been that few people in the practical field of criminal justice contribute to the literature, and the writing is done by people who may never have had a day's experience in the field. Yet both have a contribution to make, and this presentation hopes to help weld theory and practice into a cohesive field of endeavor. Karl Menninger (1966, p. 5) says that criminology is a science; Caldwell (1956, pp. 4-7) has written of it as an applied science. A symposium organized by the International Society of Criminology in London reported that criminology is an autonomous science (Carrol and Pinatel, 1957, p. 15). On the other hand, many criminologists, such as Sutherland and Cressey (1966, p. 20), believe that criminology itself is not a science. It may be that criminology can be viewed as an art based on many sciences and disciplines. Medicine is an art, not a science, but it is based on many of the natural and behavioral sciences. Criminology may be an art, also, based on the behavioral and social sciences with a liberal contribution of religion and law. In any case, it has emerged in the twentieth century as a separate discipline or field of study, however one may resolve the issue as to whether or not it is a science.

Certainly, criminal behavior cannot be understood by simply viewing the easily observable variables. Deviant behavior may or may not be pathological from the clinical viewpoint. It may or may not be ethically wrong. The understanding of criminal behavior has been attempted by conjecture and use of trial-and-error methods, much of it emotionally involved. Hypothetical constructs in the form of various theories have been offered and challenged; their use to understand phenomena difficult to understand is usual procedure. Some have proved to be helpful with the progress of research and have been refined, while others have not and have been discarded. Even the "hard" sciences (see reference to "hard sciences" in the *AAAS Bulletin,* June 1973, p. 4), as compared with the social and behavioral sciences, have used hypothetical constructs productively. In chemistry, for example, the equation, $AgNO_3 + HCl \rightleftarrows AgCl\downarrow + HNO_3$,[1] is dependent upon an electronic theory of chemical bonding in which the respective elements are ionized (Ag^+, NO_3^-, H^+, and Cl^-), and the equation is completed on the basis of the differential values of the solubility products available in the possible combinations, in this case with the $AgCl$ combination falling out of solution

---

[1]This equation simply means that when hydrochloric acid is poured into a test tube of silver nitrate, a white precipitate of silver chloride results, leaving nitric acid in solution.

as a white precipitate. (See, for example, chap. 13, "Electronic Theory of Chemical Bonding," in Quagliano, 1958.) Yet nobody has ever seen an ion!

Social factors began to be studied as separate entities in the 1830s by Auguste Comte and Adolphe Quetelet, both referring to their fields of endeavor as social physics. With a mechanistic approach, some of the concepts were similar to the laws of natural sciences expressed by Isaac Newton, though the similarity was not clearly drawn. Comte first used the term *sociology* in 1839 (Timasheff, 1955, p. 4). Social philosophy, of course, was much older and contributed to the new social science of sociology, along with history and other disciplines. Herbert Spencer (1897) viewed sociology as unifying the observations and generalizations of the other social sciences. Georg Simmel (1898) thought that sociology studied the formation and dissolution of social groups, competition, and conflict. Pitirim Sorokin (1928 and 1937–41) held that sociology is concerned with the characteristics common to all classes of social phenomena and their interrelationships. Toward the end of the nineteenth century, the influence of Darwin and the biologists and the concept of natural selection became evident in sociology.

Sociological thinking was primarily organic at that time, based on the premise that biology was the base of behavior and collective behavior could be seen as an organism (Spencer, 1892). John Dewey (1922, p. 296) said that "human nature exists and operates in an environment. And it is not 'in' that environment as coins are in a box, but as a plant is in the sunlight and soil."

Ferdinand Tönnies developed a typology of social adjustment frequently spoken of as *Gemeinschaft* and *Gesellschaft*. *Gemeinschaft* refers to group relationships developed unconsciously within the family; *Gesellschaft* refers to group relationships entered into deliberately in order to accomplish predetermined objectives.

The most influential early sociologists were Emile Durkheim, Charles Horton Cooley, and Max Weber. Durkheim clearly delineated the field as the study of social fact. Weber saw social behavior as the intention of the individual with reference to others and considered social stratification and bureaucracy as vital to sociology. Cooley saw transportation and the general economic base as basic to social interaction. The early sociological criminologists were Tarde, Durkheim, and Bonger. The early emphasis placed on socialization by W. I. Thomas, George H. Mead, John Dewey, and Charles Horton Cooley also contributed to the development of a criminological concern within sociology. The founding fathers of American sociology, Albion Small, Lester F. Ward, and A. E. Ross, were concerned about social control. Durkheim's concept of change from mechanical to organic solidarity, Tönnies's idea of change from *Gemeinschaft* to *Gesellschaft,* and Weber's view of change from traditional to legal authority were all reflected in the development of criminological theory. Conditions that influenced this development included culture conflict, social disorganization, rural-urban differences, and uneven ecological distribution of social breakdown. In the academic field, the first department of sociology was established at the University of Chicago in 1893, and other universities soon followed.

The modern sociologists have produced many views of society. The interdependence between personal and social pathology and the secondary importance of the symptom itself are vividly demonstrated in the use of the sick role as a control of delinquency (Parsons, 1951), in which an alternative to delinquency may be the hypochondriacal reaction in some people. Cooley's (1909) "looking-glass self" and Riesman's (1950, pp. 19ff.) "other-directed character" also show this interdependence.

Talcott Parsons (1951) viewed society as an interaction of stability and integration of systems. Society is a series of systems engaged in boundary struggles with each other. Social change and conflict, then, are not just changes of pattern, but represent an overcoming of the resistance of one system by another. It is during these changes that society is in flux, and this instability can be manifest in higher crime rates. Parsons had indicated that social control applies not only to deviants but also to therapy and rehabilitative processes in general, where some behavior has support, permissiveness, denial of reciprocity, and rewards judiciously balanced.

Several models have emerged in viewing relationships between people as far as crime is concerned. The extremes of these models frequently are referred to as the consensus model and the conflict model. The consensus model of society assumes (1) stability, (2) integration, (3) functionality, and (4) consensus. The conflict model of society assumes (1) change, (2) conflict, (3) dysfunctionality, and (4) coercion.

Psychological and psychiatric approaches to criminology came later than the sociological approaches. The first definitive evaluation of individual differences was presented in an article by Alfred Binet and V. Théophile Henri in 1895 in which the mental processes of an individual were correlated with full development of the individual (Anastasi, 1937, p. 9). W. Stern published his *Über Psychologie der Individuellen Differenzen* in 1900 and his *Differentialle Psychologie in Ihren Methodischen Grundlagen* in 1911 and 1921 in Leipzig. The English scientist Francis Galton (1822–1911) is best known to psychologists as a pioneer in the interpretation of behavior, including deviant behavior, in terms of heredity and the first to apply statistical methods to individual and group differences in mental traits. The first attempt in America to evaluate test scores on the basis of an independent criterion was in 1892 when Bolton (1891–92) analyzed data collected by Boas on 1,500 school children in which "memory spans" were compared with teachers' estimates of "intellectual acuteness." In 1893, Gilbert (1894, 1897) compared teachers' estimates of "general ability" on 1,200 children with eight tests of sensory and motor functions, reaction time, sensory memory, and suggestibility. Three years later, he described additional tests and analyzed several hundred children with regard to sex differences, intellectual growth, and the relationship of mental and physical development. In America the 1895 meeting of the American Psychological Association appointed a committee to study the feasibility of collecting mental and physical statistics. In 1896, the American Association for the Advancement of Science (AAAS) included psychological testing in the proposal advanced by the American Psychological Association.

In 1904, the French Minister of Public Instruction appointed a commission to formulate methods for instruction of the feeble-minded children in Paris (Garrett, 1941, p. 1). One of the members was Alfred Binet, who collaborated with Théodore Simon and produced the first intelligence test in 1905. A revision was made in 1908 and again in 1911. The development of the Binet-Simon scale was the beginning of intelligence testing. The concept of "mental age" came with the 1908 revision. Goddard translated the 1908 scale into English and brought it to the Vineland Training School in New Jersey. Terman revised the scale in 1916 (this was called the Stanford revision) and again in 1937 with Merrill (the latter is also known as the Stanford revision). Kuhlmann made revisions in 1912, 1922, and 1939. Yerkes, Bridges, and Hardwick made a revision in 1915. Herring had a revision in 1922. The term *intelligence quotient* or *I.Q.* was first used in 1914 by the German psychologist W. Stern, and Lewis Terman used it in his 1916 revision of the Binet-Simon scales, called the Stanford Binet; it has been used in intelligence testing ever since.

Following publication of Charles Goring's *The English Convict* in 1913, interest began to subside in biology and anthropology as important elements in the study of the offender, and interest in psychological efforts increased. Lightner Witmer had coined the term *clinical psychology* in 1896 and had opened a clinic in Philadelphia at the University of Pennsylvania. William Healy had begun the case study method at the Juvenile Psychopathic Institute at the juvenile court in Chicago in 1909. By 1925, Cyril Burt was approaching crime and delinquency in London as part of his work with the London County Council. By the 1930s, psychologists and psychiatrists were an accepted part of the criminal justice team.

SCHOOLS OF CRIMINOLOGY

There is general agreement among criminologists that at least two prominent schools of criminology exist: the Classical School, "began about 1755 to 1764" after Beccaria (1738–94) published his famous *Essay on*

Crimes and Punishments; and the Positive School, after the publication of Lombroso's *L'uomo Delinquente (The Criminal Man)* in 1896–97. (The first publication of this theory was in a pamphlet in 1876.) The Classical School focused on the offense and suggested equal punishments for equal crimes, developing the motto, "Let the punishment fit the crime." It held that man was hedonistic, sought pleasure and avoided pain, and had sufficient free will so that he could choose between good and evil when he knew what the consequences might be. The Positive School, or Italian School, was deterministic and held that crime was caused by biological heritage, social heritage, and other factors rather than being freely chosen by the offender. Along with Beccaria, the advocates of the Classical School included Rousseau, Montesquieu, Voltaire, Jeremy Bentham, William Blackstone, Samuel Romilly, and others. Along with Lombroso, the Positive School included Enrico Ferri (1856–1928), Rafaele Garofalo (1852–34), and others. Gabriel, Tarde (1843–1904) was a determinist but rejected the biological approach of the times and proposed his law of imitation, a forerunner of Sutherland's theory of differential association.

There have been many "schools" of criminology suggested by many writers. It would not be practical to list them all. A few that have received some support, however, can be mentioned, and the major ones supported by almost all criminologists can be examined in further detail. Sutherland and Cressey (1966, pp. 53–65) suggest that there are several schools of criminology—the Classical, Cartographic, Socialist, Typological, Sociological, Epidemiology and Individual Conduct, and Multiple-Factor schools. Their approach is portrayed in Table 2-1. Other criminologists present different classifications and different schools.

TABLE 2-1.
Schools of Criminology

SCHOOL	DATE OF ORIGIN	CONTENT OF EXPLANATION	METHODS
Classical-neoclassical	1765	Hedonism	Armchair
Cartographic	1830	Ecology, culture, composition of population	Maps, statistics
Socialist	1850	Economic determinism	Statistics
Typological			
1. Lombrosian	1875	Morphological type, born criminal	Clinical, statistics
2. Mental testers	1905	"Feeblemindedness"	Clinical, tests, statistics
3. Psychiatric	1905	Psychopathy	Clinical, statistics
Sociological and social psychological	1915	Groups and social processes	Clinical, statistics, fieldwork

From Edwin H. Sutherland and Donald R. Cressey, *Criminology*, 10th ed. (Philadelphia: J. B. Lippincott Company, 1974), p. 55. Reprinted by permission of the publisher.

With respect to whether the early criminologist was primarily interested in the offender as a person or the crime as an offense, Jeffery presents the classification shown in Table 2-2.

TABLE 2-2.
Early Criminologists' Interests

CRIME	INDIVIDUAL OFFENDER	
Bentham	Lombroso	Doe
Beccaria	Garofalo	Maudsley
Montero	Ferri	Maconochie
Durkheim	Goring	Tarde
Bonger	Aschaffenburg	Gross
	Ray	Haviland

From Clarence Ray Jeffery, "The Historical Development of Criminology," chap. 25 in Hermann Mannheim, ed., *Pioneers in Criminology*, 2nd ed. enlarged (Montclair, N.J.: Patterson Smith, 1973), pp. 459-60.

Thus criminology shifted focus from the original idea of protection of society or the welfare of the group to emphasis on the offense (the Classical School) and then emphasis on the offender (the Positive School). The Classical School emphasized the legal concerns while the Positive School rejected the legalities and focused on the rehabilitation of the individual offender. Other prominent schools frequently mentioned by criminologists are the American Sociological School and the Social Defense School. Although some criminologists consider them to be separate schools, others tend to view them as extensions of the Positive School of criminology. Table 2-3 lists all the schools and their adherents.

TABLE 2-3.
Classification of Schools of Criminology

Classical School	*Bentham, Beccaria*
Legal Aspects of Crime	*Doe, Montero*
Sociological Aspects of Crime	*Tarde, Durkheim, Bonger*
Prison Reform	*Maconochie*
Positive School	*Garofalo, Lombroso, Ferri, Goring*
Psychiatric Aspects of Crime	*Aschaffenburg, Ray, Maudsley*
Prison Architecture	*Haviland*
Criminalistics	*Gross*

A good compromise may be to view the schools of criminology as follows, keeping in mind the lack of consensus as to how they should be classified:

- Classical School—Legal approach according to the seriousness of the crime.
- Positive School—Crime is caused by a variety of factors, and the legal approach is essentially rejected.
- American School—Sociological theories of crime causation.
- Social Defense School—Crime is caused by a variety of social factors, and the legal framework should take all factors into account. Brings the law back into the Positive School.

Some discussions of each of these approaches appears to be appropriate.

The Classical School

The Classical School of criminology is so called because it was the first relatively adequate form or system of thinking in the area of criminology, just as Hebrew, Greek, and Latin are called the classical languages because they were the first to communicate adequately in modern abstract thinking. The reaction was against the many vagaries and inconsistencies in the existing practices in criminal justice; judges could introduce personal biases into the evolving process of justice. The results were manifest in harsh punishments that reflected vengeance rather than equitable justice.

As has been mentioned, Beccaria's *Essay on Crimes and Punishments* resulted in a great change in the existing legal system. Voltaire wrote the introduction to the French edition, and the French legislators worked out many of the ideas in the famous French Code of 1791. In that code, nothing was left to the judgment of the court except the question of guilt (Gillin, 1945, p. 229). The punishments were fixed in accordance with the seriousness of the offenses. The English edition of Beccaria's book was published in London in 1767 and was followed up by William Blackstone, Jeremy Bentham, and Samuel Romilly in the codification of English criminal law, which was accomplished by 1800. Thus the Classical School developed and implemented an administrative and legal system of criminology.

Beccaria held that commission of crime was a matter of free will, that people tend to seek pleasure and avoid pain, that punishment was a deterrent, that laws and their punishment should be published for uniformity and deterrence value, and that children and the insane could not be charged as criminals. The principles that Beccaria recommended were that (1) the basis of all social actions must be the utilitarian concept of the greatest happiness for the greatest number; (2) crime must be considered an injury to society; (3) prevention of crime is more important than the punishment, which means that publishing the laws so that everyone may know what they are would be to reward virtue and prevent crime by certainty of punishment; (4) secret accusations and tortures should be abolished in favor of humane and speedy trials, and turning state's evidence is only "public authorization of treachery" and should be abolished; (5) the purpose of punishment is to deter persons from crime, rather than to provide social revenge; and (6) imprisonment should be more widely employed, but it should be improved (Vold, 1958, pp. 25–26).

Problems arose from the implementation of the theories of the Classical School in the French Code of 1791. The ignoring of individual differences and the significance of particular situations required a degree of flexibility that was difficult to achieve. The fact that first offenders and repeaters were to be treated similarly on the basis of the criminal act committed was found to be unrealistic. The fact that minors, idiots, the insane, and other incompetents were treated similarly on the basis of the act committed rather than on the individual offender was also unrealistic. Consequently, the Neoclassical School was characterized by (1) modification of the doctrine of free will, which could be affected by pathology, incompetence, insanity, or other conditions, as well as premeditation; (2) acceptance of the validity of mitigating circumstances; (3) modification of the doctrine of responsibility to provide mitigation of punishments, with partial responsibility in such cases as insanity, age, and other conditions that would affect "knowledge and intent of man at the time of the crime"; and (4) admission into court procedures of expert testimony on the question of degree of responsibility. The French Code of 1810 and the Revised French Code of 1819 provided for these modifications.

In England, Jeremy Bentham (1748–1832) was probably the greatest leader in reform of the criminal law in the direction of the Classical School. His *felicific calculus,* or the idea that man's objective is to achieve the most pleasure and the least pain, was central in the criminal law at that time.

Although William Blackstone (1723–80) was a conservative, he condemned the inconsistencies of the English criminal code of the day and supported the work of Bentham. In 1778, John Howard, supported by Blackstone and Sir William Eden, drafted the Penitentiary Act passed in 1779 to establish penitentiary houses. These houses were to be secure and sanitary structures; systematic inspection was to be provided; fees were abolished; and a reformatory regime was provided. This was the first formalization of the idea of "prison" in the modern sense.

Sir Samuel Romilly (1757–1818) launched a program that resulted in the construction of the first modern English prison at Millbank in 1816. His work was followed up by Sir James Mackintosh (1765–1832) and Sir Thomas Foxwell Buxton (1786–1845). The legislative leadership on behalf of a reform of the criminal code fell upon Sir Robert Peel

(1788–1850), who established the first modern police system in London in 1829. Although "insanity" had been a legal defense in criminal cases since Edward I (1239–1307), it was not until 1843 that the present McNaghten Rules defining insanity were formulated as a result of Daniel McNaghten's shooting and killing Prime Minister Peel's secretary by mistake, thinking he was Peel. McNaghten was acquitted by reason of insanity, since he thought the prime minister was persecuting him. The resulting furor was resolved by appointing a commission to determine the meaning of "insanity," and the commission's report is now known as the McNaghten Rules.

Paul J. A. Von Feuerbach (1775–1833), a German jurist, founded a theory of penal law that he called "psychological-course or intimidation theory." It gave a secular purpose to the rigorous Kantian doctrine that punishment ought only to be given for its own sake. He protested against vindictive punishment, however, and furthered the reform of German criminal law. He urged publicity in all legal proceedings as a deterrent and was a forerunner of modern efforts in the field of comparative law.

In America, Edward Livingston (1764–1836) was best known for his contributions in codifying the law, especially the criminal law. From 1829 to 1831, he presented the revision of the penal laws for Louisiana and the United States. Essentially, he did the same thing for United States criminal law that Blackstone, Bentham, and Romilly had done for England.

In summary, the Classical School of criminology rejected the previously prevailing concepts of supernatural powers and the "will of God" as the primary forces in human behavior, including criminal behavior, and substituted the free will of man and his intent. The consequent systematization of the discipline was built on the concept of free will; it eliminated human motives of revenge and substituted rational punishments that fit the seriousness of the crimes by causing rules to be determined and written into the law. Because of its basic concept of free will and punishments to "fit the crime," deterrence becomes important in the Classical School of criminology.

The Positive School

The Positive School of criminology is so named to indicate that legal findings and observations are to be based on proof and evidence as opposed to speculation and philosophy. Consequently, the emphasis changed from the free will of the Classical School to the "causes" of crime. The Positive School denied individual responsibility, intent, and free will and espoused a nonpunitive social response to crime.

Cesare Lombroso, an Italian Jew, initiated the Positive School with the publication of his *L'uomo Deliquente (The Criminal Man)* in 1876.

He maintained that his studies of troublesome soldiers showed that behavior is caused and the typical criminal can be identified by certain definite physical characteristics such as a slanting forehead, long earlobes or none at all, a large jaw, heavy supraorbital ridges, either an excess hairiness or absence of hair, and either extreme sensitivity or a lack of sensitivity to pain. He made a more thorough study of criminals in Italian prisons, where he found similar phenomena.

Lombroso developed a classification of criminals that became quite popular. The types he named were (1) the born criminal; (2) the insane criminal; (3) the criminal by passion, including the political "crank"; and (4) the occasional criminal, including the pseudo-criminal who was not dangerous and whose acts might be in defense or honor or for subsistence, (5) the habitual criminal, who had been conditioned to crime by unfavorable environmental circumstances, and (6) the criminal who was between the born criminal and the honest man but showed a touch of degeneracy. In terms of practical application, Lombroso thought that about a third of the prisoners were "throwbacks" or biological reversions to the primitive savages, or near "animals," a third were borderline in terms of biological endowment, and a third were accidental or occasional offenders who probably would not repeat their crimes.

Although his classifications did not stand, his objective approach and scientific method were forerunners of more accurate approaches to criminology. He consistently emphasized the need for direct study of the individual and began with the basic assumption of the biological nature of human character and behavior. In later years, he modified his theory and method to include all kinds of social, economic, and environmental data, but his method was always objective and "positive" in the sense of deterministic or causal factors, and he pursued the basic idea of cause as a "chain of interrelated causes."

Enrico Ferri was one of Lombroso's students. In 1878, he published *The Theory of Imputability and the Denial of Free Will*, which was an attack on the idea of free choice in human behavior and supported the general view that human behavior was caused. A determinist, Ferri was interested in Lombroso's ideas of basic biological causation but placed more significance on the interrelation of social, economic, and political factors. Classifying criminals as insane, born, occasional, and criminals by passion, he developed the idea of preventive measures, such as free trade, abolition of monopolies, building inexpensive workingmen's dwellings, public savings banks, better street lighting, birth control, freedom of marriage and divorce, state control of manufacture of weapons, provision for marriage of the clergy, establishment of foundling homes, and provision for public recreation. He thought that the state was the principal instrument through which better conditions were to be attained. When Mussolini came into power in Italy after World War

I and became prime minister in 1922, Ferri had already undertaken the preparation of a new penal code for Italy to put into legal practice the theories he had developed in earlier years. The Ferri Draft of 1921 denied moral responsibility of the individual and rejected the concept of punishment or retribution. It was, therefore, too radical a departure from the classical doctrine of the past and it was rejected by the Italian Chamber of Deputies. He then accepted the practical compromises and was accused by C. Bernaldo de Quiros of assenting to fascism (de Quiros, 1931).

Raffaele Garofalo was also a student of Lombroso; he too rejected the doctrine of free will and supported the position that crime can be understood only if it is studied by scientific methods. He attempted to formulate a sociological definition of crime that would designate those acts which no civilized society can refuse to recognize as criminal and which can be repressed by punishment. These constituted "natural crime" and were considered offenses violating the two basic altruistic sentiments common to all peoples, namely, probity (honesty) and pity. Crime is an immoral act that is injurious to society. This was more of a psychological orientation than Lombroso's physical-type anthropology. Garofalo's law of adaptation followed the biological principles of Darwin in terms of adaptation and the elimination of those unable to adapt in a kind of social natural selection. Consequently, he suggested (1) death for those whose criminal acts grew out of a permanent psychological anomaly, rendering them incapable of social life; (2) partial elimination or long-time imprisonment for those fit only for the life of nomadic hordes or primitive tribes; and (3) enforced reparation on the part of those who lack altruistic sentiments but who have committed their crimes under pressure of exceptional circumstances and are not likely to do so again.

Charles B. Goring (1870–1919), physician of His Majesty's Prison in England, enlisted the services of Dr. Karl Pearson, the eminent statistician who developed the coefficient of correlation and other statistical concepts, and made an exhaustive study of the physical types of inmates in England. In 1913, Goring published *The English Conflict*, with findings that were distinctly contrary to Lombroso's contentions. The result was that the Lombrosian doctrine of physical types was all but forgotten. Lombroso's contribution, the introduction of objective scientific method into the study of criminology, was an extremely important one to criminology, however.

Gabriel Tarde (1912), a French jurist and scholar, held that behavior is learned, including criminal behavior. His *Laws of Imitation* and *Penal Philosophy* were both first published in 1890 in Paris. He proposed association and learning as explanations of crime in contrast to the biological approach of Lombroso. (See Wilson, 1954.) He referred to criminals as "social excrement" at one point. Tarde thought that the court's only function was to determine the guilt or innocence of the accused person and that a committee of doctors should determine the degree of his responsibility, and the disposition should be on a psychological basis. He considered equal sentencing for equal crimes unfair and simplistic. Because crime is "caused" rather than a free-will response, deterrence is not an important concept in the Positive School. Rather, the Positive School emphasizes reform of the individual offender.

The American School

The American School of criminology, stressing sociological theories of crime causation and directly related to the Positive School, was influenced by nineteenth-century thinkers such as Adolphe Jacques Quetelet (1796–1874), who was a Belgian mathematician considered to be the developer of social statistics and the first social criminologist. He viewed climate, age, sex, and the seasons as contributing to crime, according to his analysis of crimes and moral conditions in France in 1836. He concluded that society prepares the crime and the guilty person is the instrument by which it is accomplished (de Quiros, 1911, p. 10).

Isaac Ray (1807–81) was the most influential writer in forensic psychiatry in the nineteenth century (Overholser, 1973). He published his *Medical Jurisprudence of Insanity* in 1838; this was published in both America and England. He brought the mental approach in criminological thinking from phrenology to psychiatry; and the diagnosis and treatment of the criminally insane still bear the influence of Isaac Ray.

There were other men who heavily influenced the development of the American School. Among them were such men as Henry Mayhew (1812–87), a British journalist and sociologist who studied the London poor and offenders and differentiated professional criminals who earn their living through crime from those accidental offenders who commit crime because of unanticipated circumstances (Clinard and Quinney, 1967, p. 8). John Haviland (1792–1852) was the architect who designed the radial prison and contributed the concept of functional prison design. It was after he reviewed the functions of the Pennsylvania System of Penitentiary management that he designed the Eastern State Penitentiary at Cherry Hill, Pennsylvania (now in Philadelphia), the New Jersey State Prison at Trenton, the Western State Penitentiary at Pittsburgh, and other prisons throughout the United States and Europe. Hans Gross (1847–1915) originated scientific criminal investigation in his native Austria, and the publication of his *Manual for the Examining Justice* in 1883 became the standard throughout the criminalistics world. In fact, Gross established criminalistics as an applied science. Gustav Aschaffenburg (1866–1944) was a German psychiatrist interested in criminology. Henry Maudsley (1835–1918), an English psychiatrist, published his *Responsibility in Mental Disease* in 1874. He saw real difficulty in treating offenders successfully and discussed convulsive therapy, psychosurgery, and many other approaches. There were other early criminologists. Many of them are included in an excellent book edited by Herman Mannheim entitled *Pioneers in Criminology*. All these approaches were adopted in America and became incorporated in the American School of Criminology.

The American School of Constitutional Criminology, as proposed by Barnes and Teeters (1959, pp. 128–34), paralleled the work of Lombroso but emphasized degeneracy and body build. Theoreticians who directly influenced this school included Jean Esquirol (1772–1840), *Mental Diseases;* Richard Dugdale (1841-83), *The Jukes;* Henry H. Goddard, and *The Kallikaks.* All of these publications supported the theory of degeneration of families. Body-build theory was central in Earnest A. Hooton's *Crime and the Man,* and this book was followed by supporting work by William H. Sheldon (1949) and Sheldon and Eleanor Glueck (1956).

John L. Gillin identified the American School of Criminology as early as 1914, referring to the clear sociological approach taken by American researchers and writers in the field of criminology ("Social Factors," 1914; also Sutherland and Cressey, 1966, p. 59). Maurice Parmelee indicated in 1908 that sociologists were contributing more than anybody to the field of criminology in America and, consequently, that criminology is really a subdivision of sociology in American universities (Parmelee, 1908).

All these approaches to criminology are positivistic in their approach. Although the Classical School emphasized free will, the law, and equal punishment for equal crimes, the Positive School and the American School deemphasized the law, indicating that behavior is caused and that the offender should be treated if possible. Prior to the Classical School, the focus was on the welfare of society, and banishment, death, and vengeance were primary reactions to offenses. The Classical School focused attention on the offense, and reaction by society was dependent upon the seriousness of the crime. The Positive School focused on the individual offender, and social reaction to crime was in terms of diagnosis and treatment.

The Social Defense School

The Social Defense School has been considered by some, such as Hermann Mannheim (1973), as a third school of criminology after the Classical School and the Positive School. Others, on the other hand, view it as an elaboration of the Positive School. Jeffery views "social defense" as a concept that transcends both the Classical and the Positive schools, as does Marc Ancel (1954). The concept of this body of theory developed gradually; Ancel traced its beginnings back to the Middle Ages, and

Enrico Ferri of the Positive School first used the term. The first significant recognition of social defense was in 1943, when Fillippo Gramatica established the Center of Social Defence Studies in Venice. The first international social defense conference was held in San Remo in 1947 and the second was held at Liège in 1949. The Social Defence Section of the United Nations was created in 1948. Because of some disagreement as to the definition of social defense, the name was changed in 1972 to the Section on Crime Prevention and Criminal Justice.[2] Gramatica (1963) contributed to the theory of social defense, while Ancel was more active in its implementation.

Social defense is concerned with (1) the personality of the offender, (2) the penal law, and (3) the manipulation of the environment for social betterment and, therefore, for crime prevention. Social defense is seen by Ancel as a revolt against the positivistic approach, just as the Positive School was a revolt against the Classical School. Social defense is a reaction against vengeance and retribution because crime involves both society and the individual, so the approach to crime must be broader than simply convicting and punishing the offender. The basic precepts in this school can be summarized as follows (Ancel, 1966, p. 24):

1. Social defense presupposes that the means of dealing with crime should be conceived as a method of protecting society rather than punishing the individual.

2. The method of social protection involves the neutralization of the offender, either by removal and segregation or by applying remedial and educational methods.

3. The penal policy of social defense favors an individual rather than a collective approach to the prevention of crime that is aimed at the resocialization of the offender.

4. This program involves a process of an ever-increasing "humanization" of the new criminal law that involves restoration of self-confidence and personal responsibility on the part of the offender, together with the development of a sense of human values.

5. The process of humanization of the criminal justice system involves the scientific understanding of the phenomenon of crime and the offender's personality.

The basic tenet of social defense is the elimination of punishment, as such. Protection of society can be accomplished by rehabilitation and socialization better than by punishment and vengeance. Offenders are biological and social entities who learn their behavior or are having emotional problems with social adaptation. They should be studied scientifically and assisted in their social adaptation. The use of legal fictions

---

[2]The international spelling is *defence*. In America it is *defense*.

like *mens rea* or intent have no place in social defense.

The Social Defense School differs from the Positive School because it brings the law back into criminological thinking. It does not go back to the theories of the Classical School, however, because the law in social defense incorporates provision for the needs of the offender rather than emphasizing the seriousness of the crime. It is interesting to note that most of the writing in social defense has been by Europeans, while the actual implementation of many of its tenets has been manifest mostly in the United States.

EMERGENCE OF CRIMINOLOGY

The emergence of criminology as a field of study in America came in the early twentieth century, although it had flourished in Europe for over a century before in schools of law, legal medicine, and anthropology. As has been mentioned, Maurice Parmelee (1922, 1924) pointed out the contributions of sociology and anthropology in 1908, and John Gillin identified the American School as a sociologically oriented one in 1914. Parmelee also noted that the majority of research reported in the literature in this field between 1900 and 1918 had been done by sociologists, so criminology was a legitimate subspeciality of sociology. Other sociologists contributed to defining and identifying the field of criminology.

The earliest significant textbook in the field was written by Edwin H. Sutherland, and first published in 1924. After Sutherland's death in 1950, Donald R. Cressey, a former student of Sutherland's, continued the revisions. The tenth edition was published in 1978 and it remains one of the most encyclopaedic texts in the field. Donald R. Taft published his *Criminology* in 1942, with other editions in 1950, 1956, and collaborated with Ralph England for a fourth edition in 1964. Barnes and Teeters published their excellent *New Horizons in Criminology* in 1943, with subsequent editions in 1951 and 1959. Walter C. Reckless published his *The Crime Problem* in 1950, with subsequent editions in 1955, 1961, 1967, and 1973. Although there have been other good texts, these have been the leaders in the field, all written by sociologists. There have been many other excellent books, such as George Vold's *Theoretical Criminology* published in 1958 and updated in 1979 by Thomas J. Bernard; Hermann Mannheim's *Comparative Criminology* published in 1965 and updated in 1979; Sue Titus Reid's *Crime and Criminology*, Second Edition, published in 1979, and Gresham M. Sykes, *Criminology*, 1978. This type of literature in the field, in addition to many journals, has identified criminology as a distinct field of study, though it borrows from many disciplines, including sociology, psychology, law, and the medical field, particularly psychiatry.

FOUR MODALITIES OF CRIMINOLOGY

The theory and the practice of criminology in the universities and in the applied field of criminal justice appear to fall broadly into three categories. Some approaches emphasize the *control model*, in which changes in behavior and the objectives of practice emphasize external control, such as arrest and apprehension, custody, behavior modification by reward and punishment, and similar control approaches. The *medical model* or *patient model* sees offenders as maladjusted or "sick" persons who need psychotherapy, casework, education, counseling, and other approaches that will help them to deal better with their environment. In the *sociogenic approach*, offenders are seen as products of their environment; their social and economic settings need to be improved, involving such things as change of home or neighborhood, improving the conditions in the inner city or ghetto, and other modifications designed to improve their environment. The *justice model* is simply determinate sentencing to fit the seriousness of the crime without being concerned about causation or other factors. There has been no definitive study to indicate the superiority of one approach above the other. In practice, it is apparent that all four are brought to bear on the offender and the crime problem in different degrees.

CONCLUSIONS

The three natural origins of punishment or reaction to crime have been (1) the presence of a harsh environment with which humans have to deal, (2) occurrence of natural disasters, and (3) religion (Newman, 1978, p. 14). Society's reaction during early times was in retribution and compensation through slavery, which as a social institution contributed much to penology (Sellin, 1976).

Criminology emerged as a separate discipline between the eighteenth and twentieth centuries. Before the publication of Beccaria's *Essay on Crimes and Punishments* in 1764, crime was seen as sinful and motivated by supernatural spirits of various sorts. Between 1764 and 1883, the Classical School of criminology prevailed, in which crime was seen as free choice and the offenses were codified in the law with appropriate punishments attached. The biological movement of the nineteenth century found expression in criminology in Lombroso's work published in 1876, which initiated the Positive School, focusing on the offender rather than the law. Lombroso, Garofalo, and Ferri have been called the holy three of criminology (Schafer, 1968, p. 3). All were determinists in that they held that crime was *caused* by factors beyond the individual's control rather than *chosen* through free will. Lombroso emphasized biological factors. Garofalo held that criminals suffer from inherited moral degeneracy. Ferri placed priority on social and environmental conditions, such as the neighborhood socioeconomic levels, and proposed programs aimed at improvement of living and social conditions. The biological theories of Lombroso were discredited by the work of Goring, published in 1913, after which social, economic, and psychological causes of crime dominated the field. By the early twentieth century, criminology had emerged as a special discipline or area of study and practice.

Crime has been seen as an identification of problem areas in any society. This has led some writers to conclude that crime really creates the social order, and not the other way around, that one has to forgive one's enemies, but not before they have been hanged (Newman, 1978, p. 287). There is little grace in justice.

Questions

1. What is criminology?
2. How did criminology emerge?
3. Differentiate between the consensus model and the conflict model of relationships between people.
4. How did intelligence testing emerge?
5. What is the Classical School of criminology?
6. Describe the Positive School of criminology.
7. What is the American School of criminology?
8. Outline the social defense approach to criminology.
9. What were the contributions of Emile Durkheim, Charles Horton Cooley, and Max Weber (generally considered to be the most influential early sociologists)?
10. Why have Lombroso, Garofalo, and Ferri been referred to as the holy three of early criminology?

three

BIOLOGY AND ECONOMICS

After the philosophical tenets of the Classical School and Positive School had been evaluated, other factors were considered that broadened the base of understanding of deviant and criminal behavior. Even Lombroso, in his later years, included environmental factors as well as the biological factors in his explanation of crime. The base of understanding of human behavior, including criminal behavior, became refined in the biological factors, with some emphasis on intelligence as a biological or hereditary trait. The modern experimental psychologists retain the biological approach, with the rats running mazes and other experimental phenomena for which the units can be described, observed, and measured. The units of measurement are still biological rather than from value systems or "human" abstractions, so the biological and physiological approaches to human behavior still exist in many of the behavioral sciences. The relationship of biological factors, however—particularly regarding the intellectual aspect—remains at issue today. A recent controversy as to what I.Q. measures, for example, hinges on the following argument: (1) If differences in mental abilities are inherited, and (2) if success requires those abilities, and (3) if earnings and prestige depend on success, (4) then a social standing that reflects earnings and prestige would be based to some extent on inherited differences among people (Herrnstein, 1973).

Economics is the social science most closely associated and incorporated with success in society. Karl Heinrich Marx (1813–83), together with Frederich Engels (1820–95), pointed out the significance of economic conditions and class struggle in crime, poverty, and other social problems in the *Communist Manifesto*, published in 1849. Economic interpretations of social problems must include the contribution of Karl Marx. The idea of social crimes develops from economics and philosophy. As criminology developed, biology and economics had to be basic to the transition from philosophical considerations to a scientific approach in understanding criminal behavior. Through the nineteenth century, human behavior was seen as biological from the standpoint of the individual, economic from the standpoint of society, and philosophical from the standpoints of ethics and religion.

BIOLOGY

Although biology and economics both rose to new importance in the nineteenth century, it was the biological explanations that most influenced the emerging field of criminology. Body type and endocrinology, the "born criminal" biologically determined by what might now be called in the vernacular the "bad seed" was prominent in the field, as indicated by previous references to studies of "degenerate" families like *The Jukes* and *The Kallikak Family*. Intelligence testing, considered to be a measure of ability derived by heredity, began in the 1890s in rudimentary form. More recent interpretations of these biological interpretations have taken the form of chromosomal differences and brain waves that are measured by the electroencephalograph. Surgical approaches to biological concerns, such as psychosurgery and castration, have been recent refinements in another direction. Persisting from the eighteenth century and earlier is the belief that the influences of external forces—weather, climate, and the moon—upon biological functions may partially determine behavior. A brief discussion of each of the approaches seems to be appropriate.

The effect of biology on social thinking is in five areas: (1) theory of evolution, (2) "organic analogy" of society, (3) heredity and environment as complementary causal factors in behavior, (4) theories regarding racism, and (5) biodynamics like stress, anxiety, and other pathological conditions. The theory of evolution is related to the "struggle for existence" as applied to the social order. The organic analogy is related to organizations and other groups, both formal and informal, that begin, mature, and die, with their strength gaining, reaching maximum proportions, and then fading away. Heredity has been seen as the basic explanation for individual differences and a basic factor underlying social and political change in the interaction between the social "heavyweights" and the "lightweights" in the sociopolitical process. Several writers have been concerned with racial superiority and inferiority in many ways, such as intelligence and physical strength. Stress and anxiety impair judgment and social interaction. It is apparent that biology has, in fact, influenced social thinking.

Body Type and Endocrinology

The idea that body type and other constitutional types form the biological basis of human behavior is not new. In the fifth century B.C., Hippocrates proposed the dichotomy of the thick-set, heavy body build susceptible to apoplexy and similar physical disorders (*habitus apoplecticus*) and the long, slender body susceptible to respiratory diseases (*habitus phthisicus*). In the second century A.D., Galen, frequently called the father of modern medicine, proposed the well-known four temperaments, sanguine, choleric, phlegmatic, and melancholic, according to the excess of one or another of the four humors of body fluids. In 1853, Carus, a German zoologist, described three body types as phlegmatic (a person whose digestive organs are prominent), athletic (a strongly developed person), and asthenic (a long body and poorly developed bones and muscles). Body-type theories abounded in the last half of the nineteenth century, including those of Viola in Italy, Davenport in America, Pavlov in Russia, and Jaensch, Weidenreich, and many others in Germany. In 1912, Carl Jung (1875–1961) proposed two broad biological types: the introvert, who is governed by subjective factors and whose psychic energy is directed inward; and the extrovert, who is governed by external factors and whose psychic energy is directed outward. Ernst Kretschmer (1888–1964), a German psychiatrist, has probably been most influential in America with his classifications of pyknic type (large trunk with short legs), athletic type (well-proportioned body), leptosome or asthenic type (long body and little weight), and the dysplastic (marked abnormalities in development). Different temperaments were associated with each type.

Earnest A. Hooten (1887–1954) of Harvard revived theories of race and "criminal stock" in the Lombrosian sense (1939). He tended to vindicate Lombroso in an exhaustive twelve-year study in which 13,873 male prisoners in ten states and 3,203 persons not in prison were compared. He also conducted a minute anthropological study of 5,689 prisoners and divided them into nine racial types, concluding that the biologically inferior people in each race deviated farther from the mean than the races themselves. Hooten applied the body types developed by Kretschmer to criminology.

William H. Sheldon (1940, 1942, and 1949), a student of Hooten, carried the project further in several publications that connected body build with criminal behavior. The contention of all these publications was that delinquency and body build were associated. Following Kretschmer's types, the endomorph was viscertonic, short and fat, and was an extrovert. The mesomorph or athletic type was normal and well-proportioned; he was considered to be somatotonic or active, dynamic, and aggressive. The ectomorph, tall and thin, was cerebrotonic—an ingrown person who worried, had allergies, and was an introvert. In his *Varieties of Delinquent Behavior,* Sheldon described the lives and adventures of two hundred young adults in South Boston, pointing out that behavior is a function of body structure and thus attacking the psychiatric approaches.

Sheldon and Eleanor Glueck (1956) have also theorized that body build plays more of a role in precipitating delinquent behavior than has previously been acknowledged. They held that (1) differences in physique types are accompanied by differences in the incidence of traits associated with deliquency; (2) differences in body type produce differential responses to environmental pressures; and (3) differential incidents of traits and reactions to environment among physique types is related to differences among them in the etiology of delinquency (from a critique of the Gluecks' study by Albert Morris, 1957).

Physical appearance is considered to be important in interpersonal relationships, whether in politics, the workaday world, social functions, or other types of interaction with people. The reaction of others and one's own feeling about unusual appearances affects social interaction. Skin blemishes, especially during adolescence, become a source of embarrassment. Oversized ears, poor eyesight, short stature, crippled or missing limbs, obesity, cerebral palsy, and many other factors contribute to the nature and extent of social interaction. Compensatory behavior often develops in the form of delinquency (Barnes and Teeters, 1959, p. 138).

Physical disfigurement is considered by many psychiatrists as an important element in deviant behavior, including delinquency and crime (Banay, 1943). Disfigurement unquestionably contributes to greater difficulty in social adjustment. Tattoos have also been considered as a source of social embarrassment. The contribution of physical appearance to social adjustment, including crime and delinquency, is the reason many prison hospitals have facilities for cosmetic surgery. Straightening crossed eyes, removing facial and other prominent scars, straightening prominently hooked noses, setting back underslung jaws, and removing tattoos have become part of the correctional treatment process in many programs.

Endocrinology has been considered to be probably the most important factor in the behavior of man (Hoskins, 1941, p. 348); the thief and murderer have been described completely in glandular terms (Schlapp and Smith, 1928). It has been observed that approximately one-third of all prisoners suffer from emotional instability that is probably due to glandular or toxic disturbances (Schlapp, 1924). However, some outstanding biologists have indicated that the relationship between glandular dysfunction and criminality cannot be proved and that there is no evidence that anybody inherits a tendency to commit criminal acts (Montagu, 1941, p. 55).

Studies of identical twins have been used as examples of inheritance of criminality (Rosanoff et al., 1934) but criticism of such conclusions indicates that the similar environment was more important in the development of criminal behavior than similar parents (H. Newman, 1940, p. 160).

Goitein (1947) presents a "character pattern" that divides crime according to its function in satisfying biological needs at various levels of maturation in the psychoanalytic framework, yet permitting legalistic terms. Oral aberrations appear in assertive violence, anal aberrations appear as acquisitive crimes, urethral aberrations appear in fire-setting and flooding with accompanying fantasies, and gonadal aberrations appear in rape and other sex offenses whose complex dynamics are sexually motivated. Finally, somatic aberrations appear in hypochondriacal and perverse practices.

Contemporary reviews of Hooten's work have been consistently unfavorable. (For example, see Merton and Montagu, 1940.) His thesis appears to be the familiar "dregs of society" approach that may be popular with Archie Bunker types. There is no evidence that satisfies even the majority of criminologists that body type, endocrinology, or other biological factors *cause* crime. Critics of the body-type approach point out that there is no evidence of relating body type to crime or delinquency as legally and sociologically defined, and one critic referred to it as a "sophisticated type of shadow-boxing" (Vold, 1958, p. 74).

Intelligence

The area of intelligence, particularly mental retardation, has been associated with the constitutional approach of selective breeding—in which general capability is considered to be inherited. Aristotle proposed an analogy of predisposing causes and precipitating causes in human behavior to the growth of an oak tree or a birch tree from its original seed (quoted in Crombie, 1959, pp. 71–72). The rainfall provided the immediate or precipitating cause for germination and growth, but the final or predisposing cause that determined the result of "oakhood" or "birchhood" was in the seed itself. This thinking may have been behind the concept of the "bad seed."

The first clear separation of the categories of mental defect and mental disease was made in 1838 when Jean Esquirol published his *Mental Diseases*. Isaac Ray was reaching similar conclusions in America at the same time. The legal definition of insanity, supposedly related to mental disease, was formulated in 1843 when the McNaghten Rules were developed by a special commission appointed by the king in England. The term *idiot* used by Isaac Ray was subsequently entered into most statutes as *feebleminded.* Consequently, *insanity* and *feeblemindedness* are legal statuses that denote mental derangement and mental retardation, respectively, as decided by juries in competency proceedings.

In 1877, Richard Dugdale published *The Jukes,* a famous study of an allegedly mentally retarded family, which focused attention on generally poor heredity as a basic factor in intelligence and crime. Degeneracy and innate deprivation were considered as central to the causes of crime. In 1912, Henry H. Goddard published a similar study— *The Kallikak Family.* The Kallikak saga began during the Revolutionary War when Martin Kallikak met a feebleminded girl and became the father of a feebleminded son. By 1912, there were 480 known direct descendants of this temporary union, 143 of them known to be feebleminded, and many were of illegitimate birth, alcoholics, and prostitutes. Returning from the Revolutionary War, Martin Kallikak married a respectable girl from a "good" family. Among the 496 individuals in direct descent, there were no feebleminded persons, no illegitimate persons, no prostitutes, no criminals, but many lawyers, doctors, judges, and other distinguished persons. Davenport's study (1912) of the Nam family produced similar results.

In a study of the relationship of intelligence to delinquency and crime, Murchison (1924) stated that there was no relationship between intelligence and crime. In other writings, criminals as a class were found to compare favorably with the general population with respect to intelligence (Zelany, 1933).

Chromosomes and Crime

Normal males have one X and one Y chromosome, which is an XY, while normal females have two X chromosomes, or XX. The sex of an individual is determined at conception. Persons with normal male characteristics always have the Y chromosome; females never have the Y chromosome. There have been many abnormal combinations and mosaics, and these sometimes cause difficulty in defining roles in society. For example, an XXY may think he is female and may have been brought up that way and yet find difficulty in accepting the female role. Conversely, the XXY may have been brought up as a male but have reservations about the role. This is why sex-change operations are becoming more common in modern society. The recent theory is that the presence of XYY chromosomes in the male produces an overly aggressive "supermale" who finds himself in conflict with the law more frequently than do his XY brothers. Some have suggested that this finding will revive the effort to look for "the bad seed" (Roebuck and Atlas, 1969; also see Falek et al., 1970).

The first finding of the XYY chromosome in the adult male (an American) was reported in the English medical journal, *Lancet,* published August 26, 1961. Subsequently, a 1967 study at Pentridge Prison in Melbourne, Australia, proposed the XYY combination as linked to crime. Parenthetically, Richard Speck, who killed eight nurses in Chicago in 1968, is an XYY. Richard Fox (1971) reports that the XYYs in prison populations are no more violent than other prisoners but that they have a higher proportion of property offenses than the other prisoners. There is considerable doubt in the criminological field that XYY is a significant factor in criminal behavior. The 1969 national symposium held by the National Institute of Mental Health also concluded that the link between the XYY chromosome and crime could not realistically be shown ("Link Between XYY Syndrome," 1969). Much of the other literature is inconclusive (Jacobs et al., 1965; Montagu, 1968; Price and Whatmore, 1967; Stock, 1968; and Weiner et al., 1968).

Electroencephalography

The use of the electroencephalograph (EEG) to read the brain waves was introduced in 1929 by Hans Berger of Germany. The brain generates small electrical currents during its activity, ranging from one to five millionths of a volt at eight to twelve cycles per second. These alpha waves come from the back part of the head. More rapid beta waves come from the central and front part of the head, ranging from eighteen to twenty-five cycles per second. Abnormal EEG patterns can be identified and used in diagnosis of brain lesions, tumors, epilepsy, and other organic brain difficulties. Also, some connection between abnormal brain waves has been found to be associated with some kinds of deviant behavior.

The relationship of some conduct disorders to organic disease has been pointed out by Bender (1945). Others have pointed out that the EEG can be used in various ways in the area of understanding criminal behavior.

Stafford-Clark (1949) has used the EEG in attempting to understand pathological murder. His comparison of "normal" homicides or those with a perceptible motive with "serious" or abnormal homicides or those without a perceptible motive indicate variations in EEG patterns, with the "normal" homicide offenders showing relatively normal EEG patterns and the "serious" or abnormal homicide offenders showing relatively abnormal EEG patterns. These findings are shown in Table 3-1.

Further support for the contention that EEG abnormalities distinguish murderers who are either insane or apparently without

TABLE 3-1.
EEG Patterns of Offenders Committing "Normal" and "Serious" Homicides

	MOTIVATION	NORMAL	MILD UNSPECIFIED	SEVERE UNSPECIFIED	LOCAL OR EPILEPTIC
"NORMAL"	1. Incidental to another crime or self-defense.	10	0	1	0
	2. Resulting from clear motive or during a deliberate crime.	12	2	0	2
"SERIOUS" (Abnormal)	3. Apparently motiveless or slight.	4	5	4	2
	4. Associated with strong sexual element.	4	3	0	1
	5. Insane.	2	7	2	3

motive from those who show definite motive was reported in an editoral in the *British Medical Journal* in 1970 ("Violent Crime and the E.E.G.," 1970). Severity of EEG abnormality correlates with the degree of psychiatric disturbance. A group of aggressive psychopaths showed about two-thirds EEG abnormality, but approximately one-third of the violent and dangerous offenders had no such abnormality and simply reacted aggressively to a clear motive or in self-defense.

Some persons have been found to be able to control to some extent the production of alpha waves (Nideffer, 1973). This apparently occurs in the meditation states used in yoga and Zen disciplines. In America, transcendental meditation is a type of "exercise" in which the individual sits in a comfortable position with eyes closed and perceives a suitable thought or sound. Without concentrating specifically on this thought or sound, the meditator allows his mind to experience it freely, during which he has a feeling that he is rising to a finer and more creative level of life in an easy and natural manner. Wallace and Benson (1972) have found a marked intensification of alpha waves during these 15-to-20-minute meditation sessions. The experiments with alpha waves have never, however, supported extrasensory perception (ESP) or anything related to it. Neither is there validity in the claims that meditation develops "enlightenment and oneness of the universe," and is a physiological phenomenon (Nideffer, 1973).

Alpha rhythms are frequently thought to be associated with feelings of calmness and relaxation, while beta waves are associated with orienting the person to new stimuli, attentiveness, tension, aggravation, and frustration (Beatty, 1973).

Advocates of transcendental meditation argue that it allows rapid learning to take place. Benson and Wallace suggest that meditation can be an adequate substitute for drug-taking behavior (in Shapiro, 1973, p. 485).

In summary, the EEG patterns can be used for determining some abnormalities that appear to be based in brain malfunction, causing behavior deviation. Electroencephalography is best used to determine epilepsy and organic brain disorders, but it can also be useful in studying abnormalities in some behavioral deviations. Pathological intoxication from alcohol will produce an abnormal EEG pattern, as will some other psychosomatic difficulties. EEG changes following psychosurgery are dependent upon the extent of damage done to the frontal cortex. Soon after major lobotomies there may be high-voltage slow discharges from a broad area, later narrowing down to the frontal regions where they may persist for months or years. In conclusion, there is a relationship between the biological functions of the brain and deviant behavior, but it is not specific.

Psychosurgery

Psychosurgery is an operation primarily designed to cut the nerve pathways between the prefrontal lobes of the brain and the hypothalamus to reduce disturbing thoughts and hallucinations. The brain is considered to be a primary source of aggression (Mark and Ervin, 1970), as already discussed briefly in the previous section on the EEG. The operation was first performed in 1935 in Lisbon by Almeida Lima under the direction of Egas Moniz. The original operation consisted of cutting two holes in the skull, just above the temples, and then cutting a measured section of nerve fibers connecting the frontal lobes with the thalamus. Several modifications have been made since, of which the most popular is the transorbital lobotomy. In this operation, a sharp and slender instrument is driven through the eye sockets and up through the bony part above the eyes to reach the frontal lobe of the brain and then swung in an arc of about thirty degrees and withdrawn. This avoids scars on the side of the head. Within an hour or so, the patient can get out of bed and perform simple activities.

Postoperative effects have varied; some have resulted in aphasia, convulsions, increased appetite, and rectal or urinal incontinence. These variations have probably been caused by too much brain tissue being cut and some areas of the brain having been cut unintentionally. Some of the effects of lobotomies vary with different surgical procedures.

When successful, the lobotomy results in a reduction of emotional tension and anxiety. The patient frequently becomes complacent, showing a reduction of personality depth and some shallowness in emotional experience. He becomes somewhat cut off from his past and his identity. His intellectual ability is reduced but not impaired to a serious extent in terms of daily living. There is a diminished interest in his surroundings and poorer associations with other people.

There are other types of psychosurgery, particularly amygdalotomy or the lobotomy of the temporal lobes above the ears. The effects of some of these operations are shown in Table 3-2.

Stereotactic treatment, the use of electrodes for stimulation of the brain, is used for the treatment of aggression when other methods, in-

TABLE 3-2.
Summary of 47 Cases Classified by the Grade of Effects

Behavioral Abnormality in 47 Patients Grade of Effect	EFFECTS OF AMYGDALOTOMY ON			
	Laterality of Lessions (mm)			
	Medial			Lateral 20
	15–17.5	17.5–20		
A''-A (Sufficient improvement for patient to return to previous environment)	Case no. 91 93 98	Case no. 61 71 74 75 76 82 86 92 94 97 99 100	101 110 112 113 117 121 122 124 125 126 127	Case no. 73
No. of patients	3	23		1
B or B-C (Improvement, but not enough to return to previous work)	Case no. 90 102 105	Case no. 85 109 115 118 123		Case no. 65 66 67 84 89 103 119
No. of patients	3	5		7
C (Improvement slight)	Case no. 70 111			Case no. 95 104 107
No. of patients	2			3

Of the cases most dramatically influenced, the surgical lesions were 18–20 millimeters or less from the midline. In the three cases least affected, the lesions were farther away from the medial line. This indicates that the best effect is closer to the medial line in surgery, while the least effect is farther from the midline.

From: H. Narabayashi and F. Shima, "Which Is the Better Amygdala Target, the Medical or Lateral Nuclei? (For Behavior Problems and Paroxysm in Epileptics)," chap. 19 in Lauri V. Laitinen and Kenneth E. Livingston, eds., *Surgical Approaches in Psychiatry* (Baltimore: University Park Press, 1973), p. 133. Originally published by MTP Medical and Technical Publishing Company, Lancaster, England, 1973.

cluding psychotropic drugs, have proved unsuccessful (Nádvornik et al., 1973, p. 125). A summary of the target areas in the brain for the treatment of aggressive people through stereotactic methods for forty-three patients is shown in Table 3-3. Stereotactic treatment of aggressive behavior affects the functional mechanism of mental activity, but little is known about it. A new level of regulation of behavior is achieved in which the patient is more acceptable to society (Nádvornik et al., 1973, p. 127).

The primary use of lobotomies has been in retarded persons who have violent assaultive behavior patterns (Freeman, 1959). Among the effects recorded thus far of psychosurgery are the facts that patients seldom dream after a lobotomy; schizophrenic patients respond favorably; obsessive, phobic, and hysterical symptoms are invariably reduced. The best success has been with the disabling neuroses that are

TABLE 3-3.
Clinical Diagnosis and Surgical Targets in 43 Patients
Operated on Stereotactically for Aggressive Behavior

DIAGNOSIS	NO. OF PATIENTS	SURGICAL TARGET	BILATERAL	LEFT	RIGHT
Idiocy	11	Dorsomedial thalamus	2	—	1
		Anterior thalamus	2	1	1
		Amygdala	1	2	—
		Amygdala and left putamen	1	—	—
		Posterior hypothalamus	1	—	—
Imbecility	17	Dorsomedial thalamus	1	3	1
		Anterior thalamus	7	—	—
		Amygdala	3	—	—
		Amygdala and left Hippocampus	1	—	—
		Posterior hypothalamus	1	—	—
Debility	5	Dorsomedial thalamus	2	—	—
		Amygdala	1	1	1
Psychopathy	5	Posterior hypothalamus	5	—	—
Epilepsy	3	Posterior hypothalamus	1	—	—
		Posterior hypothalamus and both amygdalas and both hippocampi	1	—	—
		Posterior hypothalamus and both amygdalas and both hippocampi	1	—	—
Schizophrenia	2	Posterior hypothalamus	1	—	—
		Posterior hypothalamus and left dorsomedial thalamus	—	—	1
Total	43		31	7	5

Aggression was best reduced in idiots and imbeciles. Surgery to the thalamus has undesirable side effects in that it impairs activity, mood, and interest in his work. After posterior hypothalamotomy, the patient is rid of his aggressive behavior.
From P. Nádvornik, J. Pogády and M. Šramka, "The Results of Stereotactic Treatment of the Aggressive Syndrome," chap. 18 in Lauri V. Laitinen and Kenneth E. Livingston, eds., *Surgical Approaches in Psychiatry* (Baltimore: University Park Press, 1973), p. 126. Originally published by MTP Medical and Technical Publishing Company, Lancaster, England, 1973.

characterized by anxiety and hypertension. Psychopathy, however, does not respond to psychosurgery. Property offenders, such as burglars, thieves, forgers, and car thieves, resume their offenses after lobotomies. On the other hand, after psychosurgery, crimes of violence are rarely repeated, and sex offenses are limited to mild indecencies. The effect of psychosurgery on addiction to drugs and alcohol cannot be predicted because of thus far inconclusive results.

In summary, anxiety is reduced by lobotomies. Some observers in prisons in which lobotomies are typically performed, such as in California, have indicated that this surgery makes "vegetables" of people. Postoperative ability to respond to intelligence and other tests has been varied. In the future, there might be some legal due process and consent problems in using psychosurgery in criminal treatment.

Castration

Castration of the male has been an approach traditionally used by man for a variety of purposes. Ancient and medieval man used it to produce eunuchs of sexless people as servants to tend and guard the harems among the wealthy Moslems and ruling classes in the Middle East and Africa. Castration was used to produce male sopranos or contraltos for ecclesiastical chants in the Roman Catholic Church. Pope Leo XIII, who held the papacy from 1878 to 1903, stopped it. It has always been used to some extent in the case of sex offenders, historically for purposes of punishment rather than a treatment objective. During the past century, however, it has been used in many countries for treatment purposes, the idea being that the reduction of aggression in some sex offenders is conducive to public safety. Castration, as a treatment for serious sex offenders, has been traditionally employed by the Scandinavian countries. (See Stürup, 1968.)

The effect of castration after sexual maturity is not completely agreed upon. The result of early castration is well known. It produces a sexless person without the hormones attributed to masculinity. This would be similar to castrating a rooster to produce a capon or castrating a young bull to produce a steer, both having been castrated prior to sexual maturity.

At conception, a normal female receives XX chromosomes, develops ovaries, and secretes estrogen; a normal male receives XY chromosomes, develops testes, and secretes androgen. Differential levels of androgen are associated with differential levels of aggression. The theory is that reduction of the secretion of male hormones reduces both the desire and capability for sexual activity. Certain cells within these organs, together with other tissues, such as the adrenal cortex, secrete into the bloodstream testosterone and other hormones that influence development of secondary sex characteristics, such as voice pitch, body proportion, facial hair, and the whole pattern of sex behavior on the part of the individual. Castration of the male reduces testosterone and other androgens. If it is done after sexual maturity, the results are not completely clear. Sex behavior is influenced by psychological factors, memory, and emotional factors, in addition to biological structure. A consistent observation is that mammals of all species tend to grow fat and lazy after castration.

Punitive sterilization has existed in the United States since around 1907 (Paul, 1968), but has been focused primarily on sterilization of mothers with illegitimate children. The vast majority of these sterilizations were performed on women on welfare. Welfare departments had requested the action from the courts and supposedly had "informed consent" from the women. By 1968, there had been around 65,000 sterilizations, of which about 25,000 had been done in the 1930s. The largest number was done in North Carolina. In 1968, the rate was approximately four hundred sterilizations per year with a small minority of them done in penal institutions. More castrations have been done in California penal institutions than in any other state.

Following the general trend, sterilization done in prisons peaked in the 1930s. There were some organizations that actively promoted its use from that time into the 1950s; for example, the Society for Human Betterment, first headquartered in South Carolina, moved to New York City in the early 1950s. It is now defunct. Castration in prisons has been voluntary, primarily, based on "informed consent" of the individual involved, or else it has been done by a court order. It was never as widely used in the United States as in the Scandinavian countries. The number could be estimated at approaching probably a dozen men per year during its peak use in the 1930s, but this information is anecdotal and hearsay. There are no accurate records available; and American correctional physicians have generally found castration to be useless and abhorrent.

All surgery performed on prisoners, including castration and psychosurgery, encounters legal difficulties in due process and civil rights in the United States. The right of a prisoner to refuse treatment that involves lobotomies, electric shock, and other physical invasion of the bodily integrity has been recently supported (Singer, 1973, p. 194). It can be done in prisons *generally* only after "informed consent" has been received—and what constitutes informed consent has also been challenged. Certainly, the question of cruel and unusual punishment in violation of the Eighth Amendment could be raised and First Amendment objection to "tinkering with a man's mind" has already been raised.

Weather, Climate, and the Moon

Several early scholars used geography as an explanation of criminal behavior. In his *Spirit of Laws*, Montesquieu contended that criminality increases as one approaches the equator and drunkenness increases as one approaches the poles. Adolph Quetelet, frequently referred to as the "father of social statistics," indicated that crimes against the person were more prevalent in warm climates and increased as the equator was approached, while property crimes were more numerous in cold areas and increased as the poles were approached. This "thermic law" of crime was further studied by Mayo-Smith in 1907. A study by M. deGuerry Champneuf indicated that from 1825 to 1830, there were 100 crimes against the person in the northern part of France as compared with 181.5 against property, while there were only 48.8 crimes against property for every 100 crimes against the person in southern France. (See Barnes and Teeters, 1959, p. 143.) Lombroso, Ferri, and Aschaffenburg all made similar observations regarding their countries. Peter Kropotkin (1842–1921) proposed a formula: multiply by seven the average temperature of the month, add the average humidity, and multiply by two in order to obtain the number of homicides that will be committed during the month in Russia.

Although weather has been considered by many practitioners to be an influence on criminal behavior, there is no empirical evidence to support that hypothesis. The lack of association between crime rates and such weather conditions as temperature, humidity, and barometric pressure measured daily for one year in a city suggests that weather variation has no relationship to crime (La Roche and Tilley, 1956). Data from the National Crime Surveys from 1973 through 1975 indicate that some crimes are higher in the summer months, such as personal larceny of $50 or more, forcible-entry burglary, assault, and motor vehicle theft; larceny under $50 is highest in October (*Crime and Seasonality*, 1980).

Seasonal variations in crime are generally associated with cultural factors rather than the season itself. For example, in the U.S., rapes are highest in July and August, while shoplifting is highest in December—fewer clothes are worn in the summer; Christmas is in December. In any case, there has been no meaningful link between crime and the seasons other than cultural ones that satisfy all persons interested in crime causation.

The moon has been cited as a cause of criminal behavior by many veteran law enforcement personnel and some prison guards or correctional officers. Lieber has reported significantly higher rates of homicides in Cuyahoga County (Cleveland, Ohio) and in Dade County (Miami, Florida) during times of the full moon (Lieber, 1978). The president of Professional Astrologers, Inc., Doris Chase Doane, is reported to have said, "Ask any policeman about the marked increase in murders and rapes during a full moon" (Weisinger, 1973). When asked, however, a high official in the New York City Police Department replied in the negative: "Criminals shun well-lit areas—if anything, a full moon is a detriment to their activities." Such reports regarding lunar influence are generally expressed in anecdotes and presented in the form of belief. Unfortunately, literature or research supporting this contention is elusive to the behavioral scientist. Nevertheless, the belief is widespread and appears in many class discussions among operational-level personnel beginning to study human behavior.

The ancients worshipped the moon, among other natural phenomena, and numerous superstitions have survived regarding terrestrial and behavioral aspects of the moon, but only the movement of the earth's tides has been shown to be directly affected by the moon. Deviant behavior other than crime, however, has frequently been attributed to the moon. The terms *lunacy* and *lunatic* refer to influences of the moon on deviant behavior. The "trial of lunatics of 1883" in England authorized a new verdict, "guilty, but insane," and resulted in automatic commitment to the custody of the Home Secretary for purposes of treatment.

Myths have always been associated with the sun and the moon, but those associated with the moon are more dramatic. Some primitive peoples, particularly American Indian tribes, have thought that man descended from the sun, but the sun remains similar always. The moon, on the other hand, waxes, wanes, and disappears, only to come to life again. Consequently, primitive peoples consider the moon as a symbol of resurrection; myths concerning death and resurrection, the land of the dead, adventures of the first ancestors, mysteries of fertility and birth, initiation rites, magic, and sorcery have all combined so that, in some instances, the moon has actually usurped the role of a celestial supreme being.

An expression of solar and lunar rhythms in birds, insects, fish, turtles, and crustaceans is evident in their use of the azimuthal angle of the sun or moon as a directional guide in which their orientational angles adjust to compensate exactly for the earth's rotation relative to the sun and the moon. Still, so far the influence of the moon on human behavior has not been scientifically proved, although many studies have been made concerning lunar effects.

The earliest references to "moral lunacy," or what may have been psychopathic personalities, appeared in 1758. A case from the Richmond Lunatic Asylum in Dublin was described as one in which the line between extreme stress and insanity is difficult to define (Battie, *A Treatise on Madness*, referred to in Stearns, 1944, p. 822). Prichard (1835) developed and expanded the concept of moral lunacy in 1835, when he began to group mental diseases according to emotional differences; he did not pursue lunar causality, however.

There are few references to the moon influencing behavior in the psychiatric literature. The most recent was a study of homicides in Miami, Florida, over a fifteen-year period (Lieber and Sherin, 1972; also Lieber, 1978). The homicides were found to peak at full moon followed by a secondary peak just after the new moon. The study contended that there is a relationship between lunar cycle and crimes of violence and supported a theory of biological tides influenced by the moon. A thirteen-year study of Cuyahoga County, Ohio, demonstrated a similar tendency, but it was not statistically significant. The running activity of hamsters over a one-year period reported by Brown and Park also tended to support the theory of biological lunar tides (Brown and Park, 1967). However, the vast majority of social and behavioral scientists do not support the hypothesis that the moon affects human behavior in any way. Only those studies mentioned here suggest a realistic connection between the moon and human behavior.

In summary, there has been little support in recent years for the proposition that weather, climate, or the moon affects human behavior or, especially, the deviant behavior called criminal. Most studies in these areas were in the eighteenth and nineteenth centuries. The most recent book relating to climate and weather appears to be Mills's *Climate Makes the Man*, which was published in 1942. This book refers to the productivity of people living in the temperate and colder climates as opposed to lower productivity among people living in the tropics. Further, it discusses the effects of environmental pollution by industry, deaths from heat, migration for health reasons, cancer, and moods and behavior, but no mention is made of crime and delinquency. There is no mention of the moon, climate, or weather in a comprehensive survey of research and theory in the United States since 1945 made by the Center for Studies in Criminology and Criminal Law at the University of Pennsylvania (Criminology, 1974). The absence of concern about the weather, climate, and the moon in the criminological literature in the twentieth century suggests that criminologists and behavioral scientists have looked elsewhere for explanations. The literature focuses on social and environmental factors, psychological and emotional stresses, and some biological approaches, the latter focusing on aggression and violence. Behavioral scientists emphasize the social environment and the learning processes to explain human behavior, including criminal behavior.

Psychopharmacology

Drugs have an effect on human behavior and can be used constructively in therapy. The drugs include anesthetics, analgesics or pain relievers, stimulants, alcohol and other depressants, barbiturates and other hypnotics, opiates and other narcotics, and tranquilizers. Relief of pain and reduction of anxiety by use of these substances has been practiced by humans since prehistoric times. Prison administrators often feel that "tranquilizers were made for prisons" for the purpose of keeping violent offenders sedated.

The use of drugs in behavior therapy became significant in the 1950s with the discovery of reserpine and chlorpromazine, which became useful as tranquilizers to reduce certain kinds of behavior associated with hyperactivity and agitation. A second group of drugs, including meprobamate and other more mild sleep-producing drugs, has been used to reduce anxiety and tension. The discovery of *d*-lysergic acid diethylamide, more commonly known as LSD-25, originally derived from ergot or the fungus on rye and wheat, opened the area of psychedelic drugs. LSD was used in the 1960s as an aid to the treatment of neurosis when conventional approaches failed, as an aid in the treatment of alcoholism, and for other psychiatric purposes. The subjective effects of LSD vary with the individual, but they have included an expansion of consciousness and awareness of surroundings. Any social utility would be in the mystical-religious experience that enhances personal security and basic trust.

It was particularly when these drugs began to be used in some prisons to change people and their behavior that legal difficulties were encountered. When LSD became sufficiently available to be abused and taken without the supervision of physicians, other controversies arose. After a court order in 1966 restricted experimentation to a few laboratories, its general use became illegal.

Other types of psychopharmacology include insulin shock, which like electroshock, produces convulsions not dissimilar to the Jacksonian convulsions observed in epilepsy. The result is to reduce anxiety and tension and produce a quiet and contented person. These shock treatments have been particularly helpful both with depressions and hyperactive patients as well as in other psychiatric problems. These treatments, also, have encountered legal restrictions in some areas, so their future use will be quite selective.

Other Biological Approaches

There are some biological approaches that are concerned with mental health but not specifically with criminal behavior. There are many types of "healers," healing shrines like Lourdes, and other religious approaches to healing (Anderson, 1974). Many of these healers are successful in some cases because the difficulty is functional, such as in a conversion hysteria, where emotional pressures are manifest in physical symptoms, and the patient has sufficient faith and belief in the healer and healing operation to work through the difficulty (Holland and Ward).

Osteopathy is a form of healing begun in 1874 by Andrew T. Still, who held that all diseases are due to abnormalities in and near the joints, and the treatment for every disease is the correction of these abnormalities without the use of drugs. Modern osteopathy, however, uses surgery and drugs and views the entire body as generally having recuperative powers. Approaches used are manipulation, rest, physical support, mechanical traction, heat, diathermy, exercises, and pain-relieving and muscle-relaxing drugs. Osteopathic psychiatrists are in practice and use these same approaches, but there is no osteopathic theory of criminal behavior.

Chiropractic was introduced by D. D. Palmer in 1895 as a system of treatment of disease based on the premise that the nerve system controls all other systems in the body and interference with nerve control affects all bodily functions. Treatment consists of adjustments and manipulations of the body, particularly the spinal column, to restore normal nerve functioning. Chiropractic is concerned with mental health, and the figures released through the Palmer School of Chiropractic indicate success that matches any other approach (*Case Histories*, 1953; also see Mears, 1965). A text was published in 1973 under the title *Mental Health & Chiropractic* (Schwartz, 1973).

All these approaches are viewed by the medical professional as oversimplistic answers for complex physiological problems. The United States Department of Health, Education and Welfare reported after a study made at the direction of Congress in 1967 that chiropractic should not be honored under Medicare because chiropractic practitioners ignore a large body of knowledge related to health, disease, and health care (Monaghan, 1970). There is no evidence that sublaxation, or dislocation of vertebrae, is a significant factor in disease process. Osteopathy has been accepted to provide services under Medicare; and as of July 1, 1973, "limited services" were permitted to chiropractic practitioners. In summary, all these approaches are interested in mental health, but have not yet focused directly on criminal behavior.

BIODYNAMICS AND BIOSOCIAL APPROACHES

Biodynamics generalizes and demonstrates the clinical applicability of a wide range of phenomena in animal and human behavior. The four principles are (1) organisms are actuated by physiological need, (2) organisms react to their milieus in terms of their individual needs, capacities, and experiences, (3) when an organism's goal-directed activities are frustrated, it changes its techniques to reach its goal, and (4) when two or more motivations conflict, the organism experiences anxiety, and its behavior becomes either ambivalent, poorly adaptive, and ineffectively substitutive (neurotic) or progressively more disorganized, regressive, and bizarrely symbolic (psychotic) (Masserman, 1955).

Physical-growth problems frequently lead to inability to think clearly, to brain damage, to endocrinal imbalance that in turn leads to hypoglycemia that results in excessive swings from hyperactivity to indolence, to other hyper- or hypoactivity of the endocrinal system, and to many other possible physical problems that could lead to misbehavior, delinquency, and crime (Rees, 1982). Physical growth proceeds normally unless there is serious illness, accident, exposure to toxins, or malnutrition. Genetic abnormalities come from defects in the genes; congenital defects come from damage to the fetus that may result from drugs or alcohol consumed by the mother or from damage at birth caused by prolonged labor and improper use of forceps, breach delivery, or other problems; and after birth abnormalities may be caused by severe falls, accidents, or abuse. In some situations, an individual may be frightened, unable to think clearly, have a feeling of impending death, hallucinate, or have other conditions resulting from endocrinal imbalance. Offenders should be subjected to routine urinalyses, blood counts, tuberculin tests, tests for abnormal function of the kidneys, liver, and other organs, as well as other tests to eliminate possible physiological imbalance that might cause dysfunctional reaction to "normal" stimuli. A six-hour glucose-tolerance test can pinpoint hypoglycemia as a cause of fainting, sweating, irritability, inability to think clearly, and other problems. It has been reported that hair analysis has shown offenders to have a higher aluminum content, excessive mercury, which causes depression, and excessive copper, which is a brain irritant, as well as other abnormalities not easily detected (Rees, 1979). A complete medical, nutritional, and laboratory evaluation of all delinquents and offenders should precede any "sociopolitical" or counseling treatment.

The relationship between food, starvation, and disease is well known and is incorporated in all diet studies. Until about 10,000 years ago, man gathered and/or hunted for his food. Fire had been discovered and began to be used for cooking in a few places about 750,000 years ago, and Cro-Magnon man learned to fish about 20,000 years ago. The introduction of agriculture about 10,000 years ago resulted in a major shift to grains. In 1900, the largest food store might have 500 items, while the modern supermarkets have 10,000 different items. The diets of humans have changed over the centuries and the years.

Modern clinical nutritionists recognize that many chronic degenerative diseases arise from the disharmony between nutritional needs shaped over millions of years of available food supply and the modern food supply (Hoffer, 1978). While primitive man may have suffered from real starvation, he did not suffer from the affluent starvation so common today in industrialized nations where food is rich in calories and food artifacts. Food processing came from the discovery that pounding and grinding foods make them easier to cook, chew, and digest, but the "whole" or "natural" foods have all but disappeared. Additives are chemicals added to foods that make colorful, consistent, bland products with long shelf lives but usually have nothing to do with nutrition. Modern food processing has resulted in dietary changes that have caused many chronic disorders from hypoglycemia and functional hyperinsulinism to metabolic disorders involving sugar substitutes to psychiatric diseases and other conditions that require orthomolecular nutrition. Nutritional problems contributing to crime and antisocial behavior can be caused by an imbalance in mineral intake (Hoffer, 1979, p. 193), drinking excessive quantities of milk (Schauss and Simonsen, 1975, p. 149), excessive consumption of sugar, and other poor eating habits (see D'Asaro et al., 1975, p. 212). Because of these problems, several agencies have begun serious diet programs with offenders. In 1982, the Los Angeles Probation Department initiated a strong dietary program for the juveniles under its supervision.

Metabolic disorders lead to learning disabilities and dysfunctional behavior. Among the factors that lead to delinquency and criminality, the most prominent is the failure to be successful in socially acceptable ways. The approach most likely to give rapid results is to enhance physical well-being so there is less irritability, better stress tolerance, increased attention span, and improvement of other factors that permit longer focus on the positive relationships in society (Bonnet, 1978). Excessive use of refined carbohydrates makes poor nutrition the norm, rather than the exception, in the population of delinquents and criminals. Dietary background in the family becomes important, such as whether mother drank excessively, whether the child was breastfed or bottle fed, and many other questions. Even an examination of the stool is important; a stool that stinks suggests either indigestion, allergies, or enzyme deficiency or an insufficient amount of crude fiber, while a stool that falls apart suggests food allergies or a vitamin B6 deficiency. Among the nutritional disorders that need attention in the treatment of offenders are hypoglycemia, cerebral allergies, pyroluria, which interferes with metabolism of vitamin B6 and zinc, trace-metals imbalances, histamine disorders, manic-depressive disorders, psychomotor epilepsy, alcoholism, and overuse of drugs.

In biological treatment, the needs of the criminal are similar to those of a growing child—both are immature, biologically and emotionally (Wunderlich, 1978). In the case of criminals, habits of wrong living and wrong thinking have hardened them over the years and they do not respond to "sociopolitical" efforts at rehabilitation or "talking therapy"—counseling. Many years of wrong eating, overlooked allergies, untreated deficiencies, and toxic states combine to produce the hardcore offender who cannot or will not be helped. The basic approach to treatment includes (1) identification and management of underlying biological deviations, (2) maintenance of desirable biological functions long enough to permit revision and restructuring of old lifestyles and attitudes, (3) establishment of a program of physical fitness, (4) provision of psychological reinforcement, such as supportive counseling, (5) identification of vocational aptitudes and job training, (6) education in self-analysis and body care, (7) quick access to medical care when aberrations in functions arise, and (8) opportunity for intellectual development. Today's society is sedentary, and many biological abnormalities have arisen. Trephining, leeching, bleeding, and reading bumps on the head are biological concerns of the past in criminal behavior. Body chemical analysis belongs to today and the future.

Another element in biodynamics receiving attention recently is biofeedback. Biofeedback is based on minute measurement of bodily changes in all areas, including temperature, galvanic reflex (transmission of electrical impulses over the skin), sweating, EEG (electroencephalograph), EMG (electromyography or muscular contractions), and many other involuntary physiological functions. The polygraph (often erroneously called the lie detector) is based on biofeedback principles, using the galvanic reflex, pulse, and breathing. A person can influence, but never learn to control completely his or her own biological and mental functions (Brown, 1974, p. 464). The skin's ability to read the mind's unconscious reaction to reality, such as control of muscles, heartbeat, blood pressure, and brainwaves, has been demonstrated to some extent. Biofeedback is utilized to facilitate relaxation and detoxification from drugs, particularly methadone (Nebelkopf, 1978). Biofeedback training has been effective in controlling tension headaches, heart rate, blood pressure, and migraines. Control of these physiological stresses prevents the subject from possible inadvertent reaction to them that might result in criminal behavior. Biofeedback can reduce stress (Stern et al., 1980). In hospital and in correctional settings, biofeedback can be used in the treatment of emotional problems, stress management, and pain control.

Biosocial approaches have been prominent in the criminological literature since the latter half of the 1970s. Several scholars have indicated that learning is influenced by things other than the environment, although that is important. The organism, itself, is important in the interaction with the environment, as previously stated. It is a person's brain that is interacting with the environment and producing behavior (Ginsburg, 1979). Mednick and Christiansen (1977) have presented similar positions. The primary influences on one's behavior can be endocrinal, tissue needs like hunger, fear, excretory needs, defensive attitudes, growth and developmental problems, activity of the central nervous system, and other phenomena with which one's biological functions have some relationship. One's psychological responses to the environment depend upon one's biological and physical state; the effect of that state on one's personal goals in education, work, and play, and the cumulative effect of physiological deficiency caused by any dysgenic element in one's personality. Various scholars emphasize different aspects: Jeffery, the brain; Wunderlich, physical and emotional maturity; and Hoffer, nutrition. Hippchen (1978) tends to emphasize biochemical concerns.

There is still considerable debate about the biological approaches to crime causation. Those who adhere to biological causation tend to view with suspicion those criminologists who are concerned with the social and behavioral sciences and sometimes accuse them of engaging in "sociopolitical treatment" and "talking therapy." On the other hand, many criminologists from the social and behavioral sciences hold that there is no factor in the genes causing crime and delinquency and consider biological causes as "oversimplistic." At national meetings, some biologically oriented scholars have been called neo-Lombrosian (Jeffery, 1980, p. 10). Some have indicated that this biological determinism has been "laid to rest over and over," but "this phoenix . . . is regularly resurrected on the ashes" of all criminological theory "so far advanced, inferred, collected, or imagined" (Rosenberg and Silverstein, 1969, p. 2). Gresham Sykes (1978), indicates that "such explanations are of little use in understanding criminal behavior."

Crime is not a unitary pheonomen. Consequently, efforts to view and explain it from single or limited approaches or positions limit understanding of it. No one theory could explain all crime. On the other hand, all knowledge should be available to explain any social phenomenon to be used as it is needed.

ECONOMICS

Economics combined with philosophy to provide the social part of the explanation of human behavior, including criminal behavior, in the nineteenth century into the twentieth century. While the biological influence permeated the nineteenth-century prison and criminal justice system, economics was seen as the most likely modifier in terms of behavior. Like biology and sociology, economics as a separate discipline emerged in the nineteenth century from its previous identification in the seventeenth century as "political economy" and its earlier heritage of Greek and medieval writers.

Economic determinance of behavior, particularly criminal behavior, referred to the interactions in the distribution of goods and services to individuals within any given social system. The interpretations of economic influences on criminal behavior, however, must shift with the political structure and social formation of the four broad periods in the development of economics: (1) the classical or Greek phase, (2) the medieval phase of static structure, (3) the development of the national state and free trade influenced by the Industrial Revolution (about 1750), and (4) the modern phase of free enterprise, productivity, interest and dividends, rent, and the gross national product. The definitions of crime change with the changing economic systems.

Systematic registries of births and deaths developed in the 1500s in many European cities and states. These provided an opportunity to study social conditions and consequences. Edmond Halley (1656–1742), an astronomer for whom the famous comet was named, compiled and published in 1692–93 the first systematic "life-expectancy tables" (Whipple, 1923, pp. 3–6). Adam Smith (1723–90) used these data on social and economic conditions in writing his famous *Inquiry into the Nature and Causes of the Wealth of Nations*, published in 1776. Soon crime and delinquency statistics began to be available.

Karl Marx and Friedrich Engels emphasized economic determinism in their *Communist Manifesto* in 1849. Crime was considered by them to be a by-product of economic conditions. Marx (1904, pp. 11–13), held that the mode of production in material life determines the general character of the social, political, and spiritual processes. When the mode of production in material life comes into conflict with existing relations of production or property, people become enslaved within the system. The change of the economic foundation will result in the change of the entire social superstructure. Social reform can, then, be obtained through change in the economic life of society. In the meantime, some individuals within that society may be faced with inadequate opportunity and dilemmas that threaten the value system. Crime is one result of this situation.

A *Report of the Committee of Justices Appointed to Consider the Treatment of Juvenile Offenders* was published by the Borough of Birmingham in 1800. The *London Committee for the Investigation of the Causes of the Alarming Increase of Juvenile Delinquency in the Metropolis* was published in 1816. France published the *Comte générale* in 1825. In 1833, A. M. Guerry published in France what many considered to be the first work in scientific criminology under the title *Essai sur la statisque morale de la France.* Adolphe Quetelet developed a social statistic in 1835 and has been described as the first social criminologist who thought that society prepares the crime and the guilty person is only the instrument by which it is accomplished.

The best compilation of research on the problem of economics and crime until the 1940s was Thorsten Sellin's *Research Memorandum on Crime in the Depression* published in 1937. Sellin cited several studies relating to crime and economic conditions in England in the early nineteenth century. Russell attributed an increase in crime in England in 1842 to the general distress in commercial, manufacturing, and agricultural economics. Covering a period of thirty-seven years between 1810 and 1847, Fletcher claimed to have found a connection between the price of food (wheat) and the number of admissions to prisons. Clay measured commitment to the Preston House of Corrections in London for 1835 to 1854 and claimed that, compared to "normal times," more young persons went to court during "hard times," and the number of cases on the court calendar was even greater during "good times" because the young and thoughtless became intemperate when high wages encouraged frivolity.

Probably the most famous study was that of Georg von Mayr, who correlated the fluctuation in the price of rye with fluctuations in crime in Bavaria for the years 1836–61. This writer indicated that a half-penny increase in rye increased crime one-fifth per hundred thousand persons. On the other hand, a corresponding decrease in crime accompanied every drop in the price of rye.

Mary Carpenter (1853), longtime superintendent of the Red Lodge Reformatory for Women at Bristol, England, disputed the influence of economics and poverty on delinquency. The influence of social interaction with an institutional class of professional criminals was considered a more important concern. Charles Booth (1903) did an intensive study of the economics in London between 1886 and 1902, dividing the people of London into eight economic groups. Cyril Burt (1925, p. 92) reexamined Booth's work and discovered that approximately 56 percent of the delinquents came from the four lower economic classes that included 37 percent of the people, finding a general attendancy for delinquents to come from lower socioeconomic classes. Dorothy Swaine Thomas (1925, p. 143) studied the relationship between crime and the business cycle, finding a correlation of $-.25$ between all indictable crimes and economic prosperity in England and Wales during the period of 1857 to 1913, but the question arises as to how long it takes for the full effect of change in economic conditions to have a maximum influence on the crime rate. Vold (1958, p. 178) recomputed the data on the basis that it took two years to make an influence of economic conditions on personality and found the coefficient of correlation to be $+.18$, which is not significant. Because neither coefficient of correlation was significant, no relationship between crime and the business cycle was demonstrated.

American studies of economic conditions and crime have not been fruitful. Whether this is because the standard of living in America is sufficiently high that the majority of the population does not live on a marginal standard, whether welfare and social programs fill the gap, or whether there is realistically no connection between poverty and crime remains unanswered. American criminologists, however, do not generally consider economics to be a governing aspect in causes of criminal behavior. It is interesting to note, however, that property crimes tend to rise during economic depressions, while crimes against persons tend to rise during prosperity, with the total crime rates remaining relatively stable. Economic pressures on the individual may be traumatic, but the impact is not as dramatic when viewed from a nationwide perspective.

Recent extensive studies have revealed no relationship between low economic status and crime or unemployment and crime and only a slight inverse relationship between higher wages and crime (Orsagh and Witte, 1981). For some crime, like white-collar crime and employee theft, one must be employed. No relationship between employment and youth crime can be shown (Pabon, 1981).

Neighborhood residential mobility, structural density, and unemployment are unrelated to weapon use or seriousness of the offense (Wilson et al., 1981). Unemployment, however, is related to prison populations because there is no point in placing offenders on probation without visible means of support. During times of economic depression, there is a tendency for the proportion of property crimes to rise and, conversely, crimes against persons tend to rise during prosperity, but the total crime rate remains fairly stable (Cohen et al., 1981). It is interesting to note that during times of large urban power failures resulting in blackouts, such as in New York City in 1979, it is the liquor stores that are looted first, then come the TV stores, pawnshops, and appliance stores, then clothing stores, while grocery stores and meat markets are among the last to be looted! It is apparent that these crimes are not committed by persons seriously "in need." Economic conditions in the United States today do not really affect the overall crime rate (Long and Witte, 1981).

DETERRENCE

Deterrence as an objective of punishment was inherent in the Classical School of criminology initiated by Beccaria in 1764 (Heath, 1963, p. 60). The Positive School of criminology, however, rejected the free-will-and-choice approach of the Classical School and referred to deterrence as a "childlike faith in punishment" (Barnes and Teeters, 1959, p. 286). While the Classical School holds that man is hedonistic and can choose by free will whether to commit a crime, the Positive School holds that crime is caused by social and psychological forces impinging upon the personality. Paul Johann Anselm Feuerbach (1775–1833), a German jurist, became famous for his work in criminal law reform and his espousal of the Classical School of criminology and its concept of deterrence, especially in the Bavarian criminal code of 1813. Contemporary research and writing in support of deterrence have been primarily from economists who tend to apply a sort of social cost-benefit analysis to crime to assess the rewards, the cost, and the advantages or disadvantages of crime.[1] Deterrence research by economists has not provided

---

[1]For example, see Isaac Ehrlich, "Capital Punishment and Deterrence: Some Further Thoughts and Additional Evidence," *Journal of Political Economy,* 85, August, 1977.

a clear-cut answer, so decisions in criminal justice may continue for a long time to be made on political grounds (Fattah, 1983).

Deterrence theory contends that people make rational, cost-benefit decisions to commit a crime. In some areas, there may be "marginal deterrence," such as a person being deterred from drunk driving when laws against it are put into effect. The relatively large amount of research on deterrence and crime prevention attests to the fact that some credence is placed on deterrence. It probably has its greatest relation to politics, since harsher laws are generally passed when the public fears crime. While there is no evidence that imprisonment deters crime, the typical American is afraid of arrest and conviction that could lead to loss of reputation and/or employment (Hawkins and Zimring, 1973). Consequently, there is cause to accept some measure of deterrence. The National Academy of Sciences (1978) concluded that caution should be exercised in interpreting the deterrent effect of present criminal sanctions, especially imprisonment.

CONCLUSIONS

Biology and economics have assisted criminology in making the transition from theories of philosophy, theology, and supernatural causes of behavior in the nineteenth century. In early America, crime was equated with sin, pauperism, and immorality, without much real understanding as to causes of deviant behavior. The nineteenth century saw a transition from phrenology or reading bumps on the head to biology for purposes of interpreting behavior. Economics moved from political economics to supply and demand, trade, and a cause of crime resulting from need in the lower socioeconomic classes, which Marx viewed as a class struggle. The influence of biology was strong in the nineteenth-century prison as an explanation of crime. Economics helped to focus attention on the social problems in society. The notion of a balance between heredity and environment in causing criminal behavior began to appear in the literature in the field of crime and criminal justice. The influence of biology remains strong today, with psychosurgery, chromosomal theories, neuropsychiatry, and other physical factors being introduced into the explanations of crime. New academic journals like *Behavioral Biology* have appeared emphasizing its importance in modern thinking. The XYY chromosomal approach in the late 1960s would tend to support the "born criminal" theory of the nineteenth and early twentieth centuries. Economics has tended to give way to sociology in crime prevention, as indicated by the "opportunity programs" initiated by the government in the 1960s. The economic studies in the nineteenth century tended to show a positive connection, but economics is not so significant in the twentieth century, partially as a result of welfare and other social programs that have developed. In any case, the emerging discipline of criminology became a separate area of study and practice throughout the nineteenth century, with biology and economics making significant contributions; in the twentieth century, criminology and criminal justice have taken their place as a distinct academic discipline that includes the contributions of biology and economics together with many other areas of study.

Questions

1. What is the body-type theory of criminology?
2. How does intelligence relate to crime?
3. Trace the development of the study of poor heredity as a basic factor in intelligence and crime through the nineteenth century to modern times.
4. What is the relationship of XYY chromosomes to crime?
5. What is the contribution of electroencephalography to crime?
6. What has been the experience in treating crime by psychosurgery?
7. Does weather affect crime?
8. Does the moon affect crime?
9. How does psychopharmacology relate to the treatment of crime?
10. Evaluate the effect of economics on crime.

four

THE
CHICAGO
SCHOOL

The first large-scale research in criminology developed in the Department of Sociology at the University of Chicago in the 1920s under the leadership of Ernest W. Burgess, with Clifford R. Shaw, Henry D. McKay, Robert E. Park, Frederic Thrasher, Clark Tibbitts, and others contributing heavily. It is apparent that the interest at the University of Chicago was in response to the peculiar problems of that city, problems that later became generalized to all major cities in the United States.

Crime had emerged as a major social problem in the 1920s. There had always been crime in America, of course, and there had always been men who could not "take" civilization and the rules and regulations that control it. Daniel Boone and some other early American frontier hereos who lived off the land and shot game out of season would be locked up today. The Prohibition Era began one year after ratification of the Eighteenth Amendment. Ratification was completed on January 29, 1919. From 1920 until the ratification of the Twenty-First Amendment that repealed it on December 5, 1933, public concern for crime increased. This Prohibition Era gave rise to organized crime. Chicago had a peculiar problem because of the heavy demand for beer by its large foreign-born population. Supplying beer became a large-scale operation, and Chicago developed a surplus of operators, who took to killing each other off with submachine guns, beginning when Al Capone killed "Big Jim" Colosimo on May 11, 1920; approximately 1,000 gangland homicides occurred subsequently throughout the 1920s. There were no murder trials because there were no witnesses who would testify. Soon the gangs had reached into politics in City Hall to guarantee their survival. The culmination of this situation was the St. Valentine's Day Massacre of 1929, when seven of "Bugs" Moran's gang were shot down by Al Capone's gang in a garage on North Clark Steet in Chicago.

Public and political reaction on a national scale was immediate. In May 1929, President Hoover appointed a Commission on Law Enforcement and Observance (commonly called the Wickersham Commission after its chairman), charging it with investigating the entire field of crime and lawlessness in the United States. The report was completed in 1931, but it dodged the question as to whether prohibition should be repealed. Nevertheless, its findings on crime and law enforcement were so startling that demand for reform was soon evident. The development of crime laboratories began immediately, although the American Association of Forensic Sciences was not organized until 1948 in St. Louis. The Bureau of Investigation had been established in 1908 by Attorney General Jerald J. Bonaparte and was first headed by Gaston B. Means. William Burns became director under President Warren Harding, and J. Edgar Hoover was appointed director and the word *federal* added in 1924 after Burns was dismissed following the Teapot Dome scandals. Reorganization was given emphasis by the St. Valentine's Massacre, and a public relations campaign was deliberately initiated to glamorize "G-men" and law enforcement in general. A public relations man was added to the FBI staff and remained there for eight years to build a positive image for the FBI. The Hollywood Code was agreed upon around 1931 to 1933 to cease glamorizing criminals and gangsters in the movies, and the agreement concluded that law enforcement people should be presented as "good guys" who always won in the end.

The rise of serious research in criminology occurred simultaneously in the 1920s at the University of Chicago. The Chicago School of criminology was a part of the American School—or the sociological school, because the emphasis was purely sociological. Sociology is differentiated from other social sciences by the fact that it starts with the relative helplessness of the human infant at birth born into and dependent for survival upon a social group. The conduct of individuals, their ways of thinking and acting, the nature of social order, its structure and function and values, are understood as resulting from group life. Sociology is concerned only with the pursuit of knowledge about people and society. Values, prejudices, attitudes, social organization, human ecology, and demography are all conceptual units of interest to the sociologist. Theories of sociology are developed according to how the various scholars in this field interpret those phenomena and put them together in a meaningful system.

Anthropology is a study of cultures and comparative cultures. Consequently, there is considerable overlapping between sociology and anthropology. In fact, some universities and colleges have them both within the same department. Sociological and cultural theory are closely interdependent, but anthropology deals specifically with cultures rather than with the sociological interaction between individuals. Therefore, understanding of human behavior requires some overlap in these fields.

The significance of the culture in the social system is that it has an important bearing on individuals and the relationships between individuals in any social system. The economic and political aspects of society also are important. The internalization of cultural patterns and social objectives is basic to both sociological and personality theories. The sociological analyses of Emile Durkheim, the analytic psychology of Sigmund Freud, and the social psychology of Charles Horton Cooley, George H. Mead, and W.I. Thomas are significant in this context. Durkheim's anomie, or normlessness, has been used to explain much deviant behavior from the standpoint of the social sciences. The subconscious-motivation theories of Sigmund Freud represented a most significant contribution to the understanding of deviant behavior from the standpoint of the behavioral sciences. The "looking-glass self" of Charles Horton Cooley was basically sociological because the individual acts as others perceive him. Cultural approaches to personality taken by George Herbert Mead have had lasting impact. The four wishes of man proposed by W. I. Thomas (1937) were (1) security, (2) new experience, (3) recognition or prestige, and (4) response or intimate fellowship and love. The theory of these four wishes tends to persist in the literature pertaining to sociology and social psychology and may be helpful in explaining some behavior of delinquents in the inner city and gangs as perceived by the Chicago School of research in delinquency. At least Thomas's "four wishes" theory was prominent in the literature when the original research on delinquency areas was done in the 1920s and 1930s.

The Chicago School emphasized socioeconomic areas within the city and gangs, primarily, although there was also attention to the patterns of criminal careers and parole prediction. Sam Warner (1923) did the first significant parole-prediction study by studying the reactions of inmates to various phases of prison life in Massachusetts. His study was published in 1923, after which parole-prediction study became centered essentially in Chicago and Illinois. Ernest W. Burgess of Chicago presented the first objective method of parole prediction based on twenty-one factors that were immediately available from prisoners' files. (See Harno, et al., 1928.) Work record was considered by Burgess to be probably the most significant factor in parole success. Tibbitts (1932), also at Chicago, indicated, however, that some of the factors used by Burgess did not show a high coefficient of contingency. That indicated inadequate use of multiple correlation or tests of internal consistency, a research defect that may or may not have significantly affected the findings. It is obvious that considerable activity, including presentations of research data and subsequent criticism and evaluation, was taking place in the Department of Sociology at the University of Chicago at that time.

AREAS OF THE CITY

With the emergence of the scientific approach to sociology, Robert E. Park and Ernest W. Burgess of the University of Chicago focused attention on the community and its effect on the individual. With the community as his unit of investigation, Park studied the ecology of crime in the city. He was so convinced that factors in the environment produced criminal behavior in the individual that he took the view that laws are passed to relieve emotions and the punishment of crime is a ceremonial affair—"We might as well get up and dance!" (See Sutherland and Cressey, 1966, pp. 10, 346.) Thrasher spoke for the Chicago School when he indicated that gangland represented a geographically and socially interstitial area between the Loop and the residential districts in Chicago. Delinquency areas became the concern of Clifford Shaw (1929), who developed the theory that delinquency rates are high in the center of Chicago and progressively lower at greater distances from the center and from industrial areas. It became obvious that the rate of delinquency in various areas of the city and different neighborhoods varies widely and is tied to socioeconomic and other factors. (See Morris, 1958.) The problems of adverse conditions of urban living have been recognized as coming from: (1) the economic insecurity and instability of urban social institutions and (2) individual and social efforts to become adjusted to the requirements and pressures of urban social and economic conditions (Phelps, 1936).

A breakdown of functioning social and economic systems in an area becomes critical and far-reaching in consequences as it affects the individuals living there. A sequence of breakdowns associated with urban pathologies—such as increasing congestion, increasing costs of living, doubtful efficiency of large-scale municipal enterprises, and increasing costs that devitalize the effects of urban occupations, lagging and disorganization of urban institutions for public service and control most directly focused on the inhabitants of the slums and ghettos—influences the culture and behavior of the people. Urban environmental influences promoting crime begin with the disorganization of families in the blighted areas of urban decentralization in the absence of adequate social institutions. Poverty and emerging attitudes toward nonconformity combined with the exodus of the conforming middle class from the city to the suburbs intensify the social problems. Suicide, commercialized vice, irregular sex relations, illegitimacy, mob-mindedness, social unrest, and increased emotional tensions contribute to the indices of urban breakdown, such as congestion, broken homes, increasing complexity of social relationships, and crime and delinquency. The effect of the community on the individual is most apparent in the inner city, slum, and ghetto.

Studies of crime in the city have indicated that petty crimes against property may be concentrated near the place of residence of criminals, but the more serious crimes against property are committed some distance from the places of residence (White, 1932). Even the serious crimes, however, are perpetrated by persons residing in the central segment of the city just outside the business district (Schmid, 1960). Sutherland (1934, p. 122) also reported that the volume of crime in Chicago decreases as the distance from the inner city increases. Lottier (1938–39) found the same pattern in Detroit.

The concept of concentric circles throughout the city that describe where crime and delinquency occur began when the University of Chicago sociologists began studying delinquency and found that the areas of highest delinquency appeared in or adjacent to areas zoned for industry and commerce (Shaw and McKay, 1969). In Chicago, they occurred close to the central business district and also near the stockyards and the south Chicago steel mills. On the other hand, areas of low delinquency occurred in areas zoned for residential purposes. The concentric-circle idea arose when five zones were drawn at two-mile intervals from a focal point at the center of the city. The social data drawn from these two-mile zones indicated that the highest rate of community problems was in the central or first zone, and all problems decreased gradually with the distance from the center of the city to the outer or fifth zone. These problems included delinquency, truancy, boys' court appearances, infant mortality, tuberculosis, mental disorders, and adult criminals in various time periods between 1917 and 1938.

Closer examination of some of the data in Chicago and elsewhere reveals that little delinquency occurs in the central economic district, but most of it occurs in the area immediately adjacent to it, still in the central two-mile radius from city hall. Shaw and McKay's observation that delinquency and crime tend to appear in areas adjacent to industry and commerce tends to remain true, but the development of industry and commerce is not always in exactly concentric circles.

In American cities, the high delinquency rates tend to be concentrated in the areas of greatest poverty, whether those areas are near the center of the city or on the outskirts, although the consistent tendency is for it to be in the central city. This concentration of delinquents and criminals tends to be in areas of physical deterioration, congested population, economic dependency, rented homes, and foreign and black population areas where there are few institutions supported by local residents. These are places in which there are few antidelinquency influences. Parent-teacher associations (PTAs) do not exist, nor do other community organizations principally supported by the people in the neighborhood. The population tends to be mobile and heterogenous and unable to act in concert. School, social work agencies, and churches are supported by people who reside elsewhere. This leaves the child to grow and develop in a confused setting where a coherent system of values is hard to find. The result is a survival-of-the-fittest situation where third-grade children often pay their milk money to sixth-grade protection gangs!

People tend to maintain a loyalty to their parents, regardless of the merits of that loyalty. When a father comes from a rural state to settle in a large industrial urban area, he generally goes to the slums or a ghetto, where cheap housing is available, intending that it be temporary. After months or years of sporadic employment, the personal deterioration is frequently manifested in terms of beer, wine, and other alcoholic beverages, and, in recent years, drugs and narcotics. Young people growing up in such areas see industrial executives from the suburbs being driven by chauffeurs through their neighborhoods to the central city, which houses the securities exchange and other financial institutions. When they compare the economic levels of their fathers and the industrialists, the remark, "Nobody gets that much money honestly!" expresses a common feeling. It does not take long in this milieu, then, for young people to decide that whatever it takes to equalize the situation is just and defensible. In this neighborhood, a weapon is frequently referred to as the "equalizer." The end justifies the means, so criminal and delinquent attitudes, antisocial perceptions, and deviation from expected norms and "middle-class law" are not difficult to develop.

The various zones or areas of the city have various names. Zone I is generally the economic center of the city, such as the Loop in Chicago, Cadillac Square in Detroit, or the financial district in New York. Just outside the economic center is zone II, which is a zone of deterioration in that it was originally residential, but businesses are moving in. Consequently, some tenements, and other cheap housing are mixed with pawnshops, cheap bars, and other small businesses. The result is an "interstitial" zone, neither residential nor business, sometimes identified as slum, or ghetto, and where Skid Row is located. Beyond this zone of deterioration are usually the industrial enterprises—zone III—with working people's homes adjacent. Immediately beyond the industry and the working people's homes are frequently the homes of middle-class or upper-class residents—zone IV—such as the Gold Coast in Chicago, Grosse Pointe in Detroit, and Stamford, Connecticut, and Westchester County in the New York metropolitan area. Beyond that is zone V, the suburbs, from which commuters travel generally by car or public transportation to the center of the city where they work.

Shaw, McKay, and others analyzed the rates of male delinquency in various areas of Chicago and other cities and reached the following five conclusions:

1. The rates of delinquency vary widely in different neighborhoods; in some areas none of the boys have been arrested, while more than one-fifth of the boys in other areas have been arrested within one year. The latter areas have been designated as "delinquency areas."
2. The delinquency rates are generally highest in the low-rent areas near the center of the city and decrease with the distance from the center of the city, but they are also high near large industrial or commercial subcenters of the city and again decrease with distance from those subcenters.
3. Areas that have high rates of truancy also have high rates for juvenile court cases and adult commitments to the county jails (as well as the number of girls' delinquencies).
4. Areas that had high delinquency rates in 1930 also had high delinquency rates in 1900, although the ethnic and racial composition of the population in the area had changed.
5. The delinquency rate of any particular national group shows the same general tendency as the delinquency rate for the entire population—namely, to be high in the areas near the center of the city and lower toward the outskirts of the city (Shaw and McKay, 1942).

Taft and England (1964, pp. 153–54) expanded on Shaw's identification of criminal zones and listed seven types of neighborhoods that are conductive to delinquency:

1. Poverty areas with normal family orgainization
2. Slum areas characterized by poverty as well as anomie and heterogeneous population
3. Interstitial areas similar to the slum and cut off from conventional society by some physical or social barrier and involving conflicts of culture
4. Rooming-house areas characterized by impersonal relations
5. Ghetto areas occupied by a single minority group
6. Vice areas—police-protected areas where prostitution and gambling go on without intervention
7. Deteriorated rural areas serving as hideout or rest areas for city gangsters

The original "ghetto" was the Jewish quarter in sixteenth-century Venice, where Jews were confined (Clark, 1965). It has subsequently come to mean any area where members of a single minority group are housed apart from the general population and is generally characterized by overcrowding, deteriorated housing, and poverty.

Suggested configurations in several cities are shown in the maps that follow. It must be remembered, however, that the lines of demarcation are not sharp but blend into transitional boundaries. Consequently, any demarcation lines have to be generalized and approximate rather than exact.

The rough schemata of the Chicago area is shown in Figure 4-1. It is not intended to be an accurate map but is a rough sketch of the pattern found in the Chicago studies of delinquency areas. The actual map of the delinquency areas in Chicago in the period 1927 to 1933 is shown in Figure 4-2. The similarity of the schemata in Figure 4-1 and the map in Figure 4-2 is obvious. The data shown in Figure 4-3 show suburban-area delinquency in 1958 to 1966, indicating a growing delinquency rate in the suburbs. Figure 4-4 shows the Chicago delinquency areas in 1963-66 and indicates that delinquency in Chicago has been distributed to other areas of the city in addition to the areas immediately adjacent to the central city; delinquency has been disseminated with the introduction of automobiles and the rise of business areas in the outer city and the suburbs.

The concentric circles in the Detroit area are shown in Figure 4-5. The map of night crime in August 1973 in Detroit is shown in Figure 4-6. There is some similarity in the central city, but there are also delinquency and crime areas in other areas of the city where industry and business have developed. Industry related to the automobile industry covers all of Detroit, so the areas of high delinquency and crime are almost evenly distributed throughout the city.

New York City is the largest area under examination, and the general pattern seems to follow the principle, with some variations. For example, crime and delinquency tend to occur in the areas adjacent to the central city, but the economic center of the city "jumped" from lower Manhattan in the 1920s to Times Square and 42nd Street in the 1930s and 1940s. This left some high-delinquency areas inside the present economic center of the city. The high-delinquency areas in New York City are (1) Hell's Kitchen, which is generally on the West Side between 40th and 57th Streets and West of 8th Avenue (where *West Side Story* was probably set), (2) Greenwich Village, both East and West, generally on the Lower West Side around 14th Street, (3) the Lower East Side around 2nd Street, (4) Harlem, both East and West, north of Grand Central Park, (5) South Bronx east of Harlem, and (6) the Bedford-Stuyvesant area in east Brooklyn. Three of these areas are in what could be called

FIGURE 4-1.

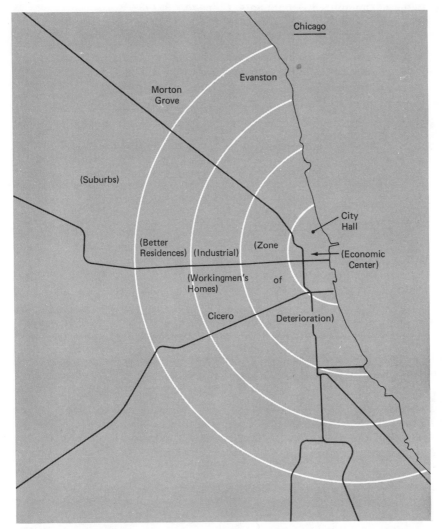

This is not presented as an accurate map but is a schemata suggesting what the pattern might be if the concentric-circle concept functioned more exactly. Figure 4-2 shows the actual delinquency areas in Chicago in 1927-1933. Figure 4-3 shows delinquency in the suburbs in 1958-1966. Figure 4-4 shows Chicago's delinquency areas in 1958-1966. Note that the 1927-1933 map (Figure 4-2) fits the concentric-circle concept, but later maps show delinquency as more decentralized, apparently reflecting decentralized business, industry, and commerce.

FIGURE 4-2.
Rates of Committed Delinquents, Chicago, 1927-33

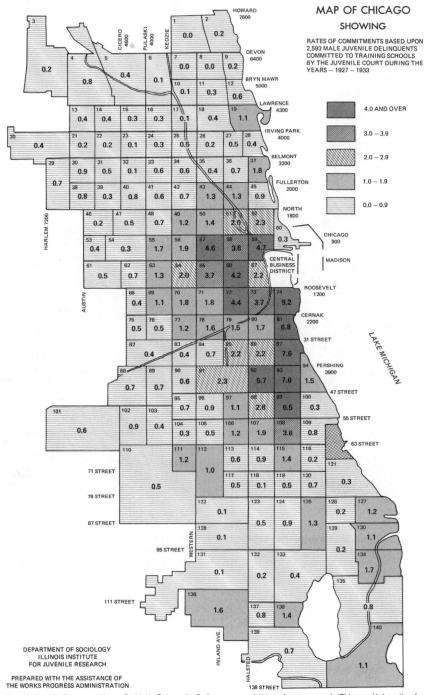

From Clifford R. Shaw and Henry D. McKay, *Juvenile Delinquency and Urban Areas*, rev. ed. (Chicago: University of Chicago Press, 1969—originally published 1942), p. 74.

FIGURE 4-3.
Indexes of Rates of Male Commitments in 47 Suburbs Based on 651
Delinquents Committed by the Cook County Juvenile Court
During the Years 1958-66

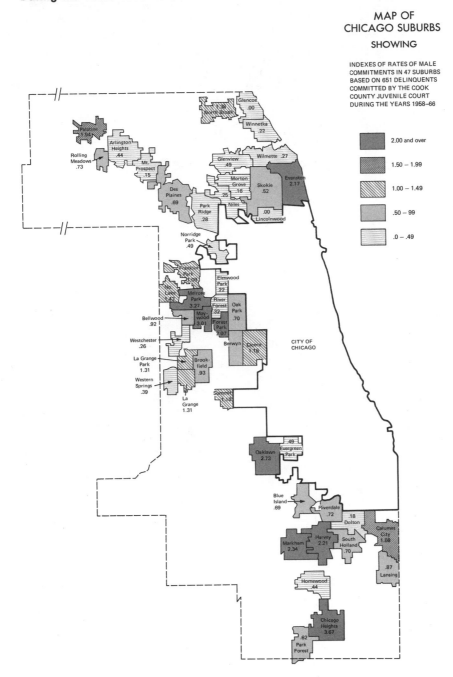

MAP OF
CHICAGO SUBURBS

SHOWING

INDEXES OF RATES OF MALE
COMMITMENTS IN 47 SUBURBS
BASED ON 651 DELINQUENTS
COMMITTED BY THE COOK
COUNTY JUVENILE COURT
DURING THE YEARS 1958–66

	2.00 and over
	1.50 – 1.99
	1.00 – 1.49
	.50 – 99
	.0 – .49

From Clifford R. Shaw and Henry D. McKay, *Juvenile Delinquency and Urban Areas,* rev. ed. (Chicago: University of Chicago Press, 1969—originally published 1942), p. 371.

FIGURE 4-4.
Indexes of Rates of Male Commitments Based on 4,256 Delinquents Committed by the Juvenile Court During the Years 1963-66

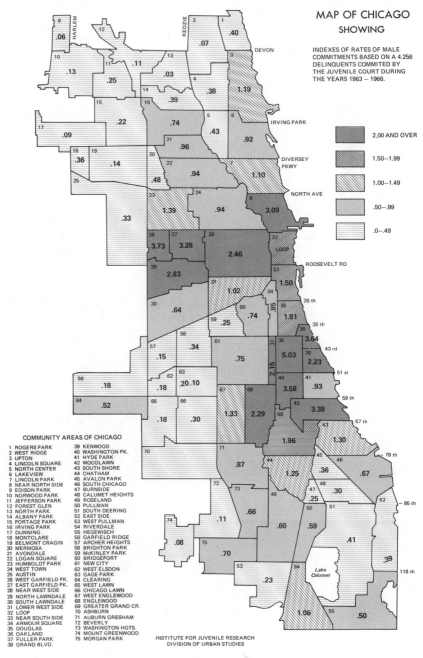

MAP OF CHICAGO
SHOWING

INDEXES OF RATES OF MALE
COMMITMENTS BASED ON A 4,256
DELINQUENTS COMMITED BY
THE JUVENILE COURT DURING
THE YEARS 1963 – 1966.

▨	2,00 AND OVER
▨	1.50—1.99
▨	1.00—1.49
▨	.50—.99
▨	.0—.49

COMMUNITY AREAS OF CHICAGO

1	ROGERS PARK	39	KENWOOD
2	WEST RIDGE	40	WASHINGTON PK.
3	UPTON	41	HYDE PARK
4	LINCOLN SQUARE	42	WOODLAWN
5	NORTH CENTER	43	SOUTH SHORE
6	LAKEVIEW	44	CHATHAM
7	LINCOLN PARK	45	AVALON PARK
8	NEAR NORTH SIDE	46	SOUTH CHICAGO
9	EDISON PARK	47	BURNSIDE
10	NORWOOD PARK	48	CALUMET HEIGHTS
11	JEFFERSON PARK	49	ROSELAND
12	FOREST GLEN	50	PULLMAN
13	NORTH PARK	51	SOUTH DEERING
14	ALBANY PARK	52	EAST SIDE
15	PORTAGE PARK	53	WEST PULLMAN
16	IRVING PARK	54	RIVERDALE
17	DUNNING	55	HEGEWISCH
18	MONTCLARE	56	GARFIELD RIDGE
19	BELMONT CRAGIN	57	ARCHER HEIGHTS
20	MERMOSA	58	BRIGHTON PARK
21	AVONDALE	59	McKINLEY PARK
22	LOGAN SQUARE	60	BRIDGEPORT
23	HUMBOLDT PARK	61	NEW CITY
24	WEST TOWN	62	WEST ELSDON
25	AUSTIN	63	GAGE PARK
26	WEST GARFIELD PK.	64	CLEARING
27	EAST GARFIELD PK.	65	WEST LAWN
28	NEAR WEST SIDE	66	CHICAGO LAWN
29	NORTH LAWNDALE	67	WEST ENGLEWOOD
30	SOUTH LAWNDALE	68	ENGLEWOOD
31	LOWER WEST SIDE	69	GREATER GRAND CR.
32	LOOP	70	ASHBURN
33	NEAR SOUTH SIDE	71	AUBURN GRESHAM
34	ARMOUR SQUARE	72	BEVERLY
35	DOUGLAS	73	WASHINGTON HGTS.
36	OAKLAND	74	MOUNT GREENWOOD
37	FULLER PARK	75	MORGAN PARK
38	GRAND BLVD.		

INSTITUTE FOR JUVENILE RESEARCH
DIVISION OF URBAN STUDIES

From Clifford R. Shaw and Henry D. McKay, *Juvenile Delinquency and Urban Areas,* rev. ed. (Chicago: University of Chicago Press, 1969—originally published 1942), p. 355.

FIGURE 4-5.

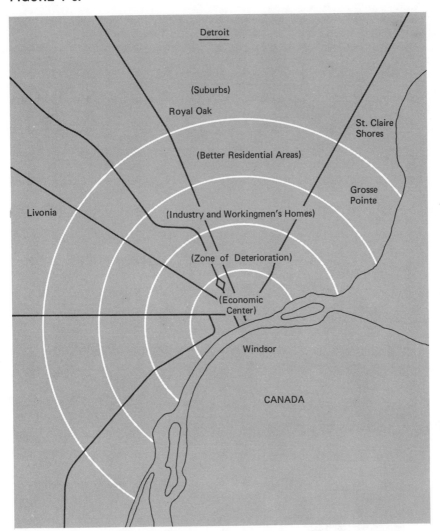

This is not presented as an accurate map of Detroit's high-crime and delinquency areas but is a schemata suggesting what the pattern might be if the concentric-circle concept functioned more accurately. Figure 4–6 shows the high night-crime areas in Detroit as of August 1973. No map of full crime and delinquency areas in Detroit was available. As in the later maps of Chicago, night crime in Detroit is decentralized, apparently reflecting the decentralization of business, industry, and commerce.

FIGURE 4-6.

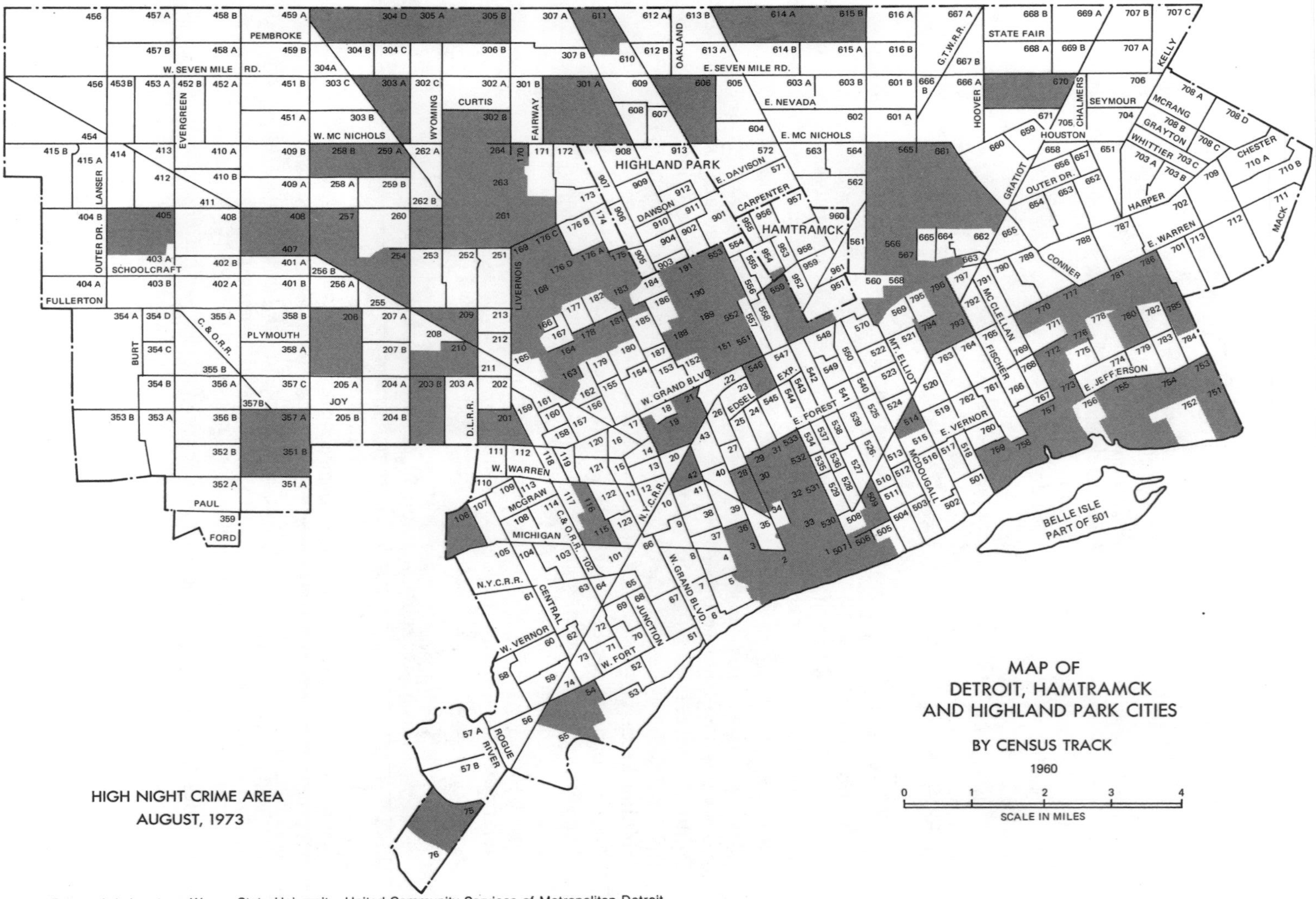

MAP OF
DETROIT, HAMTRAMCK
AND HIGHLAND PARK CITIES

BY CENSUS TRACT
1960

SCALE IN MILES
0   1   2   3   4

HIGH NIGHT CRIME AREA
AUGUST, 1973

Urban Research Laboratory, Wayne State University. United Community Services of Metropolitan Detroit "central city" in the 1970s but are not in "economic centers." (See Figure 4–7.) A map of delinquency areas in New York City was not available.

The Tenderloin area in New York City, frequently mentioned in literature and in song, is really an anachronism relating to the pre-World War I West Side area north of Greenwich Village in the theater, restaurant, and bordello area. The Tenderloin in San Francisco is a deteriorated area shaped like an inverted triangle with the hypotenuse on the south being Market Street going northeast and southwest, Geary Street on the north east-west boundary, and Post on the north-south boundary on the west.

The term *Skid Row* began in Seattle in the 1880s, when lumbering was a large business in the Northwest. Loggers would skid the logs down the hill in Seattle on specially prepared skids into the area of Elliott Bay, which opened into Puget Sound and where three sawmills were located on the shore and over pilings in the water. On Saturday night, the loggers and lumbermen would carouse, drink, and raise havoc. The area was generally on Spring, Marion, and Columbia streets between First Avenue and the bay. In present-day Seattle, Pioneer Square is near the area on First Avenue and Yessler Street and is generally associated with Skid Row. The hill is gone now, removed by water under pressure, and the old first-floor structures are covered with soil, particularly on Columbia Street, and the old second floors are now the first-floor businesses. In any case, the term caught on, and deteriorated and cheap drinking areas in most cities are now referred to as Skid Row.

The focus of the Chicago School was an ecological one, referring to certain areas of the cities adjacent to industry, business, and commerce that tend to have higher rates of social breakdown, including crime and delinquency, drinking and prostitution, and other indices of social pathology, than other areas of the city. These can be patterned on maps, and generalized concentric circles can be drawn in most cities that depict the areas.

Crime was a rural phenomenon during ancient and medieval times; this is one of the reasons many cities had walls around them. Crime occurred when highwaymen and other outlaws plundered caravans, wagons, and other groups traveling between the cities. When the modern urban city emerged in response to changing technology and economy, particularly during the Industrial Revolution in the seventeenth and eighteenth centuries, crime became primarily an urban problem.

Cities have changed drastically between the 1920s and 1980s, with considerable change having taken place in the 1960s. The older city seems to be dying, functionally, structurally, politically, and eventually ideologically (Greer, 1962, p. 208). The population complies because policy follows the market. The average middle-class white person has moved from the row houses and tenements, apartments, and subways, to the ranch house and its patio, the industrial park, and shopping

FIGURE 4-7.

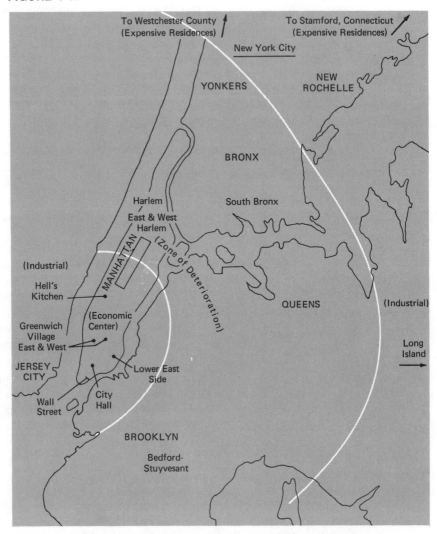

This is not presented as an accurate map of New York City's high-crime and delinquency areas, but is a schemata suggesting what the pattern might be if the concentric-circle concept functioned more accurately. No map of high-delinquency and crime rates in New York City was available. It is generally agreed, however, that the high rates appear in the South Bronx, East and West Harlem, East and West Greenwich Village, the Bedford-Stuyvesant area in Brooklyn, and the Lower East Side, with Hell's Kitchen on the West Side also contributing.

centers. Rather than there being one city as a unit, a series of complexes has arisen in the outskirts with government buildings and terminals from regional and national complexes remaining in the center, along with those poorer inhabitants of the city who cannot afford to move to the outskirts. The metropolis and megalopolis has replaced the traditional city. Social problems, however, seem to be going through the same morphology and development around the smaller units at the outskirts that the central city went through a half-century ago.

Suburban citizens have never supported consolidation or merger with the central city because it would cost them their "clean government" and small, local communities made up of friends and neighbors (Greer, p. 186). Simultaneously, inner-city residents tend to oppose merger, too, because when the affluent while middle class moves to the suburbs, the people left gain sufficient political power to run the city, and many can then move to become minority-group mayors and members of city government, even though the metropolitan area or megapolis may have a power structure that is white and middle-class.

Blacks, Mexicans, and Hispanics are the latest migrants to the metropolitan areas of America; they constitute the only parallel to the massive immigrant populations of the late nineteenth and early twentieth centuries, and they are undergoing the same social problems as did their immigrant predecessors (Greer, p. 133). The Germans and Irish fought each other and the native white Protestants in the late eighteenth century. The Italians, Greeks, and Poles fought each other and the native white Protestants in the early twentieth century. Today, the blacks, the Chicanos, and the Puerto Ricans are fighting each other and the native middle-class WASP, who wields the political power shared with the now-assimilated Germans, Irish, Italians, Greeks, and Poles.

The concentric circles of Shaw and McKay, Park, and others of the Chicago School are still viable, but not in the simple form they took in the 1920s. The introduction of wide use of automobiles and mass transit, the enlargement of the city, and the development of shopping centers around the perimeter of the city have all contributed to a decentralization of the delinquency and crime areas. Although Figure 4–5 shows only Detroit night crime and is not totally comparable to the Chicago maps, both maps indicate that the delinquency and crime areas in the city are being decentralized. The basic principle that crime and delinquency occur adjacent to industrial and commercial areas remains true, but the industrial and commercial areas, themselves, have become decentralized. Only in the middle-sized and smaller cities where industry and commerce have not been decentralized do the same concentric circles described by the Chicago School appear. In the larger areas where industry and commerce have been decentralized, the growth of crime and delinquency areas around these areas has tended to repeat the original pattern of the 1920s in microcosm.

GANGS

A classic study of the gang is Frederic Thrasher's (1927) study of 1,313
gangs in Chicago in the middle 1920s. This significant work remains
the point of departure for many other studies of delinquent gangs. One
still-valid conclusion is that gangs are merely loose federations of individual boys who are trying to work out their own emotional problems
in gang activity, with little consensus, little identification with the group,
and rapidly changing leadership.

There are many kinds of gangs, but few are organized and actually known as gangs. Much more frequently, a "clique," involving quasi-
permanent relationships between individuals interacting frequently as
a social unit, may be termed a gang by persons outside the group,
although the members do not consider themselves to be a gang. In other
instances, adolescents may go one step further in formalizing the social
organization of the gang and assume a name, such as Red Raiders or
Jets. Adults may form into gangs for special purposes, such as the "goon
squads" in the early days of the labor movement in the 1930s, when
unionization was resisted by management. Some of the gangs provide
illegal goods and services in organized crime. There are many types of
gangs, or peer groups, both informal and formal.

Shaw and McKay (1942, pp. 193–99) found that 88.2 percent of the
boys in juvenile court records in Chicago had been engaged in delinquencies in company with others and that 93.1 percent of those engaged
in stealing had been in company with others. Gangs will be discussed
at greater length in Chapter 10.

Clifford R. Shaw (1930, 1931, 1938) of the Chicago School became
interested in the life histories of persons who engaged in crime in the
Chicago area. He found that criminal careers generally start with trivial
events and expand to serious crimes. In the deteriorated areas of the
city, the gang was seen as replacing the family in providing primary
group or intimate face-to-face interaction for growing adolescents in
the neighborhood. More of career patterns will be covered in Chapter
11 on criminal careers.

The Influence of Al Capone

An interesting and relevant sidelight to our discussion of Chicago's influence on the
development of criminology is the story of Al Capone and his gang. The gang with
which Capone was identified began in 1902 when "Big Jim" Colosimo, who had been
born in Italy in 1877 and came to the United States in 1895, met a madam who
operated a house on Armour Avenue, married her, and took over management of
the establishment. His business expanded, and in 1910 he brought his gangster
nephew, Johnny Torrio, from New York City to fight off those who encroached on
his vast holdings in the city. Subsequently, Torrio became known as "the father of
modern American gangsterdom" and operated Colosimo's vast "booze and brothel"
enterprises. When the Prohibition Act was passed in 1919, Torrio tried to convince
Colosimo to go into the illegal beer and whiskey business, but Colosimo objected.

Torrio then sent for a rough enforcer from his old Five Points Gang in New York, Al Capone, who shot Colosimo on May 11, 1920; Torrio then took over the vast enterprise, going into business in illegal beer and liquor in addition to the girls. In January 1925, Torrio was seriously injured by shots thought to be from "Bugs" Moran's North Side gang. Torrio gave the twenty-six-year-old Capone the gang and his $105,000,000 personal annual income and retired to Italy.

By 1925, Al Capone controlled the South Side, and "Bugs" Moran controlled the North Side of Chicago, having taken over after Dion O'Bannion was killed by Capone's men in November 1924. Dion "Deanie" O'Bannion had put together a strong gang by 1915 and was considered to be Chicago's arch killer, having killed about twenty-five men himself and having ordered many other deaths, but he was considered to be an outstanding gentleman, attending church regularly and keeping his wife supplied with flowers. As his chief assistant, "Bugs" Moran had taken over the gang after his death.

Alphonse "Scarface" Capone (1899–1947) was born in New York City, the son of immigrants from Naples, Italy. He was the fourth oldest of nine children. His record appears as follows (Kobler, 1971):

- Disorderly conduct, Olean, New York, 1919—discharged.
- Suspicion of murder, New York City, 1919—dismissed.
- Carrying a concealed weapon and assault with an automobile while intoxicated, Chicago, 1922—charge dropped and expunged from police records.
- Arrested for blocking traffic, Chicago, 1923—charge dismissed.
- Arrested for suspicion of murder, Chicago, 1924—released.
- Arrested for suspicion of murder, New York City, December, 1925—dismissed.
- Arrested for violation of the National Prohibition Act, Chicago, 1926—dismissed.
- Arrested for murder, Chicago, 1926—charge withdrawn.
- Arrested for a violation of National Prohibition Act, Chicago, 1926—dismissed.
- Arrested for refusing to testify in killing, Chicago, 1927—dismissed.
- Arrested for carrying a concealed weapon, Joliet, Illinois, 1927—fined $2,600 and dismissed.
- Arrested with bodyguard as suspicious character and carrying a concealed weapon—Philadelphia, Pennsylvania, 1929—sentenced one year in Holmesburg County Prison but released after seven months.
- Arrested four times in May, 1930, Miami for "vagrancy"—dismissed.
- Arrested for income tax evasion and convicted October 24, 1941—sentenced to federal prison for eleven years with fines of $50,000 and court costs of $30,000. (Served eight years of the sentence.)

Capone began as a bouncer in Big Jim Colosimo's Restaurant on Wabash Avenue, a task at which he was proficient because he was quick for his 5 feet 10 inches and 225 pounds. His scars had come from an earlier similar job in Brooklyn, when he made an uncomplimentary remark about a girl, and her brother leaped over the bar with his knife to carve three ugly, jagged scars on the left side of Capone's face. Capone then became an enforcer and a gunman. He printed on his business cards "Alphonse Capone, second-hand furniture dealer, 2222 South Wabash" and even put up a few cheap displays of broken-down furniture in the brothels he managed for Big Jim and Torrio. When prohibition became law in 1920, Capone waited behind the glass doors of a telephone booth in Colosimo's night club, in response to Torrio's orders, and shot Big Jim; the following day, Torrio, with Capone as his righthand man, took over Big Jim's empire. Torrio and Capone then "owned" too many judges and police officials to worry about the law; they virtually owned Chicago's South Side. When Torrio retired to Italy in 1925 after he had been shot, Capone became the number one man in Chicago with a gross business income of $5 million a year, but he had a gang war on his hands. (It is interesting to note that at this time Walter C. Reckless, veteran criminologist now retired from Ohio State University, played violin in Torrio's and Capone's speakeasies while he was a graduate student at the University of Chicago until he earned his doctorate there in 1925.) Only George "Bugs" Moran was left on the North Side, as a result of further developments in the gang war. Early on the morning of February 14, 1929, five Capone men lined up seven of Moran's mobsters and killed them in a garage that served as Moran's bootleg headquarters. In all, Al Capone killed or ordered the deaths of 701 men in Chicago, and more than 1,000 were killed in the bootleg wars.

By his excessive and violent behavior, Capone had eliminated his opposition in Chicago's gangland. No local Chicago or Illinois law enforcement or court system could touch him because of his power. In fact, on the night of May 8, 1924, Capone walked into Joe Howard's club to ask him why he had kicked around one of Capone's men. When Howard replied insultingly, Capone emptied six bullets into Howard's head and walked out before many witnesses. A month later, Capone went to City Hall and asked a young assistant state attorney, William McSwiggin, if he was looking for him, to which McSwiggin replied that Capone was wanted for the murder of Joe Howard. Soon afterward, McSwiggin's witnesses disappeared, and McSwiggin and two other people were killed outside a Cicero bar by a gunman identified as Al Capone. Nothing was ever done.

Al Capone died in Florida on January 25, 1947, of bronchial pneumonia and brain hemorrhage, with suspected serious venereal disease. But his flagrant lawbreaking had succeeded in attracting the attention of the nation to the problem of organized crime and lawlessness in general.

CONCLUSIONS

The Chicago School emphasized certain areas of the city as centrally associated with crime and delinquency, giving sociological reasons for their conclusions. Such factors as arrests, the crime rate, welfare recipients, health problems, school truancy, and other indices of social breakdown were all shown to be directly related to specific areas of the city. This principle is supported by many studies, one of the first being Shaw and McKay's presentation of social data by zones in the city between 1917 and 1938. However, subsequent studies have shown that crime is only one symptom associated with many other indices of social breakdown. Consequently, crime cannot be successfully considered alone, separate and apart from other social problems in the city. The city shows, in recent research, no major impact from ghettoization (Beasley and Antunes, 1974). The level of racial concentration is covariant with the income and density, making it almost impossible to find an association between crime rates and racial concentration.

Some of the criticisms of the Chicago School have been that it oversimplified the development of criminality; also that the statistics from which their early data were drawn were not valid measures. Whether the statistics of arrests or of juvenile court appearances are valid measures of delinquency and crime or whether they are correlated with poverty of the families in the area are also questioned (Johnasen, 1949; Toby 1957).

The Chicago Area Project, led by the late Clifford R. Shaw in the early 1930s, was begun by sociologists from the University of Chicago to discover, measure, and treat delinquency in the neighborhoods of the city that have for more than thirty-five years produced a disproportionately large number of delinquent boys and girls in the Cook County Juvenile Court (Burgess et al., 1937). This project, directly resulting from the Chicago School influence, drew the attention of persons working with juveniles throughout the country. In 1959 the Illinois Youth Commission implemented the idea throughout the entire state of Illinois. Minneapolis has also incorporated the idea of the area projects. The New York City Youth Board began operation in 1946 with the general idea of the Chicago Area Projects as a central trust. By going directly into the neighborhoods of high delinquency, many such projects have effectively dealt with delinquency. Mobilization for Youth on the Lower East Side of New York City was begun in 1963 under a $5 million grant from the Ford Foundation and the Juvenile Delinquency Prevention and Control Act of 1961. Thus, the Chicago School has given impetus to delinquency-control projects in cities throughout the nation that are still in operation more than forty years after their beginnings in Chicago in the early 1930s.

Questions

1. When and where did the first large-scale research in criminology develop?
2. What is W. I. Thomas's theory of man's four wishes?
3. Who first focused on urban living as being associated with crime?
4. What is the concept of concentric circles as related to crime and delinquency throughout a city?
5. Why does high delinquency tend to be concentrated in the areas of greatest poverty and in proximity to industry and business?
6. What is the origin of the term *Skid Row*?
7. What changes have cities experienced between the 1920s and 1980s, and how have these changes affected the areas of high delinquency?
8. How are gangs characterized in the inner city?
9. What were the Chicago Area Projects, and what has been their impact on delinquency control?
10. What are some other projects in other cities modeled after the Chicago Area Projects?

five

DIFFERENTIAL ASSOCIATION

The theory of differential association proposed by the late Edwin H. Sutherland in 1939 in his third edition of *Principles of Criminology* was the first major sociological theory of criminal behavior to have attracted sufficient following and generated sufficient discussion to constitute a viable approach to explaining crime on the part of individuals. It has been considered to be the first purely sociological theory that centered attention on the frequency, intensity, and meaningfulness of social relations rather than on the qualities or traits of the individual or the characteristics of the external environment. Differential association fits into the ecological approach of the Chicago School in that high-delinquency areas tend to have more delinquents because they associate with more delinquents. The neighborhood and gang phenomenon provides association with others of similar interests and needs. The morphological development of individual careers still go from the small to larger and more complex activities, whether criminal or otherwise.

Differential association refers to the patterns of behavior to which an individual is exposed. As such, it is not simply a "bad company" theory, although it has been so interpreted on occasion. Its commonsense appeal has undoubtedly helped to make it popular. Essentially, it says that crime is learned behavior that is imparted by other persons with whom one associates. The Quakers, who initiated the modern penitentiary movement by reforming the old Walnut Street jail in Philadelphia in 1790, undoubtedly were using the principles underlying this theory. Their thinking was that "bad company" encourages delinquency—or "one bad apple will spoil the whole barrel." They developed a theory of moral contamination that was extrapolated into a concept that had its practical application in solitary confinement to avoid moral contamination.

Gabriel Tarde wrote in 1890 that criminal behavior is learned by association and proposed his law of imitation. Tarde represented the Positive School but proposed the theory of learned criminal behavior as an alternative to the biological approaches of Lombroso. Crime as normal learned behavior, then, differs most sharply from the biological and psychological views presented in the late nineteenth and early twentieth centuries.

Differential association continues in this tradition. It is a theory of criminal behavior based on the laws of learning or learning theory.[1] Sutherland himself had close association with the experimental psychologists at Indiana University in the 1930s, and his contemporaries and former students have suggested that these contacts influenced his professional and academic thinking in his formulation of the laws of learning into an explanation of criminal behavior.

THE THEORY OF DIFFERENTIAL ASSOCIATION

The theory of differential association was introduced by Sutherland in the following form:

1. The processes which result in systematic criminal behavior are fundamentally the same in form as the processes which result in systematic lawful behavior.
2. Systematic criminal behavior is determined in a process of association with those who commit crimes, just as systematic lawful behavior is determined as a process of association with those who are law-abiding.
3. Differential association is the specific causal process in the development of systematic criminal behavior.
4. The chance that a person will participate in systematic criminal behavior is determined roughly by the frequency and consistency of his contacts with the patterns of criminal behavior.
5. Individual differences among people in respect to personal characteristics or social situations cause crime only as they affect differential association or frequency and consistency of contacts with criminal patterns.

---

[1] Edwin H. Sutherland, *Principles of Criminology*, 3rd ed. (Philadelphia: J. B. Lippincott Co., 1939), pp. 4–9.

6. Cultural conflict is the underlying cause of differential association and therefore of systematic criminal behavior.

7. Social disorganization is the basic cause of systematic criminal behavior.

In 1947, Sutherland modified his theory of differential association to include the laws of learning; in 1960, Donald R. Cressey, one of his students, again revised the book.[2] With the latest (ninth) edition appearing in 1974, this book has been on the market for a half century—the longest running criminology text in history.

The first theory of differential association proposed in 1939 indicated that crime was basically due to social disorganization, which resulted from the social processes of mobility, competition, and conflict. This social disorganization produced culture conflict, which in turn, produced differential association so that individuals having contacts with others would be exposed to differing social values and patterns of behavior. Crime results from the association of individuals or groups with criminal patterns. The more frequent and consistent these associations, the more likely that the individual will become a criminal. Critical experiences, such as arrest, court action, and newspaper publicity, would affect the person as well, primarily in his associations. The influence of impersonal associations would have something to do with the receptivity of the individual to patterns of criminal behavior as presented in these associations. A person does not inherit criminal tendencies; individual differences among people cause crime only as they are affected by differential association and the frequency and consistency of contacts with criminal patterns. Emotional stresses in the home are significant only as they drive the individual away from home and into contact with delinquents.

In the 1947 revision of his *Principles of Criminology*, Sutherland modified his theory by adding other materials. His final theory of differential association had taken shape. It included the following points:

1. Criminal behavior is learned.

2. Criminal behavior is learned in interaction with other persons in the process of communication.

3. The principal part of learning of criminal behavior occurs within intimate personal groups.

4. When criminal behavior is learned, the learning includes: (a) techniques of committing the crime, which are sometimes very complicated,

---

[2]Edwin H. Sutherland wrote the original *Principles of Criminology* in 1924 and revised it in 1934, 1939, and 1947. Sutherland died in 1950. Donald R. Cressey revised the book as Sutherland and Cressey, *Principles of Criminology* in 1955, 1960, 1966, and 1970. The ninth edition (1974) and 10th (1978) are titled *Criminology*.

sometimes very simple; (b) the specific direction of motives, drives, rationalizations, and attitudes.

5. The specific direction of motives and drives is learned from definitions of the legal codes as favorable or unfavorable.

6. A person becomes delinquent because of an excess of definitions favorable to violation of law over definitions unfavorable to violation of law.

7. Differential associations may vary in frequency, duration, priority, and intensity.

8. The process of learning criminal behavior by association with criminal and anticriminal patterns involves all of the mechanisms that are involved in any other learning.

9. While criminal behavior is an expression of general needs and values, it is not explained by those general needs and values since noncriminal behavior is an expression of the same needs and values.

EVALUATION OF DIFFERENTIAL ASSOCIATION

Differential association has become basic to the thinking of American criminologists and other researchers in crime. Further, the theory of differential association "is currently in the period of its greatest popularity, if one can judge by the number of journal articles reporting on how it is being tested, analyzed, and expanded."

By 1970, there had been about seventy articles in the professional and scholarly journals about the theory of differential association, and the number has increased recently. A detailed analysis of these articles would be too cumbersome for the purposes of this presentation. DeFleur and Quinney (1966) indicated that differential association remained the principal organizing sociological theme for criminology; Gibbons (1968) pointed out that differential association has dominated criminology for some time.

Cressey objects to having differential association referred to as a "bad company" theory because it is an oversimplification. Rather than just association, frequency, duration, priority, intensity, motives, drives, rationalization, attitudes, and many other factors influence the quality and effect of the association. So the theory of differential association is much more involved than a "bad company" theory would be. It would probably be best described as a cultural transmission theory.

One of the problems that has had the theory of differential association in difficulty is the fact that not everyone in contact with criminality adopts or follows the criminal pattern. Vold has indicated that only a few persons in society are criminal in proportion to the general population, but association with criminals must be broader. The differential-association theory has provided an exciting episode in criminological thinking, according to Vold (1958, p. 198), but the first formulations seem to offer much more than they have been able to deliver.

Some critics have indicated that there is no doubt that individuals become what they are largely because of contacts they have, but constitutional and biological factors, as well as other psychological problems erode the impact of association with criminals or quasi-criminals (Barnes and Teeters, 1959, p. 159).

It is difficult for some scholars to understand to what criminal behavior Sutherland refers. For example, Caldwell (1956, pp. 181–85) wonders whether it applies only to systematic criminal behavior; precisely *what* behavior does it explain? It should be noted here, however, that Sutherland left out the word *systematic* in his 1947 formulations of the theory of differential association. (He also dropped *conflict* and *disorganization* in the 1947 version.)

Caldwell indicates that the differential-association theory has serious weaknesses, but it has much merit, also, particularly in its calling attention to the importance of social factors. The similarity between the processes of learning of all types of behaviors was important. Further, criminology cannot be explained entirely in terms of personality maladjustments. It may be that many offenders are as well adjusted personally as is the general population and their violations of the law are chiefly the result of the values they have learned that are not acceptable to the rest of society. Conversely, some maladjusted people in the general population are not criminal. Cressey himself indicated in 1952 that it was doubtful that differential-association theory could apply to financial trust violations and several other kinds of criminal behavior.

Some critics have indicated that the theory does not explain why persons have the associations they have (Jeffery, 1959). The theory is "arbitrary," according to Clinard (1946). There have been criticisms because it does not explain the origin of crime in the first place (Jeffery, p. 537). Some have considered the theory of differential association to be defective because it does not consider the role of free will (Caldwell, 1956). Some writers have indicated that social processes are dogmatically shaped to fit into the prejudices of the preexisting theory of differential association and that it is mutually reinforceable (Glueck, 1956). Others have criticized it because it used terms like "systematic" and "access" without providing definitions for them (Clinard, 1959). Apparently, Cressey was indicating that critics were erroneously referring to the earlier formulations of 1939, which were changed in the 1947 edition.

Some believe that it is not comprehensive enough because it is not interdisciplinary (Jones, 1956, p. 95). On the other hand, it has been held to be too comprehensive because it applies to noncriminals (Gill, 1957; Jeffery, 1959, p. 537). Some have indicated that it is not closely enough allied with the more general sociological theory and research (Schrag,

1955). Still others have indicated that it is of little or no value to "practical men" (Barnes and Teeters, 1959, p. 210).

Cressey defends the theory of differential association against practically all the criticisms on the basis that critics do not understand what Sutherland tried to say—some address themselves to the 1939 formulation prior to its revision in 1947 (Caldwell, Cavan, Elliott, Korn, and McCorkle), and some critics have erroneously assumed "theory" to be synonymous with "bias" or "prejudice." Cressey's (Sutherland and Cressey, 1966, pp. 83–97) defense of the theory of differential association is cogent, effective, and vigorous.

Several studies have indicated that operant behavior is concerned with reinforcement by consequences, which is not covered in differential association (Jeffery, 1965). Criminal behavior is maintained by its circumstances, both material and social. Punishment, on the other hand, decreases response rates only when used in a consistent manner. This concept of reinforcement should have been included in the differential association theory, according to several writers.

The application of modern behavior theory would change some of the statements in Sutherland's theory of differential association. Differential association has been inadequate in (1) the amount of empirical support for the theory's basic propositions, (2) the "power" of the theory in terms of data derived from its higher-order propositions, and (3) the controlling possibilities, including whether the theory's propositions are causal principles or can be stated in such a way that they suggest possible practical applications (Burgess and Akers, 1966). A suggested modification of the theory of differential association is provided in Table 5-1 in accordance with Burgess and Akers's suggestions.

Differential identification was suggested by Daniel Glaser (1956) as a way of avoiding some of the criticisms of the current theory of differential association. Differential identification also influences the individual's attitude toward the law (Stratton, 1967). Glaser (1964, p. 494) subsequently suggested a theory of differential anticipation as a modification to Sutherland's original theory. This refers less to the concept of interpersonal relations with the peer group and emphasizes the aspirations of the individual.

Empirical testing of differential association began to appear in the 1950s (Liska, 1969). Most of these studies have shown low correlation between criminal behavior and association with criminal behavior patterns. Theoretical interpretations have been difficult.

Nettler (1974) listed the primary criticisms of differential association as follows:

1. The differential-association hypothesis neglects individual differences.
2. The differential-association hypothesis regards opportunity as a constant.

TABLE 5-1.
A Differential-Association-Reinforcement Theory of Criminal Behavior

SUTHERLAND'S STATEMENTS	REFORMULATED STATEMENTS
1. "Criminal behavior is learned."	1. Criminal behavior is learned according to the principles of operant conditioning.
2. "Criminal behavior is learned in interaction with other persons in a process of communication."	2. Criminal behavior is learned both in nonsocial situations that are reinforcing or discriminative and through that social interaction in which the behavior of other persons is reinforcing or discriminative for criminal behavior.
3. "The principal part of the learning of criminal behavior occurs within intimate personal groups."	3. The principal part of the learning of criminal behavior occurs in those groups which comprise the individual's major source of reinforcements.
4. "When criminal behavior is learned, the learning includes (a) techniques of committing the crime, which are sometimes very complicated, sometimes very simple; (b) the specific direction of motives, drives, rationalizations, and attitudes."	4. The learning of criminal behavior, including specific techniques, attitudes, and avoidance procedures, is a function of the effective and available reinforcers and the existing reinforcement contingencies.
5. "The specific direction of motives and drives is learned from definitions of the legal codes as favorable or unfavorable."	5. The specific class of behaviors which are learned and their frequency of occurrence are a function of the reinforcers which are effective and available and the rules or norms by which these reinforcers are applied.
6. "A person becomes delinquent because of an excess of definitions favorable to violation of law over definitions unfavorable to violation of law."	6. Criminal behavior is a function of norms which are discriminative for criminal behavior, the learning of which takes place when such behavior is more highly reinforced than noncriminal behavior.
7. "Differential associations may vary in frequency, duration, priority, and intensity."	7. The strength of criminal behavior is a direct function of the amount, frequency, and probability of its reinforcement.
8. "The process of learning criminal behavior by association with criminal and anticriminal patterns involves all of the mechanisms that are involved in any other learning."	8. (See Statement 1.)
9. "While criminal behavior is an expression of general needs and values, it is not explained by those general needs and values since noncriminal behavior is an expression of the same needs and values."	9. (Omit from theory.)

From Robert L. Burgess and Ronald L. Akers, "A Differential Association-Reinforcement Theory of Criminal Behavior," *Social Problems*, 14, no. 2 (1966), 146.

3. The differential-association hypothesis seems inapplicable to the explanation of passionate crimes.

4. The differential-association hypothesis is impossible to falsify. It is an explanatory account that holds true regardless of what happens or how deviant behavior really developed.

5. The advice to be gained from the differential-association hypothesis is poor. It takes a separate action and calls it a "cause" and assumes that "definitions of the situation" have considerable impact upon specific deviant behavior [pp. 196–99].

The commonsense reluctance to accept differential association of attitudes and beliefs as an adequate explanation of criminality emerges from the observation that changing the definitions of the situation may not be the best way of preventing or reducing crime.

Burgess and Akers (1966, esp. p. 147) presented a different approach to differential association from that taken by previous scholars. They applied the principles of modern behavior theory to the differential-association theory and found it lacking in (1) the amount of empirical support for the theory's basic propositions; (2) the "power" of the theory—i.e., the amount of data that can be derived from the theory's higher-order propositions; and (3) the controlling possibilities of the theory, including (a) whether the theory's propositions are, in fact, *causal* principles, and (b) whether the theory's propositions are stated in such a way that they suggest possible *practical* applications. Burgess and Akers reformulated the theory to satisfy their questions (see Table 5-1).

The criticisms of the theory of differential association have been well summarized by Reed Adams (1973), who went through the available literature up to 1972. The primary criticisms can be itemized as follows:

1. It is difficult to reduce differential association to empirical research for validation purposes.

2. There are some misinterpretations on the part of some writers with respect to differential association. For example, it is important to emphasize that Sutherland was referring to an *overabundance* of criminal associations rather than simply criminal associations. Further, the emphasis should be on *patterns of behavior*, rather than simply criminal associations.

3. The theory does not explain why the associations exist.

4. The theory fails to account for all types of crime.

5. The theory fails to consider personality and differences between people in receptivity.

6. The theory does not specify the ratio of behavior patterns that determine criminality with sufficient accuracy and precision.

Adams (1973) has suggested that criminological theory can employ operant conditioning principles, as suggested by Burgess and Akers, which rely on punishment and reward as reinforcers of behavior. Some distinction should be pointed out between the acquisition and the maintenance of criminal behavior, however. Sutherland was primarily concerned with the acquisition of behavior. Once the behavior is acquired, however, its maintenance is dependent upon the reinforcing effect of the deviance or maintenance, while the acquisition or "association" becomes irrelevant. This distinction may point the way to future research.

Akers (1973, pp. 45–61) has since proposed a social learning theory as a modification of differential association, in which the impact of differential reinforcement, the nature and context of social reinforcement, and the effect of learning failure are major considerations. The effect has been a strengthening of differential association by the bringing of individual differences into focus. It is really a peculiar blending of behavior modification principles with differential association, both of which supposedly disregard individual differences and focus only on observed behavior, but the result appears to be a more viable approach to explaining deviant behavior.

In the ninth edition of Sutherland and Cressey's *Criminology*, which contains probably the best formulation of differential association, Cressey acknowledges Akers's contribution and comments on its significance.

Examples of cases of differential association in offenders, themselves, have been difficult to demonstrate to the satisfaction of all. Professional and organized criminals would probably be easier to use as examples because the neighborhoods and companions and others to whom they have been exposed could be shown. W. A. Rushing (1973) says that the professional thief, who generally lives in the slums or in "white-light" districts in which commercial recreations flourish, is the best example.

WHITE-COLLAR CRIME

White-collar crime was another concept initiated by Sutherland (1945). He made a systematic rejoinder to criticisms of his 1939 formulation of the theory of differential association by identifying white-collar crime as a good example of it. In 1949, he published *White-Collar Crime*, which continued his defense of the theory of differential association while discussing white-collar crime as a "thumb-on-the-scales" type of sharp business practices and cheating in the business world.

An excellent discussion of his theory and the implications involved were also included in a posthumous volume known as *The Sutherland*

Papers (Cohen et al., 1956). Sutherland had pointed out that the usual statistical reports picture the criminal populations as lower class and economically underprivileged and give a misleading impression of non-criminality on the part of the middle and upper classes. He noted the respected and highly placed business and political personages who had "chipped" morality and honesty as the "robber barons" of an earlier period had done. White-collar criminality was considered to have taken place frequently—misrepresentations of the financial statements of corporations, manipulation of stock exchanges, bribery of public officials, kickbacks, or "considerations" in the securing of desirable contracts or immunities, commercial transactions, trust funds, dishonest bankruptcies, and similar activities.

Computer Crime

The most recent development in white-collar crime is computer crime, which is big business today. Losses in computer crime were estimated in 1979 to be $621,000 per incident (Congressional Record, Jan. 25, 1979, p. S726). One of the newest training fields among law enforcement agencies is in computer crime (Colvin, 1979). Computer security cases fall into four categories: (1) sabotage, (2) information fraud and theft, (3) financial fraud and theft, and (4) unauthorized use or theft of computer services (Parker, 1979). Financial fraud and theft are becoming more prevalent as more liquid assets are put into computers. The "typical" computer criminal is thirty-five years of age, male, lives in a respectable neighborhood with a wife and two children, has been employed by the firm for three years, has an income in the top 40 percent bracket, and steals about 120 percent of his salary.

Frank Costello and "Legs" Diamond

Two examples of the operation of the theory of differential association might be shown in the cases of Frank Costello and "Legs" Diamond. Both were born and raised in the slums of large cities and began practicing larceny and shoplifting with their friends by the time they started school. Both grew up in their respective neighborhoods and graduated into higher types of crime. The patterns of behavior, the definitions of conformity and nonconformity, the companions, and all the patterns used in differential association were present in both cases.

"Legs" Diamond, originally John Thomas Noland (1896–1931), was born and raised on the West Side in Philadelphia, where he and his brother, Eddie, grew up with the Boiler Gang, practicing thievery even as young boys and establishing a police record. They went to New York City and joined the Hudson Dusters, a group that specialized in robbing delivery trucks, but soon graduated into burglary; arrests for assault and robbery followed. "Legs" deserted from the U.S. Army during World War I and was sent to Governor's Island Disciplinary Barracks in 1919, transferred to Leavenworth, and released in 1920. He began working as a lieutenant to New York City gangster Jacob "Little Augie" Orgen and continued bootlegging, smuggling narcotics, and hijacking trucks. In the gang wars in New York, Diamond became known as the "Clay Pigeon" because he had been shot at and wounded without effect more than any other of his colleagues; his ability to survive was a source of amazement. Diamond soon earned a reputation for clever planning of several types of crimes; for instance, he engineered the murder of "Kid Dropper" outside a courtroom where the police had brought him on a minor complaint deliberately filed to get him into the open. By 1927, "Legs" was a powerful figure in New York's underworld, but that apparently attracted the attention of other gangsters, and his luck deteriorated; he was shot in bed at 4:45 A.M. in Albany, New York, on December 18, 1931, by one of Dutch Schultz's men.

Frank Costello, originally Francesco Seriglia (1893–1973), was born in Calabria, Italy, but was brought to New York by his parents shortly after his birth. He grew up in East Harlem, where he was associated with a street gang. Arrests began in 1908, including assault and robbery on several occasions and one for concealed weapons in 1919, after which he spent a year in jail. He became a rum-runner for Big Bill Dwyer's gang in 1920; this was an operation financed by Arnold Rothstein, and Costello took over the gambling interests after Rothstein's death. When Mafia boss Salvatore Maranzano was killed in 1931, "Lucky" Luciano took over; as a member of Luciano's Cosa Nostra family, Costello consolidated the gambling interests of the syndicate throughout the United States in the 1930s, concentrating on New York, Florida, and Las Vegas. When Luciano was deported in February 1946, Costello took over, promising Luciano a continuing cut. His operations took some heat from the 1951 United States Senate Crime Investigating Committee under Estes Kefauver, who forced Costello into the open by requiring him to testify, but his answers were cagey and empty of information. Nevertheless, this weakened Costello, and Vito Genovese was able to assume control of the organization when one of his men shot Costello on the evening of May 2, 1957, in the lobby of the building on Central Park West where his posh apartment was located. Costello subsequently went to prison for income tax evasion, but then went into semi-retirement, continuing his association with New York's prominent businessmen and politicians. He died quietly in bed at eighty years of age on February 18, 1973.

CONCLUSIONS

The theory of differential association was first presented by Edwin H. Sutherland in 1939 as an explanation of crime based on social disorganization and learning of criminal behavior. It was revised in 1947 to include learning principles. It was the first purely sociological approach to the explanation of crime, based on frequency, intensity, and quality of social interrelationships. The differential-association approach has sometimes been referred to as *cultural transmission*. Certainly, cultural transmission of values and attitudes is basic to the dynamics of differential association. The theory has been attacked, supported, modified, and criticized for its limitations. Differential association has been most ably defended by Donald R. Cressey, a former student of Sutherland's at Indiana who has revised the book several times since Sutherland's death. The theory of differential association has attracted more attention and generated more comment, research, and writing than any other criminal theory. In recent years, the principles of operant conditioning with reinforcement by punishment and reward have appeared in the research.

The application of B. F. Skinner's behavior modification and operant conditioning approaches to differential association (Tarter, 1973) has brought even greater response recently on the part of scholars and researchers. The fact that it has often been viewed as a commonsense "bad company" theory, however erroneous according to Cressey (who uses the term *patterns of behavior* instead), has always made differential association attractive to the general practitioner and the public, even though its practical application has been limited to trying to control the association of minor offenders with more serious offenders. Glaser (1970) has suggested bringing the concepts into the area of the prison of the future. He indicates that the goals of future prisons will be (1) to evoke in offenders an enduring identification of themselves with anticriminal persons and (2) to enhance the prospects that released prisoners will achieve satisfaction in legitimate postrelease activities. In any case, research, writing, and attempts at practical application are still appearing in the literature concerning differential association.

Questions

1. What is the theory of differential association?
2. Why is the theory of differential association sometimes called a theory of learning?
3. What have been the primary criticisms of the theory of differential association?
4. Although many people considered the theory of differential association as a "bad company" theory, Cressey says it is not—for what reason?
5. How does the application of modern behavior theory change some of the statements in Sutherland's theory of differential association?
6. What is the theory of differential identification, which has been presented as a modification of differential association?
7. What has empirical testing of differential association produced?
8. How do B. F. Skinner's behavioral modification and operant conditioning relate to differential association?
9. What is white-collar crime?
10. How does white-collar crime relate to the theory of differential association?

six

ANOMIE, ALIENATION, IDENTIFICATION, AND IDENTITY

Anomie, alienation, and identification all have to do with the congruency of the individual to his or her social norms. Each has been incorporated in theories of criminal and delinquent behavior in different ways. Anomie is a personal disorganization resulting in disorientation and lawlessness, or social situations in which the norms are in conflict and a person encounters contradictory requirements or a social situation that contains no norms. Alienation is an estrangement of the individual from the outside world or a lack of integration within the personality itself. Identification refers to the merging of the individual with his group or an imitation of the behavior of others (Gould and Kolb, 1964). Identity has to do with an individual's strivings, values, expectations, actions, fears, and problems of adaptation, generally either mutually shared with or complemented by other members of a group (Ackerman, 1966, p. 204). An individual identity that is not merged in a group generally results from an identity struggle sometimes originating in unresolved conflicts in basically authoritarian and intolerant personalities, disturbed patterns of parental identification frequently involving the father, or other similar problems (Brody, 1966, p. 635). All these concepts refer to the relationship of the individual to his society and its norms. All have been used in a series of theoretical formulations that help explain criminal and delinquent behavior.

Identification, identity, and alienation have different meanings, but they are related to one another and are important in human social behavior. They can all lead to anomie or normlessness. Identification is the accepting of the roles of certain groups, such as racial, ethnic, occupational, professional, family, or gang. The individual identifies with that group to which he considers he "belongs." Identification relates to "belonging." Identity is the attempt by a person to exert his or her unique individuality. He may adopt an identity that differentiates himself from all others. Actors and show people adopt gimmicks and specific lines, such as the late Jack Benny's stinginess, Dean Martin's drinking, Rodney Dangerfield's "I don't get no respect!" and many other traits and characteristics that identify each as an individual. Alienation is the aloofness from group behavior. The alienated person does not "belong," nor does he or she consciously seek an identity by which he or she can be viewed by others. Alienation is characterized by asocial or antisocial attitudes, failure to "belong," and a lack of loyalty.

The word *anomie* first appeared in English in 1591 and was frequently used in seventeenth-century theology to mean disregard of law, particularly divine law. It was included in Dr. Johnson's dictionary of 1755 in English (*anomy*) and French (*anomie*) spelling, though the French spelling now predominates because of its introduction into the language of sociology by Durkheim in 1897. A major theoretical pattern involves social alienation which, for criminology, began with Durkheim's revival of the concept of anomie. Robert K. Merton, Richard Cloward and Lloyd Ohlin, Jacob Chwast, and others have used this approach.

The concepts of anomie, alienation, identification, and identity explain some criminal behavior by focusing primarily upon the personality of the individual, as compared with the social environmental focus found in differential association. In terms of modalities in the criminal justice system, then, differential association would be the sociogenic model, while anomie, alienation, identification, and identity would represent the patient, or medical, model. In anomie, society's normative standards of conduct and beliefs have weakened or disappeared. This is commonly manifested in individuals by anxiety, personal disorientation, and social isolation. Anomie was a term used by Dr. Benjamin Rush to mean a congenital defect in morality. Alienation is a general term now largely restricted to forensic psychiatry relating to a dissociation of one's own feelings so that they no longer seem effective, familiar, or convincing, resulting in estrangement and deep personalization, and therefore alienation from society. The alienated person may become unfriendly, hostile, indifferent, or asocial. Identity refers to the unity and comprehensiveness of the individual's perception of himself or herself; it provides the ability to see one's self as holding continuity and sameness in relationships with primary love objects. The identity crisis is a social role conflict as perceived by the person himself or herself, threatening the loss of personal sameness and continuity or of the ability to accept the role expected of him or her by society. The identity crisis frequently occurs in adolescence when a sudden increase appears in strength of drives, combined with a sudden change in the role the adolescent is expected to adopt socially, educationally, or vocationally. These independent and interdependent factors influence the social behavior of individual personalities.

The concept of anomie received its first major attention when Emile Durkheim (1858–1917), considered to be the father of French sociology, made his contribution to social theory of *collective consciousness* or *collective conscience.* Under this concept, *mechanical solidarity* (a term from physics) moves in the development of society to *organic solidarity* (reflecting the influence of biology), in which individuals become aware of social values and react to them. Durkheim's study of personality problems was found in his book *Le Suicide* published in 1897, in which three types of suicides were described: (1) egoistic suicide, which results when an individual shuts himself or herself off from other human beings; (2) *anomique* suicide, or anomie, which comes from the beliefs that one's world has fallen apart around one; (3) the altruistic suicide, which results from great loyalty to a cause. Anomic suicide, applied to crime, occurs when a person's world has fallen apart around him or her and he or she consequently exhibits suicidal or criminal behavior.

ANOMIE

Modern man has been beset with the twin problems of anomie and alienation (Krill, 1969). A frequent sense of aimless drifting and a feeling of impotence and powerlessness lead to concern about personal insignificance and a fear that one has been victimized. Diminished responsibility accompanies feelings of insignificance, but bitterness and envy arise toward others in more fortunate circumstances. To change the environment and the circumstances, quick and easy solutions are sought ranging from alcohol and drugs to crime.

The concept of anomie emerged with Durkheim in 1897 as the loss of individual identification with one's cultural group. Merton (1938) had considered anomie as an explanation of deviant behavior early in 1938. In 1949, he suggested that the condition of anomie would be a good explanation for deviant behavior in any society. In 1955, he elaborated on anomie as central in juvenile delinquency (Witmer and Kotinsky, 1955). Because criminal behavior grows out of a contradiction between the culture and the social structure and, in addition, between the cultural values and the means provided for achieving them, the individual dissociated from his cultural group may well exhibit deviant behavior. Merton further elaborated and refined this concept in 1957.

In the beginning, humans' biological impulses sought full expression, but the growing social order made necessary the management of those impulses in individuals and the social processing of tensions. With the advance of social science, sociological perspectives have entered into the analysis, and the question as to why deviant behavior varies within different social structures needs clarification. How some social structures exert pressure on certain persons to engage in nonconforming behavior must be primarily sociological, with biological and personality differentials changing the directions of behavior.

Culturally defined goals as legitimate objectives for all members of society are basic in the social formation. The culture defines and regulates the acceptable modes of reaching for those goals, and these regulations are rooted in the mores or institutions of the society. The criterion of acceptability is value laden. Deviant behavior comes when the aim is victory in competitive athletics, for example, and is construed as "winning the game" rather than "winning under the rules of the game." Consequently, there arises a difference between achieving the goal by legitimate means and by illegitimate means, the latter being called deviant behavior.

The types of individual adaptation to this frustration can be classified. Table 6–1 identifies five modes of adaptation with acceptance or rejection of the goals and the means identified by a plus signifying acceptance, a minus signifying rejection, and a plus-minus signifying rejection of prevailing values and substitution of new values.

Conformity to both cultural goals and institutionalized means, adaptation type I, is the most common and desired adaptation. Innovation occurs when a person has assimilated the cultural values regarding the goals without equally internalizing the norms governing the way

TABLE 6–1.
A Typology of Modes of Individual Adaptation

TYPES OF ADAPTATION	CULTURAL GOALS	INSTITUTIONALIZED PROCEDURES
I. Conformity	+	+
II. Innovation	+	−
III. Ritualism	−	+
IV. Retreatism	−	−
V. Rebellion	±	±

+ stands for acceptance
− stands for rejection
± stands for rejection of prevailing values and substitution by new values
From Robert K. Merton, *Social Theory and Social Structure*, rev. ed. (New York: Macmillan Publishing Co., 1968), p. 194.

of obtaining them. Therefore, adaptation II, innovation, may become criminal through white-collar crime, the "Robin Hood" syndrome, or other types of crimes. Ritualism, or the type III adaptation, involves abandoning and scaling down the goals to a point where aspirations can be legitimately satisfied with the means available. A person who plays it safe and does not rock the boat may adapt in this manner. He or she is playing the game but not particularly enjoying it.

Adaptation type IV, retreatism, shares neither society's values nor the institutional means by which they are achieved. The retreatists are not *in* society but *of* society and are the true aliens in society; they are alienated. Many are outcasts, vagrants, vagabonds, tramps, alcoholics, drug addicts, psychotics, and others who have not identified with the goals in society and have ignored the means by which they are achieved. Retreatism is a frequent adaptation, probably second only to adaptation type I, or conformity. These people have the dilemma of either being crushed in the struggle to achieve approved goals or enduring the hopeless resignation and flight from them. Rebellion, which is adaptation type V, leads people outside the social structure to envisage and try to establish a modified social structure. They are probably alienated from the present goals and the means, regarding them as purely arbitrary. Their efforts are aimed toward the introduction of a social structure and cultural standards of success and the means by which they are achieved that would make for a closer correspondence between their effort and their rewards. When the institutional system is seen as a barrier to legitimatized goals and achievement, the stage is set for rebellion and protest.

The pressures from this social structure produce strain directed toward anomie and deviant behavior. This strain does not operate evenly among all members of society. The lower socioeconomic strata are most vulnerable to the pressures toward deviant behavior because many of the desirable goals are not readily available through institutionalized means, as they are in the middle and upper classes. The social system becomes stabilized when the cultural structure attaches prestige to certain goals and alternative goals, while permitting individuals to have access to them. In such a stabilized society, potential deviants may still conform, under stress, but the central thrust is toward anomie or some disregard for social norms in the face of frustration and deprivation.

The family sometimes contributes to anomie and deviant behavior. Children learn to "cut the corners" by observing their parents cheat at the same time they are teaching that "honesty is the best policy." Learning thus to act upon stereotypes and categorizations of people and things, absorbing a questionable evaluation of the culture while developing achievable goals may be learned by the child from the parents, with the parents providing explicit positive advice and guidance at variance with their performance. The projection of parental ambition onto a child so that the child may be successful in an area where the parent has failed provides further motivation for anomie.

The concept of differentials in access to success-goals by illegitimate means may be a step beyond Merton's systematization and extension of the anomie theory to patterns of disjunction between goals and access to them by legitimate means (Cloward, 1969). The linking of concepts regarding accessibility of both legitimate and illegitimate opportunity structure suggests new possibilities for research on the relationship between social structure and deviant behavior.

Cloward (1959), a student of Merton, attempted to reconcile or consolidate the two major sociological schools of thought about deviant behavior. Edwin H. Sutherland's differential association or cultural transmission approaches were more in line with the approach by Clifford R. Shaw, Henry D. McKay, and others of the Chicago School. The concept of anomie, exemplified by the work of Emile Durkheim, focused on the way social conditions lead to desire for success where unlimited aspirations produce a breakdown in regulatory norms in Durkheim's approach; in Merton's work, attention was directed to patterns of disjunction between culturally prescribed goals and access to them by legitimate means. Cloward proposed an additional variable in anomie, the concept of differentials in access to success-goals by illegitimate means. Not everyone has the same access even to the illegitimate means. The organization of illegitimate means in slum areas consists primarily in individuals and groups who participate in stable illicit enterprises, such as gambling, the "numbers," and dice (Whyte, 1955, p. viii). The use of the concepts of legitimate goals and illegitimate means combined with differential opportunity to achieve and participate in these illegitimate means provide a conceptual structure of both legitimate and illegitimate opportunity structures. The concept of differential systems of opportunity with variation in access could provide a meeting place for differential association and anomie.

Albert Cohen (1969), who studied at Indiana in the Sutherland tradition, attempted to relate anomie theory to other traditions in the sociology of deviant behavior. He pointed out that anomie theory concerned the relationship between certain aspects of culture (goals and norms) and social structure (opportunity or access to means). Cohen indicated that "the assumption of discontinuity" implies that the deviant act is an abrupt change from anomie to deviance. The disjunction between goals and means and the choice of adaptations depend upon the opportunity structure. The development of ego's responses may open up, close off, or leave unaffected legitimate opportunities for ego, and they may do the same to illegitimate opportunities. Table 6–2 illustrates the possibilities.

TABLE 6-2.
Responses of the Opportunity Structure
to Ego's Deviance

	LEGITIMATE OPPORTUNITIES	ILLEGITIMATE OPPORTUNITIES
Open Up	I	II
Close Off	III	IV

Response I *opens up legitimate opportunities*—such as finding employment opportunities for delinquents and criminals. Response II *opens up illegitimate opportunities*—such as collusive illicit arrangements in which both parties profit (the racketeer and the law enforcement officer). In this case, a law enforcement official, a discouraged parent, or a professor may simply give up the effort to systematically enforce a rule and limit himself or herself to sporadic token gestures, simply riding it out. Response III is the *closing off of legitimate opportunities*—it might result from being dropped from membership in a professional society or a social club, being disbarred from practice in law or other professions because of deviance; being expelled from a union or other organizaton, or becoming generally *persona non grata* in legitimate areas normally open. This increases the relative attractiveness of illegitimate means. Response IV, or the *closing off of illegitimate opportunities*, is basic "social control," including locking doors, cutting off access to narcotics or other contraband, increasing the certainty and severity of punishments, and other controls that make deviance more difficult but may also stimulate the deviant to ingenuity in devising new means to circumvent the new restrictions. It is crime prevention through environmental design.

Humans are social animals because they live long lives, are early dependent upon others, and learn interdependence through this process. Dependent upon others, for many services, they must get along with others. Social conditions that allow deregulation of social life can be termed anomie. As applied to criminology, Robert Merton's hypothesis was essentially that crime breeds in the gaps between aspirations of an individual and his or her possibilities of achieving them (Nettler, 1974, p. 157). Cloward and Ohlin (1961) brought anomie into an opportunity theory; they felt that the tension between recommended goals and available means presents a strain that the individual must handle in some way and that some go in the direction of crime and delinquency by using illegitimate means to achieve recommended goals.

Cloward and Ohlin hold that a major problem for lower-class youth is the disparity between what they are led to want and what is actually available to them. When they internalize conventional goals but are faced with limited access to legitimate means to achieve these goals, the intense frustration may result in exploration of nonconforming alternatives to achieve them. Resorting to gangs and collective behavior among many youths with the same problems should be expected. The gangs generally fall into one of three patterns, according to the behavior of the group: (1) criminal, (2) conflict, or (3) retreatist. The criminal gang steals and achieves its goals by acquiring property and money. The conflict gang is aggressive and fights other gangs or may engage in vandalism. The retreatist gang engages in self-indulgent use of drugs or alcohol, thereby escaping frustration by blocking out the world.

Four general criticisms of opportunity theory are offered by Nettler (pp. 157–67). First, the key concepts are not clear. The central concepts are "aspiration" and "opportunity," but the meanings of these concepts become slippery and ambiguous when they are applied to each individual. Second, gang behavior is not always well explained by opportunity-structure hypotheses and may be an example of middle-class scholars' imposing their values and perceptions on others—there are many other reasons for gang behavior. Third, it is questionable whether delinquent behavior is produced by the opportunity structure because the concept of frustration has different meanings to different people and can be handled in different ways. Although lower socioeconomic classes contribute disproportionately to the official crime rates, only a minority of the lower socio-economic class is involved in crime. Fourth, the recommendations that large funds be spent on large-scale projects to prevent delinquency have been accepted, but these projects have had questionable results.

The Juvenile Delinquency Prevention and Control Act of 1961 resulted directly from Attorney General Robert F. Kennedy's reading Cloward and Ohlin's book; Ohlin was appointed the first director of the program in Washington, D.C., and it served as a starting point for the "opportunity" programs in the Kennedy and Johnson administrations. Millions of dollars of federal funding and some private funding, particularly from the Ford Foundation, went into delinquency-prevention projects. Nevertheless, the record has been one of uniform failure (Nettler, p. 166). There is no way of knowing, however, how much worse the delinquency rates would have been had many of these projects not been funded. Further, research in delinquency and crime is plagued by the introduction of too many uncontrollable variables so that completely reliable and valid research in delinquency prevention is nearly impossible.

Delinquents are distinguished from conformists by their distance from the norms of their social organization. The analysis of their type of delinquency and the causes of their deviance are generally individualized, but delinquents and their judgment are constant and are the result of outside pressures. Delinquency may emerge from general tendencies coming from an unstable environment, the evolution of sub-cultural delinquency, or new problems resulting from conflict situations and drugs. The environments from which many delinquents come are delinquent subcultures, which may become criminal, conflict, and retreatist gangs in the Cloward and Ohlin sense. A primary generalization can be that deviance results from anomie, alienation, or normlessness. Further, the situation of anomie affects internalized values, resulting in secondary deviance and internalization of deviant attitudes and values combined with a readiness to deviate (Gagné, 1972).

In developing his scale for measuring anomia (anomie), Srole (1956, esp. pp. 712–13) has identified the anomic individual (or the self-to-others alienation) as the feeling that (1) community leaders are indifferent to his needs, (2) the social order is essentially unpredictable, (3) that he and people like him are retrogressing from the goals they have reached, (4) that one cannot count on anyone else for support, and (5) life is essentially meaningless. It has been shown that among people at the same status level, those who have been exposed to anomic attitudes become, themselves, more anomic (Simpson and Miller, 1936).

Wirth said in 1938 that urban life leads to alienation and anomie. Fischer found in 1973, however, that there could be shown no real association between the size of the community and a sense of personal incompetence, only a small association between urbanism and isolation, and that attributing alienation to urbanism is incorrect. This may well reflect the changing city where the inner city has tended to become black and brown, the result of white flight to the suburbs. The resulting heterogeneous black or brown inner city should produce less anomie in that group.

Anomie is limited, as are most other theories, because it does not explain *why* the individual loses identification with his or her culture nor why the majority of persons exposed to approximately similar pressures do not lose identification and exhibit sufficient deviant behavior that they are arrested. Neither does anomie explain the destructive or nonutilitarian nature of some offenders. Yet the concept of anomie is useful in most instances in deviant behavior. Probably its greatest weakness in sociological theory is in the difficulty of quantifying or reducing the data to manipulable proportions and subjecting it to research method.

ALIENATION

Alienation seems to be anomie in the extreme. It is an estrangement from normal society and may involve an identification with other persons and groups similarly alienated. This is the basis for "gay liberation" and other homosexual groups that maintain lobbies for equal rights in legislatures. Kittrie (1971) referred to the alienation of some people and groups and pointed out the dangers of a "therapeutic state" in which deviants might be subjected to enforced therapy to reduce the problem of alienation.

As previously indicated, alienation refers to an estrangement of the individual from the outside world or a lack of integration within the personality itself. Alienation is the process of tagging, defining, identifying, segregating, describing, emphasizing, making conscious and self-conscious, a person who deviates from the expected behavioral norms, called "the dramatization of evil" by Frank Tannenbaum (1938); Tannenbaum's reference to this referred to the public's extreme interest in crime, particularly in the movies and in the careers of such people as Al Capone, John Dillinger, "Pretty Boy" Floyd, "Baby Face" Nelson, "Machine Gun Kelley," "Killer" Burke, and other criminal "heroes" who had been made public figures. Tannenbaum's "dramatization of evil" also has been regarded as the forerunner of labeling theory introduced by Howard S. Becker (1963). Once individuals seek support from others who feel alienated from the prevailing norms, a gang has begun to form (Sutherland and Cressey, 7th ed., p. 205). An effective interaction between the actors in a collective problem-solving process becomes the gang for alienated youths, and the gang activities begin (Cohen, 1955, p. 59).

The function of the gang in this instance serves four important functions (Cohen, 1955, pp. 60–61; also Cloward and Ohlin, 1961, pp. 140–42). First, gang members can explore the extent to which each is willing to go in accepting and implementing alternative rules. Second, they can explore the extent to which they can rely on each other for support. Third, each member has an opportunity to test the degree to which his techniques for neutralizing the influences of law-abiding society are successful and accepted by the others. Fourth, the gang can try out various courses of delinquent actions and judge the commitment that each member of the gang is willing to make to each type of action or speciality.

Alienation does not necessarily have to be in the direction of delinquency. Some of the hippie communes and similar groups are also alienated from "the silent majority" that comprises Establishment society. The Amish, the Mennonites, and other fundamentally religious groups that use only those modes of transportation mentioned in the Bible are also considered to be alienated from the rest of society—not "with it." The Church of Satan in San Francisco has been referred to as a cult of devil worshipers, but the *Satanic Bible* has outsold the *Holy Bible* on several university campuses in recent years.

Alienation appears in various philosophical treatments of the place of humans in the world, but its primary source in the social sciences was the social theory of Karl Marx (1844, pp. 67–84), and this was supported by Sigmund Freud (1923). According to Marx, some men are alienated from their work by the relationships between economic production and the systems of class domination. This separation of the workers from the products of their labor alienates them from nature and from themselves, as well. Freud indicated that alienation occurs primarily as the result of the needs of civilization. Marcuse (1955, p. 45) felt that Freud knew that the demands of the social structure on the individual could be intensified by domination of one social class over another. Many alienated tendencies remain covert and hidden because they exist only as the negative component of an ambivalent conformist-alienation disposition (Lang, 1964).

Alienation contributes to much deviant behavior and many hostile attitudes. It also determines loyalties and disloyalties that can be seen in gang wars, court actions, the political in-fighting in all organizations from industry to universities, from the military to partisan politics, and even within the family. In the Senate hearings in the Watergate case in the summer of 1973, committee chairman Sam Ervin quoted Cardinal Wolsey's famous comment of regret in Shakespeare's Henry VIII: "Had I but served my God with half the zeal I served my king, he would not in mine age have left me naked to mine enemies."

Alienation and conflict contribute to the generation gap. In labor unions, young workers resent seniority and "fat pensions" for the old and imply that the only decent thing for them to do is curl up and die (Hoffer, 1973, p. 28). Of most serious concern to society, however, may be the feeling of alienation by individuals who form gangs in an effort to be accepted and neutralize the constraints toward conformity to "equalize" their lot with the society that has alienated them.

IDENTIFICATION AND IDENTITY

Identification refers to the merging of the individual with his or her group or imitation of the behavior of others, while identity refers to the individual's own values, ambitions, and adjustment problems that are either mutually shared with or complemented by others. Consequently, identification and identity are basic to social interaction. The achievement of what one wants to be becomes his or her identity or identification. Introduced into psychology by Sigmund Freud in 1899, the idea of identity or identification is really broad and ill-defined but has served to convey the sense of merging of one's self with others or with an ideal that is satisfying (Allport, 1954, p. 293).

Identity is the concept that bridges the gap between the inner development of the individual and the forces of culture in his or her environment. It is an integrating process in which the individual becomes comfortable with his or her environment, which in turn lessens anxiety and tension. Erikson (1950) indicates that the integration taking place in the form of ego identity is more than the sum of the person's identifications; it is the accrued experience of his ability to integrate these identifications with his motivations and the opportunity offered in social roles.

It is the adolescent identity crises that contribute to much crime and delinquency. Adolescents are "fighting it out" with authority. They are too old to be children and too young to be adults. In the attempt to find their role in society and their identity, their seemingly random activities, propelled by intense motivation, almost constantly frustrated, frequently result in activities that bring them into conflict with the law. Their attempts to find out who they are and to change "the system" may result in their becoming militant activists on campus, in the streets, or in their homes, or becoming involved in professional and organized crime.

Identity refers to a self-concept expressed in the striving, goals, expectations, and values of a person or a group of persons. It may be an individual identity or a shared identity, such as in a family or group. Identity conflict may originate in disturbed patterns of parental identification. A parent may be absent or personally distant—or, on the other hand, present and overwhelming and frightening. In neither instance is he or she available as a model or object for identification for a growing child. The results vary. The identity conflict can result in prejudice, vulnerability, and dogmatism, in paranoid schizophrenia, in homosexuality, and many in other deviations (Brody, 1966, p. 635).

Adolescence has cultural ramifications that are probably more important to the criminal justice system than the physiological phenomena of being ready for sexual activity, the appearance of facial pimples and blemishes, voice changes in the male, and other manifestations of physical maturation. Extreme mood swings, confusion about sexual feelings, intense feelings of guilt and depression, and ambivalence and vacillation result frequently from an attempt to begin to learn to cope with an adult world. Under English common law, a person becomes an adult at age seven because in the economy of the Industrial Revolution, he or she could earn a living at that time by menial jobs or in an apprenticeship to a tradesman. Beginning in the twentieth century with the White House Conference of 1910, called by President Theodore Roosevelt, followed by the Child Labor Laws of 1912, the age of self-support has been pushed upward. Compulsory education laws and the need for adequate professional preparation have now pushed the age of self-support into the twenties in many cases. The resulting confusion of roles and the cultural concept of "adolescence" intensify the ambivalences of the individual and his or her need to "find himself or herself" in the adult world.

The defense of toughness and an attitude of not caring is frequently a defense mechanism acceptable to adolescents. Approval of their peer group is a requirement for most adolescents, who respond to the expectations and values of "the gang," with conformance in dress, grooming, and behavior.

The identity crisis in adolescents is of special importance to the criminal justice system. In the process of growing to adulthood, adolescents reach a point where they must "devalue" the parents, frequently by open criticism of the parents personally, intellectually, and culturally (Hahn, 1971, p. 67). The adolescent frequently identifies with a family or individuals outside the home while rejecting the parents. It is during this time that the football coach, a specific teacher, a member of the clergy, a member of the street gang, or other persons tend to personify the adolescent's developing ideal, which the growing personality attempts to emulate. As adolescents mature into adulthood, more adult perspectives develop and there is a more balanced and realistic attitude toward parents. It might be conjectured that this identity-crisis problem may have contributed to the behavior of Patty Hearst, who was allegedly kidnapped by the Symbionese Liberation Army in early 1974, called her father a liar in taped interviews, and then joined the organization in robbing a bank in San Francisco. Many adolescents have joined the drug culture and communes. Certainly, the identity crisis emerges from the cultural phases of adolescence in modern society and its manifestations are culture bound.

Identification with a case worker with whom a positive relationship has been established has been a fairly universal factor in the successful treatment of juvenile behavior disorders and personal problems (Hollis, 1964, p. 160). One of the greatest deficiencies in the lives of delinquent youth has been the absence of a close relationship with trusted adults. Central to all counseling is help answering the questions: (1) Who am I? (2) Where am I going? and (3) How will I get there? Finding one's identity through identification with another person or constructed ideal is an excellent social stabilizer.

William Cook and Bonnie and Clyde

William Cook (1929–52), who has been called "one of the most terrifying killers in modern times," though he killed only six people, was an excellent example of the effects of anomie and alienation. Born near Joplin, Missouri, he was raised with seven brothers and sisters in an abandoned mine shaft by his father, an uneducated mine worker. After staggering out of a local tavern one night, the old man hopped a freight and disappeared. Welfare workers found the children and managed to find foster homes for all of them except Billy. It was said that "he just didn't look right." He was never able to close his right eyelid, resulting in his being referred to as Evil Eye.

The courts finally found somebody to take him for pay, which was most unsatisfactory. As he grew older, he was picked up for theft and was given the choice between a foster home and an institution; understandably, he took the institution. He was considered the roughest inmate there and was ultimately transferred to the Missouri Penitentiary at Jefferson City, where he was also a severe disciplinary problem. Upon his release at age twenty-two, he determined to live by the gun; many offenses followed, mostly robbery, punctuated by some kidnapping and auto theft. Some of his potential victims escaped with their lives because they gave up whatever Cook wanted when they saw his vicious countenance. He abducted and killed Carl Mosser, his wife, and three children near Joplin on December 30, 1950. After the abduction and killing of Robert Dewey, Cook was picked up by Mexican police and was subsequently executed in the gas chamber at San Quentin on December 12, 1951.

Bonnie and Clyde wanted to go down in history. Clyde Barrow (1909–34) was born in Telice, Texas, one of eight children in a sharecropper's home. Bonnie Parker (1911–34) was born in Rowena, Texas. They met in Dallas, where she was a waitress, and began a partnership of bank robbery and murder that filled the newspapers between 1931 and 1934. Their robberies were generally small, the largest being about $1,500, but they enjoyed killing immensely and saw their bank robbing as partial repayment for bank foreclosures on small farm owners who could not meet their mortgage obligations. Many of their crimes, particularly the killings, seemed to be mindless and without sense or provocation, illustrating anomie to perfection. It has been said that in the annals of American crime there never has been "a more pathetic, illogical, and murderous pair of social truants (*New York Times,* May 24, 1934).

A trap was set up by a friend, Henry Methvin, apparently as a deal to protect his son from prosecution, and Bonnie and Clyde were killed in a roadblock ambush near Gibland, Louisiana, on May 23, 1934.

CONCLUSIONS

The concepts of anomie, alienation, identification, and identity contribute to the understanding of conflict between some people, individually and in groups, with established society and social norms. Further, these ideas contribute to the understanding of individual and group conflicts between ethnic, racial, and other minority groups. Conflicts occur when two or more people or groups want the same thing at the same time or when one encroaches on the rights and property of the others. Some of these conflicts have been resolved by confrontation, where the minority or less powerful group created a crisis of sufficient proportion that the power structure was forced or became willing to negotiate.

More constructive use of these concepts has been in community and neighborhood councils designed to ameliorate differences. For example, interracial councils were almost a necessity in the 1960s and 1970s and were successful in "keeping the peace" in many areas. Black political leadership has emerged from two sources. First, blacks won power by default in some cities when the more affluent white society abandoned the inner city and moved to the suburbs. Second, moderate-income and affluent middle-class blacks have emerged as a political force and gained the confidence of white voters, as in the 1973 mayoralty election in Los Angeles, in which a black city councilman, a former policeman, unseated an incumbent running for an unprecedented fourth term; and in Atlanta, the major southern city, in which a black was elected over white opponents, Harold Washington, a black, was elected mayor of Chicago in 1983. These same principles may be at the root of public programs in the social areas, such as public recreation, public schools, police departments, and other agencies that deal with the public and have an opportunity to increase understanding and lessen anomie and alienation in society while simultaneously respecting the identity of each citizen.

Although anomie, alienation, identification, and identity may be seen by some as conflicting with the theory of differential association, they can and do complement one another in practice. Differential association simply indicates that crime or any other human behavior is learned. Anomie and alienation focus on the development within the individual of the ability and motivation to deviate. Identification and identity are really the meeting place of individuals' motivations and the social pressures around them that merge into forming their idea of their roles in society.

Questions

1. What is anomie?
2. What is alienation?
3. What is identification?
4. What is identity?
5. Who initiated the concept of anomie?
6. Explain the problem of legitimate goals and illegitimate means.
7. Explain the types of adaptation in anomie theory: (1) conformity, (2) innovation, (3) ritualism, (4) retreatism, and (5) rebellion.
8. In what three classifications do gangs generally pattern?
9. Discuss the current thrust in the courts and several social groups toward "the right to be different."
10. What is the identity crisis in adolescents, and how does it relate to the criminal justice system?

seven

OTHER SOCIOLOGICAL APPROACHES

There are many sociological approaches to the explanation of criminal behavior that do not place differential association or anomie in the central position. Nevertheless, most of these approaches recognize the existence and importance of differential association and anomie and their relationship to their own theories. Many of the same factors or social forces are used, but they may be put together in different ways.

SUBCULTURES

Theories of subcultures hold that a person develops with his or her peers in a group or a gang in which the value system is constant among all members, though it deviates from that of the larger society. Therefore, the persons will have developed in accordance with the values and norms of those around them but without internalizing the values of the total culture. Subcultural theories, then, used both major approaches, differential association and anomie, in different proportions. Cohen (1955, esp. pp. 121–37), who viewed himself as a sociologist but not a criminologist, was concerned with "nonutilitarian" delinquency and wrote an excellent treatise on the development of delinquent behavior in subcultures. He was less concerned with the reasons for a young person's becoming a delinquent than with that individual's development of common understandings, common sentiments, and common loyalties to his or her group or subculture (p. 178). The delinquent subculture is more likely to develop in the lower socioeconomic levels of society. The action of the gang or subculture is problem solving, and the pressures are toward conformity within the group to solve status problems. The family in this culture is not as strong as it is in middle and upper social classes. Throughout society, the position of the family and the social structure determines to some degree the experiences and problems that all members of the family will encounter in the world outside the family, but this probably occurs less in the lower socioeconomic levels where delinquent subcultures develop than elsewhere (Cohen, pp. 73–77). When children from this level step outside the family or home, they must meet the world on their own terms rather than on those of their family. The gang becomes their world. Although they may or may not be "protected" within the family, they are "on their own" while interacting with others in the gang or subculture.

There are many kinds of delinquent, criminal, and deviant subcultures in contemporary society, which result in extreme normative conflict in many places. There are many gangs in New York City and other large metropolitan areas with differing ethnic and racial makeup and different value systems. The gangs and the "families" in organized crime experience jurisdictional and normative conflict. New sets of values make delinquency and crime acceptable in these areas, regardless of whether a legislature or somebody else has made them "illegal." These values are developed and reinforced periodically, mostly as new versions of the older themes. Bordua (1961) has indicated that each generation begins with the solution of its predecessors, rather than inventing new approaches immediately.

Miller (1958) was concerned with the diffusion of delinquency values within the working class, developing the idea that working-class values actually include a delinquent subculture. These values relate to the "equalizer" approach that makes these methods acceptable. The teacher-student, social worker-client, and policeman-offender relations are just a few that are inextricably bound by many traditional expectations and definitions. These tend to be different in the lower socioeconomic class from those in the middle and upper socioeconomic classes. More needs to be known about these relationships to explain more adequately subcultural approaches to delinquency. The origin of the delinquent subculture, then, lies in the values of the working class. An intense concern for "toughness," "masculinity," and "manhood" in lower-class culture is expressed in informal values that boys must "act tough"—"Don't take nothin' off nobody." These values emerge from a process of immigration from foreign lands, internal migration from rural to urban and from section to section within the country, and vertical mobility from one socioeconomic class to another (Miller, 1959). Delinquent subcultures developed because of problems of adjustment confronting lower-class males and because of conflicts between values that stress achievement and a social structure that restricts that achievement. Cloward and Ohlin (1960, p. 65) translated this idea into three main ideas concerning delinquent behavior: First, the lower classes are characterized by distinctive values. Second, these values differ markedly from the middle-class values from which the legal code and the laws of society emerge. Third, this conflict results in certain lower-class values frequently being automatically in violation of the law, such as fighting. In fact, Kvaraceus and Miller (1959, pp. 77–79) have indicated that middle-class delinquency is an upward diffusion of lower-class attitudes and practices.

There has been little in the literature on delinquency of girls. Ruth Shonle Cavan (1969) referred to the lack of studies on delinquent girls. She devoted a full chapter to an effort to extract from other studies some references to girl delinquency. The findings were that delinquent girls resemble delinquent boys in age distribution, lower socioeconomic background, and disorganized family life. While delinquent boys are striving to achieve masculine status through competitive efforts involving courage and defiance of authority, girl delinquents tend to strive toward marriage and frequently drop out of school for that purpose. The delinquent girl evades unpleasant interpersonal relations at home by seeking pleasant relationships with boys. Career delinquent boys turn into adult property offenders, while confirmed delinquent girls tend to enter minor theft, prostitution, or act as an accomplice to a criminal husband.

The fall 1973 issue of *Issues in Criminology* was devoted to women and crime. One contributor pointed out that all limited previous literature on female crime had been in the tradition of sexist, racist, and classist attitudes; and a new definition of female crime focused on the human needs that must replace those traditional attitudes (Klein, 1973). Another contributor contended that there is a tendency in the law itself to classify offenses in a way that corresponds to sex role differences (Hoffmann-Bustamante, 1973).

In reviewing the literature on delinquent subcultures in 1966, Empey (1967) found several questions unanswered. Lower-class youths are brought into court more frequently for delinquency; Empey wonders whether there is differential treatment of juveniles based on actual behavior or value differences or on other characteristics. Is the delinquent subculture *contra*culture or *infra*culture? What are the relationships between the official and the client roles in many social systems, including the criminal justice system?

The overwhelming emphasis on lower-class gang delinquency in the slums has itself hindered understanding of that delinquency and subcultural phenomena, according to Maynard Erickson (1962). He feels that sociologists have tended to assume that peer-based delinquency is predominantly gang delinquency in a delinquent subculture. The misinterpretation, combined with dependence on official records, may have produced a premature closure on fundamental issues, as is evidenced by the fact that more than a dozen published studies in recent years using self-reports of delinquency have failed to find statistical differences between socioeconomic classes in terms of delinquency. Serious revisions of contemporary sociological theories and the development of new theories that do not lean so heavily on preconceived notions about groups and the socioeconomic distribution of juvenile delinquency are needed, according to Erickson. This would depend, of course, on the relative confidence one places on official statistics and self-reporting measures of delinquency.

Haney and Gold, (1973, p. 55) have questioned the "subcultural" theories on the basis that the most delinquent teenagers regard their friends as less delinquent than teenagers in general. The stereotype of the teenager from the lower socioeconomic class as a hoodlum seems to be widely accepted by adults in America, but these teenagers do not see themselves as "tough." The question arises as to whether the characterization of "subcultural delinquency" is itself a labeling process, or whether the teenagers are really delinquent. Haney and Gold suggest the former.

CONFLICT THEORY

Conflict theory emerges from the conditions and principles developed by Georg Simmel (1858–1918). He saw conflict as a *form* of interaction as distinguished from the *content* of interaction. The content may differ, but the form of "social conflict" remains the same. Conflict theory emerges from a social psychological orientation of social interaction theory of personality formation and the social process idea in collective behavior (Park and Burgess, 1924). Groups come into conflict when one overlaps the other in areas of interest and purpose. Groups must always be in a position to defend themselves to maintain their places and positions in a constantly changing world. The loyalty of each member to his or her group is profoundly significant concerning those on whom one can and cannot depend.

Crime and delinquency as group behavior is pervasive. Shaw and McKay (1931) reported that between 80 and 90 percent of juvenile offenders before the Cook County Juvenile Court in 1928 had committed their offenses with one or more associates. About 70 percent of 1,000 juvenile offenders reported by the Gluecks (1934, pp. 100–101) had companions in crime. From the reformatory group, the Gluecks (1930, p. 152) reported that approximately 60 percent had committed offenses with companions. In a later study of delinquents, the Gluecks reported that nearly all delinquents prefer to be with other delinquents, and more than one-half of the delinquents were members of gangs as opposed to less than 1 percent of the nondelinquents being members of gangs (1950, p. 278). People tend to travel in groups, particularly when they are alienated from the mainstream of society and have to find security, identity, and acceptance in a gang.

The gang demands loyalty and adherence to an approved code of values that are at variance with the police powers of the state (Whyte, 1943). It is nearly always a minority group that is in direct opposition to the rules and regulations of the dominant majority and the established world of adult values and power (Kobrin, 1951).

Many conscientious objectors consider themselves simply in conflict with the Establishment. Their minority-group orientation makes them oblivious to continuous contact with the "out-group" majority dedicated to changing it (for example, see Hassler, 1954). Every prisoner-of-war stockade attests to the general ineffectiveness of majority-group pressures on the attitudes and loyalties of minority-group members whose "crime" consisted of the fact that they had been overwhelmed in the battle for power. Criminals of all kinds who have a group identification to bolster their morale react defensively to efforts at "rehabilitation."

Many crimes result from direct political-reform types of protest movements, some of which lead to violence. Some criminal behavior results from clashes of interests between company management and labor unions. Some crimes result as episodes in jurisdictional disputes between different labor unions. Some crimes result from clashes incident to attempts to change the social structure, such as the civil rights movement for blacks in the middle and late 1960s.

Culture conflict was the basis of Thorsten Sellin's explanation of crime. Sellin (1938) was the first to place significant emphasis on culture conflict, although Marx had previously emphasized class conflict and struggle. He considered that cultural values developed within individuals from different backgrounds (such as in the case of the native-born children of foreign-born parents), resulting in intense cultural conflict that frequently develops and expresses itself in criminal behavior. Culture-conflict theory is particularly helpful in explaining the high crime rate of the children of immigrants, particularly from various parts of Europe.

The problem of culture conflict can be easily exemplified. An Italian immigrant family, for example, lives in a Italian neighborhood in a middle-sized city. Italian is spoken, old-world food is prepared and served, and old-country values are taught to the children. The father is the real "boss" of the household and what he says goes. When the children grow to school age, they go to an American, white, middle-class-oriented school where English is spoken. School lunches consist of hamburgers and hot dogs, and women teachers are in authority. Both their new classmates and the school power structure have values and customs that are foreign to them. Consequently, when the teacher tries to teach them, they are more concerned with what is right, what is wrong, and getting along in a strange environment; they cannot put all their effort into the learning process. On the other hand, the native-born American family speaks English; has hamburgers and hot dogs at home; the wife and mother frequently handles the bills and has a job outside of the home; and contemporary middle-class cultural norms are observed. When children from that family go to school, there is no cultural shock. Everything in school is familiar—these children can learn without the impediment of the cultural conflict.

With similar intelligence, then, persons from different backgrounds learn at differential rates and efficiency. With an I.Q. of 100, the children from native-born American families can earn Bs, while the children with similar ability from the foreign or different cultures must spend their effort in trying to adapt to a new and strange culture, so they may earn Ds or fail completely. The resulting reaction is the identification of those children as minority-group members who are "tough," "aggressive," and "a little stupid." So those children react accordingly and defend themselves, thereby assuming the expected role, and reinforcing it in the view of others. They engage in deviant and delinquent behavior with greater frequency than do children from native-born American middle-class homes. This conflict, of course, is not always between ethnic and racial groups. It occurs whenever families in the same neighborhood and economic level have different styles, values, and norms of behavior. Culture conflict is not confined to immigrant groups, but is simply easier to demonstrate among these groups. Racial, ethnic, religious, economic, occupational, philosophical, and almost any other phase of culture can be the base of culture conflict.

NEUTRALIZATION

The concept of neutralization was originally developed by Sykes and Matza. According to this theory, a person is able to rationalize himself out of the moral bind of his childhood development and justify his delinquent behavior. Sykes and Matza (1957) identified five types of neutralization:

1. Denial of Responsibility—The person learns to view himself as more acted upon than actor—he is the victim of circumstances.

2. Denial of Injury—The person feels that nobody is really hurt by his actions—auto theft is "borrowing" and gang fighting may be seen as a private duel.

3. Denial of the Victim—The injury is not seen as wrong in view of the circumstances (assaults on homosexuals and others who have been seen as "out of place"; "He asked for it").

4. The Condemnation of the Condemners—The person sees condemners as hypocrites, deviants in disguise, impelled by personal spite; by attacking others, the wrongness of his own behavior is confused.

5. The Appeal to Higher Loyalties—Sacrificing demands of larger society may be neutralized by the demands of smaller groups for loyalty, fidelity, and protection.

Sykes and Matza indicated that delinquents' value system is not consistently oppositional to the dominant social order; however, they are able to situationally qualify behavioral norms in which they believe, which allows them to engage in disapproved behavior. Much delinquency is essentially an unrecognized extension of defenses to crimes, in the form of justifications for deviance that are seen as valid by the delinquent.

Reckless and Shoham (1963) identified norm erosion as supplementary to neutralization. In this process, norm erosion is a "give" in moral and ethical resistance. Drug use and alcohol, cheating on examinations, taking things from store counters, extramarital sex behavior, and similar deviations can be attributed to norm erosion. Norm erosion and neutralization represent a diminution of inner containment, thereby facilitating involvement in deviation and criminal behavior.

The forms of justification for deviance are seen as valid by the delinquent but not by the legal system or society as a whole (Sykes and Matza, p. 666). The criminal law itself already includes a major component of what has been called "flexibility," in that many rules are not held to be binding under all conditions (Williams, 1951, p. 28).

Richard A. Ball (1965) has seen Sykes and Matza's theory as not only one of neutralization but also a denial of Cohen's "delinquency subculture" thesis. According to the neutralization thesis, delinquents do not adhere to a different set of norms but adhere to conventional norms while accepting more justifications for deviance. The norms have simply been "eroded." This is at variance with the concept of subcultures and their acceptance of values different from the mainstream of society. Ball also constructed a "neutralization inventory" that was correlated with delinquency (*Empirical Exploration*, 1966). He was able to show that delinquents use more neutralizing definitions than do nondelinquents. Mannle (1972), in a modification of Ball's neutralization inventory, found that there were no perceptible age differences but that blacks neutralized more than whites.

Hirschi (1969, pp. 205–12) analyzes the theory of neutralization quite well and generally supports the theory. Using control theory, Hirschi contends that people conform when their bonds to society are strong, and he emphasizes family ties. He does point out, however, that delinquents are unusual in that they frequently act in behalf of their group, despite the fact that it is not worth the sacrifice. Hirshi has also indicated that all phases of neutralization are well related to delinquency, except denial of the victim, which may have resulted from an overly intellectual operationalization of the concept.

DRIFT

The concept of drift occurs when a lower-class young person finds it unnecessary to make a definite commitment either to delinquency or to legal conformity. He or she may "drift" in an unidentified area between these two—opposing commitment and making use of extenuating circumstances to justify delinquency (Matza, 1964, chaps. 2 and 3). Many persons, especially in the lower socioeconomic class, take advantage of the fact that criminal laws may not be rigidly enforced and that considerable discretion is left to police and courts in their application. Consequently, the delinquent extends the legal boundaries to the extenuating circumstances that fit his or her own situation and justify the delinquency behavior. The group or gang can then expand its concept of self-defense to cover aggressive attacks on another gang under the implicit justification that the other gang is threatening the attacking gang. Because of the uncertainty in the application of the law, an individual or gang may drift into delinquency without any definite decision or commitment having been made. Most delinquents eventually drift out of this delinquency as they mature; only a limited number of juvenile delinquents become committed to an adult life of crime.

Matza repudiated positivistic theory and expanded the concept of neutralization in making it a key element in drift. Neutralization allows drift because it is a process by which the delinquent is freed from the moral bind of law. Hindelang (1970) pointed out that because delinquents are more committed to their misdeeds than are nondelinquents, the concepts of drift and neutralization are not necessary for delinquency.

CONTAINMENT THEORY

Containment theory, as proposed by W.C. Reckless (1961), is based on an inner control system and an outer control system. Pushes and pulls toward delinquent or conforming behavior, both internal and external, are basic to containment theory. If inner pushes and outer pulls are toward delinquent behavior, then delinquent behavior will result. Inner containment involves good self-concept, self-control, ego strength, well-developed superego, high frustration tolerance, high resistance to diversions, high sense of responsibility, goal orientation, ability to find substitute satisfactions, and tension-reducing rationalizations. Outer containment is the structural buffer in a person's immediate social world that holds him or her within the social norms. The presentation of a consistent moral front, existence of a reasonable set of social expectations, effective supervision and discipline of children, provision for a reasonable scope of activity, opportunity for acceptance, outlets for the expression of tension and frustration, identity and belongingness are all factors in containment. Inner and outer containment apparently occupy a central position between the pressures of the external environment of a person and his or her inner drives.

Environmental pressures may be conditions associated with poverty or deprivation, conflict, external restraint, minority-group status, limited access to success in an opportunity structure, and other stresses. Distractions, attractions, temptations, patterns of deviancy, and advertising are some of the pulls of the environment.

External containment can consist of an effective family life, interest in the activities of the community, membership in organizations, and good companions. Internal containment involves the control of drives, motives, frustrations, restlessness, disappointments, rebellion, hostility, feelings of inferiority, and freedom of expression; it involves the ability to withstand the pushes and pulls, to effectively resolve conflicts to divert individuals from exciting risks and enable them to stay out of trouble. Internal containment is more important in a mobile, fluid society because alienation makes it hard for persons to participate in the group life that has the potential to hold them in line (Reckless, 1973, p. 51).

A similar theory was proposed by Beeley (1945) that categorized (1) personal factors that enfeeble self-control and (2) social factors that enfeeble social control.

Personal factors that enfeeble self-control:

1. Inherited or acquired physical and physiological handicaps; e.g., in physique, stature, deformities, and defects.
2. Physical injury or disease; e.g., accidents, occupational or other, tuberculosis, syphilis.
3. Inherited or acquired mental handicaps; e.g., feeblemindedness, psychopathic personality.
4. Mental and psychosomatic disorders; e.g., psychosis, psychoneurosis, mental conflicts, emotional disturbances.
5. Personal disorganization from excesses; e.g., sex, alcohol, narcotics, gambling.

6. Character structure: e.g., ignorance, naivete, inadequate life organization.

Social factors that enfeeble social control:

1. "Sick" societies; e.g., Great Britain and its mining community.
2. Inherent defects in economic order; e.g., poverty, unemployment, depression, aggression, exploitation.
3. Urbanization; e.g., mobility, anonymous life in cities.
4. Changing mores in group conflict; e.g., with regard to sex, use of alcohol, tobacco.
5. Family disorganization; e.g., death of a parent, divorce, nonsupport, faulty discipline, incompatability, internal conflict.
6. Community and neighborhood disorganization; e.g., depressed areas, poor housing, unwholesome companionship, lawless gangs.
7. Overlapping and conflicting governments; e.g., municipal, town, county, state, federal.
8. Inherent limitations of the criminal law, substantive and adjunctive; e.g., obsolete, unenforceable, and conflicting laws.
9. Maladministration of criminal justice; e.g., the breakdown of law enforcement, prosecution, and the courts; incompetent administration; corruption in patrol administration; organized crime and racketeering.
10. Inadequate education activities; e.g., amount, quality and rigidity of secular, religious, and vocational instruction.
11. Inadequate avocational facilities; e.g., unwholesome leisure interests, commercialized amusements.
12. Opinion making and control; e.g., press, film, radio, television.
13. Interpersonal and intergroup conflict; e.g., ethnic, religious, economic.

Reckless (1973) elaborates on his theory in a chapter called "The Pressures and Pulls behind Involvement in Crime," presenting seven tests of validity as follows:

1. Containment theory is proposed as the theory of best fit for the large middle range of cases of delinquency and crime. It fits the middle-range cases better than any other theory.
2. It explains crimes against the person as well as crimes against property, that is, the mine run of murder, assault, and rape as well as theft, robbery and burglary.
3. It represents a formulation which psychiatrists, psychologists, and sociologists, as well as practitioners, can use equally well. All of these experts look for dimensions of inner and outer strength and can specify these strengths in their terms. Differential association and/or pressure of the environment leave most psychiatrists and psychologists cold and

an emphasis on push theory leaves the sociologists for the most part cold. But all of the experts can rally around inner and outer weaknesses and strengths.

4. Inner and outer containment can be discovered in individual case studies. Weaknesses and strengths are observable. Containment theory is one of the few theories in which the microcosm (the individual case history) mirrors the ingredients of the macrocosm (the general formulation).

5. Containment theory is a valid operational theory for treatment of offenders: for restructuring the milieu of a person or beefing up his self. The most knowledgeable probation workers, parole workers, and institutional staff are already focusing to some extent on helping the juvenile or adult offender build up ego strength, develop new goals, internalize new models of behavior. They are also working on social ties, anchors, supportive relationships, limits, and alternative opportunities in helping to re-fashion a new containing world for the person.

6. Containment theory is also an effective operational theory for prevention. Children with poor containment can be spotted early. Programs to help insulate vulnerable children against delinquency must operate on internalization of stronger self components and the strengthening of containing structure around the child.

7. Internal and external containment can be assessed and approximated. Its strengths and weaknesses can be specified for research. There is good promise that such assessments can be measured in a standard way [pp. 40–62].

Containment theory is a balance between inner pushes and outer constraints and can account for all behavior, including criminal behavior. The breadth of containment theory tends to negate the importance of narrow approaches used in crime control and in treatment programs because the pushes and pulls include poverty, unemployment, guilt feelings, criminal subcultures, mass media, and many other factors not controlled by known treatment methods. Like many other theories, there are so many uncontrollable variables that it cannot realistically be tested. Consequently, they can be examined in a prediction model much more easily than in a treatment model (Schrag, 1971, pp. 81–112).

REFERENCE GROUP THEORY

Reference group theory centers attention on all groups to which individuals are oriented (Glaser, 1958). A reference group is one whose perspective constitutes the frame of reference of the actor without necessarily being the group in which he or she aspires for acceptance

(Shibutani, 1955). The reference group could be an "identification group" in which the individual takes the role of a member while adopting the members' standpoint as his or her own (Turner, 1956). Sherif (1953, pp. 205-7) considered the values and norms of people's reference groups to be their "major anchorages" in which there is an experience of self-identity and in which they are organized. With differences among groups and the general privileges and opportunities therein, Newcomb (1950, p. 226) saw the likelihood of an individual's becoming dissatisfied with membership in a particular group as increased in a dynamic society. Consequently, the strength of membership in a group as a point of reference for a particular person will decrease with the reduction of satisfaction. Newcomb further distinguished between the positive reference groups, in which a person is motivated to be accepted, and the negative reference groups, in which a person does not want to be treated as a member or stands in opposition to it. The negative reference group in criminology might be the free community that has rejected and isolated the criminal in prison. While rejecting his rejectors, this person is likely to become a candidate for procriminal reference groups. An American adolescent boy may share most of his family's common attitudes and want to be considered a member, but he may be hostile toward some of their attitudes regarding his choice of friends, his behavior in the role of a son, and other areas; thus his family becomes the negative reference group. A positive reference group may immunize the individual against the pressures of a negative reference group. Further, there is a possibility that anticriminal groups may continue to motivate some criminals even after they have become members of negative reference groups (Johnson, 1964, p. 164).

Haskell (1960-61) offers six propositions to explain his reference group theory.

1. The family is the first personal reference group of the child.
2. The family is a normative reference group (the norm conforms to the larger society).
3. Prior to his participation in a delinquent act, the delinquent boy adopts a street group as a personal reference group.
4. The street group that becomes the personal reference group of the lower-class boy in New York has a delinquent subculture.
5. A boy for whom the street group is a personal reference group is likely, in the dynamic assessment preceding a delinquent act, to decide in favor of the delinquent act.
6. The individual tends as a member of a personal reference group to impart into its context attitudes and ways of behaving which he is currently holding in sociogroup life.

LABELING THEORY

Labeling theory is apparently based on the concepts developed by Frank Tannenbaum in 1938, Lemert in 1951, Becker in 1963, Turk in 1969, and Quinney in 1970. According to this concept, nothing is criminal, but certain things have been so defined and labeled by society. Persons become criminal primarily on the basis of visibility of offending behavior and the labeling process by the system of criminal justice. Schrag (1971) identified nine steps in the labeling process:

1. No act is intrinsically criminal but is made so by the law.
2. Criminal definitions are enforced in the interest of powerful groups by their representatives, including the police.
3. A person does not become a criminal by violating the law, but by the labeling process by which authorities confer this status upon him.
4. Dichotomizing people into criminal and noncriminal categories is contrary to common sense and empirical evidence.
5. Only a few persons are caught in violation of the law, while many may be equally guilty.
6. While the sanctions used in law enforcement are directed against the total person and not only the criminal act, the severity and consequences of the penalties vary according to the characteristics of the offender.
7. Criminal sanctions also vary according to other characteristics of the offender, such as minority groups, transients, the poorly educated, residents of deteriorated urban areas, and other factors.
8. Criminal justice is based on a stereotyped concept of the criminal as a willful wrongdoer who is morally bad and deserves condemnation.
9. Once labeled as a criminal, it is difficult for an offender to "live down" the label and restore himself to respected status in the community [pp. 81–112].

As Tannenbaum pointed out in 1938, the dramatization of evil or the heralding of famous and well-known criminals proclaims criminal careers at least as one way of gaining public attention and, further, develops a reputation that keeps the individual in the criminal role. Al Capone, for example, would hardly have been accepted to study for the priesthood.

The point of the labeling theory is that it is the social definition of crime and deviance that makes certain things criminal and deviant. Becker (1963, p. 9) has indicated that deviance is not a quality of the act but a consequence of the application by others of rules and sanctions so that the person may be labeled as deviant. Sociologists are less interested in law than are lawyers, so sociologists focus greater attention on the informal mechanisms of social control beyond the narrow legal definitions to the social process of creating deviance by labeling it (Schur, 1969, pp. 112–3).

The steps by which the labeling process occurs have also been identified by Cressey and Ward (1969):

1. In the eyes of the child, behavior that is proper as play may include breaking windows, climbing over roofs or, generally "raising hell."
2. Demands for suppression of the "bad" behavior are made on the child by community members, sometimes including parents.
3. In the face of this reaction by adults, the child may feel that an injustice is being done to him and, more importantly, that his community and perhaps his parents consider him different from "good children."
4. Parents, police, and others may then scrutinize and look with suspicion upon all of the youngster's activities, his companions, his speech, and his personality, thus reinforcing the definition of him as "bad."
5. Once the child discovers that he has been defined as bad and that even his efforts to be good are interpreted as evidence of his badness, he may become even more "predisposed toward individualized crime" or even more closely integrated with his play group, which has been redefined as a "delinquent gang."
6. Once the community has defined a youngster as bad, it knows how to cope with him; it does not, in fact, know how to deal with him *until* it defines him as bad.
7. As the community copes with the delinquent, its conception of him crystallizes, as he does his conception of himself. He now defines himself as he is defined, as an "incorrigible," a "delinquent," or a "criminal" [pp. 581–83].

Lemert says that the child begins to employ his delinquent behavior as both a defense and an adjustment to the problems created by social reactions to him. As Parsons (1951, p. 286) indicates, he may compulsively conform within the deviant subgroup and become compulsively alienated from the main institutional structure.

A good example of labeling that appears frequently in the criminal justice system occurs when somebody indicates that a person "looks like" a homosexual. Indirect evidence in the form of a rumor is frequently translated into decision making regarding the treatment of individuals so labeled. It is easy and dangerous to stereotype people in this manner. In modern society, the social significance of labeling becomes increasingly dependent upon circumstances, social and personal biography, and the bureaucracy of the organized agency of control (Goffman, 1959).

Arrest may not only lead to confinement of the suspected offender, but may also bring him loss of social status, newspaper publicity, restriction of educational and employment opportunities, and future harassment (Schwartz and Skolnick, 1962). This stigmatization sometimes serves as a catalytic agent that initiates delinquent careers (Tannenbaum, 1938, pp. 17–20). Some criminologists indicate that stigmatization resulting from police apprehension, arrest, and detention actually reinforces deviant behavior and creates a "reputation" among the individual's delinquent peers (Cloward and Ohlin, 1960, pp. 124–30).

Police officers have been given considerable discretion in apprehending youths; and it has been observed that certain youths, particularly from minority racial and ethnic groups or those dressed in the style of "toughs," were treated more severely than others for comparable offenses (Piliavin and Briar, 1964). This discretion is practiced by juvenile officers as an extension of the juvenile court philosophy. The observations made by Piliavin and Briar in this study indicate that the official delinquent is the product of social judgment and that how this judgment is accepted by the police is critical in the prevention or initiation of a delinquent career.

The "self-fulfilling prophecy" that emerges from labeling was discussed by Merton (1957). But whether a person becomes delinquent because he has been so labeled or whether a competent expert has made a correct diagnosis and prognosis is a central question. Undoubtedly, a little of both viewpoints may enter into the social situation. Stigmatization of the deviant occurs in the form of name calling, labeling, or stereotyping, generally at the point where in-grouping within the delinquent gang and out-grouping through the rejection of the gang by society makes the deviant behavior manifest and attracts the attention of society (Mead, 1918).

Labeling in delinquency control programs is dangerous (Wheeler and Cottrell, 1966). In the first place, it is not clear in terms of results whether doing something is better than doing nothing or that doing one thing is better or worse than doing another. Second, because developments in the juvenile field are leading to a category of people who are "in need of service" rather than "delinquent," the implication that labeling is a legal category makes a difference in the way juveniles might be treated.

THEORY OF DEVIANCE

Deviance is related to labeling in some popular views (Scheverish, 1973). As mentioned previously, many theories are interdependent. Tannenbaum's concept of the "dramatization of evil" in 1938, as mentioned previously, surely was a forerunner of labeling and can be considered a forerunner of deviance theory as well. Edwin M. Lemert's concept of labeling and deviance in 1951 and Becker's (1963, p. 9) statement that deviant behavior is that which people label as deviant agree on the close relationship between labeling and deviance.

Primary deviance is the act of deviating in accordance with anomie. Lemert (1951) gave the name "secondary deviation" to the result of the process of deviation. When deviant behavior is used as a means of defense, attack, or adjustment, then deviation becomes secondary. The steps by which secondary deviation is reached are roughly as follows: (1) primary deviation, (2) social penalties, (3) further primary deviation, (4) stronger penalties and rejections, (5) further deviation with hostilities and resentment focusing on those doing the penalizing, (6) crisis reached at the tolerance level expressed in formal action by community stigmatizing of the deviant, (7) strengthening of the deviant conduct as a reaction to the stigmatizing and penalties, and (8) alternate acceptance of deviance and deviant social status with efforts and adjustments in this role (Lemert, 1951, pp. 75–78).

Lemert (1967, p. 3) has called for a suitable way of integrating the notion of deviation into a theory of social change, since social change begins with deviance. Groups of radicals and revolutionaries, like the Black Panthers and the various groups of people tried for revolutionary activity, exemplify increasing militancy, self-consciousness, and organization of deviant worlds that have become unwilling to let "respectable society" have its way with them (Becker, 1965). Deviance is too frequently measured by violation of laws in response by "essentially normal persons" to realistic conflicts of interest, such as violations of draft laws (Turk, 1966). Becker and Horowitz (1970) point out that San Francisco has developed a "culture of civility" in which toleration of and accommodation to minor forms of deviance, such as sex, dope, and cheap thrills, permits deviants to live more openly than they could in many other cities.

THE "NEW CRIMINOLOGY"

The "new criminology" emerged in 1973 when Taylor, Walton, and Young (1973) from York University in England published a book by that title to correct the uneven accounts of criminology's historical relationships with the social sciences. It was held that criminology should be fully social, without biological or other extraneous concepts, and should take into account economic and structural social forces. Only a few pages of the conclusions presented anything "new." Assuming a Marxian perspective, the book focused on finding the causes of crime in the social and economic structure, rather than in the individual offender. According to the authors, capitalistic countries provide a social structure that reduces people's chances of achieving full social freedom because laws are made and enforced by the "ruling classes"—the middle and upper socioeconomic classes—for the purpose of keeping the proletariat oppressed and "in their place."

It is apparent that subsequent writers have accepted the general theory of communism as presented by Marx but did not accept his realistic ideas of criminality. Marx, himself, had little interest in crime. Marx and Engels in their original *Manifesto* in 1848 discounted the criminal classes. They viewed them as social scum, or "lumpen proletariat," thrown off the lower layers of old society and holding little promise of assisting in the struggles of the oppressed because they could be bribed by the bourgeoisie involved in reactionary intrigue and would join the winning side (1950, p. 44). Further, Marx has been viewed as having been "excessively procapitalist" when he pointed out that capitalism had "subjected Nature's forces to man" through machinery, applications of chemistry to industry and agriculture, steam navigation, railways, electric telegraphs, clearing of whole continents for cultivation, canalization of rivers, and the conjuring out of the ground of whole populations and asked what earlier century had even a presentment that such productive forces slumbered in the lap of social labor.

Nevertheless, the Marxian perspective derives from the intensity of the struggle he saw between the bourgeoisie or privileged classes and the proletariat or the oppressed working classes. Depending upon the intensity of their various positions, adherents to the new criminology have been divided into (1) conflict, (2) critical, and (3) radical components. Conflict criminologists contend that nothing and no one is intrinsically criminal but that criminality is a definition applied by classes with the power to do so to individuals on the basis of illegal, extralegal, and legal criteria (Turk, 1969, p. 10). In this sense, conflict theory in the new criminology appears simply to be an extension of conflict theory as presented in traditional sociology and criminology. Further, under certain social conditions, some individuals are more likely to be criminalized by these designations (Keller, 1976, p. 102). Critical criminology seeks to maintain an alliance with the system while criticizing and attacking the system for its failure to promote social justice. Quinney (1977, p. 9) refers to critical thinking as the intellectual stance that subsequent generations inherited from the Enlightenment and points up the contradictory and irrational element in social structures that lay in the path of human liberation and perfectability. Taylor, Walton, and Young have been classified as critical criminologists. Radical criminology draws from critical criminology and applies it to a goal of revolutionizing society. Schwendinger (1974, p. 1) has indicated that radical criminology was emerging in academic criminology in the United States but was confined to a small number of outspoken students and a smaller number of determined faculty. Platt (1974) said that radical scholarship involving university-educated intellectuals is not developed because of the absence of a Marxian tradition, while the roots of radicalism are found in political struggles that include civil rights movements, third-world liberation struggles, and antiimperialist movements. Platt and Takagi have indicated that liberal criminologists are beginning to recognize the inequalities in the system and point to the increase in prison riots, failure of treatment programs, and the killing of prisoners by correctional officers as examples of growing resistance.

Religion in general has formulated our ethical systems in primitive times, ancient and medieval times, and modern times. It has been from these ethical systems that modern criminal law has been drawn, and in some countries, particularly in the Islamic world, religion remains the basis of criminal justice. Ancient Hebrew law as contained in the Pentateuch, the first five books of the Old Testament, has influenced other religions, philosophy, and criminal law in the Western world. The basic criminal law around the world is similar. There have always been questions concerning differential application of sanctions, including benefit of clergy and the nobility's being "above the law" in different times and places. There is a sincere effort in most legal systems, however, toward equal protection and application of sanctions. It seems to be apparent that it is this differential in application that the new criminology is attacking.

The new criminology has received mixed acceptance by academic criminologists. Hackler (1977) questions whether the "new criminology" is an ideology or a better explanation of reality. Further, Hackler says, the "new criminology" may lead to intellectual feuds that generate more heat than light: the adherents will be reluctant to accept contributions made by others, objecting that such contributions do not make it clear how one can tell that "truth" has been discovered. A frequent criticism, particularly of the radical stance, is that greater emphasis is placed on practice or praxis than on science and theory, making "intellectualism" a negative value. It has been observed that traditional criminologists and those adhering to the new criminology have developed mutual contempt for each other (Gouldner, 1970, p. 7).

In a study (Pelfrey, 1978, p. 205) that surveyed 310 academicians teaching criminology at the university level and followed up with intensive interviews with some of the outstanding adherents, it was found that the new criminology was seen as a viable alternative with some reservations. The results were that 178, or 57.4 percent, found it viable (43 strongly agreed and 135 agreed), 88, or 28.4 percent, found it not viable (26 strongly disagreed and 62 disagreed), and 44, or 14.2 percent, were undecided. These respondents, then, were inclined to consider the new criminology as having sufficient potential that it should not be excluded from consideration within the academic discipline of criminology. There was concern, however, that much more research in this area would be needed before it could be an unquestioned part of traditional criminology. It was pointed out by the academicians that it could not be supported simply by advocacy but that the theoretical propositions needed to be more tightly formulated and operationalized in order to permit more rigid research.

Many scholars, such as Sykes (1974), hold that the new criminology uses an oversimplified model of stratification and that there is much more diversity and variation in modern society than the simple dichotomy between the poor and weak, on the one hand, and the rich and powerful, on the other. The new criminology is apparently a viable pursuit that does not, in reality, *replace* traditional criminology but can give it another alternative perspective.

CLASSIFICATION OF THEORIES

There are several approaches to classifying sociological theories of crime. Nettler (1974, pp. 136–248) has classified theories as (1) subcultural (2) structural, (3) symbolic interaction, and (4) control. Subcultural theories are encompassed in W. B. Miller's concept of "lower-class culture," and its "focal concerns," Thorsten Sellin's (1938) culture conflict, the proposals of the Chicago School, and similar approaches. Miller (1958) indicates that the primary or focal concerns of lower class culture that produce gang formation and behavior are (1) trouble, (2) toughness, (3) smartness, (4) excitement, (5) fate, and (6) autonomy. All these pressures or concerns combine to force dependence of lower class boys in the streets to find security in the gang. Merton's concept of anomie, Cloward and Ohlin's opportunity structure approach, and similar approaches are considered to be structural theory. Symbolic interaction includes differential association and cultural transmission theories. The containment theory of Walter C. Reckless is an example of one approach to control theory, as is Eysenck and Eysenck's (1970) theory regarding the differences within individuals with respect to psychosis, extroversion, and neuroticism as related to external differences exhibited in behavioral typologies.

Hirschi (1969, pp. 225–32) contrasted strain, control, and cultural deviance theories of crime and delinquency and tended to favor control theory. Strain theory suggested that the motivation to deviance is in the individual himself—sort of an "original sin" theory. Some of the key words in this approach might be ambition, goals and objectives, striving for fulfillment, sexual need, and similar thrusts. They assume the relationship between social class and delinquency. Hirschi (p. 227) concludes, however, that research on the family and its moral beliefs render strain theory unnecessary. Cultural deviance theories are more difficult to test by empirical data, but no groups of substantial proportions in America positively encourage crime. Control theory focuses on why people do not commit crime and why the crime rate is not higher than it is, and the answers must be in the social institutions that have inculcated values in people that tend to control behavior. Supporting control theory, Hirschi emphasizes the *bonding* that occurs between people in mutually positive and reinforcing relationships that permits the formation of cohesive groups.

A questionnaire (*Study of Criminological Course Offerings*, 1974) designed to determine the favorite approaches of sociologists in the field who teach criminology listed the classifications of theories as follows:

1. Anomie/Structure—Functional/Social—Disorganization/Opportunity—Status Deprivation
2. Differential Association/Reference Group Theory/Cultural Transmission/Culture Conflict
3. Labeling Theory/Symbolic Interaction
4. Drift Theory/Containment
5. Conflict Theory/Marxist Theory
6. Social Learning Theory/Behavioral Theory
7. Ethnomethodology
8. Psychological/Psychiatric Theories [p. 7]

This classification includes all the sociological theories and touches on the psychological and psychiatric approaches.

Akers (1973, pp. 9–31), who favors social learning theory and control theory, classifies sociological theories as those that deal with (1) social disorganization and anomie—this includes Merton's, Cohen's, and Cloward and Ohlin's approaches; (2) conflict theory—this includes Quinney's, Chambliss's, Sellin's, and Vold's approaches; (3) labeling and stigmatization—this includes Lemert's, Erikson's, Becker's, Matza's, and Schur's approaches; and (4) social control theories, which include Reckless's, Hirschi's, Matza's, and similar approaches that explain why people do not commit more crime and delinquency than they do.

Strain theory includes anomie and other alienation types of theories that are structural. Conflict theory includes approaches that deal with culture conflict, lower-class delinquency, and ethnic and racial problems that produce crime.

Many theories take conformity for granted as "normal" behavior in civilized society. Deviant behavior occurs when the individual has not adequately internalized the values and norms of society and has not been adequately socialized. Some deviance occurs when the individual grows up or becomes involved in a subculture whose expectations are in conflict with dominant social norms.

Control theories, on the other hand, take deviance for granted as "normal" and try to explain why so many people conform to the social norms. The child is an amoral being who has to "learn" the social definitions of right and wrong. Control theorists point out that there is much more conflict and confusion than there is harmony and order in human society. Control theories hold that crime and deviance are the result of inadequate normative systems. The more disorganized a group is, the less an individual can depend on it for guidance. Weak social systems, therefore, rather than weak individuals, become the source of criminal behavior.

Conrad (1965) stresses that "control" is uppermost in the criminal justice system; and the internalization of control is basic for all who become clients of the system.

Jesse James and "Baby Face" Nelson

Jesse James was an excellent example of the theory of neutralization and labeling or the "dramatization of evil" concept (Love, 1926; Croy, 1949; Breiham, 1953). Because the Civil War had been lost by the South, James's justification for his crime was "The Yankees made me do it!" Jesse Woodson James (1847–82) was born in Clay County, Missouri, and served the Confederacy in Quantrill's Guerrillas with "Bloody Bill" Anderson during the Civil War, after which he robbed banks and trains and killed with impunity for a period of sixteen years. He was shot on April 3, 1882.

George "Baby Face" Nelson (1908–34) was born in Chicago as Lester Gillis. His background in a delinquent subculture, which included conflict, labeling and stigmatization, and internalized deviant values, was unmistakable. Short of stature at 5'4", he was always being snubbed and beaten by the other boys in the tough neighborhood near the stockyards. He wanted recognition in some way. He turned to the gun and used strong-arm tactics with it while working in Al Capone's organization, specializing in keeping labor leaders in line so the organization could maintain the labor rackets. His tactics were so extreme—unnecessarily so—that the organization dropped him and he looked elsewhere for his recognition. His first sentence was to the Illinois State Penitentiary on January 15, 1931, for a jewelry store robbery, but he escaped February 17, 1932, and went on a spree of robbery and murder. He was shot to death November 27, 1934, after he had killed two FBI agents. He had joined John Dillinger by the time he was killed.

CONCLUSIONS

The basic principles of each of the approaches discussed contribute to the entire field of socialization and social control. Blocked opportunity, the influence of subcultures, conflict between groups and cultures, labeling and stigmatization, deviance and internalized deviant values, the neutralization of deviance, the drifting on the line between conformity and nonconformity, containment, and reference groups all contribute to the understanding of conforming and conforming behavior.

Because crime is a social phenomenon, middle-range sociological theories are needed as a minimum explanation of crime. Within the sociological framework, however, psychological theories can contribute significantly (Bottoms, 1973, p. 29). The present hypothetico-deductive theories restrict verification, and better-grounded theories are needed (Glaser and Strauss, 1968).

There are two broad classifications of delinquents whose identifications are important because of their implications in social relationships (Johnson, 1959). First, there is the category of the unconsciously driven individuals who still comprise the vast majority of delinquents; they cannot tell anybody why they commit crimes because they do not know. Second is the category of the gang or sociological group operating at any level, comprising a minority of delinquents; the effect of the behavior of this category is very damaging to society, but group or gang members can provide reasons or rationalizations for their behavior.

The "role" versus "goal" orientation changes with changing society. Goal-oriented people obey orders and requests. Role-oriented people are more concerned with priorities as they relate to them. When the legitimacy of authority is challenged, as it has been since the 1960s and 1970s, "role" takes precedence over "goal." Sociological theory is needed to explain this.

Questions

1. What is a subculture?
2. Why do sociologists tend to assume that peer-based delinquency is predominantly gang delinquency in a delinquent subculture?
3. Why do many sociologists question the "subcultural" theories of crime and delinquency?
4. What is conflict theory?
5. What is the theory of neutralization?
6. What is the concept of drift in delinquency?
7. What is control theory?
8. What is reference group theory?
9. What is labeling theory?
10. Discuss the theory of deviance, including primary and secondary deviance.

eight

PSYCHOLOGICAL APPROACHES

The psychological approaches to human behavior focus on the individual personality. As compared with the sociological approaches, the psychologists' concern for the environment is only as a source of stimuli. Much more important to the psychologist is the reaction of the individual to pressure and stimuli that come from his or her environment.

Psychology was a part of philosophy until it broke away in the late nineteenth century and became a separate experimental science. The date of the publication of Fechner's *Elemente der Psychophysik*, 1860, is generally taken as the starting point for psychology. One of the first interesting experiments took place in 1890 when von Helmholtz first measured the rate of transmission of nervous impulse, an experiment that gave impetus, in part, to subsequent study of the rapidity of reaction to stimuli. Wilhelm Wundt began an experimental study of perception in 1862 and established the first psychological laboratory in 1879 in Leipzig. At the same time, Ebbinghaus concentrated on association and memory.

William James introduced psychology to America, and there were many laboratories established between 1888 and 1895. The systematic structure of American psychology was concerned with the generalized normal human adult "mind" as differentiated from laboratory experiments on specific phenomena. This approach began to emerge at the University of Chicago, where philosophers and psychologists were working together. American psychology was well established by 1900 and focused on the mind in use, while European psychology remained experimental. By 1910, American psychology also embraced experimental human psychology, animal psychology, and mental tests.

The *personal equation*, or the *human equation*, as a measure of individual differences between people became important after 1796, when Maskelyne, an astromer at Greenwich Observatory, dismissed his assistant, Kinnebrook, for reporting and observed times of stellar transits nearly a second later than he observed them (Anastasi, 1937, pp. 9–10). The "eye and ear" method of the time involved coordination of visual and auditory impressions and complex spatial judgments. In 1816, an astromer at Königsberg, Bessel, became interested in the differences in seconds between the estimates of the two observers. Astronomers became interested in the human equation during the last half of the nineteenth century and introduced chronographs and chronoscopes, subsequently attracting the interest of psychologists in terms of differences in reaction times. Individual differences became important to psychologists in the late nineteenth century.

Within the field of psychology, there is a wide range of approaches to individual behavior. Experimental psychologists are concerned only with those factors they can define, observe, and measure—this is a behavioristic approach. Gestalt psychologists are experimentalists also, but they are concerned with a macropsychology in which the basic tenet is that the whole is greater than the sum of its parts. Gestalt psychologists consider the experimental psychologist to be atomistic, overly concerned with details as compared with behavior as a whole. Clinical psychologists, whose field became popular during and after World War II, use an approach to personality that is closer to psychiatry than it is to the experimental psychologies. Developmental psychologists concern themselves with developmental rates, growth curves, and "readiness" that comes with maturation. They hold that individuals develop in stages; thus they are concerned with the preschool child's development and with puberty, adolescence, maturity, and old age and see capability and interests as changing with each of these stages. The common ground of psychological approaches is a focus on individuals and their reaction to their environment, development of habits, and abilities as compared with other individuals. Psychologists focus on the individual rather than on society or the environment.

Psychology remained primarily in the field of education and child development until World War II. It was the Veterans' Administration and the U.S. Army during World War II that gave impetus to clinical psychology by responding to the shortage of psychiatrists by bringing in psychologists and training them to function as psychiatrists or psychiatric assistants. The field of clinical psychology thereby received its identity. After World War II, many universities separated psychology from philosophy and introduced graduate programs in clinical psychology. A clinic that had been established in Philadelphia in 1896 to deal with children whose problems arose primarily in school was a forerunner of clinical psychology, but the significant rise in clinical psychology came during and after World War II.

Psychologists have not developed theories of crime as have the sociologists. Psychologists have developed explanations of deviant behavior, statistical measures of normalcy, and patterns of individual deviance which some might call clinical groupings or patterns of deviance. Psychologists hold that individual behavior comes first and becomes a social problem when it is indicative of incompetency or violates the law.

PSYCHOLOGICAL TESTING

In correctional settings, particularly prisons and juvenile institutions, psychologists' primary duty is testing and personality evaluation. There are only a few institutions where they have time to do any counseling or individual treatment. They sometimes participate in group counseling and instruction of other staff in in-service training. Their primary role as psychological testers is in the area of intelligence testing, vocational and clerical aptitude testing, and some personality testing.

Tests, of course, have been the primary tools of the psychologists. The early tests were individual, such as the Binet-Simon test. Case studies and interviews are considered to be the best approaches to evaluation, but they are too time consuming. The test is a shortcut to knowledge of an individual.

During World War I, the U.S. Army wanted some kind of test to determine differential intelligence of soldiers. In April 1917, the American Psychological Association appointed a committee of five psychologists, with Robert M. Yerkes as chairman, to develop a test that could be given to everyone, those who were literate and those who were illiterate. The result was the Army Alpha Intelligence Examination for literates and the Army Beta Intelligence Examination for illiterates. From 1917 to 1918, intelligence examinations were given to approximately 1,750,000 men, of whom 8,000 were recommended for discharge because of inferior intelligence, 10,000 were assigned to labor battalions requiring low-grade ability, and 1,000 were recommended for special development battalions for observation and further training. Nearly one-third were unable to read or write enough to be called literate. After the war, a large number of group tests emerged, such as the Otis Group Intelligence Scale, the American Council of Education Psychological Examination for College Freshmen, and the Otis Self-Administering Test. These tests were standardized against the 1916 Stanford-Binet examination and the 1937 Stanford-Binet. Subsequently, correlations and comparisons were made between various groups, such as racial, foreign-born and native born, occupational groups, and others. During the early years of testing, criminal offenders were believed to be less intelligent than others. Goddard (1914) reviewed several studies and found that 89 percent of criminals were feebleminded in one study, only 28 percent in another study, while the median in Goddard's list had 70 percent of the prisoners diagnosed as feebleminded. Leslie Zeleny (1933) also claimed that criminals were feebleminded. Kuhlman's (1925–26, p. 55) study found inmates in the Stillwater Prison and St. Cloud Reformatory in Minnesota to be lower in intelligence than the average. As testing became more sophisticated and comparison with other groups more exact, however, it was determined that prisoners did not have lower intelligence than the general population. The data from Kuhlman's and Zeleny's studies were computed by Vold (1958, pp. 84–87) in comparisons with the results of the United States Army tests during World War I, and equivalent intelligence ratings were found in both groups. The first full comparison of the intelligence of prisoners with that of the general population was when Murchison (1926, chap. IV) compared the test results of prisoners in five states with groups from the World War I tests and found consistently better performances by the prisoners than the draft army soldiers. Stone (1921) had performed a smaller study with similar results a few years earlier in Indiana. Simon Tulchin (1939) compared Illinois prisoners with Illinois soldiers in World War I and found similar results. Recent studies indicate that intelligence does not significantly differ between offenders and the general population from which they are drawn. A 1950 (Rouke, 1950) study suggests that there is no need for further studies of intelligence and crime because the possible contributions have been exhausted, as indicated by a review of a series of studies that conclude that the distributions of prisoner and nonprisoner populations are almost completely superimposed as far as intelligence is concerned.

Group intelligence tests that are most popular continue to be revisions of the original army tests. The Alpha Examination, Modified, Form 9, by F. L. Wells has been a popular test for literates. The Revised Beta Examination by D. E. Kellog and N. W. Morton has been popular for illiterates. The Barranquilla Rapid Survey Intelligence Test (BARSIT) by Francisco del Olmo is a popular test in Spanish for use with Latin Americans. A quick (four to eight minutes) emergency oral test is the Kent Series of Emergency Scales. There are several popular tests of academic potential and academic achievement that are given in many prisons. The most popular individual intelligence test is now the Wechsler Adult Intelligence Scale (devised by David Wechsler), a revision of the original Wechsler-Bellevue intelligence scale. The Wechsler Intelligence Scale for Children is standardized for children aged five through fifteen. The Wechsler Adult Intelligence Scale is standardized for adults aged sixteen to over seventy-five. There are also many group and individual tests of personality and other clinical diagnostic techniques. The most popular group test is the Minnesota Multi-Phasic Personality Inventory developed by S. R. Hathaway and J. C. McKinley primarily for older adolescents and adults. This test has ten scales in addition to the question score, the lie score, the validity score, and the K (discrimination) score. The ten scales are (1) hypochondriasis, (2) depression, (3) hysteria, (4) psychopathic deviation, (5) masculinity-femininity, (6) paranoia, (7) psychasthenia, (8) schizophrenia, (9) hypomania, and (10) social introversion. The MMPI has been used in many research studies in the field of criminology. The Rorschach technique is a series of ten standardized ink blots on cards used by psychologists to evaluate personality through projective techniques. For this test the individual looks at the unstructured formations of the cards, which are black and white except for red coloring on cards II and III and complex coloration on cards VIII, IX, and X. The use of cards for projective techniques began in the latter part of the nineteenth century. It was Herman Rorschach, a Swiss psychiatrist, who standardized the present cards in 1913. Dr. Samuel J. Beck was the first man to publish in English on Rorschach, and Dr. Bruno Klopfer followed soon afterward, both in the 1930s. The five major American systems for Rorschach's scoring and interpretation are now those of Klopfer, Beck, Hertz, Piotrowski, and Rapaport-Schafer. The Rorschach test is an excellent personality evaluator when used by a competent psychologist. To become competent in Rorschach technique, however, years of serious study and supervised administration are required. Unfortunately, the Rorschach test may be given by someone who has read only a single book about it! Like many other pieces of sensitive equipment, the Rorschach test can provide perceptive understanding of personality structure with the aid of a competent psychologist, but it is very dangerous and can be misleading if an incompetent person administers and interprets it—this test is only as good as the psychologist using it.

There are many other tests of intelligence: aptitude; interest, personality, and clinical deviations; academic achievement; prediction of academic success, and so forth. The few group tests mentioned are the most popular, however, and the few individual tests mentioned are reserved for only a few difficult cases in prisons, correctional, and therapeutic settings.

There are several tests and inventories that have been helpful in understanding offenders and assessing their progress in treatment.[1] The Carkhuff Empathic Understanding in Interpersonal Process Scale was developed in 1969 and assists in assessing the client's capacity for perceived empathy and two-way communication. There are many other tests on the market that measure anxiety, self-concept, and a variety of other traits and factors.

The Reid Report Inventory (RRI) was developed in 1967 to measure punitiveness as an attitude toward punishment for theft (Reid, 1967). It is a scale of 100 yes-no items that is easily administered. Ash (1974) used it to study attitudes toward theft and found that prisoners are more apt to forgive theft than are normal job applicants, regardless of age, race, ethnic group, education, or type of crime committed.

The best comprehensive review of psychological tests is that of Oscar K. Buros, ed., *The Seventh Mental Measurements Yearbook (1972)*. The *Yearbook* is a two-volume work that lists 1,157 tests, including 640 new tests, 12,539 references and reviews, has a directory of test publishers, and other information. Previous *yearbooks* were published in 1938, 1940, 1948, 1953, 1959, and 1965.

EXPERIMENTAL APPROACHES

Most, if not all, that is learned from laboratory rats, mice, chickens, and other species that are the subjects of the experimental psychologist can be applied to the behavior of humans. The conditioned response or association of reward and punishment with specific stimuli is the basic unit of learning studied by experimental psychologists. Their interest in motivation and drives, purposeful behavior, sensitivity and perception, and the influence of experience or learning is basic to their interpretation of behavior. Although conditioning is not the same in all animals capable of it, mammals can form systems of conditioned responses and can, therefore, learn to perform tasks; dogs, for example, can be trained in hunting, shepherding domestic animals, and sentry duty. Operant learning is similar to conditioning, except that initiating the response depends specifically on the animal. For example, B. F. Skinner, who originated the concept of operant learning, had a classical experiment in which a rat learned to approach and press a bar for a food reward. If the reward was given only in the presence of a

---

[1]An evaluation of all the personality tests available in English as of June 1969 is available in Oscar Krisen Buros, ed., *Personality Tests and Reviews* (Highland Park, N.J.: Gryphon Press, 1970). Most of the popular ones and some after 1969 are available from commercial organizations that limit their sales to "qualified customers," including The Psychological Corporation, 304 East 45th Street, New York, New York 10017 and other similar organizations.

signal, such as a light, the rat pressed the bar only during the presentation of the light. If hunger was reduced, it stopped pressing.

Modification of behavior by conditioning through reward and punishment begins early in the phylogenetic scale. Even snails have withdrawn from tactile stimulation of the oral veil, have shown feeding responses to food chemicals, and have acquired a classically conditioned feeding response to touch alone (Mpitsos and Davis, 1973). Abstract thinking and abstract learning, however, are dependent on symbolic interaction and communication. This symbolic interaction of language gives rise to value systems and judgment parameters that separate *human* behavior from basic *animal* behavior. The fusion of this *human* behavior with the basic *animal* behavior results in the general behavior of the genus *homo sapiens*, modern man. Although there is evidence of communication among some lower animals, their behavior remains basically *animal* behavior, while humans' behavior is predominantly based on values, attitudes, and beliefs that are modified, of course, by their *animal* behavior.

A series of stimuli contributes to the learning process. Trial and error learning is complex, but it results in habitual behavior when some types of behavior produce reward and other types bring punishment and disapproval. (It could be suggested in a light vein that while magicians pull rabbits out of hats, experimental psychologists pull habits out of rats.) Social interaction or behavior can be seen in various experiments, such as those dealing with the pecking order of chickens (Masur and Allee, 1934a and b). In one experiment, a flock of chickens were identified individually with leg tags and observed. Chicken A pecked chicken B and everybody else, but nobody pecked chicken A. Chicken B pecked everybody in the flock except chicken A, and chicken A pecked him. Chicken C pecked everybody in the flock except chickens A and B, and on through the flock until the pecking order was charted. The standing in the social order of any individual is a social function. In the affairs of men and women, a legislator may be a "heavyweight" or a "lightweight," and this may determine his or her effectiveness in political action. There are "heavyweights" and "lightweights" in every human organization. In an elementary school, many young children work out the "pecking order" at recess. When a new kid comes to town, they find out where he or she fits in the pecking order. Social status in terms of individual stability and standing in the group appear in all social groupings. Even in chickens, the mating receptivity is related to the hen's position in the flock hierarchy and will change if her relative position is changed by flock size or membership (Guhl, 1956). The pecking order also appears in the cities—in the ghetto, it is most intense. In fact, many correctional clients, delinquents, and offenders are so far down in the pecking order that they have assumed self-concepts of being "losers" and inferior. Many have tattoos like "Born to Lose" on their arms and chests.

John T. Emlen, at the University of Wisconsin, studied populations of house mice by establishing a small population in the basement of an old building (American Institute of Biological Sciences, 1963, pp. 606–8). The mice were provided with 250 grams of food each day. When the population of the mice grew to the saturation point of the food supply, mice left the colony. In the second part of the experiment, the mice were confined in pens that prevented their leaving the colony. Then, when the daily food supply became insufficient, fewer young were born and the population stabilized. In the third experiment, the mice were again confined in pens, but more than enough food was provided. As the population density increased, there was a decline in space per mouse, and the population became overcrowded. Fighting, chasing, and conflict started. Females ceased taking proper care of their nests and their young. More mice continued to be born, but more died from neglect. Finally, cannibalism occurred even in the presence of a sufficient food supply. The same phenomenon can be observed to a lesser extent in urban ghettos and in the prisons of modern America. Conflict in an overcrowded concrete jungle where survival-of-the-fittest values prevail, if to a lesser extent than cannibalism, has produced some of the same types of conflict and fighting observed among the mice.

A similar experiment with mice was conducted by John B. Calhoun, a psychologist with the National Institute of Mental Health (reported by the Associated Press, March 1, 1973). Beginning with four females and four males in June 1968, Calhoun provided an "ideal mouse universe," giving them all the food they needed. As the colony grew, the mice tended to form social groups of about twelve mice each. Each group established a territory of its own controlled by a dominant male. When the population reached 150 and all the desirable physical spaces were filled, social breakdown began. Mothers chased the young out of the nest before the young mice had a chance to learn about mother love; dominant males started breaking down, weary from defending their territories. Females started dominating the group and became more aggressive. Young males ceased to struggle for territory and were forced to a "life on the streets" on the floor of the laboratory. Rejected males became recluses or formed large motionless aggregates away from the housing units. Rejected females assembled in the housing units that were farthest from food and water. When the population reached 2,200 in late 1970, rearing of young and breeding ceased and "everything was downhill and extinction was inevitable" after that. The last mouse died in January 1973, nearly five years after the experiment began.

Neurosis can be experimentally induced in rats by using punishment in frustrating situations (Stainbrook, 1946). Hall (1933) found that neurotic rats displayed deviant behavior. They have also been found to develop hypertension and emotional disturbances when exposed over long periods of time to stress (Farris et al., 1945). When an animal is surrounded with barriers and conflict is introduced, neurotic and deviant behavior results (Maier et al., 1940). When translated into cultural situations where humans are surrounded with barriers, frustration, stress, and conflict, this deviant behavior may be aggressive, withdrawn, or criminal, or may take any of a variety of other forms. There are many other concepts in experimental psychology that are of importance in learning more about human behavior, such as the goal gradient hypothesis, which measures how much incentive is needed to overcome how much punishment to get how much reward; the examples already given indicate the viability of the approach by experimental psychologists in understanding behavior. Thorndike (1911) first developed the concept of "reward" in experimental psychology during his experiments with cats. Hull's (1952, p. 2) concept of "habit strength" and Tolman's (MacCorquodale, et al., 1954) concept of "expectancies" have emphasized predispositional approaches in psychology. Miller's (1959, pp. 204-22) "conflict hypothesis" involves strong and weak predisposing factors and precipitating factors; if both are strong, the behavior is reinforced. If both are weak, behavior is not reinforced and permits drift, as suggested in Matza's view of delinquency and drift. When one is strong and the other is weak, behavior is not intense in either direction but is tenuous.

BEHAVIOR MODIFICATION AND OPERANT CONDITIONING

Behavior modification is essentially a conditioning approach to learning and modification of behavior based on punishment and reward; this discipline has been succinctly enunciated by B. F. Skinner (1948, 1953). Operant conditioning is technically a more restricted term referring to laboratory work in conditioning but has recently been accepted in the correctional field as interchangeable with behavior modification. The early presentations by Skinner in the middle 1940s when he was at Indiana involved raising an infant in the "Skinner box," where she could grow and develop "untouched by human hands" in a truly scientific milieu. The study of behavior modification in older persons developed from that beginning. Today, behavior modification and operant conditioning have become popular in correctional programs, particularly in many juvenile institutional programs that included in the early 1970's the Robert F. Kennedy Youth Center at Morgantown, West Virginia, operated by the United States Bureau of Prisons.

Skinner has consistently championed a systemic natural scientific study of the method of human knowledge, while orthodox sociology led by Talcott Parsons in the 1950s emphasized consensus. George Homans (1971; also Friedrichs, 1974) has brought some sociologists around to the Skinnerian or "natural" view by applying conditioning principles to social interaction. Behavior modification approaches can be applied to any area of deviant human behavior (Franks and Wilson, 1973).

Behavior modification is a system of rewards and punishments, generally in the form of candy, denial of privileges, or other types of reward and punishment available within an institutional setting. In institutional behavior modification, residents "earn" their privileges and, eventually, their freedom. Operant conditioning is based on the principle that behavior is strengthened or weakened by its consequences. It is operant conditioning that is the basis of token economy.

The theoretical base of behavior modification is that a human being is born with a "tabula rasa" and learns his or her behavior from external pressures. Behavioral modification theory identifies behaviors and the conditions that influence them. It defines the acceptable and unacceptable behaviors, and counseling is designed to reinforce the acceptable behaviors. Behavior modification includes punishment, reward, aversive conditioning, extinction of unacceptable behaviors, role playing, praise, chastisement, and other techniques by which acceptable behavior is reinforced and unacceptable behavior is decreased. Low-anxiety-producing and high-anxiety-producing stimuli are used as needed. There is a vital concern with anxiety levels and levels of tension (Kroth and Forrest, 1969, p. 725).

Behavior modification in the correctional setting includes a variety of techniques, including the "time-out" room, or confinement; privileges like reward; role playing and modeling, or "setting an example" techniques; and behavior contracts, where the offender signs a contract with the correctional worker to behave in a prescribed manner for a specific reward (Ligato and Dewey, 1974). Behavior modification is based on the assumption that all behavior results from external forces and that all people react similarly to punishment and reward. Unlike some approaches to delinquency, behavior modification assumes that delinquency does not have deep roots in the individual or in society but that delinquent acts can be committed without the person's having deep commitments to delinquency. The theorists adopting this approach argue that if the patterns were really deep-rooted, there would not be the drastic reduction in arrests that has been consistently observed in people as they move from adolescence to young adulthood (ibid., 37).

Thus, the behavior modification approach is essentially a reward and punishment approach. In institutions, the major punishments and deterrents are loss of status, privileges, and living comforts. Counseling and frank discussions of opposing rewards and punishments accompany these sanctions with the view toward modifying personality traits and the method of handling social situations; the effort is to help of-fenders function more effectively in the middle-class society in their rela-tionship to police, courts, and employers (Bishop and Blanchard, 1971, p. 8). Many academic criminologists believe that the behavior modifica-tion approach would be more economical than present programs in terms of time, money, and effort (Hindelang, 1970, p. 54). Behavior modification techniques are well suited for integration into the criminal justice system because they focus upon behavior easily subjected to reward and punishment (Schwitzgebel, 1971, p. 66). In the area of operant conditioning, food, release from institutions, money, or other rewards to reinforce good behavior have been successfully used. Stan-dards must take into consideration the limits of the law and the rights of the offenders as to whether institutions can regulate coercive techni-ques under the jurisprudential values of "fairness" and "justice."

Behavior modification techniques used most frequently at the Robert F. Kennedy School Youth Center at Morgantown, West Virginia, are the class level system and token economy (Gerard, 1970). Living con-ditions, work assignments, pay, clothing, and recreation improve with each level. Under token economy, students earn points as they meet goals set in school, work, and everyday life, and these points can buy a varie-ty of goods and services available at the institution (Karacki and Levin-son, 1970).

Behavior modification is not new, but it now has a name and some documentation in terms of experimentation and the literature. It has been used informally in homes by parents with children for a long time (Savage, 1974, p. 186). Macanochie used the mark system with merits and demerits in 1843 at the Norfolk Island Penal Colony. The Irish system introduced by Sir Walter Crofton in 1854 included incarcera-tion using a program that appears similar to that used at the above-mentioned Robert F. Kennedy Training School for Boys, where behavior modification is considered to be the primary approach. From the nine-teenth century into the 1960s many institutions, particularly juvenile institutions, have used a point system or graduated programs with in-creased privileges. These programs were viewed with some derogation by professionals. Behavior modification has now been reactivated with a new name and a body of knowledge that began with Pavlov's (1960) famous experiments in conditioning. The results concerning the social behavior of human beings, who are partially motivated by values and guilt, remain questionable. One of the difficulties with all of the behavior therapies, including behavior modification, is that they are generally limited to a specific setting. The rewards that enhance conformity in an institution and the punishments that discourage deviant behavior frequently do not appear back home in the community. When a third-grade school child pays his or her milk money to a sixth-grade protec-tion gang and the sixth-grader with the money gets "mugged" on the way home, the system of punishment and reward breaks down. It has been observed that punishment-reward types of learning become situational. Over a long period of time, of course, with "normal" people, such as the cadets at the United States Military Academy at West Point, the beneficial effects of such a rigid system can be observed.

Aversion therapy has also been suggested for behavioral disorders (Rochman and Teasdale, 1969, p. 186). The system of aversion therapy is to provide noxious stimuli along with the undersirable behavior. Modern aversion therapy has used electrical or chemical noxious stimulation as negative reinforcers. Primary uses thus far have been in sexual disorders, with electrical aversion, and in alcoholism, with chemical aversion, generally in the form of Antabus. The difficulty with aversive therapy is that when the individual leaves the therapeutic situation, the noxious stimulation ceases, and without reinforcement, there is a tendency to revert to the original behavior after a period of time.

Review of the results of behavior modification approaches to changing the behavior of delinquents has been consistently disappointing (Sumphauzer, 1970). Fully 81 percent of the experimental studies fail to show any realistic follow-up, and other studies with follow-up are disappointing. Close scrutiny must be given to behavior modification approaches in the future. In the past, however, the observation has been that those subjected to behavior modification techniques will "play the game" as long as they are in the behavior modification situation and will revert to previous behavior when returned to their original setting.

Reward and punishment techniques such as behavior modification are best suited for authoritative settings, while democratic settings are controlled by interaction among members of the group from which emerge the cohesiveness, functions, and leadership of the group. In an authoritative setting like an institution, behavior modification seems to work well; but when the individual returns to the community, he or she returns to social interaction. It would take years of positive exposure for behavior modification to be effective, for example, four years at West Point.

Attempts to use behavior modification techniques in the federal prison system resulted in intense controversy in 1973 and 1974. The START program (Special Treatment and Rehabilitation Training) at the Medical Center for Federal Prisoners at Springfield, Missouri, and the Federal Center for Correctional Research at Butner, North Carolina, were attacked by the *Prisoners' Digest International* (Sept. 1973) and by the United Church of Christ's Commission for Racial Justice (*Criminal Justice Newsletter*, Dec. 31, 1973, p. 2) for the use of "drugs, brainwashing, and hypnosis" on uncontrollable prisoners to develop methods of handling other uncontrollable prisoners. The purpose of the program was to select the worst prisoners and get them back into the prison population more receptive to rehabilitation programs. The commission reported that two inmates at the United States Penitentiary at Marion, Illinois, committed suicide because they had been selected to be transfered to Butner (ibid.). Activists in prisons have called it Orwellian brainwashing and threatened strikes and riots (*Corrections Digest*, Jan. 9, 1974, p. 2).

There are procedural problems with behavior modification, electroconvulsive therapy, and psychosurgery (Wexler, 1973; also Kittrie, 1971, esp. chap. 9). They emerge from the due process concept of civil rights and are related to section 1983 of Title 42 of the United States Code, which prevents violation of civil rights under color of law, among other prohibitions. Changing a person's body or his or her personality without informed consent has encountered resistance.

DIFFERENTIAL TREATMENT

Differential treatment is the term used to identify an approach used by Quay (1965) in an institutional setting and by Warren (1969) in a community setting. It is based on the assumption that the same treatment program that is beneficial to some types of offenders may be detrimental to other types of offenders (Warren, 1971). Differential treatment is a program similar to behavior modification. In this system, the resident moves from one stage or rank in an institution or community setting to a better one or regresses to a poorer one, depending upon his or her behavior. Quay's approach to differential treatment was introduced in the Robert F. Kennedy Center in Morgantown, West Virginia, when it opened in 1968. This type of treatment uses a variety of approaches, depending upon the classification of the offender.

Warren, in her work, uses an Interpersonal Maturity approach, generally referred to as I-Level, based on differential rates of maturation. (This approach will be discussed further in the next chapter.) Quay (1964; also Peterson et al., 1959) uses a psychological classification based on four dimensions of deviant behavior: (1) inadequate-immature, (2) neurotic-conflicted, (3) unsocialized-aggressive or psychopathic, and (4) socialized or subcultural delinquency. After experience with these four dimensions at the Kennedy Youth Center, however, a fifth category was added because a fairly large number of youths exhibited behavior similar to two of the original categories, immaturity and subcultural. The category subcultural-immature, then, is an addition based on experience. The final five categories of types of behavior in Quay's system, are as follows:

1. Inadequate-immature—Preoccupied, reticent, lazy and inattentive children behave in childish and irresponsible ways. Treatment: permit him to "grow up."
2. Neurotic-conflicted—Anxiety, depression, feelings of inferiority and

guilt. Often sorry for what he has done. Treatment: be perceptive, become involved with the youth to help him understand his weaknesses, limitations, strengths, and potential.

3. Unsocialized-aggressive or psychopathic—Untrustworthy, aggressive, and manipulative. High need for excitement. Rejection of authority, troublemakers. Treatment has to be tough-minded, direct, avoiding manipulation in a highly controlled environment. Teach them to accept responsibility for their own acts and develop a genuine meaningful relationship with others.

4. Socialized or subcultural delinquency—Gang activities, adheres to the code of the peer group. Treatment emphasizes a strong personal code to earn the respect of these students and the exercise of firm control, resisting manipulation. Help them change gang-influenced value systems and teach them how to meet status and material demands in ways acceptable to society.

5. Subcultural-immature—Socially inept and inadequate, this sort of delinquent attaches to a gang to meet his needs. Family frequently severely disorganized, accounting for distrust of authority figures. Treatment involves strong but flexible individuals who enjoy working with adolescents. Emphasizes development of positive, trusting relationships with adults and overcoming social learning deficiencies [pp. 305-9].

The primary uses of differential treatment have been the Quay model at the Kennedy Youth Center under the supervision of the United States Bureau of Prisons, and the Warren model at the Community Treatment Project in Sacramento under the supervision of the California Youth Authority. Other institutions and agencies have used differential treatment in varying ways and with varying degrees of commitment. The concept has become increasingly popular in the correctional field.

GESTALT APPROACHES

The Gestalt approach to psychology developed in Germany in 1912 under the leadership of Max Wertheimer, but the movement in the United States was primarily under the leadership of three German professors who had academic appointments in American universities—Kurt Koffka, Wolfgang Kohler, and Kurt Lewin. They called experimental psychology a "bundle hypothesis," referring to specific S-R (stimulus-response) bonds, and felt that people's complex behavior requires a more circumspect approach. They saw the data of experience as organized and extended wholes that are not encountered in specific elements.

Although children may react to a few specific stimuli, adults react to patterns or total organizations of objects around them that form "Gestalten" or "configurations." *Gestalt* means that the whole is greater than the sum of its parts and has more meaning. In a motion picture it appears as though the figures are moving, but the viewer is really seeing only a series of still pictures in rapid succession. An incomplete circle or triangle is seen as a circle or triangle through "closure," which completes the picture. Sometimes this "closure" fills in details of automobile accidents and other phenomena when witnesses are testifying on the stand. Unfortunately, closure is not always accurate and can result in misunderstanding. The concept of "insight" comes when suddenly the individual "gets the picture."

The experiments by the Gestalt psychologists were primarily with chimpanzees. One of Kohler's best-known experiments with chimpanzees, on the island of Tenerife in the Canary Islands from 1913 to 1917, was when a chimpanzee learned to fit a small stick into a hole bored in the end of a larger one and retrieve a banana that was farther than either stick could reach. It was necessary for the chimpanzee to see the situation involving the task as a whole—in its entirety.

In Gestalt therapy, importance is attached to the tone of voice, gestures, facial expression, and other types of nonverbal communication. Gestalt therapy emphasizes positive directions and goals in living (Fagan and Shepherd, 1970, p. 328); it sees a causal framework in which introspection is important; the here and now is emphasized.

Gestalt psychology posits five layers of neurosis: (1) *phony*, where we play live games; (2) *phobic*, where we get in touch with fears; (3) *impasse*, where we are caught and lose environmental support; (4) *implosive*, where we despair, grieve, and loathe self; and (5) *explosive*, in which previously unused energies are freed in an impactive way (Perls, 1970).

Neurotics hold on to their guilt and resentment toward their parents. Gestalt therapy approaches aim to find out what parts of the person are disowned and then help reassimilate them. Self-growth can be achieved by meditation, by listening to ourselves, and by introspection. Impasse can be solved by staying with and tolerating the boredom and frustration. Crisis occurs when a person's customary way of living becomes less viable. In summary, Gestalt therapy attempts to develop insight and closure; to help the person learn to place things in perspective.

Gestalt therapy itself probably had its beginnings in 1951 when Frederick Perls, Paul Goodman, and Ralph F. Hefferline collaborated in a book under the title, *Gestalt Therapy: Excitement and Growth in the Human Personality*. Wolfgang Kohler and Molly Harrower, pioneers in Gestalt theory, have rejected Gestalt therapy as not being in accordance with basic Gestalt principles (see Hefferline and Bruno, 1973, p. 56). Much behavior is comprised of somatic residuals, like tics, the development of ulcers, and thumb sucking. Gestalt therapists realize that much conflict consists of clenching of voluntary muscles, which indicates anxiety; they are concerned with how physical "hang-ups" develop and are retained, as well as with what function they serve. The Gestalt therapist is particularly interested in frustration and anger (Lederman, 1969) and the total integration of all forces—social, physical, psychological, and cultural—of which behavior is the resultant (Polster, 1973).

In summary, Gestalt therapy is a nonanalytical, existential form of therapy developed by Frederick and Laura Perls. Its objective is to integrate the splits and polarities of personality and to replace environmental support with self-support and an awareness of one's self and the world.

CLINICAL APPROACHES

Clinical psychology assesses personality and works with it. Its greatest development was during World War II and afterward, when there simply were not enough psychiatrists, and the clinical psychologist developed as an adjunct psychiatrist, in essence. Clinical psychology uses the same personality framework as that used in psychiatry. Defense mechanisms and adaptive techniques to social pressures are primary concerns. Clinical psychologists assess the emotional conflicts within people and attempt to resolve them. Emotional needs and unmet needs are of primary concern. The *Psychiatric Dictionary* (Hinsie and Campbell, 1970, p. 614) describes the clinical psychologist as "one versed in psychology who deals with clinical cases and who uses his training in the theory and techniques of psychology to aid in the diagnosis and (under medical supervision) in the treatment of mental and emotional disorders. Figure 8-1 depicts the development of clinical psychology.

Stress is viewed by clinical psychologists as the primary motivation for deviant behavior. While the sociologists emphasize external stress or environmental pressures, the clinical psychologists and psychiatrists emphasize internal stresses and tensions that may have resulted from external pressures. Reactions to stress are generally (1) attack as a result of anger or hostility; (2) withdrawal, both physically and psychologically, to reduce ego involvement in the situation and to develop resistance and protective inhibition; and (3) compromise by changing the method of operation, accepting substitute goals, or resorting to generally unacceptable means. All these approaches involve seeing and defining the problem, working out alternative solutions to the problem, deciding on the safest and most rewarding course of action, and evaluating the results of the action.

Defense mechanisms are acquired to protect the person. They are essential for softening failure, reducing cognitive dissonance (perceptions of undesirable reality), alleviating anxiety, protecting against

FIGURE 8-1.
Development of Clinical Psychology

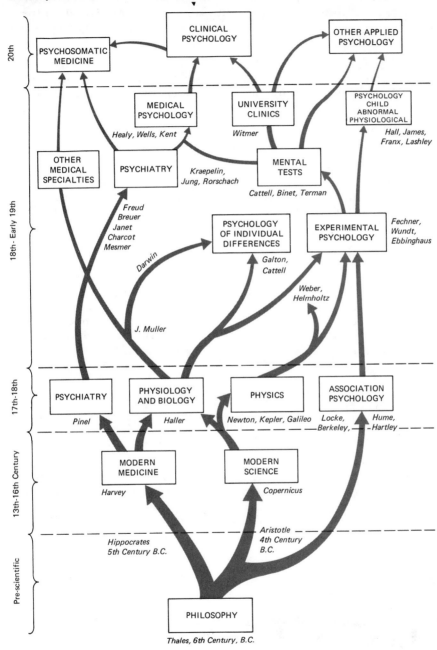

Chart 85, from chapter 85, Helen D. Sargent and Martin Mayman, "Clinical Psychology," in Silvano Arieti, ed., *American Handbook of Psychiatry*, vol. II (New York: Basic Books, Inc., Publishers, 1959), p. 1713.

trauma, and maintaining feelings of adequacy and personal worth. Defense mechanisms are really a type of self-deception and distortion of reality in order to protect the ego. There are several listings of these defense mechanisms, one of which is suggested by James Coleman:

DENIAL OF REALITY
Protecting self from unpleasant reality by refusing to perceive or face it, often by escapist activities like getting "sick" or being preoccupied with other things.

FANTASY
Gratifying frustrated desires in imaginary achievements.

RATIONALIZATION
Attempting to prove that one's behavior is "rational" and justifiable and thus worthy of self and social approval. In this mechanism, good reasons are found for activities the individual engages in or wants to engage in for probably less acceptable reasons.

PROJECTION
Projecting one's own characteristics elsewhere. Placing blame for difficulties upon others or attributing one's own ethical desires and attributes to others. Identifying with persons who are admired or projecting blame on others. Projection is most useful to the psychologist because it provides the base for the projective techniques, such as the Rorschach Test, TAT, and other projective tests, thus permitting probing of the unconscious.

REPRESSION
Preventing painful or dangerous thoughts from entering consciousness.

SUPPRESSION
Refusing to recognize or enunciate painful or dangerous thoughts that are, in fact, conscious. (Not included in Coleman's list.)

REACTION FORMATION
Preventing dangerous desires from being expressed by exaggerating opposed attitudes and types of behavior and using them as "barriers." For example, an individual may be a militant and crusading teetotaler because his father or another member in the family was alcoholic.

UNDOING
Atoning for and thus counteracting immoral desires or acts.

REGRESSION
Retreating to earlier developmental levels involving less mature responses and usually a lower level of aspiration.

IDENTIFICATION
Increasing feelings of worth by identifying with persons or institutions of illustrious standing.

INTROJECTION

Incorporating external values and standards into ego structure so that they do not act as external threats. Assuming qualities of others. Opposite or projection.

COMPENSATION

Covering up weaknesses by emphasizing desirable traits or by making up for frustration in one area by overgratification in another. An individual cannot play football, so he becomes an expert chess player.

DISPLACEMENT

Discharging pent-up feelings, usually of hostility, on objects less dangerous than those which initially arouse the emotions. The boss' wife attacks him, so he takes out his anger on his workers during the day.

EMOTIONAL INSULATION

Reducing ego involvement and withdrawing into passivity to protect self from hurt.

INTELLECTUALIZATION

Cutting off affective charge from hurtful situations or separating incompatible attitudes into logical-type compartments. Holding to attitudes and beliefs in the face of overwhelming evidence to the contrary.

SUBLIMATION

Gratifying or working off frustrated desires, frequently sexual desires, in other activities. Generally, this refers to change in means of gratification while keeping the object. For example, a person with strong sexual desires for another person who is not available may partially satisfy those desires through an acceptable means, such as dancing.

SUBSTITUTION

Gratifying or working off frustrated desires, frequently sexual desires, in other than the original desired object. For example, sexual desires for a person who is unavailable may be satisfied with another person who is available. (Not in Coleman's list).

SYMPATHISM

Striving to gain sympathy from others, thus bolstering feelings of self-worth despite failures.

ACTING OUT

Reducing anxiety aroused by forbidden desires by permitting their expression. Acting-out behavior occurs frequently in crime and delinquency.

All these defense mechanisms are "normal." Even so, most in their extremes can result in deviant behavior that violates the law. The work of clinical psychologists is basically to help clients, through counseling, to channel aggressions, frustrations, and other stresses and tensions into socially acceptable ego defense mechanisms.

Most of the psychological literature suggests that helping people does not result from financial aid, offering advice, claiming superior knowledge, using authority, coercion, bullying, manipulation, criticism, shaming or deflation, suggestion, or moralizing. Rather, people are helped by what they experience in social relationships. Consequently, helping people means to provide them with some understanding of their problem, some security and support, together with respect, consideration, recognition, appreciation, acceptance, and tolerance. In this manner, emotional defenses to stress, particularly in conflict with authority, will be reduced to the extent that the individual can adjust successfully in conforming society. Emotional hang-ups impede capacities and skills, reason and intellect, and moral values. The dissipation of disabling emotions is the primary objective of the clinical psychologist.

The defense mechanisms characteristically employed by persons in prison populations are denial of reality and projection, according to correctional counselors. Projection of blame on society, "the caught and the uncaught," and abuse of "the system" are frequent emotion-laden explanations and defenses in prison populations. Denial of reality, including "tall tales" of good jobs and beautiful women, "expensive horses and fast women," and assurances of political influence permeate prisoner conversations. These defenses are, as are all defenses, a kind of self-deception to protect the ego, and they are normally used to varying degrees by everybody.

The dyssocial offender has difficulty because of a lack of broad socialization in his background. *Dyssocial* refers to a dysfunctional relationship with social groups, rather than a dis-social or no relationship with society, which would be complete alienation. Many of these people enter cults, where they feel happier and more secure. Some of the background factors that have been associated with the dyssocial offender are the following:

1. He was raised in a section of the city where the only apparently successful person was the criminal.
2. He was reared in a structural (small and independent) society where people made their own laws—laws which in many instances showed a disregard for the social norms of the rest of society.
3. He had a family background which lent itself to the production of a person oblivious to the laws of society. In other words, dyssocial individuals are "products of their environment" (Wicks, 1974a, p. 62.)

Treatment of criminal and delinquent behavior from the standpoint of clinical psychology involves individual and group therapy sessions. In individual sessions, there is generally a well-established pattern involving (1) exploration of the problem areas, (2) confrontation, in which the therapist attempts to identify the problem and lead the offender to recognize it, (3) interpretation so that the offender is able to understand the problem and alternative solutions, and (4) termination, when the offender does not need the therapist any longer and can cope with his problems without help. The negative attitudes toward the confusion regarding social authority on the part of the delinquent results in readiness for aggressive acting-out behavior (Bromberg and Rogers, 1946, p. 674) and must be considered in the treatment process (Hardman, 1960, p. 250).

Some people can relate to others much better than other people can. This is what clinicians refer to as "insight," "clinical intuition," and/or "empathy." This ability to relate to other people in an understanding way appears to be developed throughout childhood in the family and neighborhood settings, rather than by actual teaching as such. A person with the ability to relate can be well-trained in the helping professions, but a person without that ability is generally screened out and not admitted to educational programs in clinical psychology, social work, and psychiatry. The wrong person trained is still the wrong person. There have been attempts to construct tests to differentiate persons who are highly sensitive and perceptive of what others are thinking and how they are feeling from those who are obtuse and slow to the point of insensitivity (Dymond, 1949).

A good example of the clinical approach in relation to criminology is seen in the mental health clinic that opened in the Maryland State Penitentiary in 1973 under the direction of Dr. Stephen M. Berman (Maryland Division of Correction, 1973, p. 1). Any inmate in a crisis or precrisis state, including suicidal tendencies, can come to the clinic during daylight hours. During other times, one of six psychologists or three part-time psychiatrists is on call. Special group therapy sessions are available for inmates and correctional officers. There is a positive trend now to establish such clinics in institutions, courts, and correctional agencies.

DEVELOPMENTAL APPROACHES

The developmental approaches are used primarily by child psychologists. The biological system, the psychological system or personality, and the sociological system or group interact together at every level of development, and certain "developmental tasks" are expected of the normal individual. The series of developmental tasks at various levels have been adapted from several writers and presented by James Coleman (Table 8-1).

There are several specific movements from immaturity to maturity. The individual moves from dependence to self-direction. Movement

TABLE 8-1.
Developmental Tasks of Different Life Periods

INFANCY AND EARLY CHILDHOOD –6 YEARS	Learning to walk and talk. Learning to take solid foods and to control the elimination of body wastes. Achieving physiological stability. Developing a sense of trust in oneself and others. Learning to relate oneself emotionally to parents, siblings, and other people. Forming an identification with one's own sex. Developing simple concepts of social and physical reality. Mastering simple safety rules. Learning to distinguish right from wrong and to respect rules and authority.
MIDDLE CHILDHOOD 6–12 YEARS	Gaining wider knowledge and understanding of the physical and social world. Building wholesome attitudes toward oneself. Learning an appropriate masculine or feminine social role. Developing conscious morality and a scale of values. Learning to read, write, and calculate, and learning other fundamental intellectual skills. Learning physical skills. Developing attitudes toward social groups and other institutions. Learning to win and maintain a place among one's age mates. Learning to give and take and to share responsibility. Achieving increasing personal independence.
ADOLESCENCE 12–18 YEARS	Developing self-confidence and a clear sense of identity. Accepting one's physique and adjusting to body changes. Achieving a masculine or feminine social role. Developing new, mature relations with age-mates. Achieving emotional independence from parents and other adults. Developing concern beyond oneself; achieving mature values and social responsibility. Selecting and preparing for an occupation. Preparing for marriage and family life. Learning to make choices and take responsibility. Building a conscience-value system in harmony with an adequate world picture.
EARLY ADULTHOOD 18–35 YEARS	Completing formal education. Getting started in an occupation. Selecting and learning to live with a mate. Starting a family and providing for the material and psychological needs of one's children. Finding a congenial social group. Taking on civic responsibility. Developing a satisfying philosophy of life.
MIDDLE AGE 35–60 YEARS	Accepting greater civic and social responsibility. Achieving personal goals with one's mate, and relating to one's mate as a person. Establishing a standard of living and developing adequate financial security for remaining years. Developing adult leisure-time activities and extending interests. Helping teenage children become responsible and happy adults. Adjusting to aging parents. Accepting and adjusting to the psychological changes of middle age.
LATER LIFE OVER 60 YEARS	Adjusting to decreasing physical strength. Adjusting to retirement and reduced income, and establishing satisfactory living arrangements. Adjusting to the death of spouse or friends. Meeting social and civic obligations within one's ability. Establishing an explicit affiliation with one's own age group. Maintaining active interest and concerns above one's self.
TASKS AT ALL PERIODS	Developing and using one's physical, social, and emotional competencies. Accepting oneself and developing basic confidence. Accepting reality and building valid attitudes and values. Participating creatively and responsibly in family and other groups. Building rich linkages with one's world.

From James Coleman, *Abnormal Psychology and Modern Life,* 3rd ed. (Glenview, Ill.: Scott, Foresman, 1964).

from the pleasure principle, in which one lives by seeking pleasure and avoiding pain, to the reality principle—delaying immediate gratification for future reward—is basic in emotional development. Moving from ignorance to knowledge is part of education and experience, as in incompetence to competence. The move from a diffuse sexual interest to intersexual interest and activity is necessary for adequate sexual adjustment in marriage, although sexual maturity may be limited by immaturity in other areas. Going from an amoral to a moral outlook includes the acquisition of ideas of good and bad, the internalization of these values, and the development of a conscience or superego. The move from self-centeredness to other-centeredness or the capacity to care for others is a step toward mature human behavior.

The growth of intelligence and all these factors, including physical and social factors, can be plotted on a growth curve. Figure 8-2 is an example of a growth curve.

As can be seen, girls develop probably a year and a half faster than boys around puberty. Consequently, they become "mature" before boys. In addition, there are fast-developing girls and slow-developing girls, as there are fast-developing boys and slow-developing boys. These differential developmental rates are relevant to a good criminal justice system. For example, faster-developing girls may get into sexual difficulties as juveniles. At the other extreme, slow-developing boys may have difficulty in school, become dropouts, and have a higher degree of failure in social and academic pursuits; consequently, they are represented more frequently in juvenile court and in juvenile training schools.

The Birdman of Alcatraz

Robert Franklin Stroud (1887–1963), known as the Birdman of Alcatraz, became well known as a result of Thomas E. Gaddis's (1956) popular book about him and the movie of the same name. Stroud earned his living in any way that was available in his native Alaska; he was a pimp in Juneau in 1909 when he killed a bartender who refused to pay his girl friend, Kitty O'Brien, for an evening of fun. His short temper and ruthless approach had been troublesome before, but his twelve-year sentence for this killing was his first imprisonment. He began serving his time at McNeil Island in Washington but was later transferred to Leavenworth. His interest in birds began with some sick sparrows. Subsequently, he became an expert on canaries and their diseases, and his excellent reputation in this field spread beyond the prison walls. Just before he was due for parole in 1916, he killed an officer in the dining room at Leavenworth for no apparent reason. "The guard just took sick and died all of a sudden," he said. He was tried, convicted, and sentenced to death by hanging, but his sentence was commuted to life imprisonment. During his long incarceration, Stroud wrote that his hostility and aversion to authority had undoubtedly been caused by his hatred of his father, a bad-tempered drunk who had abandoned, betrayed, and deserted Stroud's mother (Morley, 1973, p. 131). He recalled that he always had been hostile and angry; furthermore, his appearance was not conducive to a good relationship with other people; he has been described as looking a "physical disgrace"—tall, thin, attractive as a barracuda, and a "flagrant homosexual." It is apparent that his home con-

FIGURE 8–2.
Differential Developmental Rates of People Who Will Have an I.Q.
of 100 at Age 21

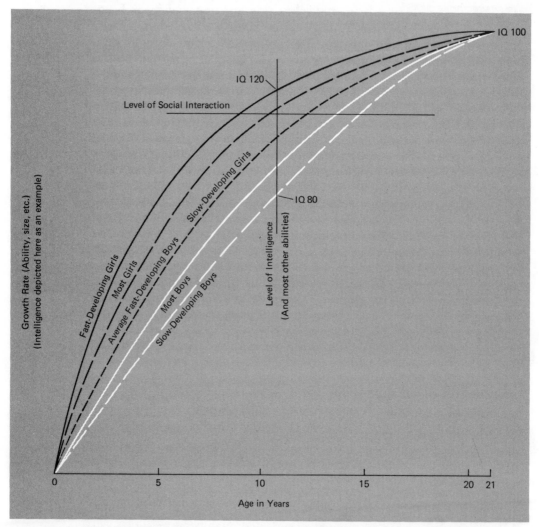

Differential developmental rates make prediction of academic and physical education success difficult. The level of social interaction indicates that younger girls may be interested in older boys and vice versa because their interests would be nearer the same level. Juvenile courts see more of the fast-developing girls and the slow-developing boys.

ditions never led to a development of the ability to have good relationships or even to form a strong and positive self-image. Thus he remained asocial, unable to communicate with people, particularly those in authority. Perhaps his birds represented his closest approach to constructive human behavior. Stroud died of old age at the United States Bureau of Prisons Medical Center at Springfield, Missouri, on November 21, 1963.

CONCLUSIONS

Human behavior, over and above basic animal behavior, involves interaction with symbols or the development of language and the subsequent development of abstract values culminating in high ideals such as concern and compassion for others. These abstract values include theology, philosophy, and ideology like liberal or conservative political or economic views. These abstract and ideological systems have sometimes been called "spiritual values" but, of course, the psychologist does not mean "spirits and demons" in this sense. Understanding of human behavior may begin scientifically, but such "nonscientific" factors as values, superstitions, and philosophies exist and must be considered. People's behavior also includes the basic conditioning that underlies the laws of learning; consequently, experiments involving rats, mice, chimpanzees, and other animals in the psychological laboratory contribute to the understanding of human behavior, but the perceptions of sociology, philosophy, anthropology, theology, and psychiatry are also needed for a complete understanding of *human* behavior.

It is apparent that ability tends to be generalized in that a capable person may be good at almost anything he or she seriously attempts. In 1922, Lewis M. Terman at Stanford University began studying 1,000 "gifted" children. Although it would have been impossible to fund, the hope was that it would be a longitudinal study that would last for years and even centuries, being picked up by contemporary scholars as time elapsed. The major report was published in 1930 (Burks et al., 1930, p. 508). A more recent report in 1973 supported the earlier findings that gifted children outperformed the population average in all areas (Fincher, 1973). They tended to be bigger and stronger, more successful in school, and better developed ethically probably because they tended to come from higher socioeconomic status, though not necessarily, and were well represented in the conventional professions such as law and medicine. On the other hand, intelligence and ability do not determine the direction in which they will be used. "Gifted" individuals can outperform most of their peers whether they are scholars or criminals. Intelligence and ability do not determine whether behavior will or will not be deviant.

One of the significant early efforts of psychology in the field of criminal justice was that of Robert Lindner and Robert Seliger (1947).

Clinically oriented, their book provided broad coverage of the field, including the clinical groupings, medical approaches, and methods of helping people. Branham and Kutash (1949), psychiatrist and psychologist respectively, also wrote a clinically oriented book that provided a still broader coverage of the field. Except for a brief and unstable publication of *The Correctional Psychologist* as the house organ of the American Association of Correctional Psychologists organized in 1950, the first significant publication specifically in correctional psychology was *Criminal Justice and Behavior: An International Journal of Correctional Psychology*, which has been the official publication of the American Association of Correctional Psychologists since 1974. In the early 1970s several books appeared that were concerned with the psychologist in corrections. (See, for example, Brodsky, 1972; and Wicks, 1974.)

Psychologists have not yet had any remarkable success in the correctional field on a national basis, but there are encouraging developments, particularly in the area of community-based correctional facilities (Brodsky, 1972, p. 159). Unfortunately, psychologists enter the correctional phase of criminal justice in a late phase of the individual's development.

Questions

1. What does intelligence have to do with crime and delinquency?
2. What is the experimental approach to psychology and how does it apply to crime and delinquency?
3. What is behavior modification?
4. What is operant conditioning?
5. What is the evaluation of the results of behavior modification approaches in crime and delinquency?
6. What is differential treatment?
7. What characterizes the Gestalt approaches to psychological therapy?
8. What is clinical psychology and how does it relate to criminal behavior?
9. What are defense mechanisms?
10. What are the developmental approaches toward human behavior, including crime and delinquency?

nine

PSYCHIATRIC APPROACHES

Psychiatry is a branch of medicine that specializes in the study, diagnosis, and treatment of mental illness or conditions that cause various kinds of behavior disturbances. The knowledge of normal development and psychological motivation applied to seemingly irrational psychopathological behavior makes possible the understanding of psychoses, neuroses, and other deviant behaviors. Psychiatry goes beyond conscious mental processes to learn about and study subconscious motivation and subconsciously repressed phenomena in order to understand personality. Psychiatrists contend that conscious mental processes and behavior that can be defined, observed, and measured represent only the tip of the iceberg, that the major part of human behavior is subconscious—disturbances of mood, affective responses, inadequate social control of emotions, conditions characterized by disorganized thinking and lapse of judgment, phobias, obsessions, delusions, hallucinations, and apparently irreversible impairment of intellectual activity comprise only a few of the concerns in psychiatry.

Modern psychiatry emphasizes the patient's genetic predisposition, the influence of his or her psychological and biochemical processes, and his or her ongoing series of life experiences beginning with the prenatal period and extending through childhood and to the present environment and cultural pressures. A human being's personality is seen as his or her characteristic recurring patterns of behavior in response to life experiences and to other persons. Psychiatry is considered a branch of medicine; psychoanalysis is a method that falls within the area of psychiatric concerns. Psychology, strictly defined, is the scientific study of behavior rather than a medical speciality.

Many modern concepts regarding psychiatric disorders developed during ancient times. As early as 860 B.C. some priests recommended kindness, physical and recreational activity, and listening to soothing music as treatment for behaviorally disturbed people. Hippocrates described many of the mental disorders that are found in modern times as early as 400 B.C. In the second century A.D., the Roman physician Galen drew attention to the brain as central in mental and behavioral functioning. The French physician Philippe Pinel (1745–1826) gave impetus to more humane and modern treatment in mental hospitals when he removed the chains from the mentally ill in the Bicêtre. The York Retreat was opened in England in 1796 through the efforts of William Tuke and his son, Henry, along with the Society of Friends (Quakers). Dorothea Dix carried on a campaign in the United States between 1841 and 1881 for the humane care of the mentally ill and of prisoners, thereby providing a psychiatric orientation to treatment programs in institutions.

Dr. Benjamin Rush (1745–1813) has been considered by many to be the father of modern psychiatry. His *Medical Inquiries and Observations upon the Diseases of the Mind,* published in 1812, was the first American book on the subject and set the stage for rational treatment of mental diseases. Dr. Rush was also an early contributor to the criminal justice system, having been one of the leaders in the penitentiary movement in 1787 that developed the first prison and the Pennsylvania system at the old Walnut Street Jail in Philadelphia in 1790.

Franz Anton Mesmer (1734–1815) had a scientific interest in the psychological factors that influenced human behavior. In Paris in 1778, he formulated the theory of a universal magnetic fluid in the body that he conceived to be of use in treatment of hysterical paralysis. Although his personal success was short and he was rejected by the profession, others studied his approach. The English surgeon James Braid used the term *hypnotism* to describe the method. A French country doctor, A. A. Liebault (1823–1904), revived it and taught many contemporaries its constructive use. Among his students was Jean Martin Charcot (1825–93), under whom Sigmund Freud studied. Charcot's success in the treatment of hysterical paralysis was reported on February 14, 1882, to the Academy of Sciences.

Sigmund Freud (1856–1939) has been credited with taking the first steps toward the theoretical structure on which modern psychiatry rests. Having studied under Charcot in Paris, he was interested in hysterical paralysis and other neurotic conditions in his subsequent practice. In 1895, he published his *Studien Über Hysterie*, in which he replaced the hypnotism or mesmerism he learned under Charcot with free association and cathartic techniques; this was the beginning of psychonalysis. Beginning in 1897, he proposed his concept of unconscious motivation, which influenced the entire field of psychiatry. His early formulations concentrated on sexual needs and their frustration, but his later writings covered a much broader spectrum. Freud's last book, *Moses and Monotheism*, published in 1939, was a masterful work with broad view and deep insight. Many psychiatrists agree that Sigmund Freud provided the framework for modern psychiatry, but he encountered difficulties when he tried to fill in the details. Even so, his brilliant and significant contributions to understanding human behavior remain basic to modern psychiatric thought.

Alfred Adler (1870-1937), an Austrian psychiatrist, founded the school of psychiatry known as the Individual School. His primary contributions are the concepts of the inferiority complex and the defense mechanism of overcompensation. He also counseled people in large groups, with individual counseling taking place in the presence of a large group of observers on the basis that they might have similar problems or might increase their understanding of human behavior.

Otto Rank (1884-1939) contributed considerably to the concept of the Oedipus complex—the libidinal feelings of the child toward the parent of the opposite sex. He considered the successful development and the resolution of this situation to be basic to the development of heterosexuality in an individual. He also considered the birth trauma to be most important.

Carl Gustav Jung (1875-1961) developed the classification of introverted and extroverted personalities, depending upon the direction of their primary focus in personal thought and activity. He rejected Freud's early theory of the psychosexual basis of neurosis and substituted an examination of man's immediate conflicts. Further, he substituted the will to live for the sexual drive in defining the libido, or life energy. According to Jung, the energy—the libido—that keeps humans going comes from the will to live rather than from the sex drive. He also focused on the possibility of cooperation between unconscious motivation and conscious behavior.

These early pioneers in modern psychiatry provided the base on which modern psychiatrists function and a point of origin for later psychiatrists who have contributed modifications and revisions of early psychiatric thought to the field so that contemporary psychiatry could develop to its present status. The American Medical Association was organized in 1847; the American Psychiatric Association was founded in 1848. The American Psychiatric Association separated psychiatry as a specialty from medicine as a whole. By the mid-1960s this association had a membership of more than 10,000 psychiatrists. By 1980, there were 27,500 psychiatrists in private practice, clinics, and hospitals in the United States, according to the American Medical Association.

Psychiatrists enjoy a central position of respect and responsibility in the field of practice in criminal justice. Some large police departments have their own staff psychiatrist, while others frequently have psychiatric assistance available by contract. Psychiatrists are central in the area of forensic psychiatry in the courts when determinations are made as to whether or not an alleged offender is competent to stand trial. In some states, like Massachusetts with its Briggs Law, a psychiatric examination is required in the cases of offenders convicted of serious and heinous crimes. Psychiatric testimony in sanity hearings is essential, though not always available. Correctional administrators frequently await a psychiatric report before releasing a potentially dangerous offender from administrative or disciplinary segregation. Parole boards use psychiatrists frequently while attempting to make decisions regarding the release of potentially dangerous persons on parole. Throughout the criminal justice system, many decisions are based upon psychiatric evaluation. It is appropriate, then, to survey the frame of reference in which the psychiatrist functions.

NORMAL PERSONALITY DEVELOPMENT

The structure of personality is composed of three hypothetical constructs: the id, the ego, and the superego (Alexander, 1952, pp. 3–34). The id (Latin third-person neuter) is the basic reservoir of drives and impulses within the person. Biologically, the id is the prime source of sexuality and aggressive impulses. Basic drives, motivations, and other personal expressions motivate the individual to action. The ego is the conscious personality concerned with perception of external pressures and expectations and internal urges, harmonizing them to ameliorate possible conflict, and guiding voluntary actions. The ego can be referred to as the conscious personality manifest in characteristic responses to stress and other stimuli. The superego is the system of internalized values the individual has learned from other people or society; it is frequently referred to by sociologists as an internalized set of values and sometimes referred to as the "conscience." It is the presence of the superego that permits the development of guilt, remorse, and feelings of morality that constitute the basic socialization process. If individuals are not adequately socialized or have not developed strong superegos, they may encroach aggressively on the rights of others. On the other hand, if they develop too much superego and too rigid a set of values, guilt feelings, emotions, and conflicts may impair their social adjustment. The id, or the internal drives like hunger, sex, and other biologically oriented motivations, and the ego, or recognition of external pressures and expectations, are present at birth. The superego is acquired through learning or conditioning after birth, particularly during the preschool period after toilet training, which is the first imposition of social control over the basic bodily needs. Development of the superego is the socialization process. The libido theory, or the generation of energy, refers to the organization of the development of behavior around the id drives of the individual, frequently referring to sex and aggression, sometimes to other drives, such as the will to live or self-preservation.

The functional interaction between id, ego, and superego is shown in Figure 9-1.

When children are born, they are mostly "id"—they do not perceive much of the outer world. Their physical needs for food, elimination, and exercise are basic. As time passes, however, they become aware of mother. During the first year, they develop the capacity to respond to many stimuli from other people in the outer world. As they grow, demands and expectations from mother, other people, and society begin to curtail thier freedom of expression and the satisfaction of their every need. They learn many dos and don'ts and social norms to which they are expected to conform. As the ego is bombarded with these demands and expectations, it transmits them, at least in part, to the subconscious. As a system of values is so internalized, the superego, or "conscience" develops. The preschool child can identify herself or himself as "good Mary" or "naughty Mary" or "good Johnny" or "naughty Johnny"; and this identification or separation of right from wrong continues throughout life.

The superego has as its functions (1) approval or disapproval of ego actions in terms of right or wrong, (2) critical self-observation, (3) self-punishment, (4) demands that the ego repent to make reparation for wrongdoing, and (5) self-love or self-esteem as the ego reward for having done right (Brenner, 1955). The superego is a split-off portion of ego that arises on the basis of identification with parents. Because the inculcation of value systems and systems of right and wrong begins at about the time of toilet training, Ferenczi referred to "sphincter morality," but this does not make itself felt until a little later. Melanie Klein (1958) thinks the superego begins earlier, probably in the second quarter of the first year.

The process of personality development is in four broad stages named after openings in the body. These are (1) oral, (2) anal, (3) urethral—sometimes called Oedipal or phallic, (4) and genital. The oral stage refers to the tasks present in the first year of life, generally identified with the mouth and sucking movement. The anal stage is obviously identified with anal needs generally regarded to begin at toilet train-

FIGURE 9-1.
Normal Personality Pattern

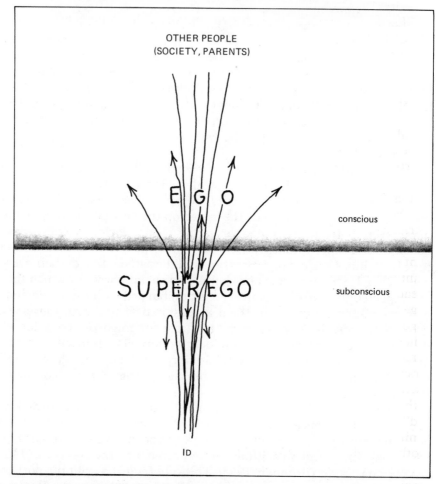

Note that the demands and expectations made on the ego are reasonable and are well internalized to form a normal internalized system of values—the superego, or "conscience." The superego "censors out" undesirable activities and urges and sometimes changes them through defense mechanisms so that they are socially acceptable and can be expressed in the altered manner.

Most offenders are "normal" as far as clinical groupings are concerned. Most property offenders and many offenders against the person for obvious and perceptible reasons can be placed in the normal clinical category.

ing. The urethral stage goes from childhood until around puberty. The genital stage is the last stage and is identified with sexual and social maturity.

Each stage can be subdivided into phases of development. The early part of the oral stage, for example, is the passive-receptive stage, in which the child does nothing but receive nourishment and attention. In the later active-incorporative phase of the oral stage, the child grasps objects and may pull them toward the mouth; he may bite the mother's breast during nourishing, which is the beginning of ambivalence. The early part of the anal stage is the passive-anal phase, characterized by identification with mother and the expression of ambivalence. The active-anal stage, which comes later, is characterized by aggression, self-assertion, and negativism manifest by the child's learning to say no. The anal-sadistic stage is characterized by testing and hitting playmates or siblings.

Movement into the urethral stage is marked by the establishment of friends, playmates, and "buddies" on the basis of selectivity rather than simply geographic proximity. It is the beginning of the establishment of the capacity for permanent relationships with others. It must be interjected here that the basic capacity for relationship with others already exists but it has to be nurtured by the mother during the oral stage of development. The Oedipal situation occurs during this urethral stage for both boys and girls. Girls become more attached to their fathers, boys to their mothers. The resolution of this situation is in the transference of the attachment to the parent of the opposite sex to other persons of the opposite sex in their own age group. This resolution is essential for emotional maturity but frequently is not achieved. The lines in the old song, "I want a girl just like the girl that married dear old Dad" exemplifies the difficulties—many girls attempt to marry men who remind them of their fathers. The unresolved Oedipal situation is another point of stress in emotional development.

The genital stage of development comes after puberty and is characterized by sexual and social maturity. It takes a long time to achieve this maturity. The earliest heterosexual attractions are transitory; subsequent attractions are physical, but may last over periods of weeks, and are frequently called puppy love, infatuation, or crushes. The narcissistic stage soon follows, in which heterosexual relationships become a series of "conquests." Girls may collect fraternity pins, costume jewelry, or other little mementos, while boys may collect such things as scarves and pictures—some have been known to paste little stars on their dashboards or cut notches in their bedposts! It is during this stage that some young people are referred to as "conceited," "arrogant," and similar names because they are obsessed with personal things such as how best to wear their hair, the best kind of smile, the figure or physique, and similar manifestations of self-absorption. It is important that this narcissistic reservoir be developed, however, because it is not until it has been satiated that a person can "give" to others emotionally. It is, therefore, a stage of emotional development through which mature people must grow. Some people grow through it and mature, some people never get through it, and some people never get *to* it. Emotional immaturity or maturity is partially defined in personal relationships with others. (See Saul, 1947; and Abrahamsen, 1958.) The growing person "falls in love" after going through the narcissistic period, and another person, of the opposite sex, becomes more important than oneself. Emotional commitment to the other person is so intense that sometimes the person is blind to faults and failings of the love object. After marriage, however, the "mask" comes off and unromantic reality must be dealt with. It is at this stage that some people have remarked, "I thought I was in love, but I was only in heat!" Successful adjustments to a permanent heterosexual relationship necessitates social and sexual maturity that comes from full and normal development through the oral, anal, urethral, and genital stages.

Deviant behavior occurs when the individual has not developed fully and normally through these stages. Emotional development may be arrested, retarded, or "snagged" at any stage. Sometimes regression occurs when the next stage is uncomfortable. The psychiatrist's approach to therapy is the identification of the area of the problem and helping the individual in therapeutic interviews to "work through" his or her problem and either correct it or learn to live with it.

The psychiatric approach posits libido as the energy that motivates life, primarily the sex drives but also other biological drives. Other terms that have been used for this energy or motivation have been *instinct*, *horme* (McDougall), and *élan vital* —the vitality of life (Bergson). At any rate, the libido is considered to be the energy that motivates sex, aggression, and survival in general. Libidinal pleasures include eating and drinking, elimination, sex, masturbation, and manipulation of erogenous zones.

The defense system is concerned with the acquisition of techniques by which conflicts between the individual and the outside world can be harmonized or accommodated. If these conflicts are not harmonized or accommodated, then mental ill health and deviant behavior must result. The defense techniques generally adopted by normal persons are well known. The defense mechanisms suggested by Coleman, a psychologist, were presented in the previous chapter on psychological approaches; those accepted by psychiatrists are similar. Franz Alexander, a psychiatrist, suggests the following: (1) repression, or excluding undesirable concepts from consciousness; (2) overcompensation, or taking a stance opposite from what is really wanted, such as guilt for not liking someone resulting in oversolicitiousness to that person; (3) rationalization, or finding an acceptable reason for doing what one wants to do, anyway, but for less acceptable reasons; (4) identification, or assuming the qualities of an opponent to reduce anxiety; (5) substitution and displacement, such as replacing murderous impulses with a minor aggression, chopping wood, or other activity; (6) sublimation, or substituting for an unacceptable tendency another one that is appropriate and socially useful, such as substituting creative arts or dancing for sexual activity or substituting sports or debate for aggression; (7) projection, or placing one's own blame on others by misinterpreting reality; (8) provocative behavior, or excusing one's own aggression by inducing another to attack or "draw" first; (9) turning feelings toward one's self, or self-criticism and self-accusation rather than attacking others; (10) isolation, or avoiding people or incidents, most common in the compulsive neuroses; (11) regression, or a return to previous modes of gratification or an earlier and happier childhood; (12) defense against guilt feelings, or expressing masochistic behavior by self-punishment; (13) defense against inferiority feelings or overcompensatory bravado, aggression, and braggadocio; and (14) conversion, or repressing ego-alien tendencies that find expression in physical symptoms like tics, spasms, convulsions, ulcers, or functional blindness, paralysis, and other incapacitations without organic basis (Alexander 1952, pp. 12–16) The normal use of these defense mechanisms results in normal adaptation in society. When they cannot be used normally to support ego integration or the personality, deviant behavior results.

Stress situations in which individuals find themselves can be diagrammed. Individuals have their own personalities and egos or individuality, together with their needs and desires; other people or society, however, restrict their freedom of action and impose demands from toilet training until death. There is frequent conflict and defense mechanisms are used for protection. Figure 9-2 depicts the individual at the left margin and society or the outside world at the right margin. Social pressures hit the individual's defenses first. If they get through the defenses, and reality is traumatic, conflicts arise within the individual. If the conflicts can be handled, then the ego survives, but if the conflicts are overwhelming, the ego could be damaged and mental ill health may result. Many offenders handle these situations at the defense level, particularly projection, denial of reality, and rationalization, thereby maintaining ego integrity. Freud has said that the neurotic or psychotic is not skilled in sublimation.

Normal persons can handle normal stresses and conflicts with the normal defense mechanisms acquired through normal development. The majority of offenders, however, do not go through this normal development and are not able to handle all the normal defense mechanisms in

FIGURE 9-2.
Schemata for Adaptation to Stress and Handling Conflict
that Might Produce Criminal Behavior

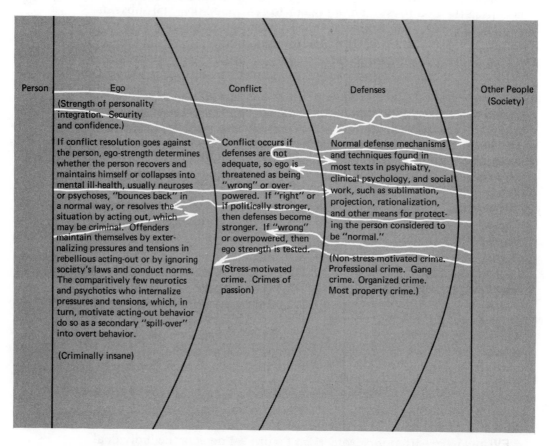

Person	Ego	Conflict	Defenses	Other People (Society)
	(Strength of personality integration. Security and confidence.)			
	If conflict resolution goes against the person, ego-strength determines whether the person recovers and maintains himself or collapses into mental ill-health, usually neuroses or psychoses, "bounces back" in a normal way, or resolves the situation by acting out, which may be criminal. Offenders maintain themselves by externalizing pressures and tensions in rebellious acting-out or by ignoring society's laws and conduct norms. The comparitively few neurotics and psychotics who internalize pressures and tensions, which, in turn, motivate acting-out behavior do so as a secondary "spill-over" into overt behavior.	Conflict occurs if defenses are not adequate, so ego is threatened as being "wrong" or over-powered. If "right" or if politically stronger, then defenses become stronger. If "wrong" or overpowered, then ego strength is tested.

(Stress-motivated crime. Crimes of passion) | Normal defense mechanisms and techniques found in most texts in psychiatry, clinical psychology, and social work, such as sublimation, projection, rationalization, and other means for protecting the person considered to be "normal."

(Non-stress-motivated crime. Professional crime. Gang crime. Organized crime. Most property crime.) | |
| | (Criminally insane) | | | |

a normal way; consequently, stress and conflict affect them more quickly. This is why they are frequently more quarrelsome and why proportionately more fights occur in prisons and in this group than in the general population. Inadequate handling of stress and conflict is characteristic.

Civilization's primary mental health problem is anxiety. People are concerned with security, accomplishment, and prestige, are worried about the future and guilt laden about the past. The alleviation of anxiety has become most important to civilized humans, as compared with primitive man, who was more fatalistic and less concerned about the future. There are various methods of alleviating anxiety. Alcohol, drugs, tranquilizers, entertainment, athletics, counseling and psychotherapy, and many other factors and programs are available for this purpose. Religion has been the greatest agent for reduction of anxiety. Crime is an anxiety-reduction agent, also, for people who perceive themselves in crisis and have to take drastic measures to alleviate it. Because they too are anxiety reducing, it may well be that alcohol and drugs have reduced the crime rate rather than increasing it, because anxiety-ridden people may resort first to alcohol and drugs and engage in crime as a last resort or to support their primary reaction. At least, some psychiatrists have so suggested.

Anxiety states are conflicts between individual needs and group mores, in which fear becomes the motivating emotion in anxiety. Precipitation of anxiety states can be by (1) guilt feelings, (2) ego involvement associated with inability to compete, (3) emotional development retardation, and (4) inability to see a way out of an intolerable situation because of restricted outlets. Guilt feelings may be associated with homosexual incidents, heterosexual experiences, desire to injure loved ones, masturbation, voyeurism, and similar unacceptable behavior. Ego involvement may involve jealousy, social or economic favor, protecting "honor" in knife fights, gambling fights, or other fights related to ego involvement. Separation anxiety can be excruciating, as many people who have experienced it in the form of homesickness know. Socialized people need other people. Further, they need to be needed. People have a basic need to invest emotionally in others, which provides the basis for socialization. Release from anxiety can be in physical symptoms like headaches, functional disorders like psychosis and neurosis, sedatives and drugs, sports, television and other entertainment, or criminal behavior in the form of suicide, homicide, desertion and abandonment, and many other releases.

DEVIANT BEHAVIOR AND CRIME

Two questions must be answered in order to understand deviant behavior:

1. How stressful is the environment?
2. How stable is the personality bearing that stress?

The sociologists and economists emphasize the first question, while the psychiatrists and the clinical psychologists emphasize the second. Both must be answered to gain an understanding of crime. The central concern of the psychiatric approach is the emotional vulnerability of the personality to outside pressures.

Deviant behavior can be classified according to patterns of deviance frequently observed in psychiatric patients. Rather elaborate classifications of deviant behavior can be grouped into (1) psychoses, (2) neuroses, and (3) antisocial personality disorder, psychopathy, or sociopathy. (See Strahl and Nolan, 1972.) In the psychoses, the defenses cannot stand up and the ego is overwhelmed. The psychoses refer to conditions that alienate individuals from society so that they live in their own world of hallucinations and delusions. Organic psychoses may result from brain lesions, extreme alcoholism, paresis resulting from advanced stages of syphilis, old age, and other physical conditions. Functional psychoses are manic-depressive psychoses and extreme depressions and schizophrenia, which is the largest group of psychoses. The schizophrenias can be divided into (1) simple, (2) catatonic, (3) paranoid, and (4) hebephrenic schizophrenia. Simple schizophrenia is a complete withdrawal from social interaction and is hardest to treat. Catatonic schizophrenia has physical symptoms in that a person can be placed in a specific position and will stay there until fatigue causes a change. Paranoid schizophrenia, even with the delusions of grandeur, is probably the most dangerous to others because individuals believe that people are against them and that they can retaliate with assault or homicide against anyone who happens to be in their delusional system. The hebephrenic is generally happy, has delusions of grandeur, and has little reason to "come back" to reality or the world. Crimes committed by schizophrenics fall into four categories: (1) violence, (2) crimes that result from gradual deterioration, such as burglary, (3) vagrancy and allied offenses such as stealing food or small economic crimes, and (4) sexual perversions of bizarre and dangerous types. The paranoid schizophrenic will take action and assault on occasion when another person is involved in his elaborate delusional system. In a depression and mania, suicide or homicide may occur; the manic phase results in exaggeration—the person is generally too excited to plan a crime but may be violent. Figure 9-3 depicts the relationship between id, ego, and superego in the psychoses.

There are several types of neurotic conditions (Alexander and Ross, 1952, chaps. 5 and 6) in which the ego is overly rigid, sometimes artificially held rigid by anxiety. Contact with the world is extremely close and some behavior results in meticulousness and nit-picking. The hysterical conditions can be divided into (1) anxiety neuroses, (2) phobias or pathological fears, and (3) conversion hysterias by which emotional pressures are released through bodily symptoms that can include hysterical blindness, paralysis, and other incapacitations, some of which can be cured by faith healers, clergy, and other nonmedical people provided the individual's faith is strong enough. The obsessive-compulsive states are a dynamic equilibrium between ego-alien or undesirable tendencies and desirable tendencies resulting in precariously balanced rituals that exaggerate social standards, such as cleanliness, punctuality,

FIGURE 9-3.
Psychotic Pattern

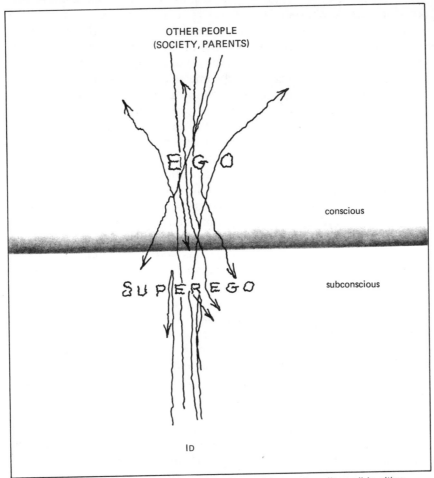

Note that the ego is unstable and shaky and does not transmit reality well in either direction. The superego does not make much difference. Rather than seeing reality, this ego experiences hallucinations and delusions. Most psychotics are not dangerous, but they may be when delusions of persecution are focused on someone else who may then be in danger. Examples of criminally insane or psychotic offenders are Howard Unruh, who shot down thirteen people in Camden, New Jersey, in 1949, and Edward Gein of Wisconsin, who robbed many graves and killed at least two women and was eating them when he was apprehended in 1957. Both have been committed to mental hospitals as criminally insane, Unruh in New Jersey and Gein in Wisconsin. Both cases are discussed later in this chapter.

and other approved tendencies. The obsessive-compulsive neurosis is of interest to the criminologist because the "irresistable impulse" frequently reported in crime is the obsessional thinking and compulsive acts that occur in this type of neurosis. The hysterias are more rare in criminology but are expressed in exaggerated expense claims, borderline white-collar crime, and the Ganser Syndrome, sometimes referred to as prison psychosis. Much crime committed by neurotics, particularly compulsive auto theft, forgery, and some sex offenses, come from this group. The depressions in the neurotic pattern result from repressed hostility. Hypochondriasis is an anxious preoccupation with one's own body and health. Fearful expectation of disease indicates a need for suffering and all one's love and attention can be centered upon oneself. Some alcoholism, drug addiction, and sexual perversions have been diagnosed as having a neurotic base and etiology. Figure 9-4 depicts the relationship between the id, ego, and superego in the neuroses.

The antisocial personality disorder, long called psychopathy until the American Psychiatric Association changed the terminology to sociopathy in 1952 and to antisocial personality disorder in 1968, is the largest single clinical grouping in prisons and correctional caseloads. (See Cleckley, 1955.) People with this disorder have been characterized as lacking in guilt and anxiety, unable to profit by experience, unable to postpone immediate gratification for future reward, and lacking in the deep emotional responses that support stable relationships, religion, and other areas requiring appreciation or a commitment. Figure 9-5 depicts the relationship between the id, ego, and superego in the person suffering antisocial personality disorders.

The American Psychiatric Association publishes the *Diagnostic and Statistical Manual of Mental Disorders* which codes mental disorders. According to this source, the largest clinical group found in prisons is the Antisocial Personality Disorder (formerly Psychopath) depicted in Figure 9-5, coded 301.70. The World Health Organization has a similar manual, *Mental Disorders: Glossary and Guide to Their Classification in Accordance with the Ninth Revision of the International Classification of Diseases.* Such coding facilitates communication and provides computer data bases in all pertinent areas. Most psychiatrists use the labels in the manual for purposes of communication but seldom use these labels while working with people. They are more concerned with emotional dynamics and the organic and functional personality problems of their patients than with labels. In fact, when psychiatrists have to make out monthly reports from mental health clinics or hospitals, they frequently have to arbitrarily assign the last few cases to the least objectionable classification. It must be noted here, also, that the majority of people in prisons and correctional caseloads do not fit into an abnormal clinical grouping, according to the majority of psychiatrists,

FIGURE 9-4.
Neurotic Pattern

OTHER PEOPLE
(SOCIETY, PARENTS)

E G O

conscious

SUPEREGO

subconscious

ID

Note the heavy demands and expectations made on the ego, which responds by internalizing a heavy component of values—superego, or "conscience." This results in difficulty in self-expression, the internalizing of hostility, and the creation of heavy components of guilt and anxiety. This personality is supersocialized to the extent that internalized hostility, anxiety, and other pressures may result in nail biting, ulcers, and other psychosomatic disorders, compulsive eating and/or drinking, drug use, or "fanatic" adherence to some belief or cult. It is the obsessive-compulsive neurotic who may commit repetitive crime like auto theft and forgery.

William Heirens is an excellent example. Burglar and murderer, he killed four females, the last being six-year-old Suzanne Degnan, in 1946. Psychiatric reports indicate that he was a neurotic of the hysteria type, emotionally insensitive, with deep sexual perversion and a "sex is dirty" attitude. (See Foster Kennedy, Harry R. Hoffman, and William H. Haines, "Psychiatric Study of William Heirens," *Journal of Criminal Law and Criminology* 38, no. 4 (1947–48), 311–41.)

FIGURE 9-5.
Psychopathic Pattern; Subsequently Called Sociopathic (1952)
and Antisocial Personality Disorder (1968)

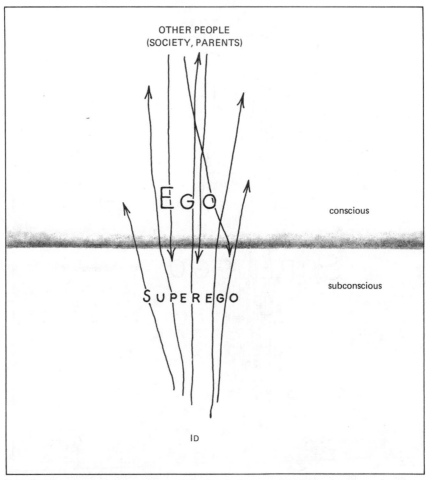

Note that few demands by society get through to form an internalized system of values or superego. In turn, deficient superego does not "censor out" much, so the personality acts out his stresses and does not develop anxiety. Thus, he becomes more dangerous to society than the normal personality. He "acts out" urges and tensions without remorse because he has little to feel sorry "with" and projects blame for any trouble he gets into onto society and "the system."

Psychopathic (sociopathic, antisocial personality disorder) persons are not as well diagnosed as are the neuroses and psychoses or those having the legal definition of insanity. From reported behavior patterns, however, it would appear that Al Capone and John Dillinger might be two examples. Both of these men have been discussed in previous chapters. Theodore Bundy, who was sent to Florida's death row in 1978 for killing two members of the Chi Omega sorority at Florida State University and a twelve-year-old girl from nearby Lake City and had been convicted but escaped from jail in Utah and Colorado, was diagnosed psychopathic by psychiatrists from Seattle and Detroit. He was connected with many other homicides of women.

but are considered clinically "normal." The dynamics discussed in connection with these groupings, however, are to some extent a part of all human behavior.

Crime began to be considered from the psychiatric viewpoint toward its understanding and treatment in the early twentieth century. Healy's *The Individual Delinquent* was published in 1915; he and his wife, Augusta Bronner, published their *Delinquents and Criminals, Their Making and Unmaking* in 1926 and their *New Light on Delinquency and Its Treatment* in 1936. August Aichorn published his *Wayward Youth* in Vienna in 1925 and in New York in 1935; his early contribution was in shifting the emphasis from constitutional factors to a dynamic understanding of the individual delinquent. Franz Alexander and William Healy published *The Roots of Crime* in 1935. Eugen Kahn published *Psychopathic Personalities* in 1931. Henderson's *Psychopathic States* appeared in 1939. Karpman published his massive four-volume *Case Studies in the Psychopathology of Crime* in 1939. Abrahamsen published his *Crime and the Human Mind* in 1944 and Bromberg published his *Crime and the Mind* in 1948. These are only a few of the more significant contributions to the psychiatric literature in the area of crime and delinquency. Today, the psychiatric literature in the field of criminal justice is voluminous.

Probably the central theme in the psychiatric approach to crime and delinquency is the emotional problems a growing personality develops when normal growth in terms of psychosexual factors is interrupted. The consequences of traumatic and critical experiences can result in the arrest (fixation) or retardation of emotional development or in regression to an earlier and happier stage of development. Much of this development concerns the development of ego strength and integration and in the comfortable and supportive internalization of values to which psychiatrists refer as superego development. It most frequently occurs in the family situation. This is why Abrahamsen (1949) contends that family tensions are a basic cause of crime.

The stage in the developmental scale at which the fixation occurs determines the type of behavior that will result. Table 9–1 indicates a tabulation of the criminoses according to the stage of fixation.

The interpersonal maturity level (I-Level) theory is a sequence of personality integrations in normal childhood development (Sullivan et al., 1957). The seven stages or levels are placed in order of their degree of maturation. Delinquency appears in levels 2, 3, and 4 (Warren, 1969). Persons at maturity level 2 are individuals who have interpersonal understanding and behavior that are integrated at the level at which the world takes care of them; they see others as "givers" or "withholders." There are two subtypes at this level: asocial, aggressive people who make demands openly and are hostile when frustrated; and asocial, passive people who whine, complain, and withdraw when

TABLE 9-1.
Tabulation of the Criminoses

STAGE OF FIXATION	PRIMAL CRIMINOSIS	CRIMINOSIS IN ACTION		CRIMINOSIS IN REACTION		CRIMINOSIS IN ACTION (MINOR)
		(Criminosis in Perversion)			(Border Criminosis)	
Early Oral			Larceny of car Unlawful entry			Vagrancy
Late Oral	Patricide Matricide Fratricid		Assault and Murder	Forgery		Disorderly conduct
		Sodomy (oral)	Burglary	Embezzling		Pickpocketing
Late Oral Early Anal and Late Anal			Intermediate types of Burglary and Robbery	Intermediate types such as Extortion	Receiving	
Late Anal		Sodomy (anal)	Robbery (with gun)	Swindling		
Urethral and Phallic		Indecent exposure	Arson			
	Incest	Manipulation	Rape	Bigamy		

Arthur N. Foxe, "Classification of the Criminotic Individual," in Robert M. Lindner and Robert V. Seliger, eds., *Handbook of Correctional Psychology* (New York: Philosophical Library, 1947), p. 33.

frustrated. Persons at maturity level 3 function as manipulators who do not understand that their own behavior has something to do with whether or not they get what they want; they try to manipulate the environment to "give" rather than "deny" what they want. There are three subtypes at this level: immature conformists respond with immediate compliance to whoever seems to have the power in the environment at the moment; cultural conformists respond with conformity to a specific reference group such as a church group or delinquent peers; and manipulators operate by attempting to undermine the power of authority and to usurp the power role themselves. Persons at maturity level 4 are individuals whose understanding and behavior integration are at the level where they judge situations from an internalized set of standards and values, understand reasons for behavior, and have some ability to relate to people emotionally on a long-term basis. The four subtypes at this level are those who are neurotic, acting-out types, who respond to underlying guilt and avoid conscious anxiety and self-condemnation; the neurotic, anxious types, who respond with symptoms of emotional disturbance produced by feelings of inadequacy and guilt; the person with the situational-emotional reaction who responds to immediate family or personal crisis by acting out; and, finally, the cultural identifier, who responds to identification with a deviant value system by living out his or her delinquent beliefs.

Several studies in California were conducted in this context, beginning with the Community Treatment Project at Sacramento. The distribution of the delinquent subtypes is shown in Table 9–2.
The results of the experiments indicated that the I-Level theory is workable. A large proportion of the delinquent population could be worked with successfully in the community and without institutionalization. A clear-cut study was the Preston Typology Study (Jesness, 1968), which indicated that homogeneity in living units of a training school decreases with increasing unit-management problems.

Guilt is a motivating force in the perpetration of crime in three ways: (1) criminalistic tendencies result from exposure to antisocial influence; (2) persons develop feelings of guilt of which they are unaware and for which they unconsciously want to be punished; and (3) aggression is relative to criminal behavior. A multiplicity of factors can be made into a formula for criminal behavior as follows:

$$C = \frac{T + S}{R}$$

where C is the criminal act, T is the criminal tendency, S is the immediate situation, and R is resistance to crime (Abrahamsen, 1960, p. 37).

When emotional development is uninterrupted, a normal individual with confidence and security emerges. The nature and intensity of any

TABLE 9-2.
Distribution of Delinquent Subtypes
in Sacramento Community Treatment Project

	DELINQUENT SUBTYPES	PROPORTION OF POPULATION (BY PERCENTAGE)
Level 2	Asocial, Aggressive	1
	Asocial, Passive	5
Level 3	Conformist, Immature	16
	Conformist, Cultural	10
	Manipulator	14
Level 4	Neurotic, Acting-out	20
	Neurotic, Anxious	26
	Situational-Emotional Reaction	3
	Cultural Identifier	6

Marquerite Q. Warren, "The Case For Differential Treatment of Delinquents," *The Annals* 381 (January 1969), 48.

interruption in emotional development determines the nature and quality of resulting aberrations in social behavior. Karpman (1939) identified interruptions in emotional development in the forms of parental rejection, parental prohibitions, parental conflicts, and unexpected loss of loved ones, with traumatic incidents occurring within family relationships.

Although a single social experience may result in varying experience patterns, each individual is committed to conformity with the evolving social frame of reference, even though it might be only the "automaton conformity" referred to by Fromm (1941, p. 185), through which he or she gains emotional security by acceptance in the social formation. By reciprocal interaction between the individual and the group, then, there evolve differential emotional and intellectual response patterns on the part of individuals and resulting variances in their contributions to the group in terms of social behavior. These relatively fixed symptom complexes or syndromes include delinquency, and they rest on motivational issues (Lemkau, 1959).

It is apparent that violence can be considered to be a public health problem that spills over into criminal activity, so the emphasis must be placed on understanding it in context of the whole socioeconomic development of people (Jones, 1971). The contributions to the literature of violence comes from psychiatry, psychology, sociology, medicine, criminology, behavioral sciences, theology, and law. Violence appears in areas of social stress between individuals, between groups, and between national states.

The personality problems of alcoholics have been diagnosed in part by the dominant theme that emerges in their hangovers. Before and while he is drinking, the alcoholic is defending himself, setting up barriers; he uses alcohol to compensate for his frustrations. Karpman (1957) identified as dominant themes in hangovers (1) escape, (2) boredom, (3) compensation for disappointments, (4) defiance against threat from others, (5) calming nerves and "settling down," (6) insecurity, and (7) elimination of anxiety from guilt. During the hangover, the defenses of the alcoholics are down, they are sick and are looking for and will accept help. Alcohol reduces anxiety. A broad review of several thousand studies of alcoholics in 1979 indicated that after years of drinking, a fairly common personality pattern emerges that shows (1) weak ego, (2) stimulus augmenting or over-reaction, (3) field dependence or need for emotional support from others, and (4) neuroticism (Barnes, 1979). These factors are the result of alcoholism, rather than predictive of it.

Crime reduces anxiety for people who perceive themselves in crisis. Credit and installment buying sometimes become misused by persons unable to postpone immediate gratification by acquisition, which also reduces anxiety. It is possible that both alcohol and the credit system have reduced the crime rate by reducing anxiety, although excessive use of either can become a crime in itself. Alcoholism frequently is present in obsessive-compulsive, industrious people of high responsibility in work that keeps them "up-tight," tense, and self-sacrificing. Many are not aware of the progressive, compulsive, and gradually insidious addictive qualities of alcohol.

Neurosis or inner-tension behavior is more common in women than in men, while crime and delinquency or acting-out behavior is more common in men (Bowlby, 1973, p. 226). This situation appears to be culture bound, in that women traditionally began life in a protected and moralistic manner, while men began life in the street as early as they could make it. Men generally have been encouraged to express themselves and be outgoing, which is consistent with the androgen secretions from the biological standpoint, while women have been expected to be passive and to remain at home, again consistent with the estrogen secretions. As previously stated, crime and other deviations are culturally defined.

Victim-precipitated offenses are sometimes the result of masochistic feelings on the part of the victim, which results in the "seduction of the aggressor" (Panken, 1973, p. 56). Many accident-prone people are in this classification, with a predilection for situations involving danger, fear, and unpleasantness.

An excellent summary of emotional problems of children, incuding delinquency, was published by the Group for the Advancement of Psychiatry in 1966 and republished in 1974; supported by a succinct outline and discussion, the following things are discussed: (1) precipitating factors; (2) predisposing factors, particularly parent-child relationships; (3) contributing factors, such as illness, depressions, and limitations in the family; and (4) perpetuating factors, particularly the secondary gain in which attention or vicarious satisfaction is obtained through pathological behavior or symptoms (Committee on Child Psychiatry, 1974, p. 124).

One of the best summaries of the psychiatric role in the criminal justice system is contained in Halleck's *Psychiatry and the Dilemmas of Crime*, published in 1967. Crime is seen as an effort to gain psychological and physical equilibrium in the face of intense stress and anxiety. Psychiatrists must serve both the patient and society and try to counter the myths about crime that have led to harmful errors in terms of reaction to criminal behavior by punishment. Halleck views psychiatrists as "in the middle" in the criminal justice system because their approach to rehabilitation of the individual tends to violate the righteous indignation of law-abiding society to treatment of the offender.

PSYCHOTHERAPY

Psychotherapy, from the psychiatric standpoint, is generally individual, client-centered, and concerned with relationships. It is permissive or directive, according to the personality of the psychiatrist and the needs of the individual. In the criminal justice system, there is more directive therapy to provide the client with a "new look" at authority that is supportive and guiding, while there tends to be more permissive therapy in the mental health system. Studies have indicated that therapists who are accurately empathetic without being manipulated and who are nonpossessively warm in attitude and not considered to be phonies by their clients, can be very effective (Truax and Mitchell, 1971, p. 310).

Psychotherapists discuss in their sessions with clients all the concerns that impinge on achieving good mental health and conforming behavior. This poses a problem sometimes not well understood by nontherapists. All impulses and needs, whether acceptable or forbidden and destructive, must be discussed regardless of their conflict with social values. Forbidden and disintegrative impulses and needs must be mastered and brought under control by being converted to acceptable impulses and needs (Mahrer and Pearson, 1973, vol. I, p. 13). This is what psychotherapy is all about. A person driven by inner forces does not have to clash with external values, and that is the problem with which the therapist must work.

In the treatment of offenders, therapists often encounter clients who do not want to accept psychotherapy. Motivating the offender toward self-improvement is a teamwork situation in which all criminal justice personnel have to support each other. Motivation is a constant process. It is enhanced when the therapist accepts the individual "as he or she is" for the moment but with a view toward the future. The therapist's own values enter the situation and he or she must combine a positive social philosophy with a degree of tolerance toward the lawbreaker. Melitta Schmideberg (1958), put it well when she said that if the therapist condemns the offender, he cannot treat him; but if he condones his offense, he cannot change him.

The attitude of the offender is important to the therapist. The client who wants to improve is the easiest to treat. The asocial offender who is dissociated from society and does not care is the most difficult to motivate. Antisocial offenders with intense hatred for society are a challenge, but the fact remains that they *are* still in contact with society and are angry about it. At least, they are motivated about something, and although it may be difficult, their motivations can be channeled into socially approved directions by competent therapists who accept them as they are without becoming punitive or sympathetic.

The personal experience of prison inmates is most vital in shaping their future lives (*Handbook of Correctional Psychiatry*, 1968). Time perception, dehumanization by regimentation and taking away decision making, routinization, boredom, automaton conformity, guilt, anxiety, worry, and responsibility are only a few of the factors that condition the incarcerated personality. Patterns of reality testing, perceptions of the world, and attitude toward society are in the balance.

Therapy should be used, rather than punishment, for the chronic criminal who has already demonstrated the ineffectiveness of prior punishment. Sturup's (1968, vol. I, p. 491) approach has been in integrating as much normalcy into the institution as possible, consistent with public safety. Six-hour leaves are usual in his institution at Herstedvester in Denmark, and staff-inmate relations emphasize normalcy, rather than the "kept" and the "keeper" relationship as much as possible. Offenders tend to remain easily frustrated, alienated, impulsive, and maintain aggressive inclinations, and imprisonment does not do much to alleviate this problem. The most helpful reaction by prison officials is, while maintaining a strong perimeter for security and the safety of the public, to provide as relaxed an atmosphere as possible within the compound and avoid using basic necessities, like food, in any punishment context.

The criteria for successful psychotherapy were outlined by Knight (1941) and repeated by Strupp (1973) as follows:

1. Disappearance of presenting symptoms.
2. Real improvement in mental functioning.
   a. The acquisition of insight, intellectual and emotional, into the childhood sources of conflict, the part played by precipitating and other reality factors, and the methods of defense against anxiety which have produced the type of personality and the specific character of the morbid process.
   b. Development of tolerance, without anxiety, of the instinctual drives
   c. Development of ability to accept oneself objectively, with a good appraisal of elements of strength and weakness
   d. Attainment of relative freedom from enervating tensions and talent-crippling inhibitions
   e. Release of the aggressive energies needed for self-preservation, achievement, competition, and protection of one's rights
3. Improved reality adjustment.
   a. More consistent and loyal interpersonal relationships with well-chosen objects
   b. Free functioning of abilities in productive work
   c. Improved sublimation in recreation and avocations
   d. Full heterosexual functioning with potency and pleasure

These criteria apply to all psychotherapy, including that with offenders.

PSYCHOANALYSIS

Psychoanalysis is both a particular theory of personality development and functioning and a particular method of therapy. It is a specialization within the field of psychiatry. Psychoanalysis originated in the perceptions and clinical observations of Sigmund Freud. He observed that most patients talk freely without being under hypnosis, and he developed the technique of free association of ideas. By encouraging patients to say anything they had in their minds without regard to relevancy or propriety, he found that disturbing events discussed with anguish earlier could be discussed later with relative ease, and the sources of psychological pain eventually surfaced into the consciousness, thereby losing their crippling effect. Ernest Jones delineated seven major principles of Freud's approach: (1) determinism—psychical processes are not chance occurrences; (2) affective processes have certain autonomy and can be detached and displaced; (3) mental processes are dynamic and tend constantly to discharge the energy associated with them; (4) repression; (5) intrapsychic conflict; (6) infantile mental processes—the wishes of later life are important only as they ally themselves with those of childhood; (7) psychosexual trends are present in childhood (Kinsey and Campbell, 1970, p. 608).

Although psychoanalysis is a specialty within psychiatry, it has made several contributions to the broad field of psychiatry, whether or not the psychoanalytic method is used. The focus on the importance of subconscious motivation is understanding human behavior has been a major contribution. The concept of id, ego, and superego were first used by Freud, as was the concept of transference, or the development of a deep attachment to the therapist, either of love or hatred, sometimes representing feelings concerning parents. Freud concluded that analysis of transference and the patient's resistance to analysis were the keystones of psychoanalytic therapy. In summary, psychoanalysis has not contributed much to the field of criminology because of its expense in practice and because not many psychoanalysts have concerned themselves with crime. The contributions of psychoanalysis to the understanding of crime have to be in the form of its contributions to understanding of human behavior as a whole.

The two persons who have contributed most through psychoanalysis to the understanding of crime have been Dr. Robert Linder, who wrote *Rebel Without a Cause* in 1944, and Dr. Benjamin Karpman, with his *Case Studies In the Psychopathology of Crime*, a four-volume work published in 1939, and his later work as editor of the *Archives of Criminal Psychodynamics* and other writings. Both concluded that psychoanalysis could be helpful in crime, but that it was more expensive than society could afford. As Dr. Karpman told this writer at the annual meeting of the American Psychiatric Society in Philadelphia in

1960, a good psychiatrist may influence the lives of 125 to 135 persons in a professional lifetime. This kind of resource is simply not available to the field of criminal justice.

Freud has written that his analytic work revealed that some delinquency and criminal behavior was motivated by the preexistence of intense feelings of guilt without tangible reason. The criminal act serves to provide a "reason" and, therefore, mitigates the diffuse guilt feeling (Rothgeb, 1973, p. 186). In some cases, the preexisting guilt was a reaction to the two great basic criminal intentions of killing the father and having sexual relations with the mother.

Psychoanalytic approaches to the understanding of juvenile delinquency have been rather popular among some psychiatrists. Kate Friedlander's *The Psychoanalytic Approach to Juvenile Delinquency* was published in 1947 as a purely psychoanalytic interpretation. *Searchlights on Delinquency: New Psychoanalytic Studies* was published in 1949 by Eissler and dedicated to August Aichorn, whose *Wayward Youth* has already been mentioned as a psychiatric approach to delinquency.

Reik (1973) has suggested that psychoanalytic concepts are needed for the understanding of the attitudes of society, judges, and juries toward suspected criminals. An "innocent" man is frequently sacrificed or a guilty one unpunished because of our fear of facing our own suppressed criminal tendencies. This underlying theme is seen in Kahlil Gibran's *Jesus, Son of Man* (although Gibran was a poet, this is not just a poem—it is a small book), and in Karl Menninger's *The Crime of Punishment.*

Harry Stack Sullivan (1892–1949) was the chief proponent of a dynamic school of psychoanalysis based on sociological, rather than biological, phenomena. Also, he emphasized present events rather than events of childhood, and current interpersonal events rather than infantile sexuality. Orthodox psychoanalysts consider this to be a superficial approach, limiting itself as it did to only one classification of events—the cultural. Harry Stack Sullivan's social approach has made his work more acceptable to sociologists than are the works of most other psychiatrists. The works of Jacob L. Moreno are also accepted by sociologists. He developed the sociogram and psychodrama and originated *Sociometry,* a journal now published by the American Sociological Society.

FORENSIC PSYCHIATRY

Forensic psychiatry is a specialty in this field, designed to serve the courts. Many courts in large urban areas have their own psychiatric services, such as the Psychopathic Clinic attached to Recorder's Court in Detroit. The purpose of the forensic psychiatrist is to provide expert opinion in connection with the state of mind of any person who has been accused of committing criminal offenses. The determination as to whether or not a person is competent to stand trial is central to the due process model in the American system of criminal justice.

The question of insanity is a chief concern to the forensic psychiatrist. From the time of Edward I (1239–1307), "madness" has been considered to be a defense to crime. As early as 1765, Blackstone stated in his *Commentaries* that a man who commits a capital offense and then becomes mad should not be arraigned for it because he cannot plead to it with proper advice and caution. Further, if he becomes mad after he has pleaded, he should not be tried because he cannot make a proper defense. This principle was brought to American jurisprudence in *Freeman v. People* in New York in 1847. The concept of "moral insanity" had existed for a long time, but it began to be narrowed to the knowledge of right and wrong in the early eighteenth century. The legal definition of insanity in English law was finally focused in the McNaghten case of 1843. Daniel McNaghten thought he was being discriminated against by the prime minister, Sir Robert Peel, and tried to kill him. However, he shot Peel's secretary by mistake. When McNaghten was acquitted on the grounds of insanity, a furor arose that demanded a definition of insanity. In 1843, the law judges of England decreed in response to a request by the House of Lords that

> to establish a defence of insanity, it must be clearly proved that, at the time of committing the act, the party accused was labouring under such a defect of reason, from disease of the mind, as not to know the nature and quality of the act he was doing; or, if he did know it, that he did not know it was wrong. [McNaghten, 1843 (England)]

Since that time, the federal courts and about a quarter of the states in the United States have supplemented the McNaghten Rule with the "irresistible impulse" test if the impulse was caused by a mental disorder. Under the leadership of Isaac Ray, New Hampshire retained the "product test" rather than adopting the McNaghten Rule, when Judge Doe wrote to Dr. Ray in 1868, "The court can only instruct the jury that a product of an offspring of mental disease is not a contract or a crime (Guttmacher, 1962, p. 8). This position was upheld by the New Hampshire Supreme Court in 1869 and 1871. The District of Columbia Court of Appeals ruled similarly in the famous 1954 Durham Rule *(Durham v. United States*, 1954), but that jurisdiction has generally returned to the McNaghten Rule, leaving New Hampshire the only jurisdiction still adhering to the product test. For all practical purposes, then, the McNaghten Rule, formulated in England in 1843, supplemented in about one-quarter of the states and the federal courts with the irresistible impulse test, is considered the basis of insanity in the United States.

An Illinois case in 1966 resulted in the Supreme Court's holding that a defendant who failed to request a hearing on his competency to stand trial was denied due process when the court did not order such a hearing on its own *(Pate* v. *Robinson,* 1966). A case in Washington of a defendant convicted of murder was similarly decided in favor of the defendant on appeal because his constitutional rights had been violated by the court's failure to conduct a hearing on his competency to stand trial *(Rhay* v. *White,* 1967).

The role of the psychiatrist in court is an uncomfortable one. Guttmacher (1962) has indicated that

> they are in a large measure abandoned in practice, therefore I think the McNaghten Rule is, in a large measure, a sham. That is a strong word, but I think the McNaghten Rule is very difficult for concientious people and not difficult enough for people who say, "We'll just juggle it." [p. 10]

In the same area, Halleck (1967, p. 223) has said that "the psychiatrist is used to lend 'scientific' authenticity to a social ritual" and that he is much more of a pawn than a knight.

In practice, psychiatrists are generally available only in the urban areas, so most states permit "physicians" to testify. "Physicians" are frequently defined as persons holding licenses in the healing arts, which are not confined to medicine, so there have been instances in which the competence of the "expert witness" to access the competency of the defendant might have been in question. It must be remembered, however, that insanity is a legal status assigned by a court, the decision generally made by a civil jury, with the trial jury's also being able to acquit by reason of insanity even when the point has not been raised. As a legal status, insanity is not exactly congruent with psychosis, which is a medical or clinical condition. Psychiatrists attempt to testify that psychotics are "insane," but the medical superintendents of most state hospitals for the insane will support the contention that although psychotics do appear in the population, so do neurotics, psychopaths, seniles, and some normals. They are all "insane."

"Criminally insane" has lost favor with the psychiatric community, and definite action has been taken by several legislatures to eliminate that designation in favor of "mentally ill offenders" or "mentally disordered offenders" (Wilson, 1980, p. 6). In addition, the criminal sexual psychopath laws that began in Illinois in 1931 and spread to about thirty seven other states have been repealed in favor of "mentally disordered sexual offender" (MDSO). California replaced them in 1963, Illinois in 1968, Massachusetts in 1977, and other states followed. While there are a few states still retaining the criminal sexual psychopath laws, most have moved toward the "mentally disordered" designation. In 1975, Michigan replaced "criminally insane" with "guilty, but mentally ill"

(GBMI), which was also picked up by Illinois, Indiana, Georgia, Kentucky, and some other states. There was further discussion of GBMI after the not guilty by reason of insanity verdict on June 21, 1982, in the case of John Hinckley, who shot President Reagan.

Many jurists have deplored the Hinckley verdict, although it was the only possible verdict under current law in the jurisdiction where the trial was held. Associate Attorney General Rudolph Giuliani (1982) has suggested four alternatives: (1) shift the burden of proving insanity to the defendant, (2) accept the "guilty but insane" verdict, (3) accept the GBMI verdict, or (4) permit the jury to return a verdict of "not guilty *only* by reason of insanity." The GBMI approach has thus far received the most favorable comment from the jurists.

ORTHOPSYCHIATRIC APPROACHES

Orthopsychiatric approaches concentrate on emotional needs and unmet needs. Orthopsychiatry is the study and treatment of mental deviations known in general as borderline states—the term is probably synonymous with "mental hygiene." The American Orthopsychiatric Association is made up of psychiatrists, clinical psychologists, social workers, and representatives from other fields.

Anxiety and pressure are central in our lives. Allison Davis referred to normal anxiety and pressure as "socialized anxiety." When the anxiety level is raised too high, however, it can become pathological. The National Institute of Mental Health has published a leaflet providing suggestions for alleviating the pressure of life as follows:

1. Air it! Don't hold the problem within, but talk about it.
2. Don't adhere to the old rules. Get away for a while.
3. Own up to your fears. It is no disgrace to admit that at some time or other you have been afraid.
4. Give in! If you yield, others will, too, and the result will be relief from tension.
5. Expand your concerns. Do something for someone else.
6. Take the "tiger" by the tail. Bring the problem out into the open and you can get rid of it.
7. Don't bet on that nag. Don't nag your family or other people. If you get off their backs, they will get off yours.
8. Give the other fellow a break. Competition and cooperation are both contagious.
9. Give up the old shell game. Emerge in order to overcome the feeling of being left out, slighted, neglected, rejected, and not appreciated.

10. Time out for fun. Relaxation absorbs pressure like a sponge does water. [NIMH, 1973]

Emotional problems leading to delinquent behavior can be identified early (Bower, 1960). They can be identified by elementary school teachers by the time a child is eight years of age and in the second or third grade. Labeling theory, of course, suggests that the growing personalities become social problems *because* they have been labeled, which leaves many agencies in a quandary. If problems cannot be identified early because of fear of labeling, then how can problems be identified early enough for counseling, casework, or therapy to be effective? It becomes obvious that the problem has to be identified early if it is to be handled adequately, but a professional approach other than "name calling" should be used.

THE MYTH OF MENTAL ILLNESS

Several psychiatrists, particularly Thomas Szasz (1962, 1970), have taken the position that mental illness is really a myth and that the symptoms adopted by people called mentally ill are manipulatory and fit into the social structure of the mental hospital. When people find that these symptoms do not work to their advantage, they drop the symptoms and improve in terms of "mental health." The position holds that an individual lives in a society that forbids illegal behavior, while institutional psychiatry forbids abnormal behavior. Szasz (ibid., p. 265) presents the example of an uneducated and overburdened housewife who suddenly escapes her life of insignificance with the dramatic pretense that she is the Virgin Mary. She then receives much attention; the outside psychiatrist says she is sick, and the institutional psychiatrists attempt to prevent her from playing the role. The conclusion is that the idea of totalitarianism in the form of fascism and communism is rejected in America, but the same ideology in the form of a therapeutic state of the mental health ethic may be accepted.

There are several other approaches in psychiatry, such as transactional analysis and reality therapy, which also concern themselves with "here-and-now" responsibility and spend little or no effort on diagnosis. This approach is closer to the behavior modification and operant conditioning of behavioral psychologists than it is to most medical thought, in which the etiology of a disease or condition is of concern in diagnosis and treatment. Szasz (1960) contends that the notion of mental health and mental illness has outlived whatever usefulness it might have had and now functions primarily as a convenient myth to disguise and render more palatable the moral conflicts that occur in human relations.

TRANSACTIONAL ANALYSIS

Transactional analysis attempts to understand the interplay between the therapist and the patient for the purpose of ultimately understanding the interplay between the patient and all external reality in terms of role theory. This approach evokes implicit expressive or emotional roles and incites repetition of old transactions and illuminates the genetic source of current behavior (Grinker, 1961). The importance of the therapist's personality, value system, and techniques of interaction are important in uncovering repressed content. This idea has become increasingly important as psychoanalysts have become aware of their effect on the analytic process itself (Marmor, 1960, p. 573). There is an International Transactional Analysis Association and a *Transactional Analysis Journal.*

Eric Berne (1961) began transactional analysis in 1961, based on ego states and the games people tend to play in life. The ego states are adult, parent, and child. His idea was to use daily games, ego states, and lifestyles in a therapeutic setting. A fast and accurate description of how a person responds to social settings can thereby be achieved, and the description can then be verbalized. Role playing takes place in a group to accommodate any conflicts between the individual and his or her group by changing some responses in terms of intensity or role. The idea was expanded in Berne's *Games People Play*, published in 1964. Thomas A. Harris, one of Berne's assistants, set the philosophy of transactional analysis with his *I'm OK—You're OK*, published in 1967. Berne's *What Do You Say After You Say Hello?* in 1972 continued to elaborate on transactional analysis in a most entertaining and informative way. As a result of its simplicity and helpfulness, at least at a superficial level, transactional analysis has become popular in several prisons, including the United States Penitentiary at Marion, Illinois, and the Illinois State Penitentiary at Vienna, among others.

Basically, each person plays three well-defined roles: parent (P), adult (A), and child (C). When two people confront each other, there are six ego states involved, three in each person when they relate to each other in agreement. It could be adult to adult, parent to child and mutually reciprocated, or any other pattern in which the transactions are complementary and allow the communication to proceed indefinitely. When a husband asks where his cuff links are and the wife replies, "Why do you always blame me for everything?" a cross-transaction has occurred. Cross-transactions reduce communication and multiple cross-transactions result in confusion and antagonism.

There are four possible life positions held in respect to the person and others: (1) I'm not OK—you're OK; (2) I'm not OK—you're not OK; (3) I'm OK—you're not OK; and (4) I'm OK—you're OK. The objective in transactional analysis is to allow the individual to identify parent, adult, and child in his transaction, both on the part of himself and on the part of others. This type of role playing results in a situation like psychodrama, in which persons can see themselves in relation to others and develop some "insight" or understanding as to their roles; this can be very therapeutic.

REALITY THERAPY

Reality therapy was developed by William Glasser (1965), who became disenchanted with psychiatry and developed a system diametrically opposed to the approach used in psychiatry. In his words,

> Plausible as it may seem, we must never delude ourselves into wrongly concluding that unhappiness led to the patient's behavior, the delinquent child broke the law because he was miserable, and that therefore our job is to make him happy. [p. 30]

Reality therapy assumes that psychodiagnostic approaches and psychotherapy are used as excuses for deviant behavior. Reality therapy is based upon getting personally involved with the clients, facing them with their responsibility, and making them accept responsibility for their acts. Key words are *responsibility, involvement, here and now,* and *facing the consequences.* Reality therapy discusses the client's current situation as one of own choosing, and the objective is to make people "feel" loved and worthwhile, which is possible under proper conditions. The thrust is that aggressive dealings with persons in a therapeutic frame of reference may result in people's loving themselves more, which has to be accomplished before they can love others.

In evaluating its effectiveness in institutions, one author (Wicks, 1969) commented, "In these days of wondrous alchemy, it may be quite possible not only to make a silk purse out of a sow's ear, but a revolutionary tool out of a pig's _____." Reality therapy is probably the most controversial approach to treatment in corrections. It receives generally favorable acceptance among practitioners in the field of corrections, but is viewed with suspicion among professional psychiatrists and clinical psychologists. Of course, this would be expected in a situation in which the originator became disenchanted with psychiatry and developed a system diametrically opposed to it. After hearing one of Glasser's lectures, an older, custodially oriented superintendent remarked that they had been doing that for years and now they had a name for it.

The strength of reality therapy is that it can be understood by correctional officers, staff, and inmates not trained in the behavioral social sciences. Its weakness, on the other hand, may be in its oversimplification of human behavior and its failure to recognize some types of mental illness that may be made worse by too-severe demands and expectations.

Reality therapy has been successfully used in juvenile courts and in probation. It has also been used in juvenile institutions, particularly the Ventura School for Girls in California, where Glasser is a staff member, the Minnesota State Training School at Red Wing, and elsewhere. It is obviously successful for some, but it may be too simplistic and demanding for some complex problems and may even be damaging to some people who cannot take it. Selection of those who can benefit by it is important.

The theory of reality therapy has been applied to schools on the basis that the cause of faulty education lies in the school programs themselves that have a high rate of failure. Glasser (1969) suggests schools without punishment but with discipline, no excuses, positive involvement and individual responsibility by students, and no failure.

DANGEROUS OFFENDERS AND THE PSYCHIATRIST

In the context of criminal justice, dangerousness involves the potential for and probability of, inflicting serious bodily harm on another person. In a ten-year study of 592 male convicted offenders—of whom 226 were considered to be dangerous offenders and were committed to a special unit for the purpose—after a psychiatric treatment period averaging forty-three months, 82 were discharged upon recommendation of the clinical staff; 5, or 6.1 percent, were returned for serious assaultive crimes, including one murder, which was considered to be a good record for these offenders (Kozol et al., 1972). The Massachusetts Center for the Diagnosis and Treatment of Dangerous Persons at Bridgewater had demonstrated that dangerous offenders could be successfully diagnosed and treated in a psychiatric setting.

Factors found by Kozol as being significant in diagnosing dangerous offenders include the following:

1. Has actually inflicted, or attempted to inflict, serious injury on another person.
2. Harbors anger, hostility, and resentment.
3. Enjoys witnessing or inflicting suffering.
4. Lacks altruistic and compassionate concern for others.
5. Sees himself as a victim rather than an aggressor.
6. Resents or rejects authority.
7. Is primarily concerned with his own discomfort.
8. Is intolerant of frustration or delay of satisfaction.
9. Lacks control of his own impulses.

10. Has immature attitudes toward social responsibility.

11. Lacks insight into his own psychological structure.

12. Distorts his perception of reality in accordance with his own wishes and needs.[1]

Conversely, factors found in a safe person include:

1. Has generally mature attitudes toward social responsibility.

2. Has developed a compassionate concern for the welfare and interests of others.

3. Has divested himself of hostilities and resentments.

4. Is relatively free of gross distortion of reality.

5. Has developed insight into his own nature.

6. Has dealt with those factors in his personality conductive to the state of being dangerous.

7. Appears to have developed strong conditioning against repetition of his original offensive behavior.

8. Accepts responsibility for his past behavior.

9. Specifically recognizes that freedom in the community involves *responsibility* as well as *gratification*.

Probably the most important factor is the analysis of the action of the aggressor as seen by his or her victim during action while inflicting injury. Psychiatrists do not use psychological tests except for specific items and do not believe there is a single test that can identify dangerousness. In combination, psychological tests are seen as sometimes useful to supplement diagnostic procedures.

Psychiatrists in the criminal justice system have noted with despair the lack of interest in the treatment of violent offenders who kill and torture. The general public and political decision-making bodies tend to demand executions or imprisonment for life or long periods. Psychiatric concerns are seldom heard on suitable institutional frames for treatment. Psychiatrists can play an active part in the treatment of violent offenders and can be influential in bringing about an acceptable kind of "law and order" that is intelligent, sophisticated, and effective (Stürup, 1973).

---

[1]Harry L. Kozol, *Provisional Guidelines for Diagnostic Identification of The Dangerous Person* (mimeographed, 5 pp.). (By permission of the author, Director of Psychiatry, Department of Mental Health, Commonwealth of Massachusetts, and Director of the Center for the Diagnosis and Treatment of Dangerous Persons, 330 Beacon Street, Boston, Massachusetts 02116)

THE "CRIMINAL PERSONALITY"

In 1976–77, Yochelson and Samenow (1976, 1977) proposed a "criminal mind" type of explanation for crime. The general idea was that there are about fifty serious thinking errors characteristic of the "criminal mind." Lying, cheating, bullying, manipulation, sexuality, self-concept of failure, lack of time perspective, failure to put oneself in another's position, failure to consider injury to others, failure to assume obligations, lack of responsible initiatives, lack of trust, pretentiousness, superoptimism, celebration after a crime, deferment of debts and obligations or failure to recognize them, irresponsibility, power orientation, fragmentation, and suggestibility are a few of those errors in thinking. In working with the criminal, the search for causes as seen by sociologists must be abandoned. If behavior is "caused" by a poor neighborhood, poor socioeconomic status, poor family background, and other disadvantages, then the offenders, themselves, become the "victims" and are not responsible for their behavior. This approach revives the moralistic view of behavior as compared with "crime causation" as depicted in the social and behavioral literature.

The contentions in Yochelson and Samenow's books have aroused considerable controversy in the field of criminology. The most favorable review was by Joseph Borkin (1976) in the *Federal Bar Journal*, who maintained that the findings were logical and challenged the traditional concepts of criminology and may prove to be shattering to the entire system of criminal justice. The majority of reviews were negative, indicating that Yochelsen and Samenow had ignored the research evidence in the literature, that no relationship could be found between the authors' methods and data, on the one hand, and their conclusions, on the other, and generally that the work had provided more heat than light (Alpert, 1977; Glick, 1979; Sarbin, 1979). There was a tendency for lawyers, jurists, and the clergy to accept the thinking expressed in *The Criminal Personality* and for social scientists and correctional administrators and practitioners to reject it.

The Criminally Insane: Howard Unruh and Edward Gein

In 1970, there were 433,890 persons in mental hospitals and 328,020 in adult correctional institutions, which is a ratio of about 1.3 to 1. In addition, there were approximately 15,000 "criminally insane," "mentally disordered offenders," or other legal designation of mentally ill offenders in maximum security mental hospitals committed by the courts. It is estimated that about 3 percent of those sent to prison are mentally ill, which would be just under 10,000. Psychiatrists have estimated that about 20 percent of all persons in prisons need long-term psychiatric care, even though they may not have been declared "insane." This would mean that 82,461 of the 412,303 persons in prison in the United States on December 31, 1982, are in need of psychiatric care. Consequently, the number of mentally disordered persons in the criminal justice system who need psychiatric help is significant.

Two dangerous criminally insane offenders who are still in state hospitals for the criminally insane are Howard Unruh of New Jersey and Edward Gein of Wisconsin.

Howard Unruh (b. 1921) was born and raised in Camden, New Jersey. He was a quiet boy, whose parents had made sure that religion was part of his daily life. Withdrawn, expressionless, and a "loner," Unruh went willingly into the army during World War II. He became a sharpshooter and spent considerable time with his rifle. Instead of going out with the rest of the boys to look for girls, he usually stayed in the barracks with his rifle, reading the Bible. Overseas he served as a machine gunner in a tank; in his diary, he listed all the Germans he had killed, together with details. Unruh was honorably discharged after the war and was given seven commendations for his coolness under fire. Studying at Temple University to be a pharmacist and continuing his Bible classes, he met the only girl he ever dated, but it led nowhere. Unruh gradually became a recluse in his parents' home, setting up targets in the basement and practicing shooting. He tried to seal himself off from the neighbors by building a high fence around the house; and those who bothered him in the slightest were added quietly to his hate list. Finally, after someone had stolen the gate to his fence, he decided to kill the neighbors. With his 9mm German Luger and another pistol, he methodically killed thirteen people. Only when he returned home for more ammunition did he stop his passionless slaughter, and by that time, the police had mobilized. He was soon captured and sent without trial to the New Jersey State Mental Hospital as criminally insane.

Edward Gein (b. 1906) was born and raised in Plainfield, Wisconsin. He was considered to be a hard-working, quiet, unassuming farmer with a smile for everyone. His mother was probably instrumental in causing his deviance; until she died, she fiercely protected him from women, making him stay at home to care for the farm. After her death, Gein began to feed a new and sinister appetite. He sealed off his mother's room and lived alone, reading books on anatomy. He no longer tended the farm but lived on governmental subsidies through the soil conservation program. Probably inspired by the contemporary news stories about Christine Jorgensen, Gein decided that he wanted to be a woman. With a friend, he started digging up the graves of women in remote areas. Then he skinned each cadaver and kept some heads, sex organs, hearts, and other parts that were of interest to him. He also committed sexual acts with the bodies. When he finally tired of looting graveyards, Gein decided to look for live victims. He shot and killed Mary Hogan, 51, and later Mrs. Bernice Worden, taking both bodies to his house. He was later discovered actually cooking and eating parts of the women's bodies. Skin ornamentation decorated his house, nine dead masks had been made from skinned faces of women, and the refrigerator was stocked with human flesh and organs. Gein had become a cannibal; parts of at least fourteen bodies were found. Gein was ultimately committed to Wisconsin's Central State Hospital for the Criminally Insane.

CONCLUSIONS

Psychiatry has made a considerable contribution to the field of criminal justice; psychiatrists are respected professionals in that administrators in all phases of the system base many responsible decisions on psychiatric testimony. Psychiatrists have not developed theories of crime, as have the sociologists, because their concern is the broader area of all human behavior, and they consider crime to be a legal label applied after a type of adaptive behavior has occurred. Their concern is generally focused on normal development and socialization patterns and normal child-parent relationships. Deviant behavior occurs when this development is fixated or arrested and when child-parent relationships are not normal.

Social workers began to be educated as psychiatrists' assistants in the 1920s for the child-guidance clinics. Similarly, during and after World War II, clinical psychologists were educated to substitute for and assist psychiatrists because of the short supply and the great need seen by the military forces and the Veterans' Administration. The result was that social workers and clinical psychologists generally accept the psychiatric viewpoint. Because the relatively large number of social workers and slightly fewer clinical psychologists in the criminal justice system do most of the casework and "treatment" in juvenile courts and institutions, in probation, prison, and parole, the clinical psychiatric approach to changing behavior is probably the most prevalent approach in practice, though not in empirical research nor in the academic study of crime; the latter has been the domain of sociologists and experimental psychologists.

Questions

1. What is the relationship between the three hypothetical constructs in psychiatry—the id, ego, and superego?
2. How can subconscious motivation result in crime?
3. What is emotional immaturity?
4. What two questions must be asked in order to understand deviant behavior?
5. Why are intrafamily tensions important to deviant behavior?
6. Describe the interpersonal maturity or I-Level approach to the explanation of crime and delinquency.
7. What is the problem of forensic psychiatrists testifying in insanity hearings?
8. What is the basic approach in transactional analysis?
9. What is the characteristic approach of reality therapy?
10. How can dangerous offenders be identified?

ten

GANGS, GROUPS, AND ROLES

Human behavior is, to a large extent, group behavior. The socialization process itself involves the assimilation of the beliefs, attitudes, prejudices, ideologies, and values of the group into which individuals are born and grow. The better they assimilate these beliefs and values, the better socialized they are. Anthropologists and biologists indicate that the genus *homo sapiens* is naturally a herding or gregarious group. This is why early humans traveled in tribes. People have a basic need to invest emotionally in other people. This explains why most societies practice monogamy. Marriage vows for life, the permanence of other relationships, and the predictability of credit ratings are important. People base their lifestyle on trust, faith, and confidence in others—this is called *socialization*. Persons who do not so live are called antisocial.

People are changed by other people, not by "programs." Programs are simply delivery systems by which people are brought into contact with other people who need them. In the absence of formal programs, people will gang anyway. There may be a type of "natural selection" going on in which people complement the emotional needs of other people, resulting in a rewarding and successful permanent heterosexual adaptation in a marriage, a social club, a quartet, an athletic team, an organization in industry or commerce, the in-group of a government, or a street gang. In any case, group behavior is an important component of human behavior. Any examination of human behavior, including criminal behavior, that does not involve group behavior, would be *prima facie* deficient.

Basic biological and emotional behavior, including sex, aggression, hunger, exercise, and free expression, conditioned responses, and similar behavior are individual and universal. Social behavior, such as the "pecking order" or the effectiveness or role an individual has in a social organization or formation is also individual, but it varies with surrounding social pressures and influences. Culture, or our way of doing things, is primarily group behavior. Individuals who assimilate the culture and accommodate to "the system" gain in social and economic power and influence. On the other hand, people who do not assimilate the culture adequately and who resist "the system" become isolates and are characterized by powerlessness within the system and may identify areas of social problems.

GANGS

Frederic Thrasher's (1927) study of 1,313 gangs in Chicago, mentioned in an earlier chapter, still stands as the classic in the field. Thrasher noted the transitory, unstable, and open-ended nature of the gang. Many of the members participated in gang activities for about three years, matured, married, and went on to young adulthood. Only a relatively few gangs, some with criminal purpose, had formal organization and were relatively stable. The majority of the gangs themselves were relatively permanent, but their membership was transitory. Thrasher's findings have been corroborated, supported, and modified by various studies since 1927. Lewis Yablonsky (1959) supported the concept of instability in most gangs. Cavan (1962) found that most gangs were loosely federated small cliques or straight clubs with informal and rapidly changing leadership, while some were more formal organizations with an aged hierarchy and specific leadership.

Clifford R. Shaw and Henry D. McKay (1942) indicated that the majority of delinquents in Chicago had engaged in delinquencies in company with others, though not necessarily with a formal gang. Approximately 88.2 percent of boys who came to juvenile court in Chicago had committed their delinquencies with others, while 93.1 percent engaged in stealing had been in company with others. Sheldon and Eleanor Glueck (1950) studied 500 delinquents and found that 492 or 98.4 percent associated primarily with other delinquents, while 500 nondelinquents living in similar neighborhoods associated with delinquents in only 37 cases or 7.4 percent of the group. William Lentz (1956) found that 22 percent of a group of rural training school boys were members of delinquent gangs, while 87 percent of urban youth were members of gangs. Eynon and Reckless (1961) found that 77 percent of all the boys committed to the Ohio Boys' Industrial School committed their first delinquent acts with companions. After the age of 13.1, 73 percent were with companions when the first delinquency occurred.

Richard Cloward and Lloyd Ohlin (1960) published a study in which they attempted to combine and synthetize Merton's anomie theory with Sutherland's theory of differential association and proposed the existence of three types of gangs: (1) criminal, (2) conflict, (3) retreatist. The criminal gang was committed to theft or other types of activity. The conflict gang was a fighting gang. The retreatist gang was made up primarily of drug users. It might be noted here that Yablonsky (1962, pp. 149–50) classified gangs into (1) delinquent gangs, (2) violent gangs, and (3) social gangs that are not delinquent. Following Cloward and Ohlin's classification, Short, Tennyson, and Howard reported (1963) that they could find no criminally oriented gangs in Chicago, and after extensive searching and inquiry, they were able to locate one drug-oriented gang. It was also noted that gangs that steal also fight occasionally (Short, 1963). The gangs described by Cloward and Ohlin were generally committed to norms in opposition to those held by the larger society but had withdrawn their allegiance to legitimacy and adopted new patterns to equalize their social status; it was held that gang behavior was motivated by failure or anticipation of failure of achieving goals by socially approved means. They may bend their efforts to reform the social order, dissociate themselves from it, or rebel against it. It should be noted that textbook classifications of gangs are much more specific than are the gangs, themselves, so that a single gang may engage in all the mentioned activities or simply remain a social gang without delinquency, conflict in fighting, or use of drugs [Short, 1963]. The role and function of gangs in the inner cities have remained quite constant, as seen by comparing Brace's *The Dangerous Classes of New York*, published in 1872, with Sgt. Collins' *Street Gangs: Profiles for Police*, published by the New York City Police Department in 1979.

Albert Cohen (1955) stressed the function of the gang in resolving the status frustrations of working-class boys. Lower-class male adolescents are at a competitive disadvantage in gaining access to legitimate success. When they attribute their failure to injustices in the social system, they may (a) bend their efforts to reforming the social order, (b) dissociate themselves from it, or (c) rebel against it. Cloward and Ohlin (1960, p. 121) pointed out that using the same criteria of evaluation without increasing opportunities available to lower-class adolescents accentuates the conditions that produce feelings of unjust deprivation and discrimination. Research has not completely supported this approach, though a tendency is found. Reiss and Rhodes (1963) found that only 28 percent of delinquents and 16 percent of nondelinquents were aware that their clothing and housing were not as good as those of their fellow students. A study at Ohio State (Landis et al, 1963) found only a slight association between delinquency proneness and perception of limited opportunity. A Chicago study (Gordon et al., 1963) indicated that the values of delinquent gangs, together with their aspirations, resemble closely the values of middle-class boys.

The function of the gang is most important, because it provides the *raison d'etre* for the gang's existence. First, it permits the gang members to explore the extent to which each is willing to go in accepting alternative rules for action. Second, it enables them to explore the extent to which they can rely on each other for support if they take a daring, rebellious, or delinquent path. Third, it gives each member an opportunity to test the degree to which his techniques of neutralizing the influences of law-abiding society are accepted by others. Finally, it enables the gang collectively to try out various courses of delinquent actions to make the commitment that each member of the gang is willing to make to each type of action (Sutherland and Cressey, 1966). For some gang members, it also furnishes an identity and provides protection in the inner city. Miller (1958) maintains that the dominant motivation underlying gang behavior is an attempt to achieve standards of values as they are defined in lower-class urban areas.

SMALL-GROUP DYNAMICS

Society derives its strength from the effective functioning of the groups it contains in homes, communities, schools, churches, industries, business concerns, union halls, civic clubs, professional groups, and the various branches of government. To understand or to improve human behavior requires understanding of groups and group behavior. Crime, mental illness, and any other deviant behavior is deviant only in relationship to others and the group. The psychological and social forces associated with groups are the substance of group dynamics.

Several different approaches to group dynamics can be found in the literature with such classification as that given by Cartwright and Zander (1960, pp. 40–42):

1. *Field theory*, originated by Lewin (1951), holds the basic thesis that behavior is the product of a field of interdependent determinants known as "life space" or "social space" with the dynamic properties furnished by concepts of psychological and social forces.

2. *Interaction theory*, which holds that behavior is the product of interaction with others in small groups (Bales, 1950; Homans, 1950; Whyte, 1951). It views the group as a system of interacting individuals where the basic concepts are activities, interaction, and sentiment.

3. *System theories* view the group as a system where central concepts are systems of orientation and systems of interlocking positions and roles (Newcomb, 1950). Communication, input, and output are central concepts in systems approaches.

4. *Sociometric orientation* was originated by Moreno (1934) and elaborated on by Helen Jennings (1943). The sociometric orientation is concerned primarily with the interpersonal choices that bind groups of people together.

5. *Psychoanalytic theory*, originated by Freud (1922), focuses upon certain motivational and defensive processes within the individual. Concepts of identification, regression, and defense mechanisms, as well as the unconscious, are central concepts.

6. *Cognitive theory* emphasizes the importance of understanding how individuals receive integrated information about the social world and how this information affects their behavior (Asch, 1952; Scheerer, 1954).

7. *Empiricistic-statistical orientation* means that the concepts of group dynamics should be from statistical procedures, such as factor analysis making use of procedures developed in personality testing (Cattell, 1948).

8. *Formal models*, with the aid of mathematics, can deal rigorously with limited aspects of groups based on some assumptions drawn from the social sciences without comprehensive substantiative theory; this has been approached by some social scientists (Hays and Bush, 1954).

Some of the dynamics include group cohesiveness, pressures, standards, motivation, leadership, and group performance. Group cohesiveness affects morale, loyalty, interpersonal attraction and rejection, hostility and prejudice, productivity and effectiveness, and all reference-group processes. Group pressures and standards have an effect on social judgment, dissension and dissonance in social context, attitude changes toward reference groups, deviation, rejection, communications standard, and social change. Individual motivations and group goals influence the effects of cooperation and competition and the achievement of goals. Leadership affects group performance, the handling of crises, and the base of social power. Even noise levels in the classrooms have been noted by experienced teachers as a measure of learning and effectiveness of the group. The higher the noise level, the less is being learned and the greater the informal interaction between the students. In summary, communication and personal interaction make group dynamics one of the most important areas of human behavior.

The criminal justice system itself is a fascinating study of group dynamics. Delinquent gangs, offenders from nondelinquent families, interaction between police, courts, and correctional programs, combined with the fragmentation within each segment, forms a "system" that frequently does not want to become a "system." Seldom does everybody work together in the criminal justice system. Seldom are the goals similar and seldom is group cohesion strong. Prisoners have a characteristic inability to relate adequately to others, even though they may manipulate others, and many are isolates or "loners." Consequently the study of group dynamics is essential in understanding the criminal justice system.

Disturbances of the equilibrium of a previously stable group may result in individual reaction on the part of individual members who consider themselves to be injured (see Bales, 1955). Divorce, for example, can change the outlook of the rejected partner significantly. In all groups, there is a tendency for individuals to assume various roles. All social relationships assume dominance-submission roles, with leadership and following characteristic of all groups. When changes in the dominance-submission patterns, role structure, and so on disturb the equilibrium of the group, then accommodation is achieved in new patterns or the group dissolves. The "political fallout" or crises requires explanation, rationalization, and scapegoating among all members of the group. Some of the reactions to disturbed group equilibrium are frequently called "crimes of passion."

GROUP THERAPY AND GROUP COUNSELING

The use of groups in the treatment process received considerable emphasis when Lloyd McCorkle and his associates used this technique with military offenders at Ft. Knox, Kentucky, during World War II and then, with Albert Elias and F. Lovell Bixby, introduced it into the New Jersey prison system as Guided Group Interaction after the war. Simultaneously, Norman Fenton introduced group counseling into the California prison system. Description of group therapy and group counseling is most difficult because the approaches have varied so widely in form and procedure. For example, some group therapists, particularly those associated with the American Association of Group Psychotherapy, hold that a psychiatrist should be the leader of the group. The American Group Psychotherapy Association is considered to be less rigid in insisting on psychiatric background for group therapy. On the other hand, the California program was designed so that groups could be led by correctional officers and other workers who volunteered for the job and who were willing to take several weeks of training in preparation for it. Consequently, the patterns and approaches of group therapy and/or group counseling does not emerge in uniform format and procedure.

Joseph Pratt (1917) has been credited with bringing together the sparse knowledge of group therapy in 1917. Pratt had previously initiated group sessions in 1905 on a weekly basis with tuberculosis patients among the poor in Massachusetts. It was nearly two decades later that psychiatrists, including Freud, became interested in groups for purposes of changing attitudes and behavior.

The literature in group psychotherapy can be frustrating because of the wide range of phenomena that are lumped together under the single name of group therapy. They range all the way from sophisticated psychiatric and psychoanalytic approaches to the relatively unsophisticated and "practical" peer-group interactions that impose pressure on an offender by other offenders in attempts to modify his or her behavior.

An interesting attempt to classify these approaches was made by Bugental (1962), who classified the approaches into five groups: (1) process-centered groups close to group dynamics or training groups, (2) activity-project groups centering around projects considered to be therapeutic, (3) interpersonal discussion groups concerned with expressing and seeking to understand relationships among members of the group, (4) expressive-projective groups that emphasize expression through projections upon ambiguous materials and activities, and (5) analytic groups that examine the reinstatement of early emotional conditioning through transferences among patients and upon the therapists.

The *process* group reviews and examines behaviors that have facilitated or blocked understanding. The therapist sets an example as a sensitive listener and perceptive reporter and maintains a here-and-now, group-centered, rational orientation in which the client tries to increase his or her personal sensitivities. The *project* group may watch a film on parental discipline or other topics or may play roles in a variety of settings. The group therapist simply provides the projects or lectures. The clients engage in memory work emphasizing manifest reasonableness and pertinence to the activities. The *interpersonal discussion* group shares emotional responses of anger, competition, affection, and other feelings. The group therapist points out commonalities and differences in the reactions, while the patients, sensing emotional parallels with the experience of others, tend to increase their understanding. The *expressive* group reveals feelings, impulses, and fantasies and may shout, curse, weep, or manifest other reactions overtly. The group therapist interprets resistances to free expression and enforces limits on acting out, while the clients overthrow superego censorship and develop spontaneity in their behavior. The *analytic* group provides subjective associations to dreams and other analytic phenomena. The group therapist is more passive and eventually interprets resistances and transferences. The patients are alerted to symbolic meanings of their contributions while seeing the therapist as a parent and the other clients as siblings. All these approaches have been used in varying degrees in correctional settings in America.

Another type of intensive group experience has been called the sensitivity training group, the T-group, or the basic encounter group (Rogers, 1966). Sensitivity training includes a wide range of experiences in human relations that increase awareness, such as group dynamics, organizational development, and verbal and nonverbal experiences. Much of the work has been based on the research of social psychologist Kurt Lewin, who proposed field theory, and has been translated into sensitivity training by Leland Bradford, former director of the Adult Education Division of the National Education Association, Ronald Lippitt of the University of Michigan, and Kenneth Benne, of the Boston University Human Relations Center. The T-group (training group) consists of a group of ten to sixteen people who meet in residential settings for approximately two weeks. The objective of the T-group is to help individual participants become aware of why they and others behave as they do in groups. T-groups have been used with judges, inmates, and other representatives of the criminal justice system to increase their understanding of and empathy with the total system.

Encounter groups, confrontation sessions, and marathon labs are generally shorter, probably twenty-four hours or a weekend, and involve direct exposure of beliefs and feelings not usually on public display. They offer great potential in the field of criminal justice for providing understanding of the common objectives and team contributions of law enforcement, court, and corrections.

Sensitivity training has been considered to be the opposite of role playing. While role playing has a person assume his or her role as a parent, an inmate, probation officer, police officer, judge, and so on, sensitivity training has the participants divest themselves of their roles. Consequently, their interaction is as men and women rather than as police, judges, correctional officers, inmates, or other roles. The participants can then discuss their views toward issues and problems as people, rather than in the ascribed social role in which they have developed and found themselves. Sensitivity training improves the way people understand themselves in relation to other people. Participants in one sensitivity laboratory reported primary changes in the areas of better listening, sensitivity to self, better understanding, and being more considerate (Wilkinson et al., 1968).

Group psychotherapy emerged during and after World War I but was not used in correctional settings until World War II (Anthony, 1971). Since the early 1950s, the use of small-group techniques in corrections has become popular in the United States. The small-group techniques at Highfields by McCorkle, Elias, and Bixby were published in *The Highfields Story* in 1958. In guided group interaction, the peer group functions as a reinforcing agent for prevalent delinquent values or positive social values, sanctions conformity to the norms of the group, and provides status and sexual identification to the group members. Group methods have been used widely and have generally resulted in enthusiastic response from staff members. Participants have also viewed group counseling more favorably than individual counseling, probably because the presence of authority is more "diluted" than in a one-to-one situation. The group meets daily and becomes the focus for change. Many experimental programs have used group methods. The Provo experiment in Utah was financed by the Ford Foundation and was initially evaluated positively by LaMar Empey and Rabow (1961). The program lasted from 1960 to 1965 but was not picked up by the state of Utah when the Ford Foundation funding ended. The Southfields experiment by Miller in 1970 and the Essexfields experiments by Scarpitti and Stephenson in 1969 were primarily based on guided group interaction originally used in Highfields. Scarpitti and Stephenson indicated in 1966 that Cressey's statements regarding the theory of differential association were best applied in small-group techniques. Immate group leaders can also use the techniques of neutralization in groups in a denial of reality and projection of blame on society. Consequently, leadership of a group must be sensitive to the directions it is taking and skillful in inobtrusively diverting this denial and projection, which frequently emerges in correctional settings as a defense mechanism.

When work is being done with a population of delinquent youth through reality therapy, the structure must be designed in such a way as to use the peer influence as the vehicle of change (Vorrath, 1969, pp. 1–2). Several types of meetings are held. The "peer-take" is the intake meeting where the youths decide whether or not to accept a new youth. The "big meeting" is held when a crisis occurs or when a youth really wants a meeting on his or her own problems but cannot bring himself or herself to request it. Meetings are regularly scheduled for all, old and new youths, and they are frequently followed by separate meetings of the older youths, and of the more recent arrivals. At the beginning of each meeting, the residents decide who is going to be discussed and why. Also, the members report during these meetings on how they have handled particular problems during the day and why. Insight is gained by restating for the group the events that have caused trouble. The process of the meetings is similar to the therapeutic approach of self-analysis but also involves the assistance of others, who interpret, reappraise, and uncover feelings. The group helps the individual gain control of his or her problems by redirection, sublimation, repression, suppression, rationalization, and other normal defense mechanisms. Delinquent youths frequently come from homes in which they have been neglected and deprived physically and emotionally and have had to battle it out with their environment in order to get any semblance of stability (Keller and Alper, 1970, pp. 8–9).

Stress is used in these groups—sometimes rather extreme stress applied by other youth. In applying pressure, however, three guidelines in the form of questions are used (Vorrath, 1969, pp. 20–25): (1) What is the individual's potential for using stress positively? (2) What is the group's strength and potential for using stress in a positive fashion?

(3) Is the focus or purpose of stress clearly defined, and are the expectations realistic? When using stress or pressure, it is important that the group move away from the connotation of punishment and toward motivation to conform.

Positive peer culture (PPC) developed from guided group interaction but differs in that it is less threatening. PPC avoids open confrontation. Rather than emphasizing peer "pressure," PPC emphasizes teaching and learning among peers. A comparison between positive peer culture and the confrontation-group approach is shown below. Proper staff roles are seen as motivating, guiding, and reversing responsibility so that the young people are inspired to take responsibility. Improper staff roles are nursing, overcontrolling, and assuming the group's responsibility. PPC is now functioning in several juvenile and adult institutions.

POSITIVE PEER CULTURE: TRUST AND OPENNESS	CONFRONTATION GROUPS: INVASION AND EXPOSURE
1. I am afraid of showing myself to the group.	1. I am afraid of showing myself to the group.
2. The group tells me that in time I will feel free with them. They will tell me about themselves.	2. The group tells me that I must be totally honest with them. They try to find out about me.
3. I feel safe as the group shows me they will not hurt me or take advantage of me.	3. I feel uneasy because they are trying to make me tell them things I don't wish to divulge.
4. The others are bringing out their problems and seem to feel good about it. Why shouldn't I face my problems, too?	4. The others say I am being phony, but I can't see any reason why I should tell them anything. Why should I face my problems?
5. My defenses do not seem necessary; so I let down my guard.	5. My defenses are not strong enough; so they break down my guard.
6. I open up to the group.	6. I am exposed to the group.
7. I have been strong enough to bring out my problems.	7. They have been strong enough to uncover my problems.
8. I feel better after opening up. I don't believe they would use anything I said against me.	8. I don't know how I feel after being exposed. I am concerned that they might use something I said against me.
9. When a new member joins the group I know he is afraid and distrustful.	9. When a new member joins the group I will know he is a phony and dishonest.
10. I will help him get used to the group just as they did when I was new. If he finds it hard to trust I will continue to help him so he does not have to be afraid.	10. I will attack him just as they challenged me when I was new. If he won't be honest I will continue to apply more pressure until I discover what he is hiding.

The following is a list of problems that frequently apply to group members.

1. Authority—Has no respect for and cannot get along with people in authority, such as teachers, counselors, parents, police, etc. (resents authority).
2. **a.** Easily misled—Is easily talked into committing delinquent acts by those he hangs around with.
   b. Misleads others—Has enough leadership ability to lead others into trouble.
3. Light Fingering (stealing)—Has stolen many things, sees nothing wrong with stealing, except getting caught.
4. Lying—Telling many lies.
5. Drinking and/or Drugs—Has a habit of drinking or using drugs when:
   a. He wants to have fun.
   b. He feels sorry for himself.
   c. He is easily misled.
   d. He is inconsiderate.
   e. Makes stupid behavior socially acceptable.
6. **a.** Inconsiderate to others—Does things which are damaging to others, both mentally and physically.
   b. Inconsiderate to himself—In becoming inconsiderate to others, he damages himself.
7. Fronting—Has a strong need to impress others in numerous ways by making up stories or by his actions.
8. **a.** Easily aggravated—Becomes easily angered.
   b. Aggravates others—Angers others easily.
9. Small feelings—Feels poorly about himself as well as others. [Miller, 1971, p. 9]

Effectiveness always draws jealous attacks from people who are threatened. This is why powerless people resent authority and why the performance of individuals in many peer groups cannot exceed the average performance of the group without causing dissension, name calling, or other retaliatory action. Personality conflicts arise from attempted manipulations and resistances in interpersonal relations, from unsuccessful attempts at communication from different and irreconcilable frames of reference, and from vicarious reactions by individuals to the successes and failures of others. This is important to know in working with delinquents, whether individually or in groups, because youngsters tend to "parentalize" an effective correctional counselor—and however desirable that might be in working with an individual, it poses a threat to the real parents who have been "unsuccessful." The problems can be worked out in groups or in family situations.

Many therapists have considered delinquents to be untreatable because they resist therapy and are hostile toward the power structure in society. Nevertheless, group methods are part of most programs considered to be successful with delinquents. The attitude of the therapist is important. No therapy should be attempted with highly resistant and hostile patients or delinquents, however, until the therapist is able to resolve his or her own conditioned aversion to them (Didato, 1972, p. 756). The most important single experience in delinquency control is a one-to-one relationship with a trusted adult (Fox, 1973, p. 10).

The use of peer pressure in correctional caseloads can reduce the task of the parole agent or line correctional worker so that the community resources and involved people can effectively curb delinquency in one segment of the correctional caseload (Gilch, 1972). The difficulty with some of the confrontation therapies, such as reality therapy and other peer-group therapies, is that the consequences of ill-timed and hurtful interventions are sometimes not accounted for (Langs, 1973). The possible consequences are paranoid and depressive feelings leading to self-depreciation, termination of counseling that is premature or not well thought out, intense defensiveness, antitherapeutic alliances in which the client submits to aggressiveness on the part of his "treators," and disruptive "acting-in" by lateness to sessions, leaving early, or complete absence.

In the community group, a constructive atmosphere of mutual confidence and helpfulness is conducive to growth toward maturity. It is achieved by (1) acceptance of each other by inmates and staff as persons concerned about each other's welfare, (2) discussions in a nonjudgmental climate, (3) an effort by the group to develop each individual's ability to understand how others feel about him or her and why they have these feelings, and (4) self-help, which is necessary in order to want to help others (Fenton et al., 1967).

Group therapy does not supplant or replace individual therapy. Group therapy does meet the needs of the adolescent, including the adolescent delinquent, for peer acceptance as his relationship with his mother, particularly, undergoes gradual severance in the normal socialization process (Kraft, 1979).

SOCIOMETRY

Sociometry is the study of the psychological structure of human society, which consists of complex interpersonal patterns rarely visible on the surface of social processes. These patterns can be studied by quantitative and qualitative procedures. Sociometry examines every relationship an individual may have with another person or persons within a social formation. Results are best obtained when individuals are placed in a situation in which they spontaneously reveal their likes and dislikes regarding other people. A fundamental part of sociometric procedure is to apply to a community an actual situation that is confronting its people at the moment. The technique was formally proposed by Moreno, (1937) who started the journal *Sociometry;* this concept developed from his previous work (1953, p. 724). Parenthetically, his first sociometric plan (dated February 1916) was proposed to the Department of the Interior of the Austro-Hungarian government to urge the application of sociometric principles to the community of displaced persons in Mitterndorf during World War I.

Partially because of his defensiveness and vociferousness, partially because of his rejection of conventional psychoanalytic and psychiatric methods, and partially because he preferred to be "on his own," Moreno was not well accepted by the psychiatric community. He was accepted by sociologists, however—probably the only psychiatrist to be so well accepted. Consequently, many of his ideas have been incorporated in sociological thinking.

The sociogram makes visible the relationship of every individual to every other individual in the group tested. The basic procedure is to ask each individual to identify the other individual he or she likes and dislikes most, second, and third. From the choices of every individual in the group tested, a pattern can be drawn of those who make reciprocal choices of each other within the first three, those who make choices without being reciprocated, those who have mutual rejections, and those who reject others without being mutually rejected. The resulting patterns give a psychological personality structure of the social group. Clique groups, rejection patterns, and leadership can be identified.

Such a sociogram was constructed by this writer in 1948 at the Cassidy Lake Technical School, a minimum-security institution in the Michigan Department of Corrections. The questions were formulated to identify those inmates of the institution with whom individuals would like to be housed in the same nine-man cabin and those they would like to avoid. The sociogram was huge but interesting. Many clique groups emerged, and many isolates or "loners" were identified, as well as inmate leaders. The isolates and the "hangers-on" were identified along with the clique groups, as were the rejection groups. The pattern was used to make housing assignments. An informal follow-up in 1952 indicated that there was a greater tendency for isolates and hangers-on to have been returned to prison for further charges and, conversely, a greater tendency for persons who could relate to others to stay out of further trouble. A similar "sociometric geography" of a community of 435 inhabitants in fourteen houses or cottages can be seen in the 1953 revision of *Who Shall Survive?* in map III (pp. 718–19), a complex foldout map inappropriate for reproduction here. In elementary school, teachers frequently make a sociogram on St. Valentine's Day, identifying who sends valentines to whom. In this manner, the social structure of the classroom can be plotted.

Gang patterns can also be plotted. It is interesting to note that frequently the person identified as the "leader," who may not be formally so identified, may have lower intelligence than the average of the group. The reason for this is apparently that persons of higher intelligence are more sensitive to significant factors in the environment and have a greater number of factors to consider when making a decision. A less intelligent but practical person can make the decision on a smaller number of factors before all the information is in and, even more significant, thereby provides emotional security and stability to the rest of the group members, who may be more "nervous" and insecure. By providing emotional stability, the "leader" tends to be surrounded with persons who need his leadership and assurance and to whom he can impart confidence. This apparently occurs in politics and other cliques, as well as in the gangs in which the criminal justice system might be interested.

An example of how a correctional administrator can use sociometric means in management occurred when this writer was faced with a problem of selecting a director of classification in a major Midwestern prison after a civil service examination. Of the fifteen employees who passed the examination, three were technically available for appointment by the civil service "rule of three," which said that any of the top three persons on the examination could be appointed to the job. Each employee was asked to name in first, second, and third order the persons of the twelve he would prefer to serve. The subsequent sociogram is shown in Figure 10-1. This figure indicates a definite split in the classification department into two cliques and a few isolates and hangers-on. The person identified as number 1 was the top man in the examination, but he was identified with neither clique and had no real contact with anybody but number 3. Number 2 was obviously the head man of one of the cliques. Number 3 was in contact with both cliques, a member of neither, and had good association with number 1. Number 4 was the leader of the other clique. The obvious decision was to appoint number 3 because he had contact with both cliques, was a member of neither, and also had contact with the man who had made the highest score on the civil service examination. He was the only man who could hold the entire group together as it was constructed. Consequently, number 3 was appointed director of classification, and the minor "brush fires" that resulted from the disappointment of other hopefuls were easily handled. In this situation, the sociometric approach provided a good management technique in a major prison. Sociometry does have much to offer to the criminal justice system in police departments, court

FIGURE 10-1.
Choices of 15 Prison Employees Seeking the Supervisory Position
by Numerical Ranking in the Examination
and First-Three Choices of Colleagues

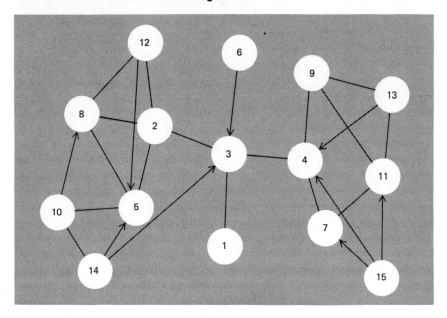

Note factionalizing of staff. Two isolates made only one choice. Number 1 on the examination was isolated, and his appointment would have destroyed effectiveness. Appointing number 2 would have favored one faction, and the others would have sought employment elsewhere. Number 3 was the only person who could hold the factions and the isolates together. Number 3 was appointed.

systems, and in correctional programs. Its use is almost essential in management of groups of inmates and correctional clients, whether formal or informal. The informal application happens when inmate leadership is identified in the prisons, gang leadership is identified in the neighborhood, and the "heavyweights" and "lightweights" are identified in all social settings related to the criminal justice system—including the legislature.

One of the earliest studies of runaways from juvenile institutions was done by Moreno (1953, pp. 518–19) at the New York School for Girls at Hudson, covering the period between July 1, 1931, and September 1, 1933. It became obvious in this study that the cohesiveness of the group and the ability of the housemother to relate to the girls was basic to the runaway problem. The highest rate of runaways was from a cottage in which there was no cohesiveness and a housemother who could not relate to girls. The lowest number of runaways was where the group was well organized and deeply attracted to the housemother. Runaways occurred in groups with the highest number of incompatible pairs and rejections. This information showed that it is the organization of the group that keeps an individual in or out of the social formation.

Moreno found that spontaneity and creativity are important concepts in sociometrics; they are related but not synonymous. A spontaneous person may or may nòt be creative, while a creative person may or may not be spontaneous. Spontaneity is the catalyzer, creativity is the substance. Another concept important in sociometrics is empathy—a one-way feeling into the private world of another person or ego. Moreno uses the concept of "tele" to mean a two-way feeling of two or more persons into each other's worlds or egos (p. 311). This is what makes up a congenial and cohesive group. Behind all social and psychological interactions are two or more reciprocating physiological organs (people and their unique characteristics) that interact with each other. These networks between people can be identified and plotted in the sociogram. Constructive and wholesome interaction in a group occurs when the internal tensional maladjustments in different individuals bring the total social formation into adjustment (p. 313).

THE FAMILY

The family is the basic social unit in which personality development begins and is shaped. Considerable emphasis has been placed on the family in determining the directions of psychosexual development and personality (Ackerman, 1958). Healy and Bronner (1936) and Gillin (1946) compared delinquent and nondelinquent siblings and arrived at the conclusion that within the same family, the emotional services determine to some extent the differential emotional maturation of each individual; this is frequently influenced by sibling order, and it helps to determine the area in which the individual may find difficulty in social adjustment. Hewitt and Jenkins (1946) held that aggressive delinquents come from rejecting families, that "socialized" delinquents come from families that have been previously accepting but have become neglecting or even rejecting, while overinhibited and neurotically motivated delinquents tend to have internalized rigid behavior controls and are unable to control resulting tensions that come from strong parental prohibitions. A fourth classification could be added for adults who come from overprotective families; the resulting dependency made unnecessary in childhood and adolescence the development of the tools of social interaction, so these individuals have to ameliorate tensions through alcohol and drugs. Some delinquency may result from disturbances that stem from incorporation or doubts and conflicts of parents regarding distinguishing right from wrong (Benedek, 1952, p. 94). Essentially similar viewpoints have been expressed in sociological terms concerning the influence on personal and social control of the individual by the primary group (Reiss, 1955, p. 269).

The hard-core multiple-problem family represents an intense manifestation of all the problems of the lower socioeconomic groups and provides in a single constellation an opportunity to study all of the social, economic, cultural, and emotional problems of the acting-out disorders. Hard-core, multiple-problem families do not move in a wide radius but remain in a relatively permanent familiar area. They tend to be large so that adequate supervision, economically and emotionally, is impossible by already inadequate parents. Mental illness does not appear very often in this type of family, but acting-out disorders appear frequently. Tension is acted out—there is frequent fighting and quarreling. Alcohol flows freely. The family is disorganized, characterized by severe marital conflict and serious neglect or abuse of children. Conflict and resentment of authority and of the establishment characterize the community.

Studies of delinquents whose parents have also been delinquent reveal the same behavior patterns and superego defects in parents and children (Porter and Kiernan, 1963, p. 539). Family systems emerge so that patterns of similar behavior appear in siblings and other family members (Johnson, 1973). Clear and specific knowledge as to how families foster or ameliorate involvement of individual members with the law is available through psychiatric and social work literature. (See Brody, 1956.) Thus, the treatment of the total family by probation, parole, and other correctional personnel can be seen to be more fruitful than treatment of the individual alone.

Cases of dominant mothers, combined with inadequate or no fathers, appear frequently in case histories involving crime and delinquency and this provides a base for the Gluecks' (1957; see esp. chap. 32) delinquency prediction studies.

In family therapy, the therapist is a go-between when two parties are in conflict. When a delinquent child and a father are involved, the go-between role of the therapist is a demanding one. In family therapy, the therapist is generally unable to avoid taking sides, but the subtle bargaining between the conflicting family members through the therapist makes it vital to avoid the appearance of taking sides. Well-handled side taking can be a source of therapeutic leverage, but poorly handled, it can be a major obstruction to conflict resolution (Zuk, 1972; see esp. pp. 383–84). Conjoint family therapy refers to working with husband and wife together (Satir, 1974; Fitzgerald, 1973). Sometimes, severe delinquency problems can be most successfully handled through this type of therapy.

NEUROTIC INTERACTION

Neurotic interaction occurs when one or more in a social formation uses ("feeds off") others for personal emotional needs. In a family under strain, a homosexual group, or other social formation that deviates from the normally expected mutually supportive group, one or more of the group use others for their own emotional needs. In a family, this may appear as nagging, one member admonishing another with righteous indignation, excessive pouting, and other manifestations of aggressive behavior. Some couples have fought intensively for all their lives and enjoyed it all the time. The interaction is neurotic because it generally involves a neurotic personality pattern. The sadistic-masochistic pattern would be the extreme, but it occurs to lesser extent in many social groups. The intensity of neurotic interaction is dependent upon the amount of cathexis, or the amount of energy devoted to the problem. The phenomenon occurs frequently in families in which one marital partner believes that the other is not assuming his or her normal and expected role.

An example of this type of interaction can be found in a study of sexual offenders in Sing-Sing (now called the Ossining Correctional Facility) done by Palm and Abrahamsen (1954). Rorschach tests were administered to all members of the family. The wives exhibited a consistent fear of men and identified with aggressive males or phallic females. The wives related well on the surface as submissive and masochistic, while latently negating their femininity by showing aggressive and masculine characteristics. They invited sexual aggression only to counter it with coldness and rejection. The attempts at sex ended in frustration, which then motivated rape of other women. The husbands complained about the wives' lack of sexual spontaneity, sleeping in their underwear, generally frigid behavior, and active provocation of sexual frustrations.

Interaction in a group can produce behavior that would never be performed alone. One example occurred in a New York school when all twenty-five boys in class opened their trousers and participated openly in mass masturbation (Stitt, 1940). The distraught teacher called the principal who, in turn, called a psychiatrist. The psychiatrist lectured the class on psychosexual development. The interpretation was that the boys were hostile toward authority, took this way to defy it, and responded better to the understanding and permissive psychiatrist than to the stern and authoritative school teacher. Whether the lectures were effective or not cannot be determined. The situation did not repeat itself, but, for that matter, it has not been reported to have been repeated elsewhere, either.

ROLE PLAYING AND SOCIODRAMA

Role is an intervening variable between a person and his or her group in that it provides a medium by which society distributes its functions in a division of labor. As a unifying factor, it channels diverse trends into recognizable patterns of behavior that become instruments of social control (Korn and McCorkle, 1959, pp. 334–35). Role is the pattern or type of behavior a person builds up in terms of what others expect or demand of him or her. Roles are learned, and have directive patterns or sequences of acts developed under the influence of significant others in the person's environment. They provide the patterns of an expected or appropriate repertoire of responses to the behavior of those with whom he or she interacts. When a person's behavior conforms with what is expected in a given situation, that person's role is complementary to the roles of others in the situation. When roles are not so expected, there is a different equilibrium of roles and people's expectations of one another, they are disappointed, and this leads to disruption of interpersonal relationships and breakdowns in group living. Crime and delinquency are examples of these disruptions of roles. Roles are explicit when they are consciously motivated and implicit when they are more remote from consciousness and awareness and are not recognized by the individual. Role confusion results in inexplicit roles occurring more frequently than explicit roles in a manner disruptive to interaction with others.

Role playing assists the individual in defining and understanding expected roles in social situations. Consequently, in role playing in prison, inmates frequently assume roles in a variety of situations that occur in the crime justice system. They may participate in an "arrest," in which some inmates take the roles of police officers, some the roles of offenders being arrested, some the roles of jailers, some the roles of the bail bondsmen, some the roles of judges, prosecutors, the defense counselors or public defenders, or any other roles that might appear in the criminal justice system. A frequent use of role playing is in the preparation for release on parole. To alleviate problems of transition, role playing may prepare a prospective parolee for his first meeting with a father with whom relations may have been difficult for a variety of reasons, an employer, or the parole officer or for any of a variety of possible situations upon release. Role playing assists in understanding various family situations. In short, role playing is a "rehearsal" that helps offenders to understand their previous difficulties and to prepare for new situations. It helps them to understand and adapt to the roles expected of them.

Sociodrama deals with the private personality of individuals and their catharsis with the persons within their milieu and with the roles in which they have interacted and may interact in the future. Sociodrama work is usually best organized in a therapeutic theater before an audience. The audience may be the therapist and staff and, perhaps, other concerned persons. Techniques of sociodrama may be (1) self-presentation where the psychiatrist asks the patients to live through and portray duplicate situations of critical events in their lives; (2) the soliloquy used by a patient to duplicate hidden feelings and thoughts that she has had or has in a situation with a partner in real life but has not expressed; (3) spontaneous improvisation in which the patient acts in fictitious or symbolic roles selected by the psychiatrist on the basis of the individual problem; (4) nonsemantic roles using pantomime, dancing, music, and other types of free expression helpful to patients with vocal defects; (5) the attempt to create an auxiliary world within which the patient might function—helpful where patients are without adequate communication (e.g., psychotic patients); and (6) sociodramatic catharsis that takes place between the actual partners in a problem, with action to resolve the current problems. These kinds of role playing can be of assistance not only to inmates, probationers, and parolees but to personnel in the criminal justice system as well in assisting in broad comprehension of the roles and functions of the various parts of the criminal justice system.

Psychodrama and sociodrama are closely related, of course, and use the same techniques. The differences are really definitional. Psychodrama refers to the procedure of role playing to resolve personal problems, like a specific domestic difficulty or insecurity; sociodrama, on the other hand, uses role playing to resolve some broader social issues, such as relationships with law enforcement, parole officers, or the court system; some racial and ethnic problems; and similar difficulties.

MOTORCYCLE GANGS

Motorcycle gangs are generally better organized than many people realize. While there are many names, the majority are members of one of four larger groups, the Outlaws, Hell's Angels, the Pagans, and the Bandidos. They have between 3,500 and 4,000 members in several states and Canada. Altogether, there are about 900 smaller gangs, mostly affiliated with the major gangs. The Outlaws have chapters in fifteen states, mostly in the East, and in Canada; the Hell's Angels have chapters in sixteen states, are heavily represented in California, and also have groups in Canada, England, Australia, Germany, and Italy. They engage in all types of crime including homicide, truck hijacking, robbery, rape, prostitution, insurance fraud, and narcotics.

A former member of the Outlaws in Canada, specifically the One Percenter group, has indicated that minor quirks of personality are emphasized for identity, including special personality patterns and nicknames—he was called Half Moon, for his smile (Montgomery, 1977). Gang members are also known for their particular skills as "good rider," "good fighter," "good typist," or "good—almost anything." Highway vandalism, motorcycle theft and stripping, reckless riding, and other "skills" become focal points within the subculture.

Girls are either attached to one rider or are community property, although most are community property and must acquiesce to each member at any time. One female member of the Bandidos, formally a part of the Outlaws, indicated that when she joined the group in 1968, she had to prostitute, dance topless, and bring home at least $100 a night or have her eyes blackened.[1]

It should be noted here that the two primary gangs had traditionally been the Outlaws and the Hell's Angels through the 1970s. With the 1980s, however, the Bandidos split away from the Outlaws and the Pagans split from the Hell's Angels, making four major gangs, rather than two. Also, the newer gangs in the 1980s have become part of organized crime, itself, in some places. Now, some of the old motorcycle gang members wear three-piece suits, drive limousines, and engage in profit-making ventures in competition with the traditional organized crime families.

Some of the motorcycle gangs engage in feuds. In 1977 in Montreal, two Outlaws killed seven Hell's Angels in a nightclub. On July 4, 1979, the Hell's Angels killed five Outlaws in Charlotte, North Carolina (Nadler, Knight-Ridder News Service, July 7, 1979). Gang members wanted for crimes have been referred to as organized criminals in uniform. Some do "jobs" for organized crime families. The Pagans have been fighting with organized crime groups in Philadelphia for several years. Motorcycle gangs are moving into organized crime in some areas.

PIRACY

The golden age of piracy was the eighteenth century (Botting, 1978, p. 14). Piracy has been in existence since before 1400 B.C., when the Egyptians established a formal marine patrol at the Delta of the Nile. Better navies and better international law have reduced it in recent years, particularly the anti-piracy agreements reached in France in 1937. Hijacked motor vessels of forty to seventy-five feet in length are favored, but there are really very few such incidents, according to the U.S. Coast Guard,

---

[1]Reported on American Broadcasting Company's 20/20 Show, July 12, 1979.

because of modern law enforcement procedures.[2]

In 1980 Americans spent $6 billion on the purchase and maintenance of the 8.3 million commercial and pleasure craft registered in the United States. Theft of boats and marine equipment ranges between an estimated $40 and $80 million annually (Lyford, 1980, pp. 10–12). Security measures of many types are recommended, but early reporting of crimes and suspicious activity to the appropriate police and security agencies is mandatory because of the magnitude of the problem that has increased significantly in recent years.

Today there are airplanes hijacked as well as vessels. According to a study by the Office of Civil Aviation Security of the Federal Aviation Administration between 1961-1982, there were 134 successful hijackings of U.S. registered aircraft, 56 incomplete hijackings in which the hijacker was apprehended or killed during the flight, and 66 unsuccessful attempts. Of the successful hijackings 19 were to Cuba. During the period, 1931-1967, there were only 11 successful hijackings worldwide, three of which were in the United States. Aircraft hijackings began on a large scale in 1968. Worldwide hijackings between 1968 and 1982 totaled 167, of these only 68 hijackings occurred outside the United States.

The Manson Family

Charles Manson and his cultists in California attracted national attention for their almost ritualistic and apparently nonutilitarian murders of seven people. This was the type of crime that no one member would have done alone but all members of such a group could do together.

Charles Manson (b. 1934) was born in Cincinnati to an unwed mother and was raised by a grandmother in West Virginia. He was sent to Boys Town in Nebraska for a brief stay after he was first arrested for stealing food. He was later sent to Indiana Boys School Reformatory at Plainfield, from which he ran away eighteen times. Later he was sent to several federal reformatories over a three-year period, including the National Training School for Boys. After his parole from the federal reformatory at Chillicothe, Ohio, in November, 1954, he organized a communelike hostelry at Spahn near Los Angeles. From there he directed the cultists in his group in the killing of actress Sharon Tate, millionaire coffee heiress Abigail Folger, Voityack Forkowsky, Jay Sebring, and Steven Parent on August 8 and 9, 1969, and Leno and Rosemary LaBianca two days later. He was convicted, together with three of his female assistants, and was sentenced to death on January 25, 1971, but the death penalty was abolished and he is now serving a life term.

It is clear that Manson was the leader or catalyzer of the group he directed. It was a cohesive group that followed the leader unquestioningly. The interdependence of the members of the group and their dependence upon Manson is a classic demonstration of group behavior. Whether interpreted by the psychiatric concept of neurotic interaction, the sociometric concept of complementary inner tensional malad-

---

[2]Letter from Captain R. H. Overton III, chief, Ocean Operations Division, United States Coast Guard, dated April 23, 1980.

justments, or the sociological concept of role and division of labor and leadership, it is obvious that this cohesive group was acting as a single organism. Certainly, the motivation for each member must have been the satisfaction of emotional needs as he related to others. It is because of this group function that persons will behave in ways reinforced by a group that they would not even consider when alone.

CONCLUSIONS

It is obvious that human behavior, including criminal behavior, on the part of individuals must be related to the group in which they participate in order to be fully understood. The individual does not function in a vacuum, but interacts with other people. The first major group is the family. The sociologists refer to primary groups as those in which the individual belongs on an immediate, face-to-face basis, such as the family, the gang, and other close groups. Secondary groups are those in which the motivation is something other than the immediate confiding found in the primary group; examples are professional organizations, business clubs, labor unions, and church groups. Tonnies's idea of *Gemeinschaft* and *Gesellschaft* (community and society) was one of the early formulations of this differentiation. In any case, the inculcation of values in an individual is implemented by his or her group. As John Dewey said, a person is in his environment not as a coin in a box but as a plant embedded in the soil, receptive to the sun and the rain. A person's environment involves other people, whether they are family, friends, business and social associates, from the neighborhood, or from total society.

Conversely, any attempt at modification of the behavior of an individual must take these groupings into consideration in order to achieve optimum effectiveness. To be effective, all the workers in the criminal justice system have to be acquainted with this phenomenon of grouping and the basic principles of group dynamics. The police require training in crowd control, crisis intervention in family disputes, and other areas of endeavor that involve disruption. For adequate disposition and treatment, court and correctional personnel need to know even more about family interaction and group behavior, including roles and the techniques by which groups and role playing can be used to accomplish the treatment objectives.

Questions

1. Why is human behavior, to a large extent, group behavior?
2. What are the general characteristics of gangs?
3. What is the dominant motivation underlying gang behavior?
4. What are the advantages of group therapy?

5. What are the differences between positive peer culture and confrontation groups?

6. What is sociometry?

7. How is the family important in criminal and delinquent behavior?

8. Why is the presence of dominant mothers or the absence of fathers frequent in the case histories of persons involved in crime and delinquency?

9. What is neurotic interaction and how does it contribute to crime and delinquency?

10. Why is role playing important in the treatment of crime and delinquency?

eleven

CULTURAL
AND
ANTHROPOLOGICAL
APPROACHES

Social or cultural anthropology is primarily concerned with culture and the comparative study of human societies. It is sometimes difficult to separate sociology from anthropology because their considerable overlapping blurs the distinctions in many areas. In fact, in many major universities sociology and anthropology are in the same department, and many other universities have only recently separated them. Many of the social and behavioral sciences, including sociology, anthropology, economics, and social psychology, overlap in some areas. In reality, the divisions between the social sciences are conveniences for purposes of manipulable conceptions rather than real and intrinsic divisions in the understanding of human behavior. Yet all have contributions to make toward understanding of crime, such as the economic law of supply and demand in areas of theft, and political science in the areas of treason. The separation of anthropology from sociology, then, is only a convenience in conceptualizing the cultural contributions to definitions of criminal behavior as compared with sociology's interest in interaction of individuals in a group.

Anthropologists hold that it is only culture that determines differential human behavior. Biological principles and successful medicine are the same around the world. Learning and the psychological processes are universal. It is only culture that provides differential stimuli that shape personalities differently. In the last analysis, all research and learning in this field is directly or indirectly oriented to one central question: "What makes an Englishman an Englishman? an American an American? a Russian a Russian?" (Kluckholn and Murray, 1953, p. xviii). Even more specific to the problem of criminal behavior, what makes a criminal a criminal or a gangster a gangster? The anthropologists find the answer in culture.

In society, people come together with varying backgrounds and from different cultures. The homogeneity or heterogeneity of a society is partially dependent upon the contributions to it from various cultures. For example, the Amish are a highly cohesive group that rejects the use of modern transportation, and their culture is as strong today as it ever was. On the other hand, the nineteenth-century whaling-ship captain wanted a "motley crew," which was a heterogeneous group that might include a Swedish first mate, Italian, German, Turkish, and Spanish crewmen, and a Chinese cook. They were from such different backgrounds that they could not get together and organize for a mutiny! Thus it can be seen that the behavior and cohesion of a social group is dependent upon the cultural influences that comprise it. Criminal behavior varies with the culture and with the mixture of cultures in a society.

Anthropology holds that legal systems differ from place to place and change from time to time to reflect differences and changes in culture (Pospisil, 1971); the culture is important, while the individual person is not. Differences in ideas of crime and delinquency have been found to be different in different cultures (Rosenquist and Megargee, 1969). An example is seen in some African criminal definitions, which with the infusion of modern civilization into ancient tribal organization and custom, represent a fascinating blend. The well-disciplined social order of the Kanuri of Bornu Province in northern Nigeria responds to the concept of *berzum*, or discipline-respect, to the extent that maximum security facilities are not necessary for prisoners (Sobe, 1962, p. 32). On the other hand, the more individualistic societies, such as Algeria, necessitate stronger controls on the individual. The definitions of crime vary accordingly. Social control involves both the training of members of society and a system of rewards and punishment that operates to produce conformity in behavior. The formal education, family life, and cultural values all contribute to this control. Social control is embedded in the social system, a by-product of the family and kinship, economic or political concerns, and ritualistic relations. The special problems of ethnic groups, such as blacks and Orientals in Western society, as well as other minority groups in situations of differentiation and discrimination, are within the scope of social and cultural anthropology.

Anthropology deals in "cultural streams" in which the individual is insignificant. While sociology is concerned with the relationship of the individual with his or her group in a social formation, and psychology is interested in the behavior of the individual, anthropologists hold that psychological principles in terms of learning are universal, sociological principles of interaction of individuals within groups are universal, and only culture or the existing "ground rules" make differences in human behavior.

PRIMITIVE PEOPLES AND THEIR LAW

Primitive law is not really "law" in the modern sense but custom and taboo. The beginnings of the development of organs of justice, however, can be seen in the emergence of primitive law. Primitive law refers to the norms and sanctions that controlled deviant behavior prior to the written word. Customs and folkways were the primary sanctions among primitive peoples, though advanced primitive peoples, such as the Cheyenne and the Comanche, had rudimentary organs of justice. Some African tribes today, for example, have organs of justice comparable to those of ancient Babylon. The essential elements of law are (1) regularity, (2) official authority, and (3) the potential application of physical force. This type of social sanction has existed in most primitive societies. Probably most of the sanctions in primitive societies were handled privately—such as when a relative of a slain person killed the culprit—and public opinion would usually uphold the punisher, and retaliation against him would be unlikely in such cases (Barton, 1930, p. 115). The primary authority for legal sanctions in primitive law is the kinship group in support of its individual members. Private law, then, dominates most primitive law. At the same time, most primitive society recognizes some acts as legally punishable by society at large.

Homicide within the group and adultery, with some exceptions, are common illegal acts in primitive society. Sorcery or antisocial witchcraft are also widespread. These acts are generally avenged privately by the victim or his kin. Primitives have killed their brothers or other near-relatives simply to obtain their magical powers in order to use them for the benefit of the group (Makarius, 1973). This is another example of a jealous response to the effectiveness of another person. Theft is not a subject of major concern in primitive law. Neither is the welfare of people not in one's own group. That is why African chieftains sold captured peoples of neighboring tribes into the slavery trade between the fourth and nineteenth centuries. The Miyanmin people, who live near the headwaters of the Sepik in New Guinea, capture, kill, and eat neighboring peoples, particularly the Telefolmin. When the Australian government moved into the area in the early 1950s, 138 Telefolmins had been consumed in the previous eleven years ("Having Neighbors for Dinner," 1975). Social and cultural practices vary between cultures and what is defined as a crime varies with them.

The major contrast between primitive and civilized law is in procedure. Forms of social control and law are related to the rest of the social structure. Simple primitive societies are decentralized, segmentary units of organization that lack overall political authority, with each family or group of kinsmen being led by its elders. Where several families are in a village, the elders from each family may meet in a tribal or village council. The autonomy of the kinship groups, however, remains primary. In primitive law, the wronged individual is avenged by his kinship group, while civilized law establishes organs of government for the purpose.

The type of enforcement found in primitive societies gives rise to the feud, where there may be a continuing succession of violence, violent retaliation, and blood revenge. The problem of society is to find legal or other procedures that are ritual devices for avoiding or terminating feuds. This has given rise to the ritual chief, such as among the Nuer in the African Sudan, and the mediation by outstanding and neutral citizens, such as among the Ifugao in northern Luzon. Centralized judicial and political authority begin to be developed in advanced primitive tribes, such as among the Cheyenne Indians, where such authority is vested in a tribal council. The legal authority resides in a high priest among the Pueblo Indians in the southwestern United States. Legal authority was in the hands of a caste of conquerors among the conquest-oriented caste societies in ancient Africa and the Mediterranean area.

There are still primitive peoples whose custom and taboo are in the stage of primitive law discussed here. Ten tribes of Indians in Brazil and one in Ecuador; the Eskimos and Athabascan Indians in Alaska; several tribes in Africa, particularly in the Congo, Uganda, and Tanzania; several tribes of aborigines in Australia; and several tribes on the island of New Guinea are among contemporary primitive peoples with these systems of social control. Cotlow (1971, esp. chap. 1) is concerned that primitive man is now an "endangered species" that is disappearing before the advance of white man's civilization.

In the United States, this change can best be observed among the Eskimos and the Athabascan Indians in Alaska. Until the arrival of white man's power approximately eighty years ago, no "organization" was needed and social control was as in an extended family. With the arrival of the white man, village councils were developed to act as a buffer between primitive customs and the white man's authority. Central to the difficulty in coexistence between the two systems of social control is that primitive sanctions are based on consensus, while "white man's justice" is based on conflict in an adversary system. The efforts to resolve this are discussed by Hippler and Conn (1973), who suggest that Eskimo justice be generally let alone unless a state agency, generally the Alaska State Troopers, is summoned by a village council to take a troublesome individual out of the village to Fairbanks for disposition. Eskimo sanctions are based on noncoercive and conflict-avoiding approaches, and Eskimos do not want third parties intervening and settling disputes. On the other hand, Western justice requires a prosecution, a defense, a judge, and the right to a jury trial. Primitive man does not understand this.

ETHNIC MINORITIES AND CRIME

Ethnic minorities and crime have been associated in the crime statistics and in the literature. Tensions exist where a minority group threatens the lifestyles and culture of the dominant group. Probably the problem resolves into one of cultural nonassimilation and social maladjustment rather than one of any inherent criminal tendency that varies from group to group (Barnes and Teeter, 1959, p. 166). The United States, of course, is probably the most heterogeneous country in the world, with its many immigration patterns and many ethnic and racial groups within the population. The tendency for people to identify and socialize with their own cultural and racial groups results in maintaining some social distance from other groups. Social distance results in cultural differentiation, and this cultural differentiation reinforces the social distance.

Racial and ethnic problems in the United States resulted from (1) expansion that included large numbers of Indians, (2) annexation that included a large number of Spanish-speaking people in the Southwest and West, (3) slavery and emancipation that brought blacks to America and gave them citizenship, and (4) immigration that brought people of all races and nationalities to make up the population. The various proportions of ethnic origin in the population in 1979 are shown in Tables 11–1 and 11–2.

Because of the ethnocentric tendencies in most groups, whites have tended to interact with and marry whites, blacks have tended to interact with and marry blacks, and other groups, similarly have been "closed" to various degrees. Regardless of the racial and ethnic background of any one person, the entire culture of the United States has been dominated by European whites. This accommodation has been difficult for many racial and ethnic groups (other than European whites) to accept wholeheartedly. Even within the European white community, there are many differences that find expression in street fights, name-calling, and mutual derision, exemplified by the well-known Irish-German confrontations in the large cities like New York and Boston between 1840–1900. The 5,921,000 Jews consider themselves different, also. This

TABLE 11-1.
Population by Ancestry—Selected Characteristics, 1979

ANCESTRY	NUMBER	MEDIAN AGE	PERCENT HIGH SCHOOL GRADUATES	MEDIAN FAMILY INCOME
English	11,501,000	40.4	75.7	$16,891
French	3,047,000	36.2	66.4	15,571
German	17,160,000	37.1	72.2	17,531
Irish	9,760,000	39.0	69.5	16,092
Italian	6,110,000	42.3	61.5	16,993
Polish	3,498,000	46.0	61.6	16,977
Scottish	1,615,000	43.5	79.9	20,018
Spanish	9,762,000	23.5	41.4	10,607
MIXED ANCESTRY				
American Indian and other	7,847,000	23.4	61.7	13,641
Dutch and other	6,759,000	27.3	68.2	15,868
English and other	28,503,000	27.1	81.4	18,680
French and other	11,000,000	24.5	76.8	17,048
German and other	34,489,000	23.0	80.2	18,375
Irish and other	33,002,000	25.7	75.1	16,860
Italian and other	5,622,000	17.7	84.5	17,833
Polish and other	4,923,000	20.3	84.3	19,968
Spanish and other	12,590,000	32.2	81.2	19,148
Total Population	216,613,000	30.3	68.7	15,764

Table No. 45, *Statistical Abstract of the United States—1982–83,* Washington, D.C.: Government Printing Office, 1983, p. 37.

TABLE 11-2.
Resident Population, by Race and Spanish Origin, 1980

White	188,372,000
Black	26,495,000
American Indian	1,420,400
Chinese	806,000
Filipino	774,700
Japanese	701,000
Asian Indian	361,500
Korean	354,600
Vietnamese	261,700
All other races	6,999,200
Spanish origin (could be any race)	14,609,000
Total Population	226,546,000

Taken from Table No. 36, *Statistical Abstract of the United States—1982–83,* Washington, D.C.: Government Printing Office, 1983, p. 32.

uneasy mixing of ethnic, racial, and religious backgrounds is not new.

Colonial America was two-thirds Anglo-Saxon, with a higher percentage in Massachusetts and Virginia. Because of this and the political background of the United States, Anglo-Saxon government and other social institutions became the cultural core of America. English history and Western civilization were taught in the schools, and the English language was spoken. All other people had to adhere to that culture in order to become effective socially, politically, and culturally. The "immigrant" groups who did not readily adapt contributed disproportionately to the crime rate.

The resulting tensions sometimes increased the social distances between people. When the late shah of Iran said, while discussing the oil crisis on the CBS program "60 Minutes" (March 10, 1974), that the "blue-eyed Europeans" were to blame for devastating and plundering the Middle East by taking oil and gas, the resentment was unmistakable. He spoke the feelings of many people around the world. During the colonial era, "blue-eyed Europeans" sent their military and commercial establishments around the world, followed by their missionaries, whose presence was considered by many people in the "colonialized" areas to be imperialism and an invasion of their cultures. Within the United States, the tensions are obvious, too, with many assuming that if one's parents came from England, they are "aristocrats," but if they came from Poland or Italy, they are "immigrants." This social situation sets the stage for the culture conflict presented by Thorsten Sellin and others and is basic to conflict theories of subcultures.

BLACK MILITANTS AND THE JUSTICE SYSTEM

The basic reason for racial stress in America appears to be the traditional social distance maintained by northern Europeans and the English toward people of other races. Northern Europeans and Englishmen have traditionally maintained social distance from the "exotic" Africans. They did not try to "civilize" or "convert" them; neither did they intermingle with them. Although the institution of slavery may have contributed by intensifying the problem, it was not really the basic cause. As an institution it has been almost universal in the history of man—part of the economic system. African chieftains dealt in slavery as early as the fourth century A.D., selling fellow Africans to European and Muslim traders along with gold and ivory. After the sixteenth century, slaves were Africa's major export (Hallett, 1970, pp. 18, 21). Some African kingdoms, such as Ashanti and Benin in West Africa and the Ovimundu states in what is now Angola, gained immense wealth from trade in slaves with European slave traders. The first black slaves brought to the Western Hemisphere arrived in South America to develop the tropical Amazon Valley's agriculture. Slavery still exists in isolated places in South America, the Middle East, and elsewhere, which is why the League of Nations held a slavery convention in 1926 and why a supplementary convention was held by the United Nations in 1956. All peoples in the world have practiced slavery at some time, with the exception of the Eskimo, the American plains Indian, and peoples in Australasia. Yet the racial strife now appears to be centered in the United States.

The first black slaves in what is now the United States arrived in Virginia in a Dutch ship in 1619. Need for agricultural labor resulted in increased trade. In 1790 alone, the number of slaves transported from the West Coast of Africa was 38,000 in British ships, 20,000 in French ships, 10,000 in Portuguese ships, 4,000 in Dutch ships, and 2,000 in Danish ships. During this early period, there were also indentured white Europeans and Indian slaves, but the European whites ceased to arrive, and the Indians were too rebellious and hard to control, so slavery was relegated to the black African.

Racial strife, then, appears to be more the result of the traditional social distance maintained by northern Europeans and the English than the institution of slavery itself. The Latins around the Mediterranean did not maintain that social distance but rather intermingled and intermarried with the black Africans. Puerto Ricans, for example, are a mixture of Arawak Indians originally from Peru and Caucasian Spanish, with some Negroid strains. Mexicans are about 15 percent white, about 29.2 percent Indian, and about 60.5 percent mixture of Aztec Tlaxcaltecas Indians and Caucasian Spanish—called mestizos—and a few blacks, some mixed with Caucasian Spanish and others with Indian strains. As a result of this intermingling and mutual acceptance, there are no racial problems in Latin America. In fact, the Latins themselves have suffered some discrimination in America, partially because they have not respected the social distance traditionally maintained by the northern Europeans and Englishmen who constitute the power structure.

American racial problems, particularly in the criminal justice system, stem from this traditional social distance, sometimes called prejudice. When a people already socially distant are brought into a country in a subservient status and purchased on the open market, there is no way that they can be emancipated by proclamation and be immediately accepted by the white power structure, so "separate but equal" school systems should not be unexpected. The Dred Scott decision of 1857 (*Dred Scott* v. *Sanford*), had already established that Negroes were not citizens and could not sue in the federal courts. The Jim Crow law of the South were upheld by the Supreme Court in 1896 in *Plessy* v. *Ferguson*, relating to separate waiting rooms, separate public bathrooms and toilet facilities, separate water fountains, and separate seating on buses, trains, and other public carriers. The plaintiff in this case had indicated that he was seven-eighths Caucasian and one-eighth African and his mixture of color was not discernible, so he had a right to the privileges of the white race, but the court ruled against him. ("Jim Crow" was a stereotypical Negro song-and-dance act presented by Thomas D. Rice beginning in 1860, based on an anonymous early nineteenth-century song called "Jim Crow." Originally applicable to any other racial or ethnic group, the term came to refer only to blacks.)

It is against this background that black militancy arose in the 1960s, a century after proclaimed emancipation in 1863, enforced after 1865. Some blacks in the South stayed with their "families" and, together with others, went into what has been called economic slavery. The Ku Klux Klan originated in the South at the end of the Civil War during the Union occupation of the South. It was disbanded in 1869 and reestablished in 1915 (Fry, 1969, pp. 135–36). The threat of violence by blacks continued to rise and reached a crescendo in the 1970s. Violence erupted in race riots in St. Louis in 1917, Chicago in 1919, and Detroit in 1943. The first major riot in a corrections facility caused by racial issues was at the District of Columbia Youth Center at Lorton, Virginia, 1962, and involved the Black Muslim sect. Impatient after a century of inadequate progress toward equality and acceptance, blacks had become militant. By the 1960s and 1970s, black militancy and violence had become a realistic social concern in America. The criminal justice system, especially, was concerned.

The most serious racial difficulties in American prisons occurred at Soledad and San Quentin in California in 1970 and 1971, involving the "Soledad Brothers," particularly George Jackson and Angela Davis; and at Attica in New York in 1971, where the prison population was 70 percent black and Puerto Rican, while the staff was all white. After the Attica situation was handled questionably by New York officials and forty-three people were killed (thirty-nine by officers and troopers), worldwide reaction pointed at racial problems in America. Examples of some international newspaper excerpts are as follows:

> The idea that blacks are prisoners in a white man's world was espoused by the late Malcolm X, and this view is widely held among black convicts. Black prisoner's crime may or may not have been a political action against the state, but the state's action against him is always political. Black militancy and prison violence were linked long before Attica. [*Athens Daily Post*, Athens, Greece, September 24, 1971]

> Nothing is more powerful than the idea that they are being repressed by a racist society. "These are not hostages, they are human beings," said a prisoner, "and we want to be treated like human beings, too." [*South China Morning Post*, Hong Kong, September 18, 1971]

The majority of prison troubles in the United States is among Negroes and Puerto Ricans. [*L'Union*, Reims, France, September 16, 1971]

The majority of criminals are white, but the majority of prisoners are black.

Something is wrong in America. [*Voix Ouviere*, Geneva, Switzerland, September 25, 1971]

Conditions in American prisons are bad and they are racist. [*La Norve Sardegna*, Sassari, Sardinia, Italy, September 21, 1971]

Rockefeller may face murder charges. [*E. L. Daily Dispatch*, Zambia, Central Africa, September 22, 1971]

World attention to problems regarding blacks and Puerto Ricans has been centered on the United States. James (1935, p. 83) pointed out that the largest Negro population was no longer in Africa, but in industrial North America, specifically, the United States. In fact, blacks were in South America before Columbus came to America, having crossed the narrow part of the South Atlantic near the equator (Van Sertima, 1976). Further, officials in San Juan, Puerto Rico, have stated that New York is the largest Puerto Rican city in the world. It is also the largest Jewish city in the world. Further, New York is the largest black city in the world (1,941,000 in 1980) followed by Chicago (1,428,000). Major American cities with a black majority in the population include Atlanta, Georgia (51.3 percent) and Washington, D.C. (71.1 percent). Chicago is the largest Polish city.

The Black Muslims are part of a socioreligious movement in the United States. This group was founded in 1931 by Wali Farad, believed to have been an orthodox Muslim born in Mecca about 1877. He came to the United States in 1930 and established his first temple or mosque in Detroit in 1931 and a second in Chicago soon afterward. Elijah Muhammad succeeded Farad in 1934, and the movement grew, becoming the rallying point for many pent-up frustrations of black people in America and for the black nationalism apparent in Africa and America after World War II. It restricted its membership to nonwhites until 1975 and has a primarily black following. The present headquarters in Temple No. 2 in Chicago. Elijah Muhammad's program, in brief, is as follows.

1. We want freedom.
2. We want justice.
3. We want equality of opportunity.
4. We want our people in America whose parents or grandparents were descendants from slaves to be allowed to establish a seperate state or territory of their own—either on this continent or elsewhere.
5. We want freedom for all Believers in Islam now held in federal prisons. We want freedom for all black men and women now under death sentence in innumerable prisons in the North as well as the South.

6. We want an immediate end to the police brutality and mob attacks against the so-called Negro throughout the United States.

7. As long as we are not allowed to establish a state or territory of our own, we demand not only equal justice under the laws of the United States but equal employment opportunities—NOW!

8. We want the government of the United States to exempt our people from ALL taxation as long as we are deprived of equal justice under the laws of the land.

9. We believe that intermarriage or race mixing should be prohibited. ["The Muslim Program," *Muhammed Speaks* 12 (June 22, 1973), 32.]

Further, all Muslim followers are admonished not to beg the white slave-master for anything.

Although the Black Muslims verbalize nonviolence, their activities concerned the American Correctional Association to the extent that a resolution was passed in its annual business meeting in Philadelphia in 1961 to the effect that the Black Muslims constituted a threat to the order and security of American prisons. The following year the Federal Court of the District of Columbia ruled that the Black Muslims constituted a legitimate religion and were entitled to First Amendment rights (*Fulwood* v. *Clemmer*, 1962). Their activities, probably unintentionally, led to the first major riot based on racial issues at the District of Columbia Youth Center at Lorton, Virginia. In his eulogy after the death of Malcolm X, LeRoi Jones said:

> Western Culture (the way white people live and think) is passing. If the Black Man cannot identify himself as separate, and understand what this means, he will perish along with Western Culture and the white man. [Jones, 1971, p. 164.]

In 1966, Huey Newton and Bobby Seale formed the Black Panthers, partly because the Black Muslims were nonviolent in intent and they thought progress was moving too slowly. The Black Panther party began with the premise that political power grows out of the barrel of a gun. Several incidents of police killing and other violence ensued, including the police shootup of Panther headquarters in Oakland, California, in the late 1960s. Black Panther activities subsequently resulted in a congressional hearing and a concerted effort on the part of law enforcement agencies to contain them (U.S. Congress, 1970). The Black Panthers attempted to change their image by such beneficial acts as giving food to poor children. Their chief ambition remains to change the American government by any means necessary. Their violent activities in American prisons are intentional. The response by the law enforcement agencies and the courts has been difficult because of procedural concerns. If an unwritten and unspoken police conspiracy to deprive Black Panthers of constitutional rights is condoned by the white-dominated community, it will be the beginning of the loss of all liberties for everybody. Unfortunately, these groups—all of them—are still simmering, but have aligned with other groups so that their original identities are not as prominent. In a turbulent culture, you can always find rebels with varying degrees of militancy. The gangs and groups from the urban areas have extended into the prisons, also, making discipline so difficult that San Quentin in California, Stateville in Illinois, Santa Fe in New Mexico, and others have had to be "locked down," which means closing programs and not letting inmates out of their cells. The "names" prominent in the 1970s have faded a little—but they are not "out of it"—but the thrust of social unrest continues on a wider scale, which makes the violence *seem* more moderate only because it makes less "news" now.

The Black Liberation Army was formed in 1971, with the more violent and more dedicated revolutionary members splitting from the Black Panther Party under the leadership of the exiled Eldridge Cleaver. This organization was responsible for the killing of several police officers in New York and San Francisco, other murders, and several bank robberies. Homicides of two young white men in Jacksonville, Florida, in July 1974, with tape recordings and notes left to indicate that this was part of a war together with other activities, indicated that the Black Liberation Army, estimated at about a thousand members, was nationwide. Arrests in New Orleans and on the East Coast temporarily slowed their activities in 1974.

The California Department of Corrections published in 1974 a pamphlet on this type of terrorism (*Terrorism in California*, 1974). This publication pointed out that the credo of urban guerrillas is taken from a manifesto prepared by Carlos Marighella, a member of the Brazilian Communist Party who broke with the parent organization because he thought the revolution should occur immediately. Under the title *Mini-Manual on Urban Guerrilla Warfare*, Marighella outlined three goals: (1) to show the masses that police and military authorities are impotent to protect themselves from urban terrorism and thus powerless to protect society as a whole; (2) to provoke by outrageous terror an overreaction on the part of police and government to "radicalize" sympathizers of revolutionary aims; and (3) to combine the first two goals ultimately to overthrow the established government. The Symbionese Liberation Army (which kidnapped Patty Hearst in 1974), probably numbering no more than twenty-five members, grew out of the Black Cultural Association at the California Medical Facility at Vacaville. The Revolutionary Union centered on application of the Marxist/Leninist doctrine as interpreted by Mao Zedong, but in 1971, Bruce Franklin split with the parent body and formed the Venceremos organization with a goal of revolution within fifteen to twenty years. The Venceremos organization staged the escape of one prisoner from Chino and the murder of his guard in 1972. The Black Guerrilla family was formed in 1971 from fragments of the Black Panther party left over from the split, but it organized a Marxist/Leninist revolutionary group under the leadership of Eldridge Cleaver and George Jackson. Other groups include the Mexican Mafia and lesser groups.

White racist groups opposing black militancy included the Weathermen or Weather Underground that began in 1969 when the group split from Students for a Democratic Society and the Polar Bear Party, but the latter group merged with the Venceremos Underground and thus had to change its racist policies. The prisoners' Aryan Brotherhood consisted of all-white inmate membership and did not espouse revolution.

The Republic of New Africa was formed in March 1968 when 500 blacks met in Detroit and declared independence from the United States. This organization claimed Louisiana, Mississippi, Alabama, Georgia, and South Carolina on the basis that this area was their traditional homeland on the North American continent and was due them in reparations settlement for slavery. The minister of information, Mrs. Fulani A. Obafemi of Jackson, Mississippi, wrote a four-page *Black Prisoners Manifesto* that defied the victimization of black prisoners. Mrs. Obafemi was active in Florida, where her husband was a resident at the Florida State Prison. The headquarters of the group was in Hinds County (Jackson), Mississippi, which was renamed "El Malik," the provisional capital of the Republic of New Africa. A meeting in Atlanta, Georgia, on Pan African activities was attended by Richard Henry, delegate from the Republic of New Africa. The African People's Socialist party, whose membership and leadership overlapped that of the Republic of New Africa, held that crime, venereal disease, and other "social symptoms" prevalent among blacks were related to the racist and exploitive nature of American culture and politics (Williams, 1947, p. 17). They hold that all blacks, wherever they are, should be considered to be African nationals. They set May 25 as African Liberation Day, to be celebrated with marches, demonstrations, and other activities (David, 1974, p. 3).

BLACKS AND CRIME

The high proportion of blacks arrested and convicted for crime has generated concern that discrimination occurs in the justice system. Of 9,683,672 arrests in 1980, there were 7,145,763 whites and 2,375,204 blacks arrested. Blacks in 1980 comprised about 11.7 percent of the total population of the United States and they contributed to 27.8 percent of the arrests. Approximately 46.3 percent of the prisoners in America in 1980 were black. The breakdown of racial disproportions in American prisons in 1980 was as follows:

RACE OR ETHNIC BACKGROUND	PRISONERS PER 100,000 IN GENERAL POPULATION
White	70.8
Black	600.0
Hispanics	182.0
Native Americans	280.0

Source: "American/European Incarceration of Whites Not Too Different," *Corrections Digest*, 11, no. 15, July 18, 1980, pp. 6-9.

The black militant has identified areas of social injustice, differences between black culture and white culture, and points out where the criminal justice system is being discriminatory (Aollett, 1971).

Most criminologists attribute the high crime rate among blacks not only to prejudice, discrimination, and differential treatment but to the fact that blacks are overrepresented in the lower socioeconomic classes from which most offenders come. In proportion to their representation in the poverty level of society, the blacks and the whites approximate each other in prison populations. Consequently, crime appears to be a function of socioeconomic class, of cultural and economic deprivation, rather than being of racial or ethnic origin. Some reservation about that thesis is expressed by Sutherland and Cressey (1978, p. 144), however, who point out that it is apparently accurate for the male offender, but that the female offender does not follow that pattern. Again, the matriarchal nature of the black family, particularly in the disorganized and disadvantaged family, where the mother can obtain domestic work or receive Aid to Families with Dependent Children (AFDC) payments from the state welfare department, results in the mother's being cast in the role of strength while the male becomes peripheral (Minuchin et al., 1967).

Race is not a factor in crime, except possibly in the cultural concomitants that come from being a member of a visible minority group. Johnson contends that the cause of the high crime rate among blacks can be attributed to (1) low socioeconomic status, (2) migration and urban disorganization in which blacks migrating from rural areas to urban industrial areas have to readjust, (3) family disorganization and poverty with the survival of the matriarchal family where the father's role is frequently casual and easily interrupted (Johnson, 1968, pp. 79–82). This situation deprives the growing black child of a basis for security, confidence, and realistic hope for the future. Drift into delinquency or the use of crime as an "equalizer" would be expected to occur in this situation more frequently than in others, regardless of race or ethnic origin.

Failure to be able to compete on an equal basis has caused more than one young black man tired of long hours and low pay to decide that

> the only way to get real money from him [an employer] is to get a gun, go down there and put it to that mother-fucker's head and take it. [Brown, 1965, p. 284]

THE FEMALE OFFENDER

Cultural factors appear to explain at least part of the differential crime rates between men and women. As indicated in chapter 3, differential androgen levels are associated with differential levels of aggression, so biological factors must also be taken into account. Women constitute about 4 percent of the adult prison population. The ratio of arrests has been generally one woman to five men, indictments about one woman to nine men, convictions about one woman to seventeen men, and prison population, one woman to twenty-seven men. Most of the reasons appear to lie in the social and cultural factors within the family that reduce the possibility of women's being involved in crime in the first place, and the "protective" tendency in American culture that decreases the possibility of their being processed through the courts to a prison sentence (Haslam, 1973, p. 2). The attitudes of society about expected behavior of girls tend to develop methods of handling problems without treating them as criminals. Further, the relationship of the girls to home and family tends to decrease their vulnerability to negative experiences that might result in criminal behavior. Charges are not made against women in many instances because the offense occurred in home surroundings. Some offenses are more likely to be handled by a warning or dismissal. "Accidents" resulting in the death of a member of the family may not really be accidental but many provide insufficient evidence to warrant laying a charge. Crime for profit may occur when women stimulate men to commit crimes for their benefit, but women are not generally guilty of the offenses themselves. Self-destructive types of offenses occur among women more than among men.

The differential treatment of women in Western civilization is reflected in the nature and extent of their crimes. In the traditionally male-dominated culture, women have been considered as strange, secretive, seductive, and sometimes dangerous (Pollak, 1950, p. 149).

The methods of women differ somewhat from those of men because of differences in physical strength and cultural definitions of sex roles. Perception of the double standard, development of revenge desires created by female occupations in domestic service, and other roles into which women are placed lead to much pent-up resentment, which, in turn, sometimes evolves into a desire for aggressive compensation (ibid., p. 160). Because of family responsibilities, duties, and exposures, female aggressive crime tends to have greater ego involvement. It is seldom that women kill strangers, for example, and the victim is frequently a husband, paramour, or rival.

It is generally conceded that women use greater deceitfulness in their offenses against property and that women tend to be more manipulative than men (ibid., pp. 8–12). Women seldom commit robbery and burglary, though they may be used as decoys or in other manners participate with men. Larceny, blackmail, and fraud tend to be committed more frequently by women.

Homicides by women are accomplished more frequently by poison as compared to men who commit homicide with firearms or knives. The victims of homicides by women are in general children, members of their own families, or persons with whom they have close personal ties. Infanticide, baby farming, assault, false accusation, and other offenses against children occur frequently among women offenders. Commercialized vice and prostitution, of course, are female offenses, though they are largely directed and controlled by men. Conversely, rape is primarily (but not exclusively) a male offense.

In terms of personal characteristics, the female offender traditionally starts later than the male offender, generally between ages twenty-five and thirty-five, as compared to the male peak between twelve and twenty-two. Sometimes female deviant behavior is intensified by physiological crisis in maturation. Married offenders are more frequent among women than among men. In terms of occupation, domestic services occupations are high, while factory work is low in female crime. In summary, although biological factors are present, the nature and extent of female crime appears to be more a function of cultural factors.

The changing role of women in the crime scene recently has been of importance, and more literature will be focused on the female offender. A review of arrest rates between 1960 and 1973 for men and for women show dramatic changes (*Crime in the United States,* 1981). During this period, the total number of arrests of males increased 27.8 percent, while the total arrests for females increased 95.3 percent. Even more dramatic were the figures for arrests of males and females under eighteen years of age. Between 1960 and 1973, the arrests of males under eighteen years of age rose 123.5 percent, while the arrests of females in the same age group rose 264.1 percent. In comparison, the increase of arrests of males eighteen and over during that period was only 12.2 percent, as compared with arrests of females eighteen and over, which increased 47.5 percent. During the ten-year period, 1971 through 1980, the arrest rate for all females was only 118.5 percent over the 1971 rate, which means that the dramatic increase in female arrests during the period, 1960 through 1980, is slowing—though still increasing faster than the 107.6 percent increase in arrests of males over the same period. To interpret these rates, it is necessary to examine the age and the sexual function. Older males and females have their lifestyles established. The newer lifestyles that emerged in the late 1960s and set the stage for new attitudes and outlooks in the 1970s affected the younger people. The changing social values regarding women, their entry into the mainstream of society with some roles equivalent to men, rejection of "Victorian values," and women's liberation, equal rights, and other "equalizing" movements are bringing the female crime rate closer to that of men, although there is still wide disparity in their respective arrest rates.

Girls' gangs are beginning to appear in the big cities. Drug abuse has been a significant component in the rise of deviant behavior, particularly that of females. When women were involved in "heavy" crime before the 1970s, they were generally used as decoys or for intelligence gathering purposes by male accomplices. More and more, however, women are getting into the "heavy" crime by themselves. Though she was not alone and had male accomplices, the news picture of Patty Hearst with a rifle during a bank robbery in San Francisco was symbolic of the changing scene. It has become obvious that those who have viewed crime, corrections, and the criminal justice system as primarily a "man's world" must begin to shift reference points and recognize the increasing significance of women in crime. Certainly, more literature concerning female criminality will appear as female crime increases.

MIGRANTS AND CRIME

Migrant labor has always been a part of agriculture in the United States because harvest time and some other times in the agricultural cycle require more labor in some seasons than in others. Also, the need shifts from the South to the North and back again in all sections of the country. Three primary streams are the ones from Florida to New York State and back, from Texas to Colorado and Michigan and back, and from California to Washington and Montana and back. The children of migrants go to several schools in a single year, have high absentee rates, probably attending about seven months a year on an irregular basis, and drop out early. They are made up of blacks, Chicanos or Spanish-speaking people, and "poor whites." The Florida to New York stream is more than half black, with many workers coming from rural Georgia. It begins in the fall in Florida in the citrus and winter vegetable areas and attracts about 85,000 workers. Mexican-Americans make up the majority of the Western migrant streams, together with some blacks and whites. They go with the streams because they are "trapped," since agriculture is the only work they know, and they do not have the capital to go into their own businesses (*Florida Health Notes*, 1960, p. 4). Their crimes and delinquencies are low and they are minor. Faced with failure outside their own group, especially in schools, migrant children seek security in their own culture, in their own homes, and with their own crew. Saturday night drunks and fights, together with a little minor theft, generally represent the extent of their "criminal" activities.

In agricultural pursuits in 1970, there were 93,000 migratory workers below the age of twenty in the United States earning an average of $8.35 per day; and there were 103,000 workers twenty years of age and older earning $13.10 per day (Statistical Abstracts of the U.S., 1973). Many of them were Mexicans who had illegally crossed the border (Portes, 1974, p. 240).

In 1982, there were an estimated 1.5 million migrant farmworkers (Satchell, 1982, pp. 6–7). Their life expectancy is about 49 years, while the average in the United States is 73 years. The median income is $3,900 per year, less than half the official poverty level. Only 14 percent of farmworkers' children complete high school. Farmworkers are not covered by the National Labor Relations Act. Their workplace has no requirements for toilets, drinking water, or other sanitary facilities. Poor living conditions, bad food, and primitive sanitation make common illnesses pervasive. Alcoholism is epidemic. The crewleader is a throwback to peonage. In fact, three crewleaders were convicted of slavery in Florida in August, 1983.

Students of the migrant labor situation have indicated that "continued exposure to what appears to be the worst condition of economic and psychological deprivation in the entire society" exists there (Nash, 1974, p. 48). People in that situation may be too "defeated" to commit significant crime.

An interesting type of migrant labor occurs in the seafood-processing plants in Unalaska, about midway down the Aleutian chain. Three larger companies and four smaller companies recruit migrant laborers from Seattle and take them by ship to Unalaska. The one-way fare from Seattle to Dutch Harbor is $231.50. At the end of six months, the companies will return the workers without charge, but if the workers quit or are discharged, they must pay their own way back. Unalaska's population ranges from 400 to 1000 at various times of the year, and there are generally 140 to 200 migrant employees of the seafood-processing plants at any one time. Some of these plants are "floating," having been World War II Liberty ships made into processing plants. Many other buildings in the area are quonset huts and pillboxes built during World War II. Some of the migrant workers get into trouble and are discharged before their six-month time period has expired, and they are stranded on the island without means of support. There were probably eighty men so stranded in 1974, living in old quonset huts and pillboxes. They constitute a problem for the criminal justice system and the small (two-to-four-man capacity) jail is hard pressed to handle the problem. An information sheet for potential employees furnished by the Vita Food Products, Inc., in Seattle is shown in Figure 11-1. This is an excellent and honest description of working conditions in the shellfish operations. Men who take employment under such circumstances are generally unattached, homeless, and migrant. They may also be described as desperate. Reasons for discharge published by Pan-Alaska Fisheries, Inc., are

1. Refusal to perform all work directed by supervisors
2. Refusal to work
3. Drunkenness or possession of alcohol on company premises
4. Disorderly conduct or fighting
5. Failure to maintain adequate personal hygiene
6. Failure to pass physical examination
7. Possession or use of narcotics or drugs

In circumstances that are more cramped than those of agricultural migrants but are otherwise not much different, the development of normal personality is most unlikely. The primary characteristics of the migrants' lifestyle are deprivation and futility. Even crime and delinquency are half-hearted.

MASS CULTURE CONFLICT: THE CUBAN-HAITIAN INFLUX IN MIAMI

Surplus people have been a problem ever since the development of agriculture made land valuable enough to be governed by a political structure—feudal fiefdom, state, or empire. These surplus people are generally (1) dissidents, who challenge the ideologies of the political structure and (2) those who consume more than they produce or are in some way dependent upon society because, for instance, they are prisoners or otherwise institutionalized. Execution or banishment was once frequently used for the dissidents, while slavery took care of the less efficient and competent persons in society. Large military establishments have also been used to absorb surplus people, as the Soviet Union does today. Beginning in the fourth century, A.D., the Christian church used the papal inquisition to eliminate dissidents, who were convicted of heresy, alchemy, witchcraft, and other "compacts with the Devil." At first, the sanction was excommunication, but executions began in 385 A.D., with Priscillian.

    Large numbers of surplus people resulted from the enclosure

FIGURE 11-1.
Information Sheet for Potential Employees

To Potential Employees:

Thank you for your interest in employment with Vita Food Products, Inc., in their Alaska Plants. In addition to the conditions described in the attached employment agreement, we offer the following information concerning employment there.

We have two plants. The barge "VITA" which is permanently moored in Dutch Harbor, and the M/V "VICEROY" which is a self contained factory ship operating at both Dutch Harbor and Adak. The conditions described below apply in general to both plants.

(1) One way transportation from Seattle to either Dutch Harbor or Adak is $231.50. Round trip $463.00. Provided you complete the entire season, which under no circumstances is less than six (6) months, the transportation is furnished by "Vita". If you quit or are discharged for cause, the transportation charges must be paid by yourself. Transportation charges there are deducted from your first earnings and will be refunded when and if you complete the season.

(2) The living quarters are cramped. The bunks are 35" X 74", with 2 to 8 per room, and limited bath and shower facilities. There are no dressers or closets, only military type lockers. We encourage you to bring seabags - NOT SUITCASES, and all washable warm casual clothing.

(3) No bedding or pillows are furnished. You may bring your own or may purchase from the plant. Most employees use sleeping bags. The plants have sleeping bags, sheets, pillows, and blankets for sale. You should bring your own towels.

(4) The work is cold and wet. The majority of all jobs require you to wear rain gear (rubber boots, rain pants, rain coat, rain hat). None of this rain gear is furnished, so bring your own or you can purchase from the plant what is required. Gloves and aprons are the only items furnished at no charge at the plant.

(5) Board and room is furnished. The food is excellent.

(6) There is no recreation, no radio or TV and no entertainment except for occasional movies. The weather is generally bad so out of door activities are limited.

(7) The work is generally monotonous and uninteresting. It is not physically difficult but it is laborious. There are no guarantees, but when work is available the shift is usually 12 hours a day. We work 7 days a week when required.

(8) Laundry facilities are available at no charge.

(9) There are no medical or dental facilities available at Dutch Harbor, and military facilities are available for emergencies only at Adak.

The plants and their location are no place for someone who must have privacy in his day to day activities. In order to last the season, one must be willing to rough it and forget many of the creature comforts available in the city. You must be willing to accept orders and work extremely hard for improved production and quality. You must be able to get along with your neighbors.

If you have any doubts above, please withdraw your application. Life is too short for both of us to have unhappiness.

VITA FOOD PRODUCTS, INC.

Courtesy of Vita Food Products, Inc.

movement in England, which began just before the Industrial Revolution. As English agriculture was transformed from a subsistence economy to a market economy, private farmers fenced in their land and expelled many former occupants, who were left to fend for themselves.

In the middle of the nineteenth century (1846–48) the Great Famine of Ireland cost more than two and a half million people their homes and in many cases their lives. Many Irish emigrated to the United States.

Governments have long been getting rid of surplus people (Rubenstein, 1982). The large-scale pogroms (massacres) in Russia under the czar, begun in 1881, resulted in the biggest migration of Jews in history. Millions of Jewish emigrants went to Germany, Austria, other countries in Western Europe, and the United States. During World War I at least a million Armenian Christians were massacred by the Turks. The Nazis systematically destroyed European Jewry between 1933 and the end of World War II by transporting the Jews to death camps, where six million were murdered. Pol Pot instituted genocide in Cambodia in the 1970s when the Hanoi regime took over South Vietnam. Amnesty International, headquartered in London, has reported many political killings and "disappearances" in Iran, Argentina, El Salvador, Uganda, Ethiopia, the USSR, and elsewhere around the world. The Cuban-Haitian influx of refugees into Miami and Dade County, Florida, in 1980, is simply another event in this continuing saga of "surplus people."

Fidel Castro began his struggle for power with a speech on July 26, 1953, and gathered strength until by 1957 his "gang" had built a base in the mountains of Oriente Province. Through sabotage and raids in 1957–58, the government became so shaky and weakened that President Batista was forced to leave Havana on January 1, 1959. Castro assumed power the same day. As a consequence, 500 Americans were evacuated, and many refugees left Cuba for Key West. The United States granted political asylum to Cuban refugees. War crimes trials began on January 22, 1959, in the Havana stadium, and 700 Batista supporters were executed. By November, all government workers left from the Batista regime were fired, their property confiscated, and another large emigration to the United States occurred. These refugees were scholars, professionals, and other responsible middle-class people. Cuba experienced a "brain-drain," and these hard-working immigrants built a solid cultural and political Hispanic base in the Miami metropolitan area. In April 1961, the Revolutionary Council of Cuban Refugees announced an invasion of Cuba, subsequently known as the ill-fated Bay of Pigs. In January 1961, Castro's adherence to communism resulted in the exclusion of Cuba by the Organization of American States (OAS) from "participation in the international American system." Between January 1, 1959, and October 22, 1962, when the "Cuban missile crisis" ended, 248,070 Cubans came to the United States.

On April 2, 1980, 2,000 Cubans jammed the Peruvian Embassy in Havana, demanding asylum in Peru or other Latin American countries. Their number increased to 10,000 in a few days. On April 20, Castro said they were free to leave, since Venezuela and Peru were accepting common criminals. A raft with five Cubans was picked up at Key West on April 2, and two boats loaded with Cubans were picked up on April 21, beginning the "Mariel boatlift." Castro wanted to expel from Cuba "criminals, mentally retarded, mentally ill, and all other social scum" (Final Report of the Grand Jury, Miami, 1982). At the same time, refugees were arriving from Haiti, the most poverty stricken country in the Caribbean. During and after the Mariel boatlift, 124,789 Cubans and 34,111 Haitians arrived in the United States.

Arriving in six stages between 1959 and 1981, 774,996 Cubans arrived in the United States, though some estimates are as high as 918,974 (McCoy and Gonzalez, 1982). The number of Haitians was about 40,023 between 1975 and 1981. On May 5, 1980, President Carter promised federal assistance that never came, and on May 14, he tried to stop the boatlift. About 2,400 refugees were criminals from Cuba's prisons and 1,094 of them were taken to the United States Penitentiary at Atlanta. Others were detained in jails and unused military installations. On June 1, a serious riot involving Cubans occurred at Fort Chaffee, Arkansas, and other disturbances were reported from Seattle to New York and back to Miami. The policies of the United States Immigration and Naturalization Service confused many people. The service granted asylum to Cubans and other refugees who could show well-founded fear of persecution if they returned to their homelands but not to refugees from "friendly" countries like Haiti and El Salvador. On June 20, 1980, 15,000 Haitians were granted reprieves by Federal Judge Alcee L. Hastings in Miami and were given the right to work.

The influx of Cubans had a vast social impact on Miami and its environs, including a sharp rise in crime, while the Haitians were quiet and caused little trouble. The rate of violent crime doubled between 1975 and 1979, and by the summer of 1979, Miami officials realized that three-quarters of the cocaine and marijuana entering the United States was coming through southern Florida. New terms, such as cocaine cowboys and narcobucks, entered the language. Violence, drug war assassinations, and assaults increased until spring 1980, when the first large-scale urban disorder in a decade occurred in Liberty City. There were 66,000 handguns sold in Miami in 1980. Crime in 1980 went up 30.5 percent over 1979 (Metro-Dade Police, 1980). In comparison to 320 homicides in Dade County in 1979, there were 515 homicides in 1980, 576 in 1981, and 533 in 1982. In comparison with 139,566 total Index Crimes in Dade County in 1979, there were 182,164 in 1980 and 180,840 in 1981. Of the Hispanic victims of murder, 89 percent were criminals; 78 percent of the killers and victims were acquainted; 32 percent of crimes were drug related; and 84 percent of the murders were committed with handguns (Wilbanks, 1982). It is general consensus that only about 25 percent of the increase in homicides was due to the Marielitos and that some of the increase came from other factors, such as the increased narcotics trade.

The cost to the local and state taxpayers was seen as "staggering" and the absence of federal aid was similarly "staggering" (Grand Jury Report, 1980, p. 17). The immigrant experience of the Cubans, with its corollaries in family disruption, downward social mobility, and other problems in adjustments, taxed local resources beyond their limits, and outside assistance was almost nonexistent. The Fascell-Stone Amendment provided some federal financial assistance beginning in early 1981, but it was seen as "totally unacceptable" (ibid., p. 7). Jackson Memorial Hospital spent $21 million in medical services to the Cubans and Haitians, and the federal government reimbursed $14 million.

The future of Miami and Dade County looked good (Neil, 1982). The arrival of professional and middle-class Cubans after Castro took power had established a strong political and economic base in the Miami area. The majority of the Marielitos who came with the boatlift in 1980 have begun to be assimilated, and the serious criminals and mental cases have been isolated and detained. The grand jury report indicated that Dade County has survived one of the most terrifying periods in its history and is now in the forefront of national and international political, cultural, and economic progress in this area. Miami is bicultural and bilingual; has money from various sources, even in laundered "narcobucks"; and has an energetic population that can make it the international crossroads of the Americas. While New York City has close ties with Western Europe, Chicago is the farmers' economic and cultural base in central United States, and San Francisco serves the Pacific basin, Miami in the future will serve the Caribbean basin and Latin America as its cultural, economic, and political center. Sixty percent of the population is Hispanic, 20 percent black, and only 20 percent is Anglo/white, and there are no Anglo neighborhoods. Already, 25 percent of Miami's business is international banking, and the area, particularly Coral Gables, has been referred to in the *Harvard Business Review* as one of the "global cities of tomorrow" (Neil, 1982). The hard-working Cubans and the "brains" that came after Castro's takeover have furnished a solid base for the future of Miami. Its Cuban mayor, Maurice Ferre, is a capable man, who sees the future of Miami as the crossroads of the Western Hemisphere. Because of the newly increased importance of the area, "We are looking forward to April 15, 1992, when King Carlos of Spain will come to Miami to celebrate the five-hundredth anniversary of Columbus's voyage to the New World" (ibid., 1982, p. 26).

DYSSOCIAL OFFENDERS

Dyssocial offenders are individuals who are not classified in a clinical group of personality disorders and are considered to be normal but are the product of a lifelong environment that has fostered social values in conflict with the usual codes of society (Coleman, 1964, p. 369). This would include many people in organized crime and the rackets, along with many in moonshining and bootlegging, gambling, prostitution and vice, the narcotics trade, and other undercover businesses. The dyssocial offender has a dysfunctional contact with society in that he or she is a part of it but does not have a good and wholesome relationship with it, as compared with what some have called the dissocial offender, who is dissociated and estranged from society (criminally insane). Dyssocial offenders are business people. Any "rehabilitation" would be to control their activities so that their profits would be reduced or so that they are put out of business. This is generally difficult to accomplish, because it is difficult to find complaining witnesses among those who buy the goods and services they want or others who are afraid to testify. When Governor Dolph Briscoe of Texas closed Edna's Fashionable Ranch Boarding House at LaGrange, Texas, for example, about seven hundred citizens signed a petition asking that the closing order be rescinded (Scott, 1973). (Edna's was probably the most famous of American houses of ill-repute, having served six generations of Texans.) Edna's had become an integral part of the community. The citizens wanted to protect an old establishment that had served their interests well.

ORGANIZED CRIME

Organized crime deals in illegal goods and services, including gambling, loan sharking, narcotics, and all forms of vice; it is deeply involved in legitimate business and labor unions as well (*Task Force Report*, 1967, p. 1). Frank Costello (1893–1973) was considered by many to be a leader in organized crime, specifically the Mafia syndicate; he dined in the best restaurants in New York City, was shaved daily at the Waldorf-Astoria Hotel, lived in an expensive apartment at 72nd Street and Central Park West, and was seen in the company of many judges, public officials, and prominent businessmen. In short, he was accepted as a prosperous and successful man (ibid., p. 2). He died peacefully in his sleep at the age of eighty.

Organized crime operates in all sections of the country, with police departments in 80 percent of the largest cities reporting organized crime in their cities. The wealthiest and most influential core groups operate in New York, New Jersey, Illinois, Florida, Louisiana, Nevada, Michigan, and Rhode Island (ibid., p. 7).

In recent years, the Mafia has been credited with being the major organized crime group. While full consensus on the origin of the Mafia may be lacking, a credible version is that it began in Sicily about 1298 when the towns people of Palermo formed a vigilante group to kill French soldiers in reprisal for the rape-slaying of a young Sicilian bride. The cry of the vigilante group was "Morte alla Francia Italia Anela" (MAFIA), which meant "Death to the French is Italy's cry!" Spreading throughout Sicily and southern Italy, this vigilante group existed for hundreds of years under various conditions and promulgated various causes. The group really consisted of an underground force that harassed the French oppressors; it effectively plundered, robbed, kidnapped for ransom, and engaged in other terrorist activities. The population considered the Mafia to be heroes in much the same manner that the old English made Robin Hood a legend. In recent years, however, it has become apparent that the true Mafia never got out of Sicily. Organized crime groups in America evidently simply adopted the name.

The Mafia was first reported in the United States by Chief of Police David Hennesey of New Orleans in 1890. The revelations by Joseph Valachi during the McClellan Committee hearings in 1963 were not new to the police in America. There are several good books that describe the operation in detail (for example, see MacLean, 1974). It is general knowledge that it was Salvatore Maranzano in New York City who initiated the idea of "families" after Giuseppe "Joe the Boss" Masseria was gunned down April 15, 1931. Maranzano named the five family bosses in New York and assumed the title *Capo di Tutti Capi* ("Boss of all the Bosses"). Soon afterward Maranzano eliminated "Lucky" Luciano and Vito Genovese for insubordination, whereupon four men identified with Luciano and Genovese killed Maranzano, and on the same day forty-two other Maranzano Mafiosi were killed in other cities throughout the country. Despite considerable evidence, some sociologists hold that the Mafia may be a myth promulgated by criminology textbooks and that more research needs to be done to determine whether the Mafia really exists (Galliher and Cain, 1974). Al Capone was not in the Mafia. It is apparent that the "Mafia" label has been overextended and does not include all organized crime.

Organized crime has a deeply entrenched position in American society (Conklin, 1973; Tyler, 1962; Salerno and Tompkins, 1969; and Homer, 1974). Although there is evidence of national organizations, most organized crime appears to be more localized. Bribery and corruption make it difficult to prosecute mob leaders, and the consumer demand for illegal goods and services prevents public outcry against it and, more immediately, reduces the possibility of complaining witnesses. When the syndicate "owns" key police oficials and judges, as Al Capone was reputed to have done, convictions are impossible even when witnesses are available.

Organized crime survives through fear and corruption and also because it provides sufficient services in addition to "protection by terror" to discourage legitimate complaints in court. There are twenty-seven major "families" now working in the United States, with eight states being the major areas of activity.

Organized crime is a functional part of American society that has been generally used by successive waves of immigrants as a means of upward mobility, with the Italians taking the early lead (Ianni, 1974). They were briefly challenged by the Irish during the 1920s. Today, the big business, except for prostitution, is still in the hands of the Italians, but blacks and Spanish-speaking racketeers are becoming increasingly involved in organized crime. A feature story from the *New York Times* in 1973 indicated that black racketeers were "taking over" in Newark, New Jersey.

Organized crime is the second largest business in America, behind oil, which gained revenues of $365 billion in 1978, while organized crime gained $150 billion (Cooke, 1980). By comparison, the automobile industry grossed about $125 billion, and other industries followed. White-collar crime grossed probably $100 billion (Saxon, 1978; also Duncan and Caplan, 1980). Street crime, while grossing only about $3 to $4 billion, is a type of crime that generates much fear in the public because it is visible. Organized crime provides goods and services for which people will pay, and white collar-crime is virtually invisible.

The difficulty in handling organized crime, of course, is that it serves a consuming public that will pay for the illegal goods and services. In addition, it has an enforcing system that silences any potential witnesses. Former U.S. Attorney General Robert F. Kennedy testified in 1963 that protection of the witnesses who had cooperated with the federal government was nearly impossible; some had changed their appearance, changed their names and identities, and some had even left the country (*Task Force Report*, 1967, p. 1). Obtaining evidence for conviction under due process of law in the American legal system remains almost impossible.

Murder, Inc.

Murder, Inc., was organized sometime around 1933, when it was approved by "Lucky" Luciano, and it operated in total secrecy until 1940. It was established as an enforcement arm to protect the syndicate's growing interest against rival mobsters. The first goon squad was headed by Benjamin "Bugsy" Siegel and his partner, Meyer Lansky. Based in Brooklyn, it was available to all members of the syndicate throughout the United States. Some of the prominent names connected with Murder, Inc., were "Lucky" Luciano, Albert Anastasia, Vito Genovese, Louis "Lepke" Buchalter, Abner "Lony" Zwillman, Meyer Lansky, and Frank Costello. Murder, Inc. became big business under the guidance of Buchalter. There were many "hit men" in the group, but one of the most energetic was Pittsburgh Phil (whose real name was Harry Strauss), who killed about 500 people for hire before Murder, Inc. was exposed early in 1940.

CONCLUSIONS

Cultural factors and anthropological approaches are important in criminal behavior and must be taken into consideration by the criminal justice system. Racial and ethnic differences and delinquent subcultures, have been a part of crime in America throughout the twentieth century and organized crime has been an outlet for some of the most recent immigrant groups. It is our culture that gives us our frame of reference, our way of thinking and eventually our lifestyle. Although it can be changed by other factors, our way of doing things—our culture as we learn it—constitutes the most significant factor in a person's successful adaptation to society.

The United States has the most heterogeneous population in the world. Ethnic and racial groups tend to identify with their own heritages and traditions. Simultaneously, social distance between these groups appear in varying degrees. Social distance reinforces the cultural differentiations between groups that identify with their historical traditions, and in turn, cultural differentiation reinforces the social distance. The result is tension and stress between ethnic and racial groups that produces violence and crime. As previously mentioned in chapter 1, crime identifies the stress points in a society, which are frequently the result of social, economic, and cultural inequities, differentiation, and conflict. A heterogeneous society is more likely to generate higher crime rates through cultural conflict than a homogeneous population.

Questions

1. What are the characteristics of primitive law?
2. How does the primitive blood feud relate to the development of law?
3. Why are ethnic minorities disproportionately associated with crime in the statistics and in the literature in America?
4. What is culture conflict theory and who developed it?
5. What was the reaction of the international press to the manner in which the riot in Attica, New York, was handled in September 1971?
6. Why are blacks disproportionately represented in the arrest and crime rates?
7. What are the cultural factors associated with the low crime rate among females?
8. What is the contribution of migrant laborers to the crime problem?
9. What is the dyssocial offender?
10. Discuss organized crime in America.

twelve

PHILOSOPHICAL, RELIGIOUS, AND MOTIVATIONAL APPROACHES

Values and value systems are the central concerns of philosophy, religion, and motivational approaches. Philosophical, religious, and motivational approaches are the oldest attempts to understand behavior and to offer suggestions for the modification of deviant behavior. When Neanderthal man first began to "care" about his fellow man and initiated funeral rites around 60,000 B.C., the beginnings of religion were emerging. The earliest organized primitive religion appears to have originated around 23,000 B.C., according to the findings of archeologists. Spoken language was in the process of developing between 100,000 and 30,000 B.C., and it provided humans with the power of abstract thinking which, in turn, permitted them to develop values and to think in terms of the past and the future. Intelligent humans developed anxiety and would call upon the gods for assistance, protection, and support. Religion then gave meaning and purpose to man's existence. It gave meaning to life.

Philosophy emerged in sophisticated form among the ancient Greeks in the fifth and fourth centuries B.C., the most popular ancient philosophers being Socrates, Plato, and Aristotle. During the rise of the great religions, philosophy and theology became intertwined. Theological systems were developed to explain the existence of evil and sin in a world in which God was omniscient, omnipotent, and omnipresent. The resulting creeds took many approaches, developing many types of philosophies and theological systems. Philosophy emerged semi-independently during, the Reformation, generally considered to be in the thirteenth and fourteenth centuries A.D., and the Renaissance. It was René Descartes, a French philosopher, who separated natural law from divine law, maintaining that God had given man his free will and permitted him to function under natural law, so any deviation would be man's responsibility. Later philosophers also attempted to understand the universe and the behavior of man, developing many systems that could explain deviant behavior.

Motivational explanations of deviant behavior became significant when laws concerning vagabondage were passed in Europe and England beginning around the fifth century A.D. and continuing into the nineteenth century (Ribton-Turner, 1972). The thesis was that poor people who could not pay their debts were intentionally lazy and not motivated to behave in a socialized manner. Their ineffectiveness in dealing with their environment, then, became a matter of motivation. The early punishments in the workhouses in England and on the Continent were based on this premise.

The contributions of philosophy, religion, and motivational approaches to understanding and treating criminal and delinquent behavior remain important to this day. Many religious organizations have private institutions for delinquent boys and girls. Many of these institutions and their counseling programs use the inspirational-repressive approach to modify behavior, as compared with the psychological, psychiatric, and sometimes only custodial approaches in other public and private institutions. The concept of moral reeducation is prominent, for example, in Canadian and European French-speaking areas. Motivational approaches are used in many drug treatment programs like Synanon and Daytop Village and in many organizations of people with problems, like the Fortune Society in New York and Alcoholics Anonymous, where persons who have experienced these problems help to support psychologically other persons with similar problems. The peer-pressure programs in some juvenile institutions would be in this category. Many of these approaches disregard the background of the offender with the "let's forget the past" approach and offer hope for the future.

PHILOSOPHICAL APPROACHES

Philosophy is a Greek word referring to the love and pursuit of wisdom. Early philosophers and theologians recognized no division of knowledge, because all scholarship attempted to understand the reality of the universe. Philosophical approaches are deductive in that a basic truth is accepted, and logical arguments and thinking are developed from the basic truth. Science, on the other hand, is inductive in that basic data are gathered, hypotheses are developed after observation, and the basic truth or laws are derived from the available evidence or data. For example, the study of human behavior in many denominational colleges and universities and religious schools with a philosophical and theological orientation accepts the existence of the soul. (For example, see Moore, 1948.) They contend that attempts to study human behavior without considering the soul and the power of God are grossly deficient. On the other hand, psychology in tax-supported universities and schools is based on proximate causes and available data.

The justification of sentencing and punishment has been the central concern of philosophers interested in criminal behavior and the justice system. Immanuel Kant (1724–1804) was the chief proponent of "critical," "transcendental," or "formal" idealism, and Georg Wilhelm Friedrich Hegel (1770–1831) systematized philosophical approaches, relying heavily on Kant. Hegel has been called the "father of political fascism," and Hitler had read his writings extensively. Kant and Hegel were the two most severe philosophers in their judgments of crime and punishment, both viewing punishment as a right of the criminal. Hegel stated the proposition well:

> Punishment is the right of the criminal. It is an act of his own will. The violation of right has been proclaimed by the criminal as his own right. His crime is the negation of right. Punishment is the negation of this negation, and consequently an affirmation of right, solicited and forced upon the criminal by himself. [Quoted in Ezorsky, 1972, p. 358]

This retributive approach is simply that punishment is only justified by guilt as a doctrine of "annulment" or "getting even," which is not utilitarian, according to many philosophers, but there is debate as the whether retribution is or is not utilitarian.

Teleological philosophical approaches are concerned with evidence of design in nature, that events are shaped by purpose, and that natural processes are part of a total plan conceived as determined by a final plan and designed by a Divine Providence. Therefore, retribution is utilitarian to the teleological philosophers. Plato, Jeremy Bentham, and others who see punishment as utilitarian hold that punishment is a deterrent, both to the individual concerned and to others (Rowls, 1972, p. 358). Parents generally regard punishment of children as justified only in view of the future good of their children and to make life in the home more tolerable and to distribute jobs and sacrifices equally (Brandt, 1959, pp. 490–95). Bentham's famous criterion of "the greatest good for the greatest number" appears applicable in the utilitarian approach to punishment.

Teleological retributivism involves vengeance as a natural consequence of crime and sin. St. Thomas Aquinas held that punishment for punishment's sake was unacceptable, but in the case of punishment directed toward good, so that the sinner may reform or be restrained from harming others, vengeance may be lawful. Armstrong (1961) has written that justice gives those in authority the right to punish offenders up to some limit, and an offender may be punished less, but it is never just to punish a man more than he deserves.

Still other philosophers have indicated that neither utilitarian nor retributive approaches are just. George Bernard Shaw (1946), the English author and philosopher, wrote:

> Either Come Off It, or Go Inside and take the measure you are meting out to others no worse than yourself. [p. 71]

Wasserstrom (1964) has called for treatment of the offender, with no punishment for the crime because there are too many uncontrollable factors involved and most attempts at justification suggest that punishment of people, guilty or innocent, is designed for the deterrence of others, which is hardly morally defensible. Clarence Darrow, in discussing the many jails in Chicago and the treatment of offenders, particularly holdup men, said:

> But more grim and farcical still than the senseless talk about the holdup man is one other fact. Chicago has hundreds of Christian churches—we are a Christian people. It is nineteen hundred years since Christ's teachings were given to the world—we profess to be the disciples of that lowly man who believed in no jails or clubs—who taught infinite love and infinite mercy—who said if a man asked for your coat, give him also your cloak—and yet today we know nothing better than hatred, repression, brute force, jails and clubs. We single out a considerable class of our fellow men to shoot on sight. Of course, the world will continue to treat its so-called criminals in this enlightened humane way. Therefore would it not be well to rechristen our churches, and stop calling them after Christ? [Ezorsky, 1972, p. 364]

Philosophers regard punishment for crime in many different ways. Some call for nonutilitarian vengeance. Others see nature as the "pattern of things" in a teleological or purposeful manner, either utilitarian for deterrence or retributive for vengeance. Still others hold that punishment does no good, and they are not concerned with the utilitarian or retributive goals nor the teleological or purposeful intent of it. Philosophical approaches are broad and are concerned with the moral issues of crime and punishment as they relate to the value system. Some people, such as Hugo Adam Bedau (1967) of Tufts University, are currently active in studying the death penalty. Philosophical and ethical issues pervade the entire area of criminal behavior and the justice system.

ORGANIZED RELIGION AND SOCIAL CONTROL

The first group beyond the family and kinship group able to hold the loyalty of man was the religious group. The world's oldest profession was the priesthood in whatever form it appeared—the religious leader, shaman, medicine man, or other spiritual leader who interpreted the voice of the gods and the supernatural to primitive man. A system of values and morality had to emerge prior to prostitution, which some have called the "world's oldest profession," so the priesthood preceded prostitution! The ethical systems that developed in early religion were really distillations of the customs that had been found to work best as the ground rules for group living.

Religion synthesized and codified the basic ethical system that functions in all societies. It is interesting to note that although the rituals and the deities differ among all the great religions, there are no significant differences in the ethical systems of Judaism, Christianity, Islam, or any other of the major faiths. Consequently, any review of specific ethical systems would apply to all religions, though the specific references to the Talmud, Torah, Bible, Koran, and so on, would differ. In fact, Judaism, Christianity, and Islam have essentially the same prophets, having come from the same religious base, historically. The Council of Nicaea in 325 A.D. separated Christianity from Judaism and the peoples who lost at that Council tended to accept Islam when it rose in 622 A.D. with Jesus Christ as a prophet. An example of the universal values and the ground rules appears in the Sermon on the Mount in the Christian faith as reported in Matthew 5: 3–12.

Using these approaches as ground rules, social living and adherence to religious principles were easier. The very ability to accept adversity according to these tenets was one of the factors that caused Marx and Engels in *The Communist Manifesto*, published in 1849, to refer to religion as "the opiate of the people." In any case, the Sermon on the Mount appears to be an excellent and concise statement of ethical principles in social living as they emerged everywhere in ancient civilization.

A thousand and more years earlier, the laws of Moses were developed, between 1500 and 900 B.C. As pointed out in the first chapter, Moses' trip to Mount Sinai and his being given the Ten Commandments has been placed at about 1215 B.C. In the Judeo-Christian tradition, they appear in the Old Testament and are similar to the ethical formulations in the other great religions. The Ten Commandments appear in Exodus 20: 3–17 and in Deuteronomy 5: 7–21. (Some chaplains in correctional institutions view God as authoritarian. Several have indicated that if God were permissive, he would have handed down the Ten Suggestions! Other chaplains see God as loving and forgiving but admonish their flock to do the best they can.)

The manner in which these basic tenets are implemented in working with people is dependent in large measure on the personality of the practitioner. Prayer has little meaning for a delinquent child or adult criminal, but many religiously oriented practitioners have made this a basic approach. In response to inquiries about the services of the chaplain, several prison inmates have told this writer, "If there is a God, he sure as hell wasn't on my side." From the psychological standpoint, the "power of prayer" is apparently in suggestion. A delinquent who is strongly religious in the first place can benefit from suggestion, but the entire procedure may alienate a delinquent who rejects the concept of religion and prayer. This discussion must relate only to proximate causes and not to theology that includes ultimate causes and the theological power of prayer.

The death penalty is prescribed in Exodus 21: 12, 14, 15, 16, and 17, and Exodus 22: 18, 19, and 20. All other major religions reject the death penalty, including Christian canon law, Islam, and the ancient *Chinese Book of Five Punishments*. The "eye for eye, tooth for tooth" concept of retaliation appears in Exodus 21:24. Compensation and retribution are prescribed for most property crimes in Exodus 22: 1–15.

From primitive times into the nineteenth century, religion provided the primary leadership in social control. About the time of the Industrial Revolution and the emergence of the modern national state, this function was taken over by lawyers, concurrent with the rise of the criminal law. Obedience to divine law and religious precepts is promulgated in all writings basic to the great religions. In addition, religious organizations promote obedience to secular law as well. For example, *The Book of Common Prayer* of the Episcopal church supports secular government with statements such as the following:

> Endue with the spirit of wisdom those to whom in thy Name we entrust the authority of government, that there may be justice and peace at home, and that, through obedience to thy law, we may show forth thy praise among the nations of the earth. [p. 36]
>
> To honor and obey the civil authority: To submit myself to all my governors, teachers, spiritual pastors and masters: To order myself lowly and reverently to all my betters: To hurt nobody by word or deed. . . . [p. 580]
>
> The Power of the Civil Magistrate extendeth to all men, as well Clergy as Laity, in all things temporal; but hath no authority in things purely spiritual. And we hold it to be the duty of all men who are professors of the Gospel, to pay respectful obedience to the Civil Authority, regularly and legitimately constituted. [p. 610]

Confidence in the achievement of justice permeates religious writing. It is well-stated in the following familiar verse by Friedrich von Logau:

Though the mills of God grind slowly,
  Yet they grind exceeding small,
Though with patience He stands waiting,
  With exactness grinds He all.

There has always been religious and church-related work with juvenile delinquents and adult offenders. In America, the Christian church played an important role in the development of correctional practice because crime, like poverty, was considered to be endemic to society (Rothman, 1971, p. 15). The Christian church at that time was interested in intimidating the offender into being obedient, insuring public safety, and carrying out God's law. A primary approach was taken from Matthew 25: 41, which said, "Watch and pray, that ye enter not into temptation: the spirit indeed is willing, but the flesh is weak." Prevention of delinquency was the primary thrust of the early church, but repentence was the primary approach to those who had already offended. That is why the first institution established by the Quakers in Philadelphia in 1790 was called a "penitentiary."

Religious and church-related work with delinquents and adult offenders continues on a large scale today. The halfway house movement received some impetus from Dismas House in St. Louis (1959), St. Leonard's House in Chicago (1961), and other similar projects in other areas. Many projects have involved personalities, such as Father Flanagan's Boys Town in Nebraska, Billy Graham's initiation of Youth for Christ, and many other clergymen who have devoted their lives to helping people avoid involvement with the criminal justice system. (See Wilkerson, 1963).

The Salvation Army, Volunteers of America, Society of St. Vincent de Paul, the Home Mission Board of the Southern Baptist Convention, the Jewish Board of Charities, and similar established organizations have been serving juvenile and adult offenders for a long time. They were joined in the 1960s and 1970s by some "way-out" groups that have attracted many adolescents, such as the "Jesus Freaks," "Street Christians," and "Jesus People," who are part of a movement that began in San Francisco in 1967. The Catholic Pentacosts also joined the way-out groups. The majority of effective work in this field by religious and church-related groups is done by the established groups that have made a direct commitment to working with offenders.

There are some other church groups that have neither expressed interest in nor contributed significantly to this area of endeavor. Most of these are conservative groups that agree with Max Weber's (1930) concept of the "Protestant ethic," which maintains that the goals of personal and material success are available to all who work for them and that the achievement of material rewards is a sign of moral worth. Undesirable people can be identified and "frozen out" or otherwise eliminated from the church. There are a few churches, then, not interested in the juvenile delinquent and the adult offender, but most major churches established in America do contribute in some measure to the assistance and rehabilitation of people in trouble.

Most chaplains are primarily concerned with positive motivation (Leibold, 1971, pp. 67–68). Motivation does not exist without deep personal relations and concern for the value of other people and relationships with them; it comes from the aspirations and inspirations of people. Yet motivation and relations with other people for the most part are stifled in prison. This makes the work of the chaplain in prisons most difficult. All obnoxious behavior, whether a baby screaming or a person committing a crime, is really a cry for help—"Someone listen to me, make me feel important, worthwhile. Someone, please love me!" (Helline, 1972).

Garmon (1968) points out that Jesus spent a lot of time with outcasts, social undesirables, and sinners, and calls for the Church to go to these people.

In summary, the least the Church is saying is to leave the offender alone and without vengeance, as incorporated in the ancient *Babylonian Talmud: Shabbath:* "Leave the drunkard alone: he will fall by himself." The most the Church is saying is to take the offender in, comfort him and give him peace, mercy, love, and a promise of resurrection. How these varying views are implemented are as varied as the views themselves. There is no single "religious approach" to the offender nor to the criminal justice system, but varying degrees and methods of interest, offering assistance, and performing the service.

EVALUATION OF RELIGIOUS APPROACHES

The psychological and social factors in religion, not the theological factors, appear to depend upon the emotional and social needs of the individual. Religion tends to answer the questions, (1) Who am I? (2) Where am I going? and (3) How will I get there? Religion gives meaning to a life that would otherwise be meaningless. Participation in church activities, like participation in any other activity, is not the same for everybody. Many people are goal oriented and focus on the ends intended by a church in terms of its purpose and promise. Others are role oriented and are more interested in the visibility of being identified and associated with a church. Still others are activity oriented and enjoy the participation without major consideration either for the goal or the role.

The differences appear to lie, at least in part, in the emotional and social needs of people.

The first major contribution to the understanding of personality factors in religion was made by the famous Harvard physiologist and psychologist, William James (1842–1910), who wrote *The Varieties of Religious Experience*. This remains the classic work in the psychology of religion today, and subsequent research has served to support James' observations. Much of the recent research has appeared in the *Journal for the Scientific Study of Religion*, established in 1957, but even more significant research was distributed over the first half of the twentieth century after William James' contribution.

In terms of development, Mudge (1930) found that 77 percent of a group of fourteen-year-olds had a "clear image of God," indicating concrete thinking rather than abstract thinking, while older persons did not have such a clear image. McLane, O'Brien, and Wemple (1954) indicated that 95 percent of Sunday School children said that when they talked to God, they found out what was right to do, which connected religion with morality. Franklin (1929) found that the comprehension of parables was greater than comprehensions of precepts in children four to twelve years old, and the increases were independent of church attendance.

Radke, Traeger, and Davis (1949) found that projective pictures shown to 250 white and black children in kindergarten, first, and second grades, and of Catholic, Protestant, and Jewish background, indicated confusion. Cultural concepts are learned early in childhood, and they reflect the subcultures in which people live. The child accepts adult attitudes toward other groups; and the extent of learning about groups and the degree of depersonalization of attitudes increases with age. Children show vital interest in cultural differences and negative self-feelings appear in minority groups. The differences are due to cultural and social problems rather than religion.

Hartshorne and May (1930) reported after a massive project that religious training and moral concepts seemed to be unrelated to each other. In an independent study of deceit, Hartshorne (1928) found that religion was secondary in this behavior, but that deceit in cheating, lying, and other patterns occurred in accordance with (1) classroom association; (2) personal handicaps, such as low I.Q., poor resistance to suggestion, and emotional instability; (3) other limitations that impede expected performance; and (4) miscellaneous factors. Nobody is honest or dishonest by "nature"; deception is a natural way of adaptation in stress.

Starbuck (1908 and 1897) indicated that religious conversion does not usually occur beyond eighteen to twenty years of age. The motives for conversion come from within, generally around thirteen years of age, but by eighteen years of age, the social factors are more important. The nonconversion religious growth experience appears in the female between ten and twelve years of age and in the male between ten and fifteen years of age. This suggests that during a period of transition from childhood to adolescence, religious phenomena are most important. Starbuck used a large questionnaire study and found that the peak of religious conversion experience for girls was between thirteen and sixteen years of age (puberty at fourteen, generally) and for males sixteen years of age (puberty fourteen to eighteen years). Puberty and conversion may supplement each other in time, though they may be mutually conditioned by culture or physiology.

Ostow and Scharfstein supported Starbuck's findings and James' observations a half-century later in their publication, *The Need to Believe* (also Linn and Schwartz, 1958). Religion was seen as an agent for the dissipation of guilt and reducing anxiety. Conservatives in religion are more dependent and emotionally upset than liberals, indicating that the more fundamentalistic religions provide greater emotional support for people who need it.

Havighurst and Taba (1949) found that religious training and moral concepts are closely related in seventeen-year-olds, indicating that late adolescents are "getting it together." This is supported by Gilliland (1940), who found that the religious ideas of college students were not correlated with the attitudes of their professors.

One point of view is that criminality represents a failure on the part of the Church to train members of society to behave normally, which means that a "lack of religious training" is the basic cause of crime. It is true that church members are committed to prison less often than nonmembers (Minor, 1931). That may be because of a selective factor, in that people who have not assimilated the values of the culture, including church attendance, tend to become involved in trouble more frequently than those who have assimilated the values and attend church. Middleton and Fay (1941) found that delinquent girls had a slightly more favorable attitude toward religious issues than did nondelinquent girls. On the other hand, a study of 915 girls attending classes in religious instruction indicated that such training did not contribute to the individual's ability to apply principles of moral law to life situations (Diaz).

Of 716 delinquent children studied by Kvaraceus (1944), 91 percent claimed affiliation with some church, 54 percent said they attended regularly, 20 percent occasionally, and only 26 percent rarely. In Detroit, Wattenberg (1950) studied 2,137 male delinquents and found that 69 percent claimed they attended church regularly or occasionally, 65 percent of the recidivists said they attended regularly or occasionally, while 71 percent of the nonrecidivists attended regularly or occasionally. Sheldon and Eleanor Glueck (1950, p. 166) in Boston found that 39 percent of the delinquents studied said they attended church regularly, 54 percent said they attended occasionally, and 7 percent never attended. A study of 162 delinquent girls in a private institution indicated that 76 percent claimed church affiliation, but only 2 percent actually attended church regularly (Dominic, 1954). It appears to be unfortunate that many of these types of studies rely on *claims* of the offender, rather than checking the claims out with the church and its pastor. Although the research may suggest more church attendance and affiliation, in the experience of chaplains in institutions attempting to "reestablish" church affiliations, very few of the claimed affiliations were even recognized by the pastors contacted.

Another study indicated that prisoners in forty-five prisons claimed some religious affiliation to the extent of 87 percent, as compared with 40 percent in the general population of the United States at that time (Kalmer and Weir, 1936, p. 19). This study suggests that prisoners want to "look good" for the parole board. Unfortunately, the experience of chaplains in prisons and correctional institutions suggests discrepancies between "research findings" and reality in the field. Caution is advised in accepting *claimed* data on religious affiliation and participation.

Prisoners who attended church regularly prior to their crimes tend to succeed in probation and parole more frequently than those whose attendance has not been regular. Compulsory church attendance, both outside and inside the prison, produces negative reactions to religion (Ernst, 1930). In addition, the self-image of religiosity assists in the reduction of delinquency (McCann, 1956).

In the United States, there is considerable variation in the representation of various religious groups in prison populations (Radzinowicz, 1937). Catholic groups have the largest proportion, with Jewish and Oriental religious disproportionately lower than would be expected from their proportions in the general population. The large number of Catholic prisoners can be explained by the fact that two-thirds of the membership of Roman Catholics and Baptists come from the lower class (Smith, 1949). The immigrant groups that include the Irish, Italian, Polish, Mexicans, and other Spanish-speaking groups are generally Catholic. Although it must be pointed out that Puerto Ricans are citizens and not immigrants, their contribution to the crime statistics is also high, and they are predominantly Catholic. The reasons for the high proportion of Catholics in the prison population is a function of culture rather than of religion. The low rate of crime among Jews has been attributed to close family ties and other cultural factors (Goldberg, 1950; Jaffe and Alinsky, 1939). Frequent church attendance has been associated with success on parole in the majority of parole prediction studies (Sutherland and Cressey, 1966).

A study of 4,200 persons aged thirteen to seventeen in three western Michigan communities reported in 1973 by Vener, Stewart, and Zaenglein indicated that religious training and respect for authority inhibit the desire to smoke, drink, use soft drugs, and engage in premarital sex in middle-class Midwestern juveniles (*Juvenile Justice Digest*, Sept. 1973).The younger juveniles were more identified with religious orthodoxy than older juveniles. Following of orthodox religious creeds tends to decline with age but remains more strong among girls than boys. Girls were more oriented toward authority than boys. Age was found to be a definite factor in respect for authority and in following orthodox religious practices, with the older juveniles being less identified with either.

The only study in which the claims of the delinquent or offender have been actually checked out with the pastors and the Sunday School teachers with whom they claimed to be affiliated was Conn's (1958) study of delinquents processed through the courts of a southern city. The claimed attendance was similar to that reported by Kvaraceus. Conn spent several weeks tracking down pastors and Sunday School teachers who could verify the claims of the offenders. He found that only 5 percent of the offenders were even known by the pastors or the Sunday School teachers, and none of them had attended regularly.

In summary, the research on the effectiveness of religion in the lives of offenders suggests that culture and personality needs are most important in determining the role of religion. Among seminary students, seven who experienced religious conversion, seven who had not experienced this conversion, and six who had experienced it but had regressed to their previous state were compared, and the difference was determined to be in the child-parent relationships within the family (Allison, 1965). Those who had experienced conversion tended to have weak and inadequate fathers, and the conversion had substituted a strong paternal figure with clear values and firm judgments. On the other hand, the attitudes of prisoners in a maximum-custody prison ranged from fundamentalistic salvation to open antagonism to a God who had deserted them as individuals (Fox, 1961, p. 148). More than religion itself apparently determines the effectiveness of church-related and religious programs in the field of criminal justice.

DEMONOLOGY

Demonology, sorcery, and witchcraft have prevailed through primitive, ancient, medieval, and some modern thinking regarding deviant behavior and crime. Primitive peoples thought that those who were deviant were demon possessed. Voodoo in Haiti incorporates thousands of demons, several of which can possess a person simultaneously. The

Old Testament says that a sorceress shall not be permitted to live (Exodus 22:18). The witchcraft trials at Salem, Massachusetts, in 1692 were the last time people were put to death in the United States for witchcraft or sorcery, although witchcraft trials continued until 1800. During the witchcraft era in Salem, the Reverend Samuel Parrish preached emotionally every Sunday and brought the nagging fears and conflicting impulses of the community into an overwhelming drama in which Christ and Satan were pictured as struggling for supremacy. Parrish has been credited with provoking the witchcraft trials, though not deliberately (Boyer and Nissenbaum, 1974). Before the year was over, however, nineteen women had been convicted and hanged as witches. One was hanged after having been acquitted. Six men also died.

Exorcism is the ritual by which evil spirits of demons are expelled from persons who have come under their power. In the early Church, there was considerable use of exorcism, and a special class of the lower clergy appeared as exorcists around 250 A.D. Jesus had expelled demons by power of word and indicated that this act was a sign of the coming of God's kingdom. The modern Church still retains the ritual of exorcism, but it is carefully regulated and its duty to "cast out devils" has given way to the preparation for baptism. Before proceeding with exorcism, the priest or minister must carefully investigate to determine whether or not he has a case of real possession. An Episcopal church in a Chicago suburb received national publicity in 1974 by its use of exorcism to eliminate vandalism from St. Anselm's Episcopal Church in Park Ridge (Charles Nicodemus in the *Chicago Daily News*, March 23, 1974). The interest in exorcism is apparent from the sales of William Peter Blatty's book, *The Exorcist*, published in 1971; it was also made into a popular movie.

Probably the most authoritative discussion of demonology is in Traugott K. Oesterreich's *Possession and Exorcism*, originally published in 1921 in Germany, most recently published in the United States in 1974. It was used as a resource book by Blatty when he wrote *The Exorcist*.

Sargent (1974), a British psychiatrist, sees a common ground in possession, sudden conversions, faith healing, and even the "Beatlemania" phenomenon when teenage girls become excited and scream hysterically over some popular male entertainer or group. He has reported that when some girls reached climactic suggestibility during snake-handling rituals and emotional messages of redemption, they were ready for immediate sexual activity, but at a later time these same girs were offended by any such suggestion.

Demonology is still discussed seriously as a viable theory and the exorcism procedures outlined. Working with demon-possessed people is discussed at some length in Oral Roberts's *Twelve Greatest Miracles of My Ministry*, published in 1974. (See also Richardson, 1974.) With its strong base in the culture, demonology will undoubtedly be used by some for a long time to explain deviant behavior.

EMOTIONAL MATURITY INSTRUCTION

Emotional Maturity Instruction (EMI) was designed by Dan MacDougald of the Yonan Codex Foundation of Atlanta on the basis that good input of information is necessary for adequate judgment formation. The concepts of good input and the mind's control system were drawn from the ancient Aramaic teachings secured from the English translation of an Aramaic text of the New Testament, called the Khaboris Manuscript. This manuscript was considered to be the social teachngs of Jesus and was translated from the Aramaic as a project of the Yonan Codex Foundation.

Words are cues of concepts of the mind's inventory of symbols. Words and concepts such as *self, neighbor, God, love, law, sin, failure, forgive, reason, judgment,* and *attitudes* are studied in order to clarify their meanings. The instructor substitutes the Aramaic concepts for the previous English translations of the teaching of Jesus on attitudes, goals, and words. Psychology, logic, and reasoning are used to illustrate that the rules are good for the individual and will improve his or her wisdom and judgment. EMI operates between the guidelines of the laws of the mind's control (divine law), on the one hand, and in the science of psychology, on the other.

EMI breaks down to five basic points, presented by Warren (1970) as follows:

1. Criminality originates in the mind and is a product of ignorance and stupidity.
2. The inhibitory system of the human routinely and automatically blocks over 99 percent of available facts from perception, reason, and judgment, leaving less than 1 percent of available fact for use in determining behavior.
3. This filter system must be controlled by each individual in accordance with proper directions or rules, or else his mind will not receive proper information and may develop into an antisocial personality.
4. Each word in the directions for properly controlling this filter must be accurately understood or the directions cannot be followed.
5. The directions for properly controlling this filter system were set down in the first century Aramaic teaching of Jesus. [p. 122]

EMI was sufficiently well publicized in annual meetings of the American Correctional Association in 1970, 1971, and 1972 that Ben Frank (1971) attempted to evaluate it. Quoting from a letter received from Leonard J. Hippchen and Wilber D. McCarty, proponents of EMI, he identified the theoretical base as follows:

> The psychopathology of the prisoner is hypothesized to stem from human reality meaning distortions learned during the early socialization period. These distortions are seen to have resulted in an impairment in the constructive neural structural operation in the mind and in development of anti-social attitudes and behavior patterns. The rehabilitation approach aims to achieve a permanent modification in the neural structures in the mind through training in language meanings which will aid the individual to move in the direction of achieving greater harmony with the laws for his constructive psychological thinking and behaving. The goal is to educate him to a point where he will be able to control his thinking and behavior so that he may be both more self-enhancing and socially adjustive. [p. 5]

Test-retests, using the MMPI (Minnesota Multiphasic Personality Inventory), have shown positive results, but challengers think the people taking the test-retest have "learned the right answers" during EMI, and whether they can translate them into right behavior has been in doubt. Optimistic results, however, have been widely claimed.

MOTIVATIONAL PROGRAMS

Motivational and self-improvement programs have always been popular. They have ranged from the well-accepted inspirational sermons in church on Sunday and the Dale Carnegie-type course to the "con artists" who make money on other people and are frequently in litigation. Nevertheless, self-improvement and motivational programs are popular and do contribute to many prison programs.

Dale Carnegie began his first class on October 22, 1912, in the YMCA in Manhattan. He published his famous *How to Win Friends and Influence People* in 1936, and it is still selling at the rate of over 250,000 copies a year. Information about these courses is available from Dale Carnegie & Associates.[1]

Norman Vincent Peale wrote several books from the religious viewpoint, the most important being *The Power of Positive Thinking* in 1952. Over two million copies have been sold. Essentially, this book advises people to have faith in themselves, break the worry habit, get other people to like them, "energize" their lives, avoid the "jitters," and take similar approaches to positive attitudes toward life. Peale also wrote *The Art of Real Happiness, Faith Is the Answer* (with Smiley Blanton),

---

[1]Department A, 1475 Franklin Ave., Garden City, N.Y. 11530.

Faith Made Them Champions, A Guide to Confident Living, Guideposts to Confident Living, Guideposts to a Stronger Faith, New Guidelines, and *Stay Alive All Your Life,* all with essentially the same theme.

A multimillionaire insurance man from Chicago, W. Clement Stone, who contributed $2 million to the 1972 Nixon campaign, has also contributed to motivation toward success. Stone founded the Stone Brandell Foundation and the W. Clement & Jessie V. Stone Foundation, both in Chicago, as helping institutions in the field of corrections. Together with Napoleon Hill, he published *Success through a Positive Mental Attitude* (PMA) in 1960. He published *The Success System that Never Fails* in 1962. In the early 1970s, a series of courses entitled *Guides for Better Living* was initiated by the W. Clement & Jessie V. Stone Foundation; these are similar to the Dale Carnegie courses. They have been implemented in many prisons.

The number of books on self-improvement and motivational programs is almost inexhaustible. Bill Sands contributed *My Shadow Ran Fast* (Prentice-Hall) and *The Seventh Step* (Prentice-Hall), Frank Betteger wrote *How I Raised Myself from Failure to Success in Selling* (Prentice-Hall), Louis Binstock wrote *The Power of Faith* (Prentice-Hall). Claude M. Bristol and Harold Scherman contributed *TNT, the Power within You* (Prentice-Hall). Dorothea Brande wrote *Wake Up and Live* (Simon & Schuster). Claude M. Bristol contributed *The Magic of Believing* (Prentice-Hall), which has been used by many football coaches. Georg S. Clason did a magnificent job in *The Richest Man in Babylon* (Hawthorne). Emile Coue's *Self Mastery through Conscious Auto-Suggestion* (American Library Services) was very good. William H. Danforth's *I Dare You* (I Dare You Committee, Checkerboard Square, St. Louis, Missouri) was very popular. Jim Jones's *If You Can Count to Four* (Whitehorn Publishing Co.) was persuasive, as were Martin Kohe's *Your Greatest Power* (Ralston) and Orison Swett Martin's *Pushing to the Front* (Success Company). Robert E. Moore and Maxwell I. Schultz wrote *Turn on the Green Lites in Your Life* (Prentice-Hall) and Ben Swedland wrote *I Will* (Prentice-Hall). As well, there was Alex F. Osburn's *Your Creative Power* (Scribner) and Samuel Smiles's *Self-Help* (Belford, Clark); Bishop Fulton J. Sheen's *Life Is Worth Living* (McGraw-Hill) is outstanding, as is Harold Blake Walker's *Power to Manage Yourself* (Harper) and Mary Alice Walker and Harold Blake Walker's *Venture of Faith* (Harper). Poets and writers like Kahlil Gibran are especially inspiring. Many prisons have courses, some taught by prisoners, in self-improvement and motivational programs.

The place of motivational programs in the criminal justice system is certainly open. Legislators and congressmen have viewed motivational programs in prisons and correctional institutions as being helpful.

CONCLUSIONS

Religious, philosophical, and motivational programs have always been a part of social control in helping people deal effectively with their environment. Ethical systems have been central in this endeavor. The systematic study of the nature of value concepts—"good," "bad," "ought," "right," "wrong," and so on—has been central in the socialization process from Neanderthal man to the present. This is content of religion, philosophy, and motivational programs.

The persistence of faith healing of various approaches, healing of physical and behavioral ills by nonmedical professions and means, has persisted in the face of scientific and medical rejection. Some physicians have explained this phenomenon on the basis of the interpersonal relationships between the people involved. Many psychosomatic ills and behavioral disorders *can* be cured by faith in the absence of real physical disorders and can provide security to those with some emotional disorders. Alcoholics Anonymous and many other self-help and motivational programs function on this basis. Many people turn to faith healers because they think the professional has let them down, while many spiritualists and faith healers offer patients more warmth and comfort than does the physician or professional therapist (Nolan, 1974, pp. 305–6).

Much more study should be done in the field of ethics in order to obtain an adequate and well-rounded concept of criminal behavior and the justice system. Supplementary reading in this field in relation to criminology would be rewarding for interested persons.

Questions

1. Why are philosophy, religion, and motivational approaches important in social control?
2. Why is philosophy concerned with the justification of sentencing and punishment?
3. What is teleological retributivism?
4. What was the contribution of organized religion to social control?
5. What was the theoretical base among the Quakers who developed the first "penitentiary" in 1790, to initiate the penitentiary movement?
6. What are the contributions of religious and church-related efforts to the problems of delinquents and adult offenders in America today?
7. How can positive motivation be generated in the offender?
8. Evaluate religious approaches to working with the offender.

9. What is the effect of compulsory church attendance, either inside or outside prison?

10. Discuss the nature, extent, and effectiveness of motivational programs in America.

thirteen

CRIMINAL CAREER PATTERNS

An examination of criminal career patterns may be of assistance in understanding the development of criminal behavior. Although criminal career patterns can be classified in several ways, probably the most productive would be the duration and intensity of criminal activity. Such a classification might be as follows:

1. The juvenile and adult violations that continue throughout life
2. First offense as a young adult in his or her twenties, continuation of a criminal career throughout life
3. Latecomer to crime with the first offense in his or her thirties or forties and with a continued criminal career throughout life
4. Juvenile and adolescent violations but no further offenses during adulthood
5. Occasional or situational offender who may be a "one-timer" at any stage of life

This classification of intensity and duration of crime represents patterns of offenders that appear in the criminal justice system.

Other concerns in criminal career patterns are qualitative and motivational. Sex offenders, narcotics offenders, dangerous offenders, drug abusers as compared with addicts, and other specialized offenders need closer examination in terms of career development. Much of human behavior is stereotyped and in the form of habit. Many people have a "readiness" to react to stress in particular ways. When these habitual patterns of behavior deviate sufficiently to bring about contact with the criminal justice system, society's agencies of social control become concerned. Some understanding of them, then, is essential.

AGE AND RECIDIVISM

The age of people at time of arrest has lowered significantly recently. In the 1950s and early 1960s, the ages that showed the highest arrest frequency were between twenty and twenty-two. In 1972, the age at which arrest took place most frequently was in the fifteen-to-nineteen range with the mode at sixteen years with a total of 403,311 arrests, the highest of any age group. Approximately one-quarter of all arrests are of persons under eighteen years of age—more than one-third of the arrests (35 percent) are of teenagers or younger children. The distribution of total arrests is shown in Table 13–1. It is interesting to note that persons ten years of age and under have a slightly lower but comparable arrest rate as that for persons sixty-five years and older.

Forty-three percent of offenders under age twenty who were arrested in 1970 to 1972 were repeat offenders (*Uniform Crime Reports—1972*, p. 36). Recidivism by type of crime is shown in Table 13–2.

The earlier a person gets into the criminal justice system, the greater are the chances that he will continue in it. The number of persons released in 1963 and rearrested within four years according to age group is shown in Table 13–3.

The type of release in 1963 of persons rearrested within four years is shown in Table 13–4.

The percent of repeaters released in 1963 and rearrested within six years is shown in Table 13–5.

Some persons who commit certain types of offenses seem to travel around more, indicating greater mobility than others. The number of repeaters released in 1963 by charge who were arrested in another state than the one from which they were released in 1963 is shown in Table 13–6. Fifty-two percent of offenders released in 1963 and apprehended again within four years were in different states, indicating a high degree of mobility.

The Federal Bureau of Investigation developed a summary of 68,914 offenders who were arrested in 1971. Offenders' records were converted to computer form for the "Computerized Criminal History (CCH) File." Of 68,914 offenders arrested during 1971, 47,197 or 68 percent were repeat offenders. The average criminal career in that group was six years and two months in duration, which represents the number

TABLE 13-1.
Total Arrests, Distribution by Age, 1980

AGE GROUP	NUMBER	PERCENT DISTRIBUTION
Under 10	55,088	0.6
10–12	139,942	1.4
13–14	408,897	4.2
15	377,792	3.9
16	493,073	5.1
17	550,921	5.7
18	589,996	6.1
19	575,105	5.9
20	531,092	5.5
21	490,597	5.1
22	447,045	4.6
23	413,528	4.3
24	378,315	3.9
25–29	1,392,514	14.4
30–34	905,411	9.3
35–39	584,122	6.0
40–44	417,202	4.3
45–49	316,799	3.3
50–54	257,349	2.7
55–59	180,724	1.9
60–64	103,684	1.1
65 and over	93,985	1.0
Total	9,703,181	100.0

From *Crime in the United States—1980, Uniform Crime Reports for the United States,* Washington, D.C.: Federal Bureau of Investigation, released September 10, 1981, pp. 200–201.

TABLE 13-2.
Present Repeaters by Types of Crime
(Persons Arrested 1970–72)

CRIME	PERCENTAGE OF REPEATERS
Robbery	77%
Forgery	74
Auto Theft	73
Burglary	71
Fraud	69
Assault	68
All Other Crimes	66
Gambling	65
TOTAL AVERAGE	
Weapons	62
Larceny	61
Narcotics	60
Embezzlement	34

Uniform Crime Reports—1972, p. 37.

TABLE 13-3.
Percent Repeaters by Age Group
(Persons Released in 1963 and Rearrested
within Four Years)

AGE	PERCENTAGE OF REPEATERS
Under 20	70%
20–24	67
25–29	65
30–39	61
Total of all ages	60
40–49	51
50 and over	38

Uniform Crime Reports—1967, report released August 27, 1968, p. 38.

TABLE 13-4.
Percent of Persons Rearrested within Six Years
by Type of Release in 1963

TYPE OF RELEASE	PERCENTAGE
Acquitted or Dismissed	92%
Mandatory Release	76
Fine	78
TOTAL AVERAGE	65
Parole	63
Suspended Sentence and/or Probation	57
Fine and Probation	38

Program and Project Plan for Fiscal Year 1971 (Washington, D.C.:
National Institute of Law Enforcement and Criminal Justice, January
1971), p. 24.

TABLE 13-5.
Percent of Repeaters by Type of Crime
Six Years after Release

CRIME	PERCENTAGE OF REPEATERS
Auto Theft	82%
Burglary	79
Assault	76
Narcotics	72
Forgery	70
Robbery	66
TOTAL AVERAGE	65
All Other Offenses	65
Larceny	62
Liquor Laws	48
Fraud	48
Gambling	48
Embezzlement	25

Program and Project Plan for Fiscal Year 1971, p. 24.

TABLE 13-6.
Mobility of Repeaters Rearrested within Four Years
after Being Released in 1963 by Specific Charge

CHARGE	TOTAL REARRESTED	PERCENT REARRESTED IN SAME STATE	PERCENT REARRESTED IN ANOTHER STATE
Auto Theft	4,434	23	77%
Burglary	367	50	50
Forgery	1,629	51	49
Robbery	248	52	48
Assault	159	57	43
Larceny	1,420	63	37
Narcotics	1,042	66	34
Fraud	297	70	30
Liquor Law Violation	1,131	72	28
Gambling	137	86	14

Uniform Crime Reports—1967, p. 38.

of years between the first arrest and the last arrest. The offenders had been arrested an average of four times. The 68,914 offenders had a total of 294,000 charges during their criminal careers, with 79,242 convictions and 28,488 imprisonments of six months or more (*Uniform Crime Reports—1971*, p. 36). The percent of repeaters by type of crime is shown in Table 13–7.

It is obvious that the crimes most susceptible to recidivism are forgery, auto theft, robbery, burglary, and assault. The career criminal is generally a property offender, which is how he can make his living. He is a failure, in that he is in and out of custody all his life.

There were 2,906.7 major crimes per 100,000 population in 1971, which means that the average rate of major crime is about 3 percent of the total population. Approximately 13.5 percent of that crime is violent crime. The greatest amount of violent person-to-person crime in the United States is in the South. The greatest amount of property crime has consistently been in the West and the Pacific areas. Because property crime is the greatest portion of crime, this gives the West and the Pacific areas the highest per capita crime rate in the country. California, Florida, Michigan, and New York have the highest crime rates in the country.

Recidivism rates are difficult to identify because they depend upon the length of time under consideration. In any one year, around 63 percent of persons arrested have been arrested before, and around 68 percent of persons admitted to prison have been there before. This does not mean that two-thirds of all persons arrested or coming to prison are recidivists. One-third of the persons arrested or coming to prison

TABLE 13-7.
Percent Repeaters by Type of Crime
(Persons Arrested in 1971)

CRIME	PERCENT OF REPEATERS
Forgery	76%
Auto Theft	75
Robbery	75
Burglary	73
Assault	71
Fraud	70
Gambling	69
All Other Crimes	69
TOTAL AVERAGE	68
Weapons	68
Larceny	66
Narcotics	63
Embezzlement	33

Uniform Crime Reports—1971, p. 37.

each year are first-timers. On the other hand, the approximately two-thirds of the rearrests and returns to prison tend to be the same people. Therefore, one-third of those arrested are new people each year, while the recidivists tend to be the same people over a period of years. In terms of numbers of people, then, the recidivists and the first-timers would be roughly equivalent in number over a two-year period. Over a three-year period, the number of first-timers would exceed the recidivists. In the population as a whole over a long period of time, then, the number of first-timers would exceed the recidivists. The recidivists would generally outnumber the first-timers in major prison populations. The recidivists tend to be a small but persistent minority with hard-core problems in terms of socialization.

The majority of recidivists can be classified in terms of personality as (1) the inadequate, dependent repeater; (2) the dyssocial or subcultural repeater, (3) the compulsive recidivist who repeats the same crime over and over, and (4) the impulsive recidivist who may repeat a variety of crimes over and over again. The personality patterns that support these varying kinds of recidivism would differ between the categories and would differ within each category in a variety of ways.

The inadequate, dependent repeater is probably the most frequent and numerous of all recidivists. He is frequently arrested for drunk and disorderly, "public intox," vagrancy, petty larceny, disorderly conduct, and similar minor offenses. It is not unusual for many of these people to have accumulated more than 100 arrests and convictions on minor charges before reaching the age of fifty. The personality patterns in these minor recidivists differ quite widely, also. Some have been considered to be in the incipient stages of simple schizophrenia, particularly in vagrancy and petty theft. Many are alcoholics of long standing. Most are known to the local jailers, while only a few ever get to prison. Some are "protected" by the police as good sources of information about more serious offenses by others.

The dyssocial or subcultural repeater is a person engaged in a business where arrest is an occupational hazard. Moonshiners come to federal prisons repeatedly for making whiskey for which the tax has not been paid. Prostitutes frequently have a series of arrests. Many people living in this pattern of crimes frequently have only a few arrests because they have been protected by the "organization." Gambling, the numbers, selling marijuana or other minor drugs, sometimes hard drugs, bootlegging, and pimping are only a few of the crimes in which these repeaters participate. They are called dyssocial or subcultural because they are getting along well in their own group, providing goods and services that people will buy, but the practice violates the laws of larger society.

The compulsive recidivist begins early in his offenses and remains with them throughout his life. Glaser (1972) has referred to these people as "adolescent recapitulators." The progression of recidivism seems to follow the same general pattern as the development of a chronic neurosis (Alexander and Ross, 1952, p. 121). The progression begins with (1) the situation in life and in the prison with which the individual cannot cope, (2) failure to solve the problem after sincere and diligent effort, followed by (3) replacement of realistic efforts by substitute regressive behavior, falling back on more immature solutions, (4) intensification of the original problem by failure of substitute methods, (5) repeatedly grasping for an answer—any answer—and, finally, (6) the compulsive repetition of the one answer he has found, whether it works or not. In this pattern, the offender tends to repeat the same type of offenses over and over.

The impulsive recidivist, who may repeat a variety of different types of crimes throughout his lifetime, tends to function in a manner characteristic of the psychopath, sociopath, or antisocial personality disorder. He is impulsive, without anxiety, and is willing to do anything without regard for others or for society. His antisocial and asocial outlook permits him to commit property and assaultive offenses.

The dynamics of repeated misconduct appear to be related to social maturation, psychopathic or sociopathic condition, the obsessive-compulsive neurotic component, and sometimes even incipient psychosis. The reality principle does not operate in that the individual does not postpone immediate gratification for further reward but reacts to immediate stress and needs according to the pleasure-pain principle. The individual does not seem to "learn by experience," nor is he able to develop "insight" other than superficial verbalization. The various combinations of immature, psychopathic or sociopathic, and neurotic dynamics in behavior offer possibilities for an explanation of recidivism in and out of prison that seems to have more meaning than conditioning, behavior modification, or free will. It is obvious that recidivism appears in people who do not respond normally to society's system of rewards and punishments. The high recidivism rate and the fact that it is the same people who come back after punishment and more punishment raise questions as to the efficacy of punishment. Society has a system of rewards and punishments to modify behavior in conforming ways. A minority of individuals simply do not have the capacity to conform. This is why punishment is not an effective deterrent. For these people, there is need for a moratorium on the system of rewards and punishments to permit emotional maturation to occur in a controlled environment. Recidivism is aggravated by conventional reward and punishment.

Offenders with juvenile records were found by the Gluecks (1934, pp. 184–85) to have had an appreciably higher recidivism record than did the ex-inmates of a reformatory without a juvenile record, suggesting that the earlier a person gets into the criminal justice system, the longer he stays in it. Middle-class white delinquents and youthful offenders are less likely to repeat criminal acts if they are never caught and put through the juvenile justice system (Haney and Gold, 1973). So many myths persist in the criminal justice field about what the delinquent is and to what he might respond that wrong programs are frequently aimed at the wrong people and the wrong groups. These myths start with false assumptions as to what a "delinquent" is. Once a potentially "good" youth is caught up in this system, the chances are greater that he will remain there. When this assertion can be made about middle-class white youths, it makes the plight of the lower-socioeconomic-class minority youth even worse, for he apparently has little chance at the very start. For this reason and others, officials concerned with juvenile delinquency are actively searching for ways of diverting people from the justice system as early as possible.

Some men "age" more rapidly than others and settle down earlier. After the "age of discretion," usually about the thirty-sixth year, factors favorable to rehabilitation of offenders who continue in crime lose their effect (Glueck, 1937, p. 123). Those few who continue in crime after age thirty-six seem to be beyond correctional programs. The Gluecks found that the passing of years or maturation was probably the most effective rehabilitative agent. The process of maturation continued up to about the thirty-sixth year, when recidivism decreased sharply (Glueck, 1940, p. 264). This raises an interesting question regarding rates of maturation or "settling down" based on statistical data. The arrest rates drop significantly after the thirty-sixth year of age. Comparably, the insurance premiums for automobiles driven by males drop significantly for the entire population at twenty-five years of age. It appears that an argument could be made that the emotional maturity, the cultural assimilation, or the "settling down" process on the part of offenders as a group may be a decade later than the general population.

CAREER STUDIES

Study of individual cases of crime and delinquency has been made on many levels and from many approaches—sociological, psychological, psychiatric, and autobiographical. For example, Healy (1915) began the individual case study method in 1909 in the juvenile court in Chicago, later became director of the Judge Baker Guidance Center in Boston, and first published his findings on the individual delinquent in 1915. He emphasized the effect of mental dissatisfaction, irritative mental reactions to environment conditions, obsessional imagery, adolescent mental instabilities and impulses, emotional disturbances, worries, repressions, antisocial grudges, mental peculiarities or aberration, and mental defects. Together with his wife and partner, he later indicated that by reviewing family and developmental histories, examining the environment, and taking physical and psychological measurements as well as doing medical and psychiatric examinations, delinquency can be better understood (Healy and Bronner, 1936).

The first sociologist to develop an intense interest in case studies was Clifford R. Shaw of the Chicago School. In 1930, he published a study of young persons who "roll" drunks. Later (1931), he and an associate published a study that was the result of interviews with young adults in conflict with the law. His conclusion was that most gang memberships last about three years, and most delinquent careers last not much longer. In 1938, he published a study of cases in which two or more brothers were in conflict with the law. His conclusion was that brothers from the same family tend to commit the same types of offenses, and these can be related to the family structure.

Sheldon and Eleanor Glueck (1930) studied 500 criminal careers and found that the socioeconomic status of the parents of offenders was generally low. Similar findings were later gathered for 500 women delinquents (1934a), and for 1,000 juvenile delinquents (1934b). In a study of 510 inmates released from the Massachusetts Reformatory during the two-year period of 1921–22 and traced in the free community every five years over a fifteen-year postrelease period, almost 80 percent of the releasees were found to be unrehabilitated after five years. Of the 418 men who could be traced over the fifteen-year period, 135 or 32.3

percent persisted in serious criminality, twenty-one men, or 5 percent, had abandoned criminality after the first ten years following release, then lapsed back into criminality. Approximately 22 percent did not come into conflict with the law again and the rest, approximately 60 percent, continued in conflict with the law but with less serious offenses (Glueck, 1943).

Data from 761 delinquents in Passaic, New Jersey, indicated that the occupational ratings of their fathers were considerably lower than for the average of the city (Kvaraceus, 1944). Only 26 percent rarely went to church, and 54 percent attended regularly, according to their claims (Kvaraceus, 1950). All delinquents in Kvaraceus's Passaic study had failed at least one grade, and most did not go beyond junior high school (Kvaraceus, 1945).

Criminals who make their livings at criminal pursuits and are not in organized crime, such as safecrackers, bank robbers, burglars, hotel prowlers, and confidence men, tend to learn their crafts just as any other skilled man would (Letkemann, 1973, p. 161). They take pride in their workmanship, respond to better safes, electronic alarm systems, and the manipulation of accounts and credit systems. Some, such as the "moonshiners," regard occasional incarceration as a hazard of the job but one worth taking for the other benefits of the business. Autobiographical reports by prison inmates themselves have also been revealing. One of the early and more popular such works was Victor Nelson's (1932) entertaining and apparently accurate description of the prison of the late 1920s and early 1930s. Although the descriptions of the physical surroundings were interesting, the social interaction between inmates and between inmates and guards indicated deprivation and exploitation that had to change a person's perspective on life. From a different part of the country, Burns's (1932) description of a Georgia chain gang during the same period revealed to the country the horrors of the road maintenance system that had replaced the horrors of the lease system of the South. He had escaped from the chain gang in Georgia and taken up residence in New Jersey, where he was protected by officials who refused to return him to Georgia on grounds that to do so would be in violation of the "cruel and unusual punishment" clause of the Eighth Amendment. Burns's descriptions were reminiscent of J.C. Powell's (1970) story of the first convict labor camp in Florida at Live Oak. Powell was the captain of that camp and his descriptions of interaction between the captain, the inmates, and the neighbors, as well as the company that had leased the prisoners for work, indicated a lasting impact on the people subjected to that system.

Probably the best of the autobiographies written by inmates was by Tom Runyon (1953), an Iowa lifer who finished his sentence in the early 1960s because of a heart attack. His analysis of the development of his criminal career that included robbery, murder, escape, and other offenses was incisive. Even more poignant was his description of the development of the "criminal mind"—the same institutionalization process, or "prisonization process," described by Clemmer (1958). Runyon's (1956) chapter about prison life in Caldwell's *Criminology* is also well worth reading. Here Runyon noted that the word *respect* is probably the most significant word in the world and that it should apply equally to all men. He said that he would build an edifice where justice would have a fighting chance—if he had a chance.

Psychiatrists have done many case studies of offenders. One of the earliest and most significant was the four-volume *Case Studies in the Psychopathology of Crime*, published by Benjamin Karpman in 1939. A psychoanalytically oriented clinical psychologist, Robert Lindner, published a widely read case study in 1944. The psychiatric literature has many other case studies of offenders.

The use of autobiographical material by counselors in prisons is usual. Inmates generally have a lot of time in their cells. A counselor may assign to clients the task of writing out their autobiographies. Using that as a basis for questioning and suggestion, both the counselor and an offender gain some insight and achieve some objectivity regarding the criminal's life and career. In some instances, inmates exchange autobiographies and criticize each other. They are especially useful in group sessions where one person may submit his or her autobiography to the entire group, and an evening or two of group counseling might be spent on it.

The use of case studies from any vantage point provides assistance in gathering the multiple factors present in criminal careers. Various patterns also emerged; most of these concern the development of personality and the individual's readiness to react to sudden stress. Developmental psychologists indicate that the basic pattern of reacting to stress is already developed by the time the child goes to school. It is refined and probably modified a little as experience is gained and behavior is modified. Nevertheless, within limits, the personality pattern appears to be shaped by hereditary factors in terms of physiological factors and, to some extent, intelligence and environmental and family factors as well as a multiplicity of other factors. Inmates themselves tend to think their behavior "is 97 percent the result of environment."[1]

The disadvantages of the case study are that (1) explanations of individual cases and specific delinquencies are also subject to the orientation and biases of the observer, and (2) most of the case studies are made by persons employed by agencies dealing with offenders, which

---

[1]Quotation by a Maryland inmate in the film *On Trial: Criminal Justice*, produced by Berkeley Associates, Berkeley, Calif., 1970, and available through the College of State Trial Judges, Reno, Nev.

means that they are concerned with policy and procedure and that they are more interested in temporary modification of delinquency treatment than they are in delinquency causation (Sutherland and Cressey, 1966).

Observation of viewpoints by the professionals, such as sociologists, psychologists, psychiatrists, and other students of crime, suggests that emphasis is placed by them on the conditions that predispose an individual to crime, such as poverty, urban slum or ghetto living, and other general environmental conditions built up over a long period of time. There is a tendency on the part of the offenders themselves to see more immediate causes and events to be important. The offenders' concern with precipitating causes and the professionals' and academicians' concern with predisposing causes sometimes interferes with communication between the practitioners in the criminal justice system and the offenders.

Autobiographical material has been shown to be most helpful in the client's "taking a second look" at his or her past development and behavior with the assistance and counsel of a therapist or caseworker (Novey, 1968). The reconstruction of events and incidents results frequently in the client's reconceptualizing the world, perceiving that he has not really been "picked on," that his negative self-image has been inappropriate, and that the roles played by other significant persons in his life can be viewed in better perspective. The patient's or client's capacity for social adaptation, based on his realistic appraisal of past events, can have a major influence on his future outlook and behavior.

THE PRESSURES OF PRISON

We have seen that it is basic that the earlier people become involved in the criminal justice system, the longer they stay in it. The reasons are obviously two-pronged and mutually reinforcing. In the first place, the emotional and social problems of individuals have impeded their successful adjustment to society. Second, and reinforcing the first, the prison environment intensifies the problems, dichotomizes the individual from social authority, and produces an "institutionalized" apathy and dependency that reduces the possibility of successful adjustment in free society.

Prison society is characterized by a theoretical forced equality where "everybody is treated alike." Total control is the objective of the custodial prison, and there is a heavy reliance on force. Psychological and material deprivations jeopardize self-esteem, personal defense systems and social adaptations, life goals, heterosexuality, and emotional security. "Born to Lose" tattoos can be found frequently on prisoners.

These frustrations and deprivations give rise to the inmate subculture, which reflects the attempt to live with them. The ex-prisoner's status problems are shared with other prisoners because they have all been rejected by society. The prisoners, in turn, reject their rejectors. The forced intimacy with other prisoners living as a mass and controlled by a strong guard force there for the purpose results in each inmate's behavior being subject to official and informal criticism.

Adaptation can be achieved by identifying with fellow inmates. Mutual loyalty, affection, respect, and common standing in opposition to the force of their rejectors results in what is commonly known as the inmate code. The inmates are united in their common opposition against their captors. Self-interest, of course, dictates that inmates do not alienate their captors unnecessarily—they still "play the nods" and comply minimally with regulations to the extent that they must. At the same time, communication with authority is reduced to a minimum. Noncooperation with authority and maintenance of loyalty to the inmates underlie adaptation. Anybody who cooperates too much with officials is "frozen out," which is a severe psychological punishment, because social contact is lost in a setting that is already deprived. At the extreme, an inmate may be beaten or killed, depending upon the situation, for too much cooperation with authority at the expense of other inmates.

The deprivation of goods and services, of heterosexual relationships, of the autonomy of relative freedom from rules, and the deprivation of security by being forced into association with vicious and unpredictable fellow inmates destroys a person's expectations of society and he or she is relegated to an unstable world (Sykes, 1958, pp. 65–78). Prison inmates indicate that the greatest pressures in the prison come from (1) mistreatment by officers and (2) mistreatment by other inmates, which is made possible by inadequate controls within the prison (Chang and Armstrong, 1972, p. 18). The consequence is that the effectiveness of constructive programming in prison schools, educational programs, and counseling is lessened by the damaging effects of having to be exploited and on the defensive all the time. That becomes a lifestyle in prison after a while.

Oscar Wilde's *Ballad of Reading Gaol* is appropriate in describing prison settings:

> *With bars they blur the goodly sun*
> *And blur the goodly moon;*
> > *And they do well to hide their Hell*
> > *For in it things are done*
> *That Son of God, nor Son of Man,*
> *Ever should look upon.*
>
> *Each wretched cell in which we dwell*
> *Is a foul and dank latrine:*
> > *And the fetid breath of living death*
> > *Chokes up each grated screen;*

And all, but Lust, is turned to dust
In Humanity's Machine.

. . . .

The vilest deeds, like poison weeds
Bloom well in prison air.
It is only what is good in man
That wastes and withers there.

Sykes (1956) points out that the prisoner most likely to become deeply enmeshed in criminal modes of behavior is the one who is alienated both from fellow prisoners and from prison officials. He relates to nobody.

"Prison has taken away my sense of responsibility," according to Edwin L. Addington, an inmate in the Kentucky State Prison at Eddyville who had also done time in Arizona and Kansas (*Kentucky Inter-Prison Press*, Oct. 1973). The moods, ideas and feelings of prison inmates or residents tend to emphasize futility and apprehension of how they will be accepted when they are released (Griswold et al., 1972). The amelioration of these feelings involves understanding and treating the whole person and not just the symptoms of deviant behavior that brought him or her to prison. Failure of the prison to provide sufficient enlightened staff to counter the futility and to provide individual respect, treatment, and minimum standards of human dignity can only counteract any constructive intention of the criminal justice system regarding the people it holds. Polarizing power holders against the powerless has brought acute conflict that will intensity as it continues (Glaser, 1971).

Is the objective of corrections to "find and arrest" or to "punish and release"—or are they not incompatible? There is a cyclical fluctuation of attitudes as offenders leave prison, get rid of the prison culture, experience social rejection or "freezing out," find support among other former inmates, return to their "prison" attitude, and continue their criminal career. Stanton Wheeler (1961, p. 711) suggests that sociological research should aim at the process of reentry into the community more than at the problem of assimilation of values in prison.

SEX OFFENSES

Sex offenses generally reflect confusion and dysfunction in psychosexual development.[2] The psychiatric view toward sexual development and behavior is that sexual identification is dependent upon (1) physical sex-

---

[2]Statutory rape is generally not included in this category because it most frequently is the result of intercourse with girls below the age of consent, which is generally eighteen years of age in most jurisdictions. Statutory rape refers to inadequate consent, generally because the girl is not legally competent to give consent, whether by age or incompetence.

ual characteristics, (2) mental sexual characteristics in terms of masculine or feminine attitudes and acceptance of culturally defined roles, and (3) the kind of sex-object choice. When the sexual identification in all three characteristics is direct and clearly masculine or feminine, no adjustment problems occur. Because most deviants from this direct and clear identification would like to appear to be conforming for social and economic purposes to the American culture, there are more people with sex-role problems and problems in psychosexual development than many people realize. The causes can be social, psychological and emotional, and biological, or a combination of these. The social and psychological results of sex-role confusion can be almost devastating to the individual so afflicted. Feelings of social ostracism can result in behavior ranging from doing anything that will help the individual to be accepted through feelings of futility to open resentment and rebellion.

Sex-role confusion and dysfunction can take many forms. Many of the minor forms make up the criminal sexual psychopath caseloads that exist in about two-thirds of the states. Exhibitionism is viewed by psychiatrists as an infantile fixation or arrested emotional development caused by an individual's difficulty in breaking with the parent of the opposite sex and focusing on the opposite sex in his or her own age group (Hinsie and Campbell, 1970, p. 287). Voyeurism or "peeping Tom" behavior is viewed as an intermediary sexual aim that becomes so intense that it surpasses in importance the normal sex act and serves to sublimate some sexual energy into other channels (ibid., p. 806). Pedophilia is sexual desire for children, generally in deviant men impotent with women.

Homosexual behavior can result from many different patterns of sex-role confusion, with the causes being social, emotional and psychological, situational, and/or biological. From the psychiatric standpoint, both male and female homosexuality are prevalent in all societies, and the causes are so diverse that a simple statement here would be inappropriate.

Homosexuality can be psychological, cultural, or situational without biological influences. On the other hand, many homosexuals have biological pressures that vary from the normal. Psychological homosexuality can be demonstrated in the case of a man whose mother died at his birth and whose mother's sister raised him. The aunt chastised him occasionally with the reminder that he had killed one good woman already and that he owed the world something. It is apparent that he grew up attempting in some way to replace his mother through compensatory behavior. Cultural homosexuality is mentioned rather frequently in the Old Testament and is legendary in ancient Greece. Situational homosexuality can be found in any unisexual prison, male or female.

Homosexual behavior is perhaps more prevalent in women's institutions than in men's institutions (Ward and Kassebaum, 1964), possibly because only the most serious problem cases among female offenders are sent to prison, as compared with the sentencing of males, just as the percentage of women in prison sentenced for homicide exceeds the percentage of men in prison sentenced for homicide. It has been seen as the major adaptation in women's prisons as a familial substitute (Ward and Kassebaum, 1965, p. 102). A description of a woman's initial experience in prison has been described in a popular magazine (*Cosmopolitan*, Feb. 1972, pp. 145–48) as follows:

> I'd never been with a woman before, but that night three of them tried to get to me and I wouldn't play, they held me against the wall and burned my breasts with cigarettes. I screamed but nobody came. And later that night they attacked me again and I was scared, so I let them do what they wanted to me. [William Murray, "Women in Prison"]

Female inmates seem to suffer more loss of identity and loneliness than males do. They need to be needed, and they are emotionally lost when cut off from their families. Consequently, homosexual affairs have been sufficiently frequent in women's institutions that the study of the handling of the termination of a lesbian relationship has been incorporated in some in-service training programs for parole agents supervising female parolees.

Male homosexuality appears to be more public than female homosexuality and more frequently involves strangers. This is why police departments keep public restrooms in bus stations and other public areas frequented by male transients under surveillance. Many contacts are made there. Some have called them tea rooms (Humphreys, 1970).

Homosexuality appears in all cultures to some extent. There are large enough numbers so that national associations of homosexuals have existed for a long time, such as the Mattachine Society, Atheneum Society of America, Inc., and Gay Liberation. Many of these societies maintain lobbyists in legislatures for the purpose of gaining equal rights and equal protection under the law. Many countries and many states have already decriminalized homosexual activity when it is between consenting adults. A journal that discusses the psychological, sociological, and anthropological aspects of homosexuality and gender identity is now being published.[3]

Forcible rape is a sex crime, according to official crime statistics; however, it is not seen as a sex crime by the rapists but rather as a crime of violence and aggression that releases pent-up anger. Rape of a victim who is a stranger is simply a matter of aggression, and she is only

---

[3]*Journal of Homosexuality*, Haworth Press, 130 West 72nd Street, New York, N.Y. 10023.

secondarily a sex object. Victims do not matter much to the rapist. Victims can be eight years old or eighty, beautiful or ugly, any race or nationality. Sex is not the primary object; everyone knows, including the rapist, that a twenty-dollar bill is cheaper than a twenty-year sentence.

Rape is generally a nonsexual use of sex, in which the expression of aggression and hostility is more important than sex itself. Nonsexual use of sex, of course, is common. It can be used for narcissistic expression, reduction of anxiety and tension, and other purposes (Fisher, 1973, pp. 438–39). Some women use sex for manipulatory purposes and, for that matter, to earn money or influence. Psychiatrists suggest that masturbation is sometimes practiced to demonstrate independence from one's mother. Some religious beliefs consider the nonsexual use of sex to be immoral, so it might produce guilt and discomfort.

Sexual assaults are not caused by deprivation but are an expression of anger and aggression generated by the same basic frustration that exists for the person within the community, particularly by the inability to achieve masculine identification and pride through avenues other than sex (Davis, 1968).

The hermaphrodite is a biological phenomenon in which an individual has the reproductive organs of both sexes (Hinsie and Campbell, 1970, p. 343). There are two forms: nonfunctional and functional. The nonfunctional group includes three forms: (1) accessory, when there is a testis and a rudimentary ovary that does not produce ova; (2) accidental, with sporadic occurrence of ova in the testis or spermatic tissue in the ovary; and (3) teratological, when the reproductive system is an intricate mixture of male and female structures. The functional group includes (1) unisexual monoecism, when a genetic female sometimes produces spermatozoa in the ovary or when a genetic male produces ova in the testis, in which case the individual could function at a low level first as a male and then a female or first as a female and then as a male; (2) consecutive monoecism, when a male later functions as a female (these are primarily males or neuters); and (3) spatial monoecism, manifesting functional hermaphroditism characterized by the presence of both male and female reproductive organs.

The success of such people in adapting varies widely. One individual who is twenty-five years old, for example, was raised as a girl but is now a "male" medical laboratory technician and doing well. The parents saw evidence of female genitalia at birth and interpreted the little penis as an overdeveloped clitoris. After finishing school, the person shed female garb on the basis that marriage was out of the question and a better living could be made by a man. The penis is similar to that of a five-year-old boy; vestiges of female genitalia are still there; facial fuzz is shaved once a month; and an adequate social adaptation, though limited, has been made. Others in similar condition have not been so successful, and their reaction to their affliction has resulted in contact with the criminal justice system where, unfortunately, the basic reasons for difficulty generally are not understood.

SEX REASSIGNMENT BY SURGERY

There is a large class of gender-disturbed persons with whom Western civilizations have generally dealt harshly, including the homosexual, the transvestite, and the transsexual. The homosexual is in love with another person of the same sex. The transvestite desires to dress in clothing of the opposite sex, masks homosexuality, and attempts to stress bisexuality. The transsexual is a person who believes he or she really belongs to the opposite sex and desires to have sex reassignment surgery that is now attainable. Approximately 1,800 Americans have undergone sex reassignment surgery (*Information on Transsexualism*, 1973, p. 4). The transsexual condition is based on biological and psychological factors, and most specialists agree that the condition is irrevocably established early in life, probably during the first two years (ibid., p. 7. Also, Benjamin, 1972).

The first successful operation was in Denmark in 1930 (Hoyer, 1933). The first such operation in the United States was at the Gender Identity Clinic in 1967, a year after the clinic opened. By 1972, there were fifteen places in the United States where these operations could be performed (*Gender Identity Clinics*, 1972, p. 4). Clinical evidence indicates that sex reassignment for transsexuals is justifiable and that the majority of patients make an adequate social adjustment afterward (Money and Gaskin, 1970–71). Although it is common knowledge that men have become women, there have also been lesser-known cases in which women have become men. A full discussion of sex reassignment by surgery is not appropriate here, but there is considerable literature for those who are interested in learning more about it. (See Money and Erhardt, 1973; Green and Money, 1969.)[4]

Problems in the criminal justice system arise for sex reassignment, not only because of the sex role confusion involved but also because of the length of time the complete alteration requires. Directors of corrections in several states have been faced with difficult decisions in this regard. The operation takes a minimum of two years for men. It begins with intense psychiatric interviews to determine whether or not the individual can make the transition psychologically. Hormone treatments by injections of estrogen are accompanied by electrolysis of the beard and occasional cross-dress for acclimating the patient to his new sex

---

[4]Information is also available from the Erickson Educational Foundation, 1627 Moreland Avenue, Baton Rouge, La. 70808.

role. Social and vocational rehabilitation for two years precedes the final surgery. In the meantime, breasts are built surgically. All these procedures are surgically and psychologically reversible, but the final removal of the genitalia is irreversible, so removal and reconstruction of the genitalia is always done last. In the meantime, some of these patients get into trouble. One correctional administrator, for example, received a patient at the men's prison with full female breasts, beard removed, and hormone treatment in progress, but with the male genitalia intact. The administrator simply let him go to a large Midwestern city to have the operation completed and brought him back to the women's unit. Another administrator kept a person in similar condition without permitting the operation to be completed, and had disciplinary problems with the prisoner, who was eventually paroled. After completing the operation, "she" violated parole and had to be returned to the women's unit.

The change of the female to a male is yet not satisfactory, either cosmetically or functionally. The operation begins with counseling and hormonal treatments. Hysterectomy and breast removal are necessary. The development of the penis or simulacrum of a copulatory organ may be either with cartilage or bone or by extending the urethra with an artificial tube. In neither case is it a sensitive organ, remaining numb and nonfeeling.

Sex reassignment is considered to be appropriate for some transsexuals and hermaphrodites. Without it, both have sex-role confusion problems and resulting trouble. With it, the confusion, while present, is reduced.

DANGEROUS OFFENDERS

Dangerous offenders were discussed in Chapter 9 in relation to the psychiatric approach. It was pointed out that dangerous offenders had been identified and treated with some success at the Massachusetts Center for the Diagnosis and Treatment of Dangerous Persons at Bridgewater. There are also other approaches that seem to be productive.

Studies of aggression and violence have identified three basic variables: (1) the instigation to aggression, (2) the internal inhibitions against that aggression, and (3) stimulus factors that either facilitate or impede aggressive acting out (Megargee, 1972, p. 5).

Instigation to aggression may be innate, "instinctual" in accordance with psychoanalytic theory; it may be a result of reaction to an aggressive environment, frustration-aggression approaches, social learning, and residual aggressive instigation (ibid., pp. 6–13). Factors that reduce aggression can also be innate, environmental substitutes, or vicarious substitutes, such as contact sports. Inhibition of aggression seeking to be released can be brought about by environmental reaction and fear of punishment, extinction through nonreward after several experiences, guilt, and positive rewards for nonaggression, such as social status.

Overaggressive and undercontrolled people can be identified with personality tests. High scores on the overcontrolled-hostility (O-H) scores on the MMPI (Minnesota Multiphasic Personality Inventory) and a review of the record can be helpful. Projective tests, particularly the TAT (Thematic Apperception Test) and the Rorschach can identify aggressive people. A competent psychologist well trained and supervised in projective techniques can use these tests to identify people with infantile aggression and repressed hostility in the presence of anxiety, which is characteristic of a "walking bomb" type of dangerous person. Depression is repressed hostility and can absorb aggressive action, thereby becoming a substitute for dangerous behavior. Suicide would be more likely. This identification can be achieved in diagnostic interviews, but the projective tests are more incisive and can be supplemented with diagnostic interviews. The dangerous offender can be identified only with the investment of time and professional competence.

There are a wide variety of theories to explain aggression, violence, and dangerousness. The reason is that aggression is not a unidimensional phenomenon, but has wide ramifications and can come from all directions (ibid., p. 34). The patterns of cause and the patterns of expression of aggression, violence, and dangerousness are a central concern to professionals and practitioners in the criminal justice system and, even more so, the general public, whose major fear of crime focuses on murder and violence.

Measuring the seriousness of crime is still quite tenuous. For example, when Loeb and Leopold killed fourteen-year-old Bobby Franks in Chicago in the 1920s, the American public was outraged. On the other hand, Pittsburgh Phil, working as a "hit man" for Murder, Inc., killed probably five hundred people in the 1930s, and very few people even knew about it. A recent study based on judgment by raters listed the perceived seriousness of 140 crimes. Apparently the judgments were made on the basis of morals rather than simply physical injury, since the third and fourth most "serious" crimes were considered selling heroin and forcible rape after breaking into a house, respectively (Rossi et al., 1974). "Dangerousness" is apparently too vague for clear scientific prediction. Further, it is not a unitary concept but is relative in varying social environments.

To measure "dangerousness," Ray asked twenty staff members of the Florida Division of Mental Health to rate 161 crimes according to "dangerousness." Half the readers were male and half were female, and in turn, half of these groups were mental health professionals (psychologists, social workers, psychiatrists), and the other half were educated in other fields. Table 13-8 shows the average ratings for the most serious crimes. The remaining crimes on the list averaged less than 5.00 on a scale of 9 for the most dangerous to 1 for the least.

The release of offenders on parole, of course, has to take "dangerousness" into consideration for the safety of society and "seriousness" for public relations. Sometimes, they coincide. Also, the "dangerousness" of the person is not always the same at the time of release as the "dangerousness" of the offense. Consequently, research into per-

TABLE 13-8.

Rankings of Crime by Dangerousness (on a scale of 9 for the most dangerour to 1 for the least dangerous)

RANK	CRIME	JUDGMENT SCORE
1.	Assassination of a public official	8.90
2.	Planned killing of an acquaintance	8.65
3.	Planned killing of a policeman	8.65
4.	Planned killing of a spouse	8.55
5.	Planned killing of a person for a fee	8.55
6.	Impulsive killing of a policeman	8.45
7.	Impulsive killing of a stranger	8.30
8.	Rape of a minor less than eleven years old	8.25
9.	Deliberately starting a fire that results in a death	8.25
10.	Forcible rape of a stranger in a park	8.20
11.	Impulsive killing of an acquaintance	8.10
12.	Forcible rape of a neighbor	8.10
13.	Deliberately starting a fire in an occupied building	8.00
14.	Killing someone after an argument over a business transaction	8.00
15.	Rape	7.95
16.	Arson	7.90
17.	Forcible rape after breaking into a home	7.75
18.	Attempted rape of a child	7.70
19.	Impulsive killing of a spouse	7.70
20.	Blackmail	7.60
21.	Torturing or unlawfully punishing a child under sixteen	7.55
22.	Kidnapping for ransom	7.50
23.	Hijacking an airplane	7.45
24.	Assault with a gun on a policeman	7.40
25.	Killing someone in a barroom free-for-all	7.30
26.	Knowingly selling contaminated food that results in a death	7.30
27.	Assault with a gun on a stranger	7.25
28.	Child molesting	7.20
29.	Killing spouse's lover after catching them together in bed	7.20
30.	Assault with a gun on a spouse	7.05
31.	Assault with a gun in the course of a riot	7.05
32.	Forcible rape of a former spouse	7.05
33.	Assault with intent to commit a felony	7.00

TABLE 13-8. *(cont.)*

RANK	CRIME	JUDGMENT SCORE
34.	Armed robbery of a bank	7.00
35.	Armed robbery of a supermarket	7.00
36.	Assault with a gun on an acquaintance	7.00
37.	Armed robbery of an armored truck	6.95
38.	Armed robbery of a company payroll	6.95
39.	Causing an accidental death while driving when drunk	6.90
40.	Beating up a child	6.90
41.	Armed holdup of taxi driver	6.75
42.	Armed hijacking of truck	6.65
43.	Armed robbery of a neighborhood druggist	6.65
44.	Assault and battery	6.60
45.	Beating up a policeman	6.55
46.	Armed street holdup stealing $200	6.45
47.	Armed street holdup stealing $25 in cash	6.40
48.	Making sexual advances to young children	6.30
49.	Killing a pedestrian while exceeding the speed limit	6.30
50.	Beating up a stranger	6.30
51.	Manufacturing and selling drugs known to be harmful to users	6.25
52.	Causing the death of an employee by neglecting to repair machinery	6.25
53.	Driving while drunk	6.20
54.	Resisting arrest with violence	6.15
55.	Selling heroin	6.15
56.	Breaking and entering a bank	5.95
57.	Aggravated battery	5.85
58.	Manufacturing and selling of drugs known to be dangerously defective	5.85
59.	Causing the death of a tenant by neglecting to repair heating plant	5.80
60.	Mugging and stealing $200 cash	5.75
61.	Using heroin	5.75
62.	Interfering with railroad tracks	5.70
63.	Mugging and stealing $25 in cash	5.70
64.	Seduction of a minor	5.60
65.	Practicing medicine without a license	5.60
66.	Beating up a spouse	5.55
67.	Unlawful possession of explosives	5.45
68.	Beating up an acquaintance	5.40
69.	Performing illegal abortions	5.40
70.	Burglary of a home, stealing color TV set	5.40
71.	Reckless display of weapon	5.35
72.	Blackmail	5.30
73.	Knowingly selling defective used cars as completely safe	5.25
74.	Selling LSD	5.25
75.	Reckless driving	5.15
76.	Selling secret documents to a foreign government	5.13
77.	Burglary of an appliance store, stealing TV sets	5.10
78.	Using LSD	5.10
79.	Beating up someone in a riot	5.05
80.	Burglary of a home, stealing a portable transistor radio	5.00
81.	Spying for a foreign government	5.00

Thomas S. Ray, *Ratings of Dangerousness of Crime.* Tallahassee, Florida: Florida Division of Mental Health, 1975. By permission of the author.

sonality changes regarding dangerousness must continue and, even more important, the implementation of what is already known and its dissemination to opinion makers and the public must be a part of any successful treatment and release of persons who have committed dangerous offenses—and this must be done commensurate with the public safety.

A Dangerous Offender: Carl Panzram

Carl Panzram (1891–1930) was probably the most dangerous criminal in America in the twentieth century. More people were killed by Al Capone's organization, the Mafia, Murder, Inc., and other organizations, but Panzram was a loner and not associated with any organization.

Panzram was born on a small farm in Minnesota of hard-working and poor parents of German descent. All his family, five brothers and a sister, along with his parents, were honest and hard-working. The parents separated when Carl was seven or eight, and his immediate family then consisted of his mother, and one brother. Panzram was forced to work hard, and said he took "a sound beating every time I looked cockeyed." He suspected there was something wrong with the treatment he received from others. One night he broke into a neighbor's house and stole everything of value. He was sent to the Minnesota State Training School at Red Wing at age twelve. Panzram summarized his attitude as he left the institution two years later in these words:

> After serving two years there, I was pronounced by the parole board to be a nice, clean boy of good morals, as pure as a lily and a credit to those in authority in the institution where I had been sent to be reformed. Yes, sure, I was reformed all right, damn good and reformed, too. When I got out of there I knew all about Jesus and the Bible—so much so that I knew it was all a lot of hot air. But that wasn't all I knew. I had been taught by Christians how to be a hypocrite and I had learned more about stealing, lying, hating, burning and killing. I had learned that a boy's penis could be used for something besides to urinate with and that a rectum could be used for other purposes than crepitating. Oh yes, I had learned a hell of a lot from my expert instructors, furnished to me free of charge by society in general. [Gaddis and Long, 1970]

He ran away from home a year later and subsequently served time in Montana State Reformatory, United States Disciplinary Barracks at Leavenworth, Montana State Prison at Deer Lodge, and Oregon State Prison at Salem, where he led riots and became incorrigible in provoking several incidents. He later served at Sing Sing Prison and Clinton Prison at Dannemora as a hard-case inmate.

After he broke out of the Oregon State Penitentiary in 1918, he spent some time as a seaman, later robbed a house and bought a yacht. Then he began to hire sailors, get them drunk, commit sodomy on them, and kill them. This pattern of sexual deviance followed by robbery and murder was repeated time after time all over the world; it is estimated that Panzram committed sodomy on more than one thousand male human beings, killed at least twenty-one people, and committed thousands of burglaries, robberies, larcenies, and arsons.

Panzram enjoyed crime, hated people, and had no desire whatsoever for reform. His mother was a highly religious person who apparently "fed off" others emotionally. His father deserted the family and, one by one, his five older brothers left.

There was apparently no affection in the family, and little Carl first grew envious of the common emotions of love and compassion, then developed a hatred for any kind of emotional display in the form of affection. He was whipped, beaten, and often starved in the institutions and elsewhere. He developed a motto. "Rob 'em all, rape 'em all, and kill 'em all!" Panzram wanted to be executed; at his execution on September 5, 1930, he pulled the hangman up the scaffold steps, spat twice, and then was hanged.

CONCLUSIONS

Criminal career patterns provide some understanding of the etiology of criminal behavior. Observation and analysis of criminal careers in case histories and autobiographies afford a continuity of social, emotional, and physiological factors that could be obtained in no other way. The case study in psychiatry and clinical psychology, the longitudinal follow-up of criminal careers over a period of years, and the social patterns that are seen as emerging most frequently in cases of offenders adds to the knowledge of deviant behavior. It is apparent that understanding of the theories and the factors in crime is augmented by a review of criminal career patterns.

Questions

1. In what way can criminal career patterns be classified in terms of age of first involvement in the criminal justice system?
2. What crimes have the highest rate of recidivism?
3. At what age do most studies indicate there is a significant drop in the arrest rate? Why does this occur?
4. Why are family and developmental histories important in understanding delinquency?
5. What does long-term interaction in the prison with other inmates and guards do to an individual's personality?
6. How can autobiographical material from offenders be used by correctional counselors?
7. What are the factors in prison life that have the greatest impact on the offenders residing there?
8. How are sex offenses related to family and psychosexual development?
9. What are the dynamics of homosexuality?
10. In what situations might sex reassignment by surgery be indicated?

fourteen

TYPOLOGIES, CLASSIFICATION, AND PREDICTION

Typologies, classification, and prediction assist in making the definitions and theories in criminology and criminal justice useful in terms of research, policymaking, and practice. Research programs have contributed to the typologies of offenders. They help to reduce the infinite variety of problems and factors through conceptualizations that focus on developmental patterns and on the patterns of dynamics and symptoms that emerge from diagnostic efforts in this field. Warren (1972) points out that these typologies or patterns represent an increasing body of knowledge in criminology, which integrates many approaches.

As in medicine, these diagnostic typologies and classifications are useful in understanding deviant behavior and probable optimum approaches for treatment and correction. Typologies and classifications of some sort have been part of the attempt to understand behavior and the nature of the universe since primitive times. Even the ancient Greeks typed and classified human behavior on the basis of temperament as related to the balance of humors or biles that comprised the human body, as discussed in chapter 1. Body types have been considered important since the time of Lombroso, William Sheldon's (1949) classifications are comparatively recent. Even Shakespeare's Julius Caesar exclaimed

Let me have men about me that are fat;
Sleek-headed men and such as sleek o'nights:
Yon Cassius has a lean and hungry look;
He thinks too much: such men are dangerous

SHAKESPEARE, *JULIUS CAESAR,*
(act I, scene ii)

TYPOLOGY

Personality typing and classification have been used for a long time to distinguish types of mental illness, personality patterns, introversion, extroversion, and the like (Jung, 1923). Gibbons (1965, chap. 3) has suggested a typology in terms of offense patterns, self-image, normative orientation, and other social psychological characteristics. The fifteen adult types and nine juvenile types proposed by Gibbons are as follows:

ADULT TYPES	JUVENILE TYPES
Professional thief	First-time gang delinquent
Professional "heavy" criminal	Conflict gang delinquent
Semiprofessional property criminal	Casual gang delinquent
Property offender—"one-time loser"	Casual delinquent, nongang member
Automobile thief—"joy rider"	Automobile thief—"joy rider"
Naive check forger	Drug user—heroin
White-collar criminal	Overly aggressive delinquent
Professional "fringe" violator	Female delinquent
Embezzler	"Behavior problem" delinquent
Personal offender—"one-time loser"	
"Psychopathic" assaultist	
Violent sex offender	
Nonviolent sex offender—nonviolent rapist	
Nonviolent sex offender—statutory rape	
Narcotic addict—heroin	

A description of each type is provided; sometimes the types are not sharply delineated and tend to overlap or be unclear. This is to be expected because criminal delinquent behavior is a continuum rather than a neat series of compartmentalized areas.

Cavan (1962) provides a typology that focuses primarily on public reaction. Her analysis of interaction between the public and the offender is as follows:

1. Criminal contraculture (professional crime, robbery, burglary)
2. Extreme underconformity (occasional drunkenness)
3. Minor underconformity (embezzlement)
4. "Average" conformity (minor pilfering)
5. Extreme overconformity (attempts to reform society by persuasion and legal means)
6. Ideological contraculture (efforts to remodel society, possibly through illegal means)

This typology is important because it allows society's reaction to the offender's self-concept and behavior to become a realistic part of the offense pattern and the criminal justice system.

Roebuck and Cadwallader (1961; also Roebuck, 1967) based their typology on 400 arrest histories selected from 1,155 black prisoners entering the District of Columbia Reformatory in Lorton, Virginia, between January 5, 1954, and November 8, 1955. Their classification was a dual one, with all cases first grouped into four general classes and then into thirteen specific patterns. The four general classes were:

1. Single pattern—An arrest history showing a high frequency of one kind of criminal charge
2. Multiple pattern—Arrest history of two or more single patterns
3. Mixed pattern—Arrest history in which changes do not form a frequency pattern—a jack of all trades in crime
4. No pattern—A residual category of those with less than three arrests, which were too few to support an analysis

The thirteen specific criminal patterns were:

1. Single pattern of robbery
2. Single pattern of narcotic drug offenses
3. Single pattern of gambling
4. Single pattern of burglary
5. Single pattern of sex offenses
6. Single pattern of auto theft
7. Single pattern of confidence games
8. Single pattern of check forgery
9. Multiple pattern of drunkenness, assault, and larceny
10. Double pattern of larceny and burglary
11. Double pattern of assault and drunkenness
12. Mixed pattern
13. No pattern

Gibbons and Garrity (1963) indicate that differences between offenders and nonoffenders can be found in their development and the environments in which they have developed. People can be classified as those whose life orientation is guided by criminal groups and those whose life orientation is largely guided by noncriminal groups. They suggest that the offender is defined by society as part of (1) that group of offenders defined as criminals from the time of the first criminal act and (2) that group of offenders not defined as criminal until later in life, although committing criminal acts early.

Reckless (1961) has suggested three criminal careers: (1) ordinary, (2) organized, and (3) professional. Ordinary criminals, of course, are those serving in prison for burglary, larceny, robbery, auto theft, homicide, rape, assault and similar "common" offenses. Organized crime is represented by the syndicate—by Al Capone's organization, Frank Costello's operation, and similar business operations in illegal goods and services. Professional crime is property crime where the offender makes his living through burglary, larceny, "con" games, embezzlement and graft, or other property offenses.

Lindesmith and Dunham (1941) devised a continuum of criminal behavior ranging from the individualized criminal to the social criminal. The individual criminal commits crime for various personal reasons with the behavior finding little cultural support. The social criminal, on the other hand, finds his crimes supported and prescribed by group norms, and he achieves status and recognition within the group where criminal values prevail. Lindesmith and Dunham refer to the habitual-situational criminal to classify those who are not professional but are constantly in trouble.

McKinney (1966) has provided eight classifications based on the criminal career of the offender, group support of criminal behavior, correspondence between criminal behavior and legitimate behavior patterns, and societal reactions, McKinney's classifications are:

1. Violent personal crime
2. Occasional property crime
3. Occupational crime
4. Political crime
5. Public order
6. Conventional crime
7. Organized crime
8. Professional crime

Violent personal crime includes murder, assault, and forcible rape. Occasional property crime includes auto theft, shoplifting, check forgery, and vandalism. Occupational crime includes embezzlement, fraudulent sales, false advertising, pricing fixing, fee splitting, black market activity, prescription violation, and antitrust violation. Political crime includes treason, sedition, espionage, sabotage, military draft violation, war collaboration, radicalism, and other forms of protest that might be defined as criminal. Public order crime includes drunkenness, vagrancy, disorderly conduct, prostitution, homosexuality, traffic violation, and drug addiction. Conventional crime includes robbery, larceny, burglary, and gang theft. Organized crime includes racketeering, organized prostitution, organized gambling, and control of narcotics. Professional crime includes confidence games, shoplifting, pickpocketing, forgery, and counterfeiting.

Morrison divided persons who commit criminal homicide into the classifications given in Table 14–1: (1) mentally ill homicide offenders; (2) deliberate antisocial lifestyle homicide offenders; (3) "Square John" homicide offenders, whom he considers accidental or one-time personal offenders; and (4) subcultural assaulter homicide offenders, whose offenses are victim precipitated or otherwise circumstantial. His complete typology is shown in Table 14–1.

TABLE 14-1.
A Typology of Individuals Who Commit Criminal Homicide

GROUP A.	MENTALLY ILL HOMICIDE OFFENDERS	Psychotic Homicide Offender Psychopathic Assaulter Violent Sex Offender
GROUP B.	DELIBERATE ANTISOCIAL LIFE-STYLE HOMICIDE OFFENDERS	Felony Homicide Offender Professional Hired Assassin Political Assassin
GROUP C.	"SQUARE JOHN" HOMICIDE OFFENDERS	Personal Offender One-Time Loser Accidental Homicide Offender
GROUP D.	SUBCULTURAL ASSAULTER HOMICIDE OFFENDERS	Victim-Precipitated Homicide Offender Violent Subculture Homicide Offender Mob Riot Homicide Offender

The McGill Clinic in Forensic Psychiatry in Montreal, headed by Bruno Cormier (1961), offers the following classifications:

1. Primary delinquent (immature, unable to tolerate anxiety or depression).
2. Secondary delinquent (delinquency through adolescence, then no trouble).
3. Latecomer to crime (persons who begin criminal careers after thirty years of age).

The latecomers in delinquency have been viewed as posing three different patterns:

1. Their criminality can be understood in terms of defective character development.
2. Delinquency can be understood as a product of a psychotic state or mental illness.
3. The individual is ill-equipped to deal with the normal demands of life.

The latecomers in adult crime pose four different patterns:

1. Neurotically conflicted individuals who are handling their problems by antisocial acting out.
2. Episodic recidivists who are prone to recurrent reactive depressions.
3. Episodic late offenders with manic-depressive personalities.
4. Persons who commit crimes in the course of a psychosis or as part of recurrent schizophrenic states.

This typology is obviously psychiatric in orientation as compared with some of the other sociological approaches presented here.

Don Gibbons has offered a rather elaborate typology that defines the characteristics of several offender types. He follows the typology with suggested treatment dimensions and diagnostic types. His typology is presented in Table 14–2. The corresponding treatment dimensions and diagnostic types are shown in Table 14–3.

Ferdinand (1966) has discussed delinquent typologies from the standpoint of social structure, degree of alienation, delinquent patterns, and class origins of the group members. His typology is shown in Table 14-4.

While developing their typology, Roebuck and Cadwallader examined social and personal attributes of the family situation for armed robbers and for other offenders and found significant differences. Greater criminality in the family, more problems known to social agencies, unsettled childhood experiences, heavy drinking, and other indices of social breakdown appeared in the homes of armed robbers. The list of attributes, together with their percentage of incidence, is shown in Table 14-5. Clinard and Quinney then proposed eight criminal types, following McKinney, consisting of those who are involved in (1) violent personal crime, (2) occasional property crime, (3) occupational crime, (4) political crime, (5) public order crime, (6) conventional crime, (7) organized crime, and (8) professional crime. This typology is shown in Table 14-6.

Marguerite Q. Warren has compiled several of the important typologies presented by psychiatrists, psychologists, and sociologists.

TABLE 14-2.
Defining Characteristics of Offender Types

TYPE	OFFENSE PATTERN	SELF-DEFINITION AND ATTITUDE
Semiprofessional property offender (Antisocial)	Robbery, burglary, larceny, and allied offenses; unskilled repetitive crime with small profit	Self-definition as a criminal, but as a victim of society; hostile toward police and correctional authorities
Auto thief—joyrider (Antisocial)	Repetitive auto theft for pleasure; "car clouting" and other auto offenses for profit not included	Self-definition as a criminal, and as tough, manly; concerned with others' perception of him as a "tough guy"
Naive check forger (Prosocial)	Passing bad checks, usually without skill; often passes checks while drinking	Self-definition as a non-criminal, and as a person burdened with personal problems
Embezzler (Prosocial)	Illegal conversion of property from a position of financial trust	Self-definition as a non-criminal, as different from "real criminals"; rationalizes acts as not really criminal
Personal offender ("one-time loser") (Prosocial)	Crimes of violence under situational stress—murder, man-slaughter, assault	Self-definition as a non-criminal, but as deserving of punishment; no pronounced anti-social attitudes
Psychopathic assaultist (Asocial)	Offenses against persons or property or both, characterized by violence in "inappropriate" situations	Self-definition as a criminal, but as a victim of the treachery of others; views others as generally untrustworthy.
Violent sex offender (Prosocial)	Sexual assaults upon physically mature females, characterized by extreme violence, mutilation, etc.	Self-definition as a non-criminal
Non-violent sex offender (Prosocial)	Sex offenses—such as child-molesting—usually with immature victims; statutory rape and similar offenses not included	Self-definition as a non-criminal; frequently rationalizes himself as Christian and his offense as not sexual but "educational"
Heroin addict (Antisocial)	Use of heroin or other opiate; property offenses as source of income for purchase of drugs	Self-definition as a criminal, but sees criminal status as unjust; holds that drug usage is a relatively harmless personal vice

Don C. Gibbons, "Some Notes on Treatment Theory in Corrections," *Social Service Review*, 36 (September 1962), 295–305. Reprinted by permission of the University of Chicago Press.

TABLE 14-3.
Treatment Dimensions and Diagnostic Types

SEMIPROFESSIONAL PROPERTY OFFENDER	
Formal treatment program	Guided-group-interaction form of therapy in group composed of other "antisocial," "right guy" offenders
Adjunct program	Vocational training or educational program
Goal	Modification of attitudes toward police work, crime, and society; development of "prosocial" attitudes

TABLE 14-3. *(cont.)*

Periods	Institutional group therapy carried on most intensively during last few months of incarceration and continued during parole
Frequency	Intensive in the pre-release period, with group meeting at least several times a week
AUTO THIEF—JOYRIDER	
Formal treatment program	Guided-group-interaction form of therapy in group composed of other "antisocial," "right guy" offenders, but with some members who have been non-joyriders
Adjunct program	Recreational program with active participation in athletics
Goal	Demonstration of inappropriateness of "tough guy" criminal activity, aid to offender in developing a self-image which is tough and masculine but consistent with socially acceptable behavior
Periods	Same as for semiprofessional property offender
Frequency	Same as for semiprofessional property offender
NAIVE CHECK FORGER	
Formal treatment program	Client-centered individual therapy, group therapy in groups composed of other forgers, or both
Adjunct program	Alcoholics Anonymous
Goal	Breaking down the offender's rationalizations for forgery, discouraging dependent behavior, building up a fund of acceptable solutions to problems
Periods	Intensive treatment if on probation or institutionalized, continued during parole, including group treatment, at least in part, and involvement in Alcoholics Anonymous during parole
Frequency	Several times a week
EMBEZZLER	
Formal treatment program	Intensive treatment not usually required; superficial assistance from time to time from treatment workers; isolation from more criminalistic types of prisoners
Adjunct program	Assignment to clerical or other service position in the institution
Goal	Preservation of the offender's prosocial self-image and attitudes
Periods	During parole some help in adjusting to altered social and economic status
Frequency	Infrequent—once a week or less
PERSONAL OFFENDER ("ONE-TIME LOSER")	
Formal treatment program	Similar to that for embezzler
Adjunct program	Assignment to institutional position
Goal	Similar to that for embezzler
Periods	Intensive treatment during parole
Frequency	Infrequent—once a week or less

TABLE 14-3. *(cont.)*

PSYCHOPATHIC ASSAULTIST	
Formal treatment program	Some form of group treatment combined with intensive psychiatric counseling
Adjunct program	None specific
Goal	Development of "normal" personality structure; resocialization of essentially undersocialized person, including development of loyalty attachments, role-taking abilities
Periods	Intensive treatment during entire period of incarceration and parole
Frequency	Relatively intense—several times a week
VIOLENT SEX OFFENDER	
Formal treatment program	Psychiatric therapy conducted by psychiatrist or clinical psychologist
Adjunct program	None specific
Goal	Modification of bizarre sexual orientations
Periods	Intensive treatment during entire period of incarceration and parole
Frequency	Relatively intense—several times a week
NON-VIOLENT SEX OFFENDER	
Formal treatment program	Intensive psychiatric therapy, particularly at initial stage of incarceration; possibly supplemented with group treatment in group of other non-violent sex offenders at later stage of prison term
Adjunct program	None specific
Goal	Modification of offender's self-image of inadequacy and sexual impotency; breaking down rationalizations regarding deviant sex acts; directing offender toward more aggressive and dominant relations with adults, particularly with his spouse
Frequency	Relatively intense—several times a week
HEROIN ADDICT	
Formal treatment program	Individual therapy designed to deal with personality problems, along with guided group interaction designed to modify group-supported norms and attitudes regarding drug use and criminality
Adjunct program	Vocational or educational program
Goal	Modification of "antisocial" attitudes, particularly attitudes toward drug use, law enforcement agencies, and drug addiction treatment programs; reduction of severe personality problems
Periods	Individual treatment and withdrawal from use of narcotics during early period of incarceration; group treatment toward end of prison term and in parole period
Frequency	Relatively intense—several times a week

TABLE 14-4.
A Social Typology of Delinquency

TYPE	SOCIAL STRUCTURE	DEGREE OF ALIENATION FROM COMMUNITY	DELINQUENT PATTERNS	CLASS ORIGINS OF MEMBERS
Mischievous-Indulgent	Weakly organized, clique structures at best.	Somewhat alienated from conventional peers and adults.	Delinquent exploits exhibit style and taste, indulgent toward appetites.	Primarily upper upper-class youths, upwardly mobile lower status youths.
Aggressive-Exploitive	Well organized into clubs and gangs of adolescent society.	Delinquent activities are unknown to conventional adults, minimally alienated.	Emphasis upon proving oneself through sexual, drinking, and physical competition.	Lower upper-, upper middle-class, and upwardly mobile youths.
Criminal	Loosely organized in terms of clique structure.	Well integrated with criminal adults, not rejected by most conventional adults in immediate neighborhood.	Emphasis upon skill in criminal techniques, pursuit of criminal activities related to adult criminal practices.	Upper lower- and upwardly mobile lower-class youngsters.
Fighting	Very well organized with formal positions and strong solidarity.	Condemned and despised by immediate community, high degree of alienation.	Major emphasis upon attitudes and skills needed in physical combat.	Upper lower- and upwardly mobile lower lower-class youngsters.
Theft	Loosely organized in terms of friendship cliques.	Not rejected by immediate community, not seriously alienated.	Indulgence of appetites, theft for excitement, assaultive when challenged, vandalism toward schools.	Upper lower- and upwardly mobile lower lower-class youngsters.
Disorganized Acting-Out	Very loosely organized, little structure at all.	Behavior not easily distinguished from normal adult patterns.	Indulgence of appetites, impulsive assaults, thefts and use of narcotics.	Lower lower-class.

Theodore N. Ferdinand, *Typologies of Delinquency: A Critical Analysis* (New York: Random House, Inc., 1966). p. 143. Reprinted by permission of the publisher.

TABLE 14-5.
Percent of Offenders Exhibiting Selected Social and Personal Attributes by Single Pattern of Armed Robbery Offenders and All Other Offenders

SELECTED SOCIAL AND PERSONAL ATTRIBUTES	ARMED ROBBERS (N = 32) (PERCENT)	ALL OTHERS (N = 368) (PERCENT)	X^2
Reared in more than one home	78	37	0.01
Mother figure southern migrant	91	39	0.01
Mother figure domestic servant	97	73	0.01
Dependent family	94	72	0.01
Family broken by desertion	47	34	0.05
Demoralized family	84	46	0.01
Criminality in family	78	40	0.01
Mother figure dominant	81	52	0.01
Inadequate supervision—father	97	73	0.01
Inadequate supervision—mother	91	69	0.05
Conflict in family	59	58	0.00
Hostility toward father	94	38	0.01
Hostility toward mother	19	20	0.00
Disciplinary problem at home	56	27	0.01
History of running away	84	42	0.01
Weak parental family structure	87	50	0.01
No parental family ties	78	70	0.01
Reared in urban area	100	82	0.00
Reared in slum area	100	59	0.01
Living in slum when arrested	94	74	0.05
History of school truancy	91	47	0.01
Disciplinary problem at school	94	43	0.01
Street trades as juvenile	87	47	0.01
No marital ties	91	70	0.05
Juvenile delinquent companions	97	56	0.01
Member delinquent gang	97	30	0.01
Adjudicated juvenile delinquent	94	40	0.01
Committed as juvenile	91	32	0.01
Police contact prior to 18	100	51	0.01
Criminal companions as juvenile	97	36	0.01

Julian B. Roebuck and Mervyn L. Cadwallader, "The Negro Armed Robber as a Criminal Type: The Construction and Application of a Typology," *Pacific Sociological Review*, 4, No. 1 (Spring 1961), 23. Reprinted by permission of the publisher, Sage Publications, Inc.

Some have been discussed here and some not, while others that have been discussed do not appear in Warren's compilation. In any case, the compilation provides some knowledge of the general pattern of offender typologies. Warren's typology compilation is shown in Table 14-7.

Glaser presented an excellent crime classification in 1972, which is useful for translation into public policy and social action.[1]

---

[1]Daniel Glaser, *Adult Crime and Social Policy* (Englewood Cliffs, N.J.: Prentice-Hall, 1972), pp. 27–66. Reprinted by permission of the publisher.

1. *Adolescent recapitulators* periodically repeat through adulthood the same pattern of offenses begun in adolescence. Many men in prison are in their twenties and thirties struggling in disorganized fashion toward the adolescent dream of a secure manhood, followed by a zig-zag path, alternatively "good straight" and then committing offenses in stress situations.

2. *Subcultural assaultors* live in a section of society where violence is emphasized more than in broader society, sometimes considered obligatory in response to verbal insults. Homicide and assaults occur more frequently in these subcultures.

3. *Addiction-supporting predators* commit property crimes to finance drug and alcohol needs.

4. *Vocational predators* support themselves and whatever families they might have by taking money and property from others. The confidence game, professional bank robbery and safe-cracking, shoplifting, burglary, and armed robbery are a few of the offenses people commit.

5. *Organized illegal sellers* engage in organized crime at different levels, generally working within an organization dealing in illegal goods or services. Systematic market research could provide better understanding of the needs, demands, and factors related to this type of criminal activity.

6. *Avocational predators* engage in part-time acquisition of property and money to supplement their primary source of income. Many shoplifters, muggers, burglars, and employee-pilferers fall into this category, as well as most "white-collar" crimes, such as price-fixing and "thumb-on-the-scales" offenses.

7. *Crisis-vascillation predators* are law-abiding people who commit crime to resolve an unusual crisis, such as embezzlement, one-time robbery, or other property offenses designed to resolve a crisis.

8. *Quasi-insane assaultors* are the murderers and sexual assaultors who do not fit into the subculture violent pattern and are not "understandable" in common-sense terms. Most highly publicized murders are of this type, such as England's "Jack the Ripper," Chicago's Loeb and Leopold, the Boston Strangler, and California's Manson Family.

9. *Addicted performers* are arrested primarily for traffic offenses under the influence of alcohol, public drunkenness, disorderly conduct, and vagrancy.

10. *Private illegal consumers* include most users of marijuana, LSD, amphetamines, and other relatively nonaddicting drugs that do not have to be supported by crime.

Morris Caldwell (1956) indicated that prison populations break down into informal inmate groups, as follows:

1. Politicians or "big shots"
2. Right guys

TABLE 14-6.
Typology of Criminal Behavior Systems

CLASSIFICATION CHARACTERISTICS	1 VIOLENT PERSONAL CRIME	2 OCCASIONAL PROPERTY CRIME	3 OCCUPATIONAL CRIME	4 POLITICAL CRIME
Criminal Career of the Offender	LOW Crime not part of offender's career; usually does not conceive of self as criminal	LOW Little or no criminal self-concept; does not identify with crime	LOW No criminal self-concept; occasionally violates the law; part of one's legitimate work; accepts conventional values of society	LOW Usually no criminal self-concept; violates the law out of conscience; attempts to change society or correct perceived injustices; desire for a better society
Group Support of Criminal Behavior	LOW Little or no group support, offenses committed for personal reasons; some support in subcultural norms	LOW Little group support; individual offenses	MEDIUM Some groups may tolerate offenses; offender integrated in groups	HIGH Group support; association with persons of same values; behavior reinforced by group
Correspondence between Criminal Behavior and Legitimate Behavior Patterns	LOW Violation of values on life and personal safety	LOW Violation of value on private property	HIGH Behavior corresponds to pursuit of business activity; "sharp" practices respected; "buyer beware" philosophy' hands off policy	MEDIUM Some toleration of protest and dissent, short of revolution; dissent periodically regarded as a threat (in times of national unrest)
Societal Reaction	HIGH Capital punishment; long imprisonment	MEDIUM Arrest; jail; short imprisonment, probation	LOW Indifference; monetary penalties, revocation of license to practice, seizure of product or injunction	HIGH Strong disapproval; regarded as threat to society; prison
Legal Categories of Crime	Murder, assault, forcible rape, child molesting	Some auto theft, shoplifting, check forgery, vandalism	Embezzlement, fraudulent sales, false advertising, fee-splitting, violation of labor practice laws, antitrust violations, black market activity, prescription violation	Treason, sedition, espionage, sabotage, radicalism, military draft violations, war collaboration, various protests defined as criminal

5 PUBLIC ORDER CRIME	6 CONVENTIONAL CRIME	7 ORGANIZED CRIME	8 PROFESSIONAL CRIME
MEDIUM Confused self-concept; vacillation in identification with crime	MEDIUM Income supplemented through crimes of gain; often a youthful activity; vacillation in self-concept; partial commitment to a criminal subculture	HIGH Crime pursued as a livelihood; criminal self-concept; progression in crime; isolation from larger society	HIGH Crime pursued as a livelihood; criminal self-concept; status in the world of crime; commitment to world of professional criminals
MEDIUM Partial support for behavior from some groups; considerable association with other offenders	HIGH Behavior supported by group norms; status achieved in groups; principal association with other offenders	HIGH Business association in crime; behavior prescribed by the groups; integration of the person into the group	HIGH Associations primarily with other offenders; status gained in criminal offenses; behavior prescribed by group norms
MEDIUM Some forms required by legitimate society; some are economic activities	MEDIUM Consistent with goals on economic success; inconsistent with sanctity of private property; behavior not consistent with expectations of adolescence and young adulthood	MEDIUM Illegal services received by legitimate society; economic risk values; large-scale control also employed in legitimate society	MEDIUM Engaged in an occupation; skill respected; survival because of cooperation from legitimate society; law-abiding persons often accomplices
MEDIUM Arrest; jail; prison; probation	HIGH Arrest; jail; probation; institutionalization; parole; rehabilitation	MEDIUM Considerable public tolerance; arrest and sentence when detected; often not visible to society; immunity through politicians and law officers	MEDIUM Rarely strong societal reaction, most cases "fixed"
Drunkenness, vagrancy, disorderly conduct, prostitution, homosexuality, gambling, traffic violation, drug addiction	Robbery, larceny, burglary, gang theft	Racketeering, organized prostitution and commercialized vice, control of drug traffic, organized gambling	Confidence games, shoplifting, pickpocketing, forgery, counterfeiting

Marshall B. Clinard and Richard Quinney, *Criminal Behavior Systems: A Typology* (New York: Holt, Rinehart and Winston, Publishers, 1967), pp. 16–17. Reprinted by permission of the Dryden Press.

TABLE 14-7.
Cross-Classification of Offender Typologies

SUBTYPES	JESNESS	HUNT	HURWITZ	MACGREGOR	MAKKAY	QUAY	REISS
1. Asocial		Sub I	Type II	Schizophrenic		Unsocialized psychopath	
Aggressive	Immature, aggressive				Antisocial Character Disorder-primitive Aggressive Passive-aggressive		
Passive	Immature, passive						Relatively integrated
2. Conformist		Stage 1			Antisocial Character Disorder-organized Passive-aggressive	Inadequate-immature Subcultural	Relatively integrated
Nondelinquency-oriented	Immature, passive						
Delinquency-oriented	Socialized conformist						
3. Antisocial-manipulator	Manipulator			Autocrat	Antisocial Character Disorder-organized Aggressive		Defective superego
4. Neurotic		Stage II	Type III		Neurotic		Relatively weak ego
Acting-out	Neurotic, acting-out			Intimidated		Neurotic-disturbed	
Anxious	Neurotic, anxious Neurotic, depressed						
5. Subcultural-identifier	Cultural delinquent	Stage II	Type I	Rebel	Subcultural	Subcultural	Relatively integrated
6. Situational		Stage II					
Types not cross-classified					Mental retarddate Psychotic		

310

WARREN	APA	ARGYLE	GIBBONS	JENKINS AND HEWITT	McCORD	RECKLESS	SCHRAG	STUDT
I₂ Asocial, aggressive Asocial, passive	Passive-aggressive personality Aggressive Passive-aggressive	Lack of sympathy	Overly aggressive	Unsocialized aggressive			Asocial	Isolate
I₃	Passive-aggressive personality	Inadequate superego			Conformist			Receiver
Conformist, Immature Conformist, Cultural	Passive-dependent		Gang offenders	Socialized			Anti-social	
I₃ Manipulator	Antisocial personality	Inadequate superego			Aggressive (psychopathic)	Psycho-path	Pseudo-social	Manipulator
I₄ Neurotic	Sociopathic personality disturbance	Weak ego control	Joyrider			Neurotic Personality	Pro-social	
Neurotic, acting-out Neurotic, anxious			Behavior problems	Overinhibited	Neurotic-withdrawn			Love-seeker
I₄ Cultural identifier	Dyssocial reaction	Deviant identification	Gang offenders	Socialized			Anti-social	Learner
I₄ Situational, emotional reaction	Adjustment reaction of adolescence		Casual delinquent Heroin user female delinquent			Offenders of the moment Eruptive behavior		

Marguerite Q. Warren, "Classification of Offenders as an Aid to Efficient Management and Effective Treatment," *Journal of Criminal Law, Criminology and Police Science*, 62, No. 2 (June 1971), 250. Reprinted by special permission of the *Journal of Criminal Law, Criminology and Police Science*, ©1971 by Northwestern University School of Law.

311

 3. Moonshiners
 4. Dope peddlers
 5. Larceny boys
 6. Gambling syndicate
 7. Leather workers
 8. Religionists
 9. Homosexuals and wolves
10. Weapon manufacturers
11. Spartans (weight lifters)

Caldwell also emphasizes the following elements of the prisoner's code:

1. Fraternization with personnel prohibited
2. Never squeal
3. Assistance in escape planning
4. No information to administration
5. Strong spirit of cooperation and loyalty between inmates
6. Cooperation with treatment people, "playing the nods," the best way out

The proposals for criminological typologies have been numerous and varied; the list presented here could be multiplied fivefold or tenfold (see Bottoms, 1973, p. 27), but the purpose here has been simply to provide examples of the types of classifications and typologies of delinquent and criminal behavior that have been offered in the literature. Typology is a tool, like the use of prediction techniques, by which offenders can be categorized for purposes of treatment and public policy. Further, typologies widen the focus of understanding of crime beyond the legal categories in which offenders are placed by the police and the courts. They assist in determining what factors are important in diagnosis and treatment.

CLASSIFICATION

Classification is the placement of individual offenders into program categories presumably in accordance with their typologies. Typologies involve diagnostic and prescriptive components, and classification involves the action or program components.

Corrections or the criminal justice programming are not sufficiently advanced or staffed to make adequate use of the typologies offered by the researchers and the clinicians. As in agriculture, the economy, and elsewhere in human endeavor, people simply do not do as well as they know how to do. Their full knowledge is seldom brought to bear efficiently to solve problems. This is nowhere more true than in the criminal justice system. With all the knowledge accumulated thus far in the study of criminal behavior and its treatment, the majority of classifications are legal or in terms of the escape risk of the individual. Legal and security classifications predominate in the criminal justice system, and they are based primarily on age and criminal history, including the most recent offense.

The legal classifications begin with the relative seriousness of the offense. In descending order of seriousness, the major legal classifications of offenses are:

1. Treason (included in the Constitution)
2. Felony (as defined by statute)
3. Misdemeanor (as defined by statute)
4. Ordinance (municipal or city law)
5. Rules and regulations (administrative codes generally without penal sanctions)

The definitions of specific crimes were synthesized by the International Association of Chiefs of Police in 1930 and adopted by the Federal Bureau of Investigation when crime statistics began to be colleced in 1930 and published in the *Uniform Crime Reports*. The major crimes, until recently called Part I crimes, now called Index Crimes because of better consistency in reporting, are:

- Murder
- Forcible rape
- Robbery
- Aggravated assault
- Burglary
- Larceny
- Auto theft

The lesser crimes, formerly Part II crimes such as arson and kidnapping are lesser either because of their infrequency or because they are misdemeanors. These lesser offenses are classified as follows in the FBI *Uniform Crime Reports:*

- Other assaults (less than aggravated assault)
- Arson
- Forgery and counterfeiting
- Fraud
- Embezzlement
- Stolen property: buying, receiving, possessing

- Vandalism
- Weapons: carrying, possessing, etc.
- Sex offenses (except forcible rape and prostitution)
- Narcotic drug laws
- Gambling
- Offenses against family and children
- Driving under the influence
- Liquor laws
- Drunkenness
- Disorderly conduct
- Vagrancy
- All other offenses
- Suspicion
- Runaways (juvenile)

The effect of a crime against society is also the basis for legal classification. There are two classifications in this grouping: (1) *mala en se* and (2) *mala prohibita*. *Mala en se* identifies those crimes that are directly damaging to society, such as murder, theft, and conventional crimes. *Mala prohibita* refers to those crimes of a regulatory nature, which are not directly damaging to society, such as moonshining, prostitution, gambling, narcotics and drug laws, and vagrancy. Victimless crimes are *mala prohibita*. Offenses under the *mala en se* category have become standard in all socities. Offenses under the concept of *mala prohibita* are culture bound and vary more widely from society to society.

Most prison administrators in the United States classify people according to escape risk and their judgment of dangerousness. Accordingly, there are generally five categories. These classifications would generally be defined as follows:

MAXIMUM

Persons who are dangerous within the prison population, a high escape risk, and those who need to be controlled for the safety of themselves or others may be locked in a solitary confinement cell and not taken out except in company of an officer and with the use of restraint equipment, such as handcuffs, belly belts, and leg irons.

CLOSE

Those persons who can "lock" (live) inside the walls and cell blocks but who may work in gangs under supervision inside the walls. In the South, when the road gangs were prevalent, close-custody inmates could be worked on the roads under supervision of guards with firearms, sometimes called a gun squad.

MEDIUM

Persons who can lock (live) inside the walls, work in gangs under unarmed supervision outside the walls, or work alone inside the walls, the latter giving rise to their designation as "inside trusties."

MINIMUM

Persons who can live outside the walls and work outside the walls without supervision.

COMMUNITY CUSTODY

Persons who can live in a community-based facility downtown or within commuting distance from the city, can go into the urban area for work or study and occasional visits without supervision. In the NewGate Program (University Study), the convicted offender may live in a university dormitory and report once a week to his or her counselor while studying at the university.

The effort of the institution is always directed toward reducing custody. Maximum and close custody are expensive, while minimum and community custody are considerably less expensive. In fact, community custody may not be expensive at all in some jurisdictions, because the person working there gives the state $3 or $4 a day for maintenance and $1 a day for transportation, as well as supporting his family back home on his earnings, thereby reducing welfare costs. Further, prisoners are more readily paroled from medium, minimum, and community custody than they are from maximum or close custody. Very few are paroled from maximum custody and then under most unusual circumstances. Rehabilitation and economy, then, are both served by reducing custody for every individual as much as possible.

Prisons in the Federal Republic of Germany classify prisoners into three groups: (1) G-1, or those not in need of resocialization; (2) G-2, or those in need of resocialization who can be reintegrated into society, many being recidivists in property crime; and (3) G-3, or offenders who can probably not be resocialized (Opp.)

Classification for purposes of rehabilitation and treatment refers to the separation of offenders by a variety of criteria to avoid moral contamination, exploitation, and other problems. In Spain the men were separated from the women as early as 1519 in jails and workhouses. Separation of the sexes in the United states began with the penitentiary movement in 1790. Children began to be separated from adults in the early part of the nineteenth century with the establishment of private Houses of Refuge in Danzig in 1824 and New York in 1825, public training schools for juveniles in New York, Massachusetts, and Maine in the period from 1846 to 1849, and educational programs for youths at the Elmira reformatory in New York in 1876. Separation for purposes of education on the basis of intelligence appeared in France when Binet and Simon were commissioned in 1904 by the French Ministry of Education to develop an intelligence test to determine which problem children were educable. The first intelligence test was produced in 1905, was revised in 1908, translated into English, and brought to the Vineland training school in New Jersey by Goddard in 1911. The Borstal system of open institutions was initiated in England in 1908, and similar institutions began in Belgium at the same time, both separating offenders for treatment purposes. A rudimentary form of classification was initiated in the Pennsylvania's Eastern Penitentiary in 1909 (Barnes, 1927, p. 336). New Jersey introduced the first classification system as a result of studies of the Prison Inquiry Commission in 1917. The original New Jersey classification was as follows (Ellis, 1931):

1. The difficult class who are hostile to society and require close custody
2. The better class who are good prisoners with reasonably good prognosis but are serving for long terms and require close study
3. The simple feeble-minded whose condition is not complicated by psychopathic traits
4. The senile and incapacitated class
5. The psychotic and epilepsy class who shall be transferred to the hospitals for the mentally ill
6. The defective delinquent class whose low intelligence is combined with high emotional instability and may need long periods of custody and training under an indeterminate sentence

The Federal Bureau of Prisons began developing a classification system in 1929 under Sanford Bates, and this program went into effect through a congressional act in 1930. Classification quickly spread to New York, Massachusetts, Pennsylvania, Michigan, Indiana, Illinois, and other states. Classification in the Federal Bureau of Prisons was under the heading of (1) custody and discipline, (2) transfer to other institutions, (3) social service, (4) medical treatment, and (5) training programs, including employment, education, religion, and recreation (*Handbook of Case Work*, 1934). In 1931, psychiatrists and psychologists had visited the Illinois institution frequently (Huffman, 1970, p. 86).

The Illinois legislature passed a classification program that became law in January 1933. Minnesota established a State Board of Classification in 1935. Indiana began classification in December 1936 and Michigan in 1937.

Classification has become an administrative vehicle by which treatment resources get to the inmate. It is a delivery system for services based on the needs of the inmates or residents as they fall into broad program categories. The administrative structure classification has developed through five stages in American prisons:

1. The preprofessional approach, in which the administrative staff, frequently including the warden and deputy warden, met and recommended assignments, originally without much guidance, except where help was needed in the prison, generally by a ten- to twelve-member committee without professional guidance;
2. The traditional classification committee, also a large committee that recommended assignments, but with a sociologist or psychologist to gather information about each inmate;
3. The integrated committee, which for the first time really became a part of the prison in that its assignments were more than recommendations but were, in fact, implemented by the deputy warden, who generally changed cell assignments with job assignments so that all persons working on one assignment could be in the same housing unit, thereby simplifying the movement of inmates;
4. The professional classification committee, which reduced the size of the committee to probably three, including a high-ranking custodial man, the director of classification, and the inmate's counselor; and
5. The team treatment approach, in which each inmate generally is assigned a team including a correctional officer, a classification and parole staff member, and an educational or other staff member, with the team determining program and assignments for the duration of his or her incarceration.

In 1969, the United States Bureau of Prisons implemented a system of classification to diagnoses that could be computerized. Placing offenders into treatment categories of (a) intensive, (b) selective, or (c) minimal as to likelihood of change according to staff judgment was the next logical step in systematization. The RAPS system is used to develop a code that can be translated into categories I, II, or III, depending upon whether there should be great, medium, or no expenditure of resources above the essential level of services. The "R" (rehabilitative potential or rating) in this code is based on the staff's professional opinion regarding the prospects of his change. The "A" refers to age as under thirty, thirty–forty-five, or over forty-five. The "P" is the number of prior sentences, ranging from none to two or more. The "S" refers to the nature of the sentence in terms of special classification (Federal Juvenile Delinquency Act, Youthful Offenders Act, or Narcotic Addiction Rehabilitation Act) or length of sentence. The code combinations are fed into computers and elicit names of the category I inmates, who are reviewed every thirty days and have first priority in assignments; category II persons, who are reviewed every six months and do not have first priority on assignments; and category III inmates, who are reviewed annually and have last priority on assignments, generally being used as needed to maintain the institution. In summary, classification has ranged from informal "guessing" in the nineteenth and early twentieth centuries to a more sophisticated and refined method of classifying persons in accordance with their needs.

The Oregon State Correctional Institution at Salem, opened in 1959, classified inmates according to the major source of their difficulties: (1) conflict with individual and societal values, (2) conflicts stemming from relationships with others, (3) problems caused by need for material things, and (4) problems based on one's self-concept (Long, 1965). Morris had suggested that offenders be classified as (1) legalistic or technical offenders, (2) situational offenders, (3) pathological offenders, (4) avocational offenders, and (5) career offenders, which represents a gradual progression from the simple and relatively nonproblematic cases to the serious and problem cases. (Morris, 1967). Some states, such as Pennsylvania, separate those delinquents under I.Q. of seventy and treat them separately in institutions for the defective delinquent.

The basic classification used at the Kennedy Youth Center in Morgantown, West Virginia, is based on Quay's classification (1965), which is as follows:

1. Unsocialized psychopathic delinquent
2. Neurotic-disturbed delinquent
3. Inadequate-immature delinquent
4. Socialized-subcultural delinquent
5. Subcultural-immature delinquent

With the exception of some special projects funded by governmental and private agencies, the Kennedy Youth Center program comes closest to implementing research and clinical knowledge into the action program in the correctional setting.

PREDICTION

Prediction of successful adjustment after involvement in the criminal justice system is a logical result of typology and programming classification. Prediction of success on parole was probably the first phase to receive intensive study, with Sam Warner doing the first study in Massachusetts in 1923. Warner pointed out the advisability of studying the reactions of the inmates in various phases of prison life. Ernest Burgess (Bruce et al., 1928) and his colleagues were the first to use objective methods of parole prediction on the basis of seventy-one factors that could be obtained from the prison records. Clark Tibbitts (1932) however, indicated that Burgess and his colleagues did not show a high coefficient of contingency, which indicated inadequate use of multiple correlation or tests of internal consistency.

Hewitt and Jenkins (1946) studied 500 juveniles from the Michigan Child Guidance Institute and found three well-defined types of maladjusted children: (1) those displaying unsocialized aggressive behavior, which included about 10.4 percent of their cases; (2) those showing socialized delinquency behavior, comprising 14.0 percent of their cases; and (3) those showing overinhibited behavior, including 14.6 percent of the maladjusted children. The aggressive child was found to be one who is unwanted and experiences no affection. The socialized delinquent is accepted in his early years, at least by his mother, and when his parents become indifferent, he becomes a loyal gang member. The overinhibited child comes from a repressive family, often shows physical deficiencies, and feels neglected and a little "different." These categories have been seen as helpful in analyzing personal versus property crimes, violent versus nonviolent crimes, and accomplice versus nonaccomplice dichotomies, as well as the areas of nonconforming social behavior.

Healy and Bronner (1936, pp. 171–72), a husband-and-wife psychiatric team, have indicated that successful adjustment by juvenile offenders depends less upon the rehabilitative program than on the type of case it is from the etiological and developmental standpoint. Experience in the criminal justice system assists in determining if an individual can be rehabilitated. Those who have been in the system longer are more difficult to improve, so the arrangement of custodial programs can be made accordingly (Reckless, 1942). Family background of delinquents studied by the Gluecks (1934, p. 80) indicated a heavy incidence of foreign-born parentage. Unfavorable parent-child relationships were conducive to failure; more than 90 percent of the individuals studied by the Gluecks were from homes that were broken or poorly supervised. The moral standards and conduct of the families as a whole were considered to be poor. In 318 cases followed for fifteen years, the Gluecks found the use of leisure time was very important in successful postincarceration adjustments, with a high coefficient of mean square continuity (Glueck, 1937, p. 85).

An interesting experiment on prediction of criminality was done by Ferris Laune (1936), who proceeded on the hypothesis that inmates could predict the success on parole of fellow inmates better than the parole board could. After finding a group of inmates who predicted success on parole directly, he identified the hunches used by the inmates with a view toward objectifying them and using them in a scale. It is interesting to note that inmate X, a valuable assistant in this study, was Nathan Leopold. The hunches were as follows:

1. Excessive interest in clothes—minus
2. Stupidity—plus or minus (qualified according to setting)
3. Timidity—plus or minus

4. Industry—plus
5. Sex craving—minus
6. White lights (cabarets, dance halls, etc.)—minus
7. Family broken—minus
8. Lack of love for relatives—minus
9. Family ties—plus
10. Learned lesson—plus or minus
11. Previous hoodlum activities—minus
12. Recidivism—minus
13. Rural type—plus
14. Previous work record—plus
15. Happily married—plus
16. Character—plus or minus
17. Pleasing personality—plus
18. Sharp practices—minus
19. Emotional instability—minus
20. Shrewdness—plus
21. Good job in prison—minus
22. Gangster—minus
23. Critical qualities (discrimination in choice of friends)—plus
24. Selfishness—plus (protects against "going along" for people)
25. Trade—plus
26. Conceit—minus
27. Self-respect—plus
28. Phlegmaticness—plus
29. Argumentativeness—minus
30. Outside environment—plus or minus
31. Minor racketeering—minus
32. Love of comfort—minus
33. Age—plus or minus (older persons more helpful)
34. Working ability—plus or minus
35. Break in criminal record—plus
36. Religiosity—plus
37. Wanderlust—minus
38. Attitude toward future—plus or minus
39. Length of time to be served—plus or minus (little time left to take chances)
40. Tendency to be an agitator—minus
41. Criminal activity in the family—minus
42. Physical defect—minus

Probably the outstanding parole prediction study was that done by Ohlin in Illinois (1951, p. 52). He identified factors in the record of individuals and correlated them with successful completion of parole and violation of parole. His predictive factors included the classifications of (1) type of offense, (2) type of sentence, (3) type of offender, (4) home status, (5) family interest in the offender, (6) social type, (7) work record, (8) type of community (urban or rural), (9) parole job, (10) number of associates, (11) personality, and (12) psychiatric prognosis. Ohlin's breakdown of these factors according to their favorable to unfavorable ratings is shown in Table 14-8.

A scale to measure general adjustment in prison was developed

TABLE 14-8.
Rating of Prediction Items,
Joliet-Stateville and Menard Divisions,
Illinois State Penitentiary System

PREDICTION FACTORS AND ITEMS	RATING OF ITEMS		
	Favorable	Neutral	Unfavorable
Type of offense			
Homicide and assault	1		
Robbery		0	
Burglary			x
Larceny and stolen property		0	
Forgery and fraud		0	
Sex offenses	1		
Miscellaneous		0	
Sentence			
All definite sentences	1		
All other sentences		0	
Type of offender			
First	1		
Technical first		0	
Occasional		0	
Juvenile recidivist		0	
Recidivist			x
Habitual			x
Home status			
Superior	1		
Average		0	
Inferior		0	
Broken		0	
Institution		0	
Left home		0	
Family interest			
Very active	1		
Active		0	

TABLE 14-8. *(cont.)*

PREDICTION FACTORS AND ITEMS	RATING OF ITEMS		
	Favorable	Neutral	Unfavorable
Sustained		0	
Passive		0	
None			x
Social type			
Erring citizen	1		
Marginally delinquent	1		
"Farmer"	1		
Socially inadequate	1		
Ne'er-do-well		0	
Floater			x
Socially maladjusted			x
Drunkard			x
Drug addict			x
Sex deviant		0	
Work record			
Regular	1		
Irregular		0	
Casual		0	
Student		0	
None		0	
Community			
Urban		0	
Rural		0	
Transient			x
Parole job			
Adequate		0	
Inadequate			x
None		0	
Number of associates			
None		0	
One or two		0	
Three or over	1		
Personality			
Normal (no gross defects)	1		
Inadequate		0	
Unstable		0	
Egocentric		0	
Gross personality defects		0	
No record		0	
Psychiatric prognosis			
Favorable	1		
Problematic		0	
Doubtful		0	
Guarded		0	
Unfavorable		0	
No record		0	

by this writer in 1943, and the scale was found to be a successful predictor of parole success as well (Fox, 1943, chap. 6; 1954, p. 287). Twenty factors were used; they were subjected to the methods of the criterion of internal consistency, using the critical ratio to arrive at diagnostic weights. Eleven factors proved to be diagnostic. The resulting scale is given in Table 14-9.

Sheldon and Eleanor Glueck published a five-factor delinquency prediction table (Table 14-10), which received considerable attention. Sociologists and researchers attacked the Gluecks' prediction scale as being deficient in adequate research methodology. Considerable conflict occurred between the New York City Youth Board, which found it helpful, and the researchers, who found it inadequate. It is apparent that the difficulty lay in the differences in viewpoint between the empirical research model and the clinical approach. The scale seemed to work for the Youth Board but lacked the research sophistication needed to be accepted by people looking for "hard" facts.

The Kvaraceus Delinquency Scale, called the KD Delinquency Proneness Scale and Check List, consists of seventy-five multiple-choice items for children to check and seventy items to be checked by someone other than the child, usually the teacher. The items cover personal, environmental (home and family), and school factors. Examples of the multiple choice items in the scale are:

Parents usually understand their children:

1. Very well
2. Quite well
3. Not very well
4. Not at all

Failure in school is usually due to:

1. Bad company
2. Lack of abilities
3. Lack of hard work
4. Unfriendly teachers

All items differentiate between known delinquents and nondelinquents, and each is given a score. The total of the scores provides a total score for each child. Children with extremely high scores are considered to be delinquent or predelinquent, while children with extremely low scores might be selected with certainty as to their future nonconforming behavior. Children with middle scores might not be predictable. Kvaraceus (1956) himself, questioned whether complete accuracy can be obtained by any prediction test but believed that children who need help can be identified.

TABLE 14-9.
Scale to Measure General Adjustment in Prison

ITEMS	DIAGNOSTIC WEIGHTS
Work reports:	
Good	24.3
Average	16.2
Poor	8.1
Block officer's reports:	
Good adjustment	13.5
Average adjustment	9.0
Poor adjustment	4.5
Misconduct:	
No misconduct reports	13.5
Minor reports	9.0
Major reports	4.5
Visits from outside:	
10 or more per year	13.2
1 to 9 visits per year	8.8
No visits	4.4
School reports (prorated if no school):	
Good	12.9
Average	8.6
Poor	4.3
Type of misconduct:	
No misconduct reports	11.4
Rebellion against authority	7.6
Violent against persons	3.8
Correspondence:	
70 or more letters in or out per year	10.8
40 to 69 letters in or out per year	7.2
Less than 39 letters per year	3.6
Chaplain's appraisal:	
Good religious status	9.9
Fair religious status	6.6
Poor religious status	3.3
Financial budgeting:	
Save $25.00 or more per year	8.7
Save $10.00 to $24.00	5.8
Save less than $10.00	2.9
Work stability:	
6 months or more on one job last year	8.4
6 months or more on two jobs last year	5.6
6 months or more on more than two jobs or less than 6 months last year	2.8
School stability (prorated if no school:)	
6 months or more last year	7.2
Less than 6 months last year or part-time student	4.8
No school contact	2.4

TABLE 14-10.
Social Prediction Table

Discipline of Boy by Father	
Overstrict or erratic	72.5
Lax	59.8
Firm but kindly	9.3
Supervision of Boy by Mother	
Unsuitable	83.2
Fair	57.5
Suitable	9.9
Affection of Father for Boy	
Indifferent or hostile	86.2
Warm (including overprotective)	33.8
Affection of Mother for Boy	
Indifferent or hostile	86.2
Warm (including overprotective)	43.1
Cohesiveness of Family	
Unintegrated	96.9
Some elements of cohesion	96.9
Cohesive	20.6

Sheldon Glueck, ed., *The Problem of Delinquency.* Boston:
Houghton Mifflin, 1959, p. 1026.

Gordon Russon, a Canadian psychiatrist, proposed a three-phase classification based on emotional maturation as previously discussed by Sullivan, Grant, and Grant (1957). His classification is shown in Table 14-11.

TABLE 14-11.
A Suggested Design for Clinical Classification of Offenders

ATTITUDE	INTERPERSONAL MATURITY (SULLIVAN, GRANT, AND GRANT)		ADEQUACY OF PATTERN OF INTERACTION (SOCIALIZATION SCALE)	
Antisocial Asocial	Stage	I— Maladjusted to the point of total inadequacy and infantile pattern of living.	1.	Submissive-passive. Acceptance of domination by others. Easily led.
Pro-social (nondelinquent)	Stage	II— Expect the non-self world to adapt to their needs. Physical-material value system. World owes them a living.	2.	Power oriented— decompensating. Dominates by making others feel responsible for them. "Look, you son-of-a-bitch what you made me do!"
	Stage	III— Rely on intellect and wit, sizing people up, knowing the rules, being smart, working the angles. Relatively insensitive emotionally.	3.	Power oriented— overcompensating. Domineering attitude. Overrides and pushes others.

TABLE 14-11. (cont.)

ATTITUDE	INTERPERSONAL MATURITY (SULLIVAN, GRANT, AND GRANT)	ADEQUACY OF PATTERN OF INTERACTION (SOCIALIZATION SCALE)
	Stage IV—Capacity for emotion and attendant conflicts, but fearful of emotion. Overdependent. Emotional relationships of short duration.	4. Cooperative. Realistic expectations from one's own and partner's abilities and contributions.
	Stage V—Relatively self-sufficient. Aware of differences in interpersonal relationships. Good candidates for casework and psychotherapy. [Two more stages, but they are not delinquent]	

Gordon W. Russon, "A Design for Clinical Classification of Offenders," *The Canadian Journal of Criminology and Corrections* (July 1962), 179–88.

CONCLUSIONS

The typologies that describe the diagnostic problems of people, the classifications that reflect the programs into which they might fit, and the predictions of success or failure of the criminal justice system to bring them together constitute the operational definitions in the criminal justice system. It is apparent that the best predictors of successful social adjustment in or out of prison are work habits, ability to manage personal affairs as indicated by such things as personal budgeting record and credit ratings, and ability to avoid attracting police or prison guard attention to deviant behavior. These seem to be the primary determinants of being involved in or avoiding involvement in the criminal justice system. Not only are they concerned with the criminal justice system, but these factors also determine success or failure in the total structure of society.

Questions

1. What functions do typologies serve in the field of criminal justice?

2. What patterns appear among latecomers in delinquency and among latecomers in crime?

3. What is the value of legal classification of crimes?

4. Differentiate between crimes that are *mala en se* and those classified as *mala prohibita*.

5. How are prisoners classified according to escape risk and dangerousness so they can be assigned to different types of security?

6. What is the RAPS system of classification?

7. What is the basic classification presented by Quay and used at the Robert Kennedy Youth Center in Morgantown, West Virginia?

8. Evaluate some of the delinquency prediction scales.

9. Evaluate some of the parole prediction scales.

10. What are some of the factors that appear most frequently in predictive instruments as being most diagnostic?

fifteen

LEGAL
AND
POLITICAL
APPROACHES

Law defines the relationship between the individual and society. It is a reflection of the values of a culture and the problem areas in society. The legal system in any society is a response to the value system of the people comprising it. Formal law is a clearly discernible system of rights and wrongs, duties, and obligations with intent of universal application and a prescribed method of enforcement and procedures for adjudication of disputes. On the other hand, a flexibility of its application and enforcement incorporates a concept of justice to the extent that each individual involved in it tends to give to the system what he or she thinks is wanted, so that there is "no injustice done." (See Green, 1964, p. 66). Functional law, then, combines the legal system as a reflection of the values of the culture with the flexibility of the individuals involved in the judgments, the implementation, and the receiving of justice. Law and political considerations determine the result. The political process of the state incorporates the concept of justice, seeking law and order along with the safety and protection of the individual. One legal historian remarked that the resulting "metaphysics of the state of the theology of jurisprudence" and sovereignty of the state might reside in the king's mistress or the politicians who kiss babies (Seagle, 1946, p. 21). The legal and political impact on the individual in terms of social control becomes, then, not as universal nor as fixed and prescribed in procedure as some may desire.

Law is basic to criminal justice. Without law, there would be neither criminal justice system nor criminal justice procedures. The easiest way to eliminate it would be to eliminate the criminal law, but then society would be left in anarchy. Conversely, it might be said that crime is needed to preserve order, since the criminal law is needed! In any case, crime identifies and holds the limits of individual and group behavior to promote the social organization necessary for a durable society. The social formation is held in shape by the experience of individuals in interpersonal relations with others, permitting them to anticipate the general behavior of others. Such anticipation leads to common attitudes and prejudices, trust, faith, belief, customs, and the ability to predict what the other person will do. Crime is a symptom of personal and social breakdown or pathology in this pattern in which the individual deviation damages the group. The negative prohibitions in law that determine crime are never enacted until there is need for these prohibitions to preserve order or to make orderly change in society.

Law as a profession and as a social institution has developed through three broad stages from fragmentized beginnings to modern maturity (Selznick, 1959). The first stage was the exploration of philosophy and the working out of the best "ground rules" needed for an organized society to endure. The ancient codes and law givers and the medieval philosophers and theologians provided this service. The second stage was the work of the craftsmen in applying accumulated knowledge to particular and practical social problems. This era, generally considered to be between 1650 and 1820, resulted in the Napoleonic Codes, the English criminal law and procedure, and other systems of law. It was at this point that law replaced theology as the primary agent of social control. The third stage, or modern law, incorporates the development of intellectual autonomy and maturity of law, in which legal scholars, frequently in high courts and in law schools, explore the legality of authority, the role of the social sciences in creating a society based on justice, and the function of law and legal systems in establishing and sustaining the framework for such a society. The definitions of crime and the identification of areas of social stress follow the development of law through these stages. Crime is the final definition assigned, so that society is given the authority to intervene in the life of a citizen, and force can be applied to the individual to effect conformity for the safety and welfare of society.

THE EMERGENCE OF CRIMINAL LAW

The origins of law preceded writing in tribal customs and taboos of primitive man. When writing began around 4000 to 3500 B.C. in Sumer, which was subsequently Babylon in the area known today as Iraq, the earliest beginnings of written legal instruments were pleadings and records in the form of contracts and deeds, probably as early as 3500 B.C., and early fragments of enacted laws appeared soon afterward, probably around 3100 B.C. Although there is a tendency to call these early enactments "codes," it becomes a matter of definition. There is general agreement that the beginnings of more systematic written law have been found between 2500 and 2300 B.C. Seagle (1946, p. 104) indicates that the first real ancient system of law was the Code of Hammurabi, inscribed about 1750 B.C. on a pillar of black diorite almost eight feet high, though the Sumerian Code was earlier. The Sumerian Code could be placed between 2500 and 2300 B.C., when it was relatively systematized, but it dates back as much as another thousand years in terms of fragmented written law.

The old Assyrian laws were developed between 2169 and 1870 B.C., and the middle Assyrian compilations were between 1450 and 1250 B.C. The Law of Moses developed between 1500 and 900 B.C. Hittite law promulgated by the kings of Hatti at Shattushash were also in this period. The laws of Draca and Solon in Greece were adopted by the Romans around 450 B.C. and have been known as the Twelve Tables. The Manu Smriti or Hindu code of Manu is of uncertain date but has been ascribed to the period between the second century B.C. and the second century A.D. The Chinese, meanwhile, developed stable government with the Hsia family about 2205 to 1766 B.C., the period that saw the beginning of agriculture. Confucious (551–479 B.C.), wrote his *Great Learning,* and his grandson, Tzu Ssu (483–402 B.C.), wrote the *Doctrine of the Mean;* these combined to provide social and ethical guidelines and became state doctrine in 136 B.C. Ancient law inherited the concept of primitive law, but fairly well advanced organs of justice were nevertheless developed. The famous passage in Homer's *Illiad* that describes the trial scene depicted on the shield of Achilles, probably about 2000 B.C., included two talents of gold, which suggests that compensation may have become a desirable substitute for the blood-feud. The blood-feud, however, continued throughout the ancient world and is well documented in the Old Testament. The courts have proved more important than the law itself, inasmuch as the rules for settling controversies have constantly changed, but the fundamental method of settling them in a court or tribunal has remained stable for centuries. The court has been considered the first, and probably the last, great legal invention (ibid, p. 69).

It was ancient Rome, however, that developed the legal profession. The lawyers, as officers of the court, studied all the ancient law and assisted citizens in ameliorating their disputes. After the fall of the Roman Empire about 477 A.D., the invading Germanic tribes adopted some Roman law in the *lex Salica* of the Salic Franks about 450 A.D. and the *lex Visigothorum* of the Visigoths about 466 to 483 A.D. In 330 A.D.

the capital of the Roman Empire had been moved from Rome to Byzantium, subsequently called Constantinople after Emperor Constantine I, who reigned from 324 to 337 and who recognized Christianity. The empire was never again ruled by a single emperor.

It was Emperor Justinian I, who reigned from 527 to 565 A.D., who appointed a commission of ten men to reduce the old law of the ancient world and the new law of Rome to the *Codex Constitutionum*, which was finished in 529 A.D. A new commission to refine it further, consisting of sixteen lawyers, was appointed in 530 A.D. The result was 9,123 extracts from thirty-nine writers summarized in the *Digest*. The eventual work was the *Corpus Juris Civilis*, which consisted of four books: *Codex Constitutionum, Digest Institutes*, and the *Novels*, most of which were issued by 545 A.D. and all within the lifetime of Emperor Justinian. It is now more widely known as the Code of Justinian and is one of the most influential legal documents in history. After the fall of the Roman Empire and the decline of secular law and control plunged Europe into the chaos that was the Middle Ages, and throughout the medieval period, these four books of the Code of Justinian were the only legal materials available. It is interesting to note that, although very few copies were available after the eleventh century A.D., the Code of Justinian influenced the legal thinking of Europe for a thousand years almost without interruption and still forms the primary base of English and Continental common law.

The Holy Roman Empire was established in 800 and brought the first semblance of order since the fall of Rome in 476. The Code of Justinian was adopted almost intact. The theologians were meanwhile trying to resolve what they saw as the conflict between the presence of evil in the world and the omnipotence of a good God and were developing theological systems that had social implications as well. Thomas Aquinas published his *Decretum Gratianum*, identifying the law of nature of the ancients with the law of God to work out an interrelationship between natural law and divine law as it affected man. It was an uncompromising appeal to reason and "divine wisdom."

After the breakup of the Holy Roman Empire, the idea of a united Christendom under the spiritual guidance of the Church accompanied the emergence of national states. It was at this point that Machiavelli's *The Prince*, published in 1513, indicated that moral and ethical principles were subordinate to political expediency. Hugo Grotius (1583–1645), the Dutch jurist, expounded the social contract theory of the origin of the state, and this idea of contract or government by the consent of the governed was supported by Thomas Hobbes of England (1588–1679), John Locke of England (1632–1704), Charles deMontesquieu of France (1689–1755), and Jean Jacques Rousseau of France (1712–1778).

In the fourteenth and fifteenth centuries, parliamentary government began in England. Prior to that time, sanctions, limitations, or laws were edicts by the monarchy. Early parliamentary legislation, devised to secure the social order, forbade making war against the king, forbade serfs from leaving the land in search of work, and forbade anyone not owning property from keeping dogs. During the sixteenth and seventeenth centuries, legislation was aimed at consolidation of the Church and state. Treason and heresy became crimes, as did swearing, adultery, and witchcraft. During the eighteenth and nineteenth centuries, piracy, forgery, and banking offenses were made crimes. In the twentieth century, white-collar and commercial crimes resulted from a changing social order. Simultaneously, the Industrial Revolution and the emergence of capitalism made lawyers private practitioners in the legal profession.

The public criminal law evolved from these earlier beginnings to its present form. Early criminal jurisdiction in Greece and Rome by popular assemblies was exceptional. In Rome, the magistrate hearing criminal cases was controlled so that justice did not become arbitrary. Procedures were only *accusatory*. In the fifteenth and sixteenth centuries, when criminal law became *inquisitory*, with a system that called for proof and provided definite procedure, criminal trials in England and elsewhere in Europe were still judicial duels without statutory basis.

It was Beccaria in 1764, in his famous *Essay on Crimes and Punishments*, who called attention to the need for written statutory law. On the basis that man sought pleasure and avoided pain and therefore was hedonistic, Beccaria insisted that a person could read the law and be apprised of punishments, then make a free choice as to whether or not he wanted to commit a crime. Further, the written criminal law would tend to make punishments uniform and reduce them to proper proportions so that the punishment would fit the crime, rather than continue the excesses that individual courts had caused in the preceding century or two without the limitation of criminal statutes.

English law was then codified by William Blackstone, Samuel Romilly, and Jeremy Bentham. Simultaneously, the French *Code Penal* and the Napoleonic Codes were established in France. The civil code in France was proclaimed March 21, 1804, under the title, *Code Civil de Francais*. The *Code Napoleon* was established in 1807. Throughout Western civilization, similar developments occurred. Due process in English law was well established by the War of 1812. In fact, English and American criminal law and procedure were codified and implemented during the period between the American Revolution and the War of 1812.

Justice Oliver Wendell Holmes (1920, p. 139) questioned whether the criminal law has done more harm than good. Roscoe Pound (1930) indicated that modern criminology is supposed to be urban, national, and professional, while until the Industrial Revolution, crimes were rural, local, and amateur, suggesting that the development of the criminal law was anachronistic or is chronologically out of place and needs updating and modernizing.

In the late eighteenth century, after the criminal law had emerged, there was considerable focus on its possibilities. Immanuel Kant thought that man partook of two worlds, the sensible and the intelligible, or the objective and the subjective. Freedom and law meant to Kant freedom from arbitrary subjection to another individual. Hegel thought that history was the process of action and reaction between opposites, translating them into thesis and antithesis, resulting in their synthesis. For example, abstract right is the thesis, morality is the antithesis, and the conflict produces the synthesis of social ethics. It was in these philosophical strains that the criminal law was developed and nurtured.

WHAT IS A CRIME?

Crime is a legally recognized symptom of social and personal pathology in which the individual damages the group (Fox, 1963). The manner in which the group is damaged is dependent upon the conditions of both acceptable and intolerable behavior as viewed by the group. Social organization is necessary for a durable society, the roles and statuses of individuals within the group representing a functional division of labor and leadership that contributes to the total social formation. This social formation is held in shape by the experience of individuals in association with other participants in a structured manner that leads them to anticipate the behavior of others in certain situations. Such anticipations lead to such intangible but real phases of interpersonal interaction as trust, faith, belief, common attitudes and prejudices, more specifically manifested in such tangible factors as contracts and credit ratings. Any deviation that damages the group can be defined as crime.

The practical approach to problems regarding a definition of crime involves the questions: (1) What behavior ought to be made criminal? (2) What should be determinative of variations in treatment? (3) What methods of treatment should be prescribed? (Wechsler, 1952) The resolution of these problems would reflect only the attitudes and procedures of a culture at a specific place and time. It is impossible, or at least unfortunate, to "freeze" a definition, the determinative factors, and the method of treatment because societies change. The present state of the social sciences precludes the complete formulation of criminal law. There must be room for sufficient flexibility to incorporate advances and changes in a body of knowledge of the social sciences and to reflect the changing attitudes and values of the society served by that criminal law. Definitions of crime should cover conduct that is harmful to society and conduct that indicates that the individual is a danger to society in sufficient proportion to warrant the intervention of social authority for the protection of society. The definitions of conventional crime and political offenses in all societies reflect this effort.

Some of the factors in the definition of a crime are whether there is a victim, whether criminal intent is present, and who sees it. This relationship between victim, intent, and audience is outlined by Glaser in Table 15-1.

Contemporary problems in crime definitions seem to represent gaps and struggles between traditional and progressive concepts. The law looks backward for precedent; the social and behavioral sciences look forward for prediction. Although these approaches are not incompatible, their blending into a progressive society with stabilizing controls necessitates a broader viewpoint than is available from a single discipline or profession. Neither the social sciences nor the law have yet been able to provide it adequately. The law provides stability, while advancing scientific knowledge provides progress. Their integration will provide a dynamic but stable society.

Social scientists are not concerned with the rational product of the work of centuries in developing a body of law. They are not especially concerned with "abstract justice." Rather, they are more concerned with the development of law in defining those attitudes and practices of the society in which the law appears and which it supports. There is an interrelationship between the norms of social behavior and the legal norms. The lawyer is inclined to agree with Hobbes that individuals seek to conform to the law, while the social scientist is inclined to regard law as the reflection of the customs and normal behavior of the people. Perhaps it is more accurate to state the result as an interaction between normal behavior and the legal norms.

The definitions of crime vary with the cultures in which it is used. Killing another person in most states is illegal, except in war, execu-

TABLE 15-1.
Victims, Intent, and Dependence on an Audience in the Legal Distinctions of the Major Categories of Crime

Defining Features	IS CRIMINAL REGARDLESS OF AUDIENCE		Is Criminal Only if It Offends an Audience
	Result of Criminal Intent	Not Result of Criminal Intent	
Has Definite Victims	Predation	Criminal Negligence	Illegal Performance
Does Not Have Definite Victims	Illegal Selling and Illegal Consumption	Not Crime	

Daniel Glaser, *Adult Crime and Social Policy* (Englewood Cliffs, N.J.: Prentice-Hall, 1972), p. 5.

tion after judicial pronouncement of the death sentence, or when juries consider the killing to be justifiable or excusable. Among some Indians of Labrador, during their primitive days, killing elderly parents was expected when they became an economic liability on the tribe. Similarly, the practice of the Eskimo before white man's welfare programs came was for the elderly and nonproductive mother to kiss her family goodbye and go sit on the ice and wait to die. There is no crime at all among the Ifugao in northern Luzon. Patterns of crime vary widely among the various tribes in equatorial Africa. Homosexuality used to be punished in this country but not in southern Europe and Scandinavia. It was accepted as part of the culture among the ancient peoples of Greece, Rome, and the Near East.

These variations reflect the attitudes of the societies in which the criminal definitions are made. The cultural values of a given society reflect the cultural aspirations of that society. The societies differ as to respective values. Values held in high regard by many people in India and China may be in sharp contrast to those held by the majority in the United States. The sanctity of contract, for example, is held in high regard by Americans primarily because of the emphasis placed upon it by the Supreme Court under Chief Justice John Marshall, while contracts and treaties among many peoples are considered to be guidelines for operating procedure that can be legitimately altered or ignored as the situation under which the agreement was made also changes.

In summary, crime is a legal definition of intolerable behavior on the part of individuals or groups that varies too widely from expected behavior to be conducive to the smooth functioning of society or that violates the traditional beliefs and sentiments of the group. Morality and the criminal law are not congruous, although morality is frequently associated with the concept of crime. Crime is not exclusively the transgressions against a particular moral code as the moralist would have it; nor is it entirely the infringements against carefully stipulated and defined criminal statutes, as the lawyer might have it. The definition of crime solely in terms of the criminal law is too constrictive to be useful to the social scientist, as demonstrated by interest in research on hidden delinquency. The social scientists believe that intolerable behavior evolved long before its legal recognition was stipulated in the statutes and that it is the attitude of society which came first, rather than the statutes, and which controls the definition of crime. Although lawyers see their work as a profession, social scientists see the law as a social institution that traditionally lags behind contemporary attitudes and values.

Crime is a legal artifact (Brodsky, 1972, p. 1). It is a category that permits the intervention of society's agents of social control into the private life of a citizen. Convicted persons cannot be behaviorally grouped as "criminals," nor can "criminal" labels be automatically assumed to be behavioral entities (ibid., p. 2). This is why the social and behavioral scientists view classification of people by their offenses as nonsensical to the point of being foolish and nonproductive. Murder, burglary, larceny, auto theft, drug use, prostitution, and all the other legally categorized behaviors labeled as "crime" can be caused by a variety of factors rather than by a simple suggestion of "the kind of person" an individual is. The lawyer and the courts, however, view the alleged offender as either convicted or not convicted—either legally guilty or innocent. Though this appears to the social and behavioral scientist to be an oversimplification, it is useful for purposes of legal disposition.

It is obvious that crime is the final definition assigned to any objectionable behavior so that force can be applied to the individual to effect conformity with and perpetuation of the existing social formation. Crime is the ultimate definition in social control so far as the individual is concerned.

PUBLIC POLICY AND CRIME

The way a crime is handled in society varies from jurisdiction to jurisdiction and from time to time, even though the same laws are in effect. Basic to due process or procedure as delineated by the Constitution and court decisions relating to it, all criminal procedure codifications include the preliminary examination and a formal indictment or information procedure, but either or both are sometimes informally waived without consent. In some jurisdictions, a defendant would have to go to court to get them, which is rarely done. Local practice varies with local customs and values.

One of the most dramatic differentials in the United States between local practice and the overall law is found among the primitive peoples of Alaska, discussed in Chapter 11 as part of the anthropological and cultural approaches to crime. For example, a member of the village council of Fort Yukon—the largest city north of Fairbanks and the largest community on the Yukon, with 600 people, mostly Athabascan Indians—told this writer that the council members cannot "buck" the white man, so they do the best they can to reduce the irritations and conflicts.[1] They do not like the white man's criminal justice system, and they dislike his wildlife management system even more because it cuts into their food supply. In the area of criminal justice, they resolve their conflicts and troubles among themselves. If an individual is beyond their

---

[1] Personal interview between the writer and Clarence Alexander, an Athabascan Indian and a member of the Fort Yukon village council in Alaska, March 20, 1974.

local control, however, they summon an Alaska State Trooper to come in with his plane and "blue ticket" him out of the community; disposition is then made in Fairbanks in white man's courts and correctional system. An interesting example of village rules in this area were the ones I found in force when I visited Venetie, about forty-five miles northwest of Fort Yukon on the Chandalar River, in December 1973.

1. No alcoholic beverages, liquor, homebrew, or wine allowed in village of Venetie.
2. If persons drink they will be fined $50. If they have no money they will cut wood for community or work for it fixing community hall.
3. Second time is state law.
4. Third time is blue ticket from village of Venetie for 2 years.
5. We don't like to bother state law. We will try to fix our trouble ourselves. But if person get smart we will have to get state law.
6. Under age drinking is against the law. If it happens we will use state law.
7. Discharging firearms—No person shall shoot any gun within or near the village.
8. Damaging property—No person shall damage or destroy the property of others. This includes personal property and buildings.
9. No five card poker games allowed. No blackjack and no dice allowed.
10. If caught playing above games persons will be fined $4 apiece for each player every time caught.
11. Pan game [a type of card game] is allowed. They will play only at house appointed by the council. Hours—5:00 P.M. to midnight. Closed Sunday. The rakeoff will go to dog races. After the dog races it will go to community fund.
12. If stranger comes to Venetie he will vote after 6 months in Village of Venetie.

The purpose of these rules, of course, is to keep the local system of social order as intact as possible, while using state law when it is convenient.

Public policy is decided primarily by majority vote of legislative and congressional committees based on information provided by testimony of expert witnesses and expressed opinions of their constituents. Agencies of social control in a democratic society must use wide discretion to accommodate public opinion. They are simultaneously the authoritarian arm of the power structure and servants of the people (Berkley, 1969, p. 232). In a democratic society, they must be responsive to the public they serve. This includes the citizen-offenders they serve. Otherwise, they will have to respond to civil suits, riots, and lesser expressions of public opinion. The Supreme Court is in a similar position. The function of the Supreme Court can be described as interpreting the values of a nation at any given time, which is why opposite decisions can be arrived at several years apart on the same issue.

The rulings of the United States Supreme Court under Chief Justice Warren Burger have been considerably more pleasing to police than were the rulings under Chief Justice Earl Warren (Green, 1974). The 1961 Mapp ruling that prevented prosecutors from using illegally seized evidence and the 1966 Miranda ruling that eliminated confessions made in the absence of warnings of the individual's right to counsel and to remain silent were especially upsetting to police. On the other hand, civil libertarians were pleased with the Warren court and concerned about the Burger court.

The decisions in the criminal justice process are made by the police as to whether to arrest, the prosecutor as to whether to prosecute even after an indictment by a grand jury has been filed, the judge and jury as to whether to convict, the judge as to sentencing within the limits of the law, and the correctional practitioners and administrators as to institutional or community types of treatment or processing and the person's eventual release from the system. All these decisions are made by agencies of the power structure "in the interests of society." The concept of justice is most difficult to define and impossible to implement to the satisfaction of all.

The use of special jury services has grown in recent years. Such services specialize in measurement of pretrial publicity, venue demography, and dossiers of qualified prospective jurors in the area of jurisdiction. For example, it has been stated that John Mitchell and Maurice Stans may have been assisted in obtaining an acquittal in the Vesco case in New York in April 1974 through the help of Marty Herbst, president of Conceptual Dynamics, Inc., of New York, who worked on the construction of the jury (Kevin P. Phillips, syndicated columnist, May 12, 1974). A telephone survey of the area residents' reaction to the defendants by age, religion, ethnic background, income, education, and political outlook was completed. When jury selection took place, the defense looked for jurors who habitually read the *Daily News* rather than the *New York Times*, who were concerned more with inflation than with the Watergate scandal, and who were politically to the right. The jury selection also eliminated Jews and preferred high school graduates over college graduates. One is reminded of Archie Bunker, the popular television character. The jury selection on the part of the defense was considered "brilliant, the government's selection not" (Walter Scott, *Parade*, June 16, 1974, p. 2). How much this jury selection contributed to the verdict cannot be legally assessed, but jury services such as this are on the increase in the larger cities. In any case, the publicity raised by the Mitchell-Stans jury selection brought to public attention a practice that had been going on for a long time. Social scientists have been in the jury selection services and are increasing because of the demand. This has produced debate about producing biased juries, how much their impact is, and other ethical questions (Kann, 1974; for an example of instruction for jury selection by the prosecution, see Sparling, 1974).

The problem of fitting social reality into the matrix of the law has plagued the criminal justice system since its inception. Roche (1958, pp. 3–4) has said that judges and lawyers must view the formalism of the law that derives from the black thread of magic and the red thread of religion; the result of this viewpoint is that the legal arbiters of culture have a sense of certainty not shared by the social scientist.

Many citizens are conservative and "hard-nosed" with "criminals," calling for stiffer penalties. The late J. Edgar Hoover probably exemplified this view better than most. A mosaic of his quotations were printed in one journal as follows:

> Criminals are not just criminals. They are: "Scum from the boiling-pot of the underworld," "public rats," "lowest dregs of society," "scuttling rats in the ship of politics," "vermin in human form," "the slimy crew who feed upon crime," "desperadoes," "vermin spewed out of prison cells to continue their slaughter," "the octopus of the underworld." These "post-graduates of outlawry" and "professors of crime" thrive "in the great fog of crime," and "the swamp and morasses of suffering" amidst the "appalling scourge of perjury" and the "oleaginous connivings of venal politicians," aided and abetted by "sentimental yammerheads" and "moronic adults" of "asinine behavior," "maudlin sentiment," and "inherent criminal worship." Away with these "moo-cow sentimentalities" with their "mealy mouthings" and their "whining pleas for sympathy"; these "hoity-toity professors." [*Journal of Criminal Law and Criminology* 28, Jan.–Feb. 1938]

Hoover continued to denounce "the cream-puff school of criminology" that wants to turn offenders loose on society. In a much more professional vein, then-FBI Director Clarence M. Kelley pointed out that in the ten years ending with 1973, more than 860 local, county, and state law enforcement officers had been killed as a result of felonious criminal acts.

The John Birch Society was in agreement with J. Edgar Hoover. In July 1974, its bulletin included the following:

> Members of the John Birch Society have been pointing out for years that the federal government has been the policeman's worst enemy because of the government's liberal and radical programs which encourage the growth of crime and the brazenness of criminals. Liberalized parole and probation procedures have made convicted criminals almost immediately eligible for release. And, of course, the Supreme Court decision that

abrogated the death penalty, and the Court's other rulings which freed many dangerous prisoners on absurd technicalities, demonstrate even more the correctness of our claim that the Nixon administration, as well as many previous administrations, is responsible for the crime wave and the terror that is crashing down on the American people today. [p. 20]

This general opinion also exists among some of those whom Hoover called "hoity-toity professors." In a major university in 1974, when plans were being made to introduce a curriculum in criminology or criminal justice one dean objected strenuously to calling it "Criminal Justice" because he did not believe in "justice" for "criminals"!

On the other hand, experienced and veteran correctional administrators join the majority of social and behavioral scientists in the position that long and stiff sentences are not only futile but are damaging and counterproductive. (See, for example, Bennett, 1958, p. 3.) In fact, they contribute to the resentment and hostility already present in people in trouble. Prisons "institutionalize" people, as has been mentioned in chapter 13, leaving them dependent and apathetic or angry, resentful, and rebellious.

Public policy regarding severe treatment of offenders is encountering legal and humanitarian difficulties, in addition to the evaluations of the correctional administrators and the social and behavioral sciences. For example, there are procedural problems associated with behavior modification, electroconvulsive therapy, and psychosurgery, among other approaches (Wexler, 1973; also Kittrie, 1971, esp. chap. 9). Modern court action is designed to guarantee (1) due process, (2) equal protection, and (3) humane treatment. Recent Supreme Court cases are important, but discussion of them would be inappropriate here. Many of the inmate suits against correctional administrations have been on habeas corpus action, the basis of cruel and unusual punishment in violation of the Eighth Amendment, failure of due process in violation of the Fifth Amendment as the Fourteenth makes it applicable to the states, equal protection before the law in violation of the Fourteenth Amendment, and the Civil Rights Act of 1871 (42 U.S.C. 1983).

A sample case is *Johnson* v. *Dye.* Johnson was convicted of murder in Georgia in 1942 and was sentenced to life imprisonment. He escaped in 1943 from a chain gang and was arrested in Pennsylvania as a fugitive in 1946, where Georgia authorities filed for extradition for return to Georgia. Johnson said that he had been the victim of cruel and unusual punishment while on the chain gang and that his life would be endangered either by mob violence or brutal treatment by prison personnel if he returned to Georgia. The Court held in favor of Johnson.

The general principle of protection of the individual extends beyond the criminal law and into the realm of private life not related to the criminal justice system. The private life of a citizen is not reason to disbar him or her from professional practice. In a recent Florida case, a lawyer was found to have committed immoral acts with his stepdaughter. She subsequently became pregnant, and the lawyer divorced his wife and married the stepdaughter, although the whole family group continued to live together. When the matter was brought to the bar association with a petition for disbarment, the Court decided that the private life of a lawyer was not grounds for disbarment because it had nothing to do with his professional competence (*Florida Bar* v. *Hefty*, 1968).

There is a strong movement toward the idea that the law has overstepped its bounds regarding the control of individual behavior. Morris and Hawkins (1970) hold that the law has become a moral busybody. They challenge the right of society to intervene with individual citizens in many of the "offenses" that are not damaging to society, such as drunkenness, narcotics and drug abuse, gambling, disorderly conduct, vagrancy, abortion, sexual behavior, and offenses by juveniles that would be crimes if they were adults. Further, they suggest that the money bail system should be abolished, most offenders should receive community-based treatment, no term of less than one year should be imposed by the courts so that only more serious cases would be processed, alternatives to institutionalization should be developed, laws restricting sale of prison-made goods should be abolished, all jails and other correctional services in the United States should be integrated and not have to stop at county and state boundaries, additional probation and parole officers should be recruited to bring the average caseload down to thirty-five per officer, probation and parole services should be available to every offender, and all releases from institutions should be on parole for a fixed period between one and five years. Similar recommendations were made by Geis (1972), who wrote for the Center for Studies of Crime and Delinquency of the National Institute of Health.

Many law enforcement personnel agree with the following statement by Benjamin and Masters (1964):

> To impose arbitrary and needless restrictions and penalties on normal human behavior is not only to tamper with the freedom of others, it is to risk social calamity. When a society passes laws that too many of its healthy and reasonably moral members will necessarily violate, the society invites disrespect for and violation of its other laws. [pp. 370–71]

The problem of intent is mentalistic and difficult to define, but it is basic to Anglo-Saxon law. As indicated earlier, there is conflict between the social and behavioral scientists, who view behavior as caused, and the lawyers and theologians, who subscribe to intent and free will. The problem is intensified when an individual "intended" at the time, but found he was wrong, like the man contemplating a divorce who said, "I thought I was in love, but I was only in heat!"

Free will embodies the legal concept of intent. Legal intent in the criminal justice system, then, is incompatible with the concept of caused behavior in the social and behavioral sciences. Resolution of this dilemma means engaging in conceptual gymnastics because the framework of the law is built on precedent to last for centuries. Social scientists and behavior changers have to "reinterpret" their diagnoses and prognostications to fit into the legal structure, just as psychiatrists do when testifying in cases of insanity or incompetency, or they lose whatever effectiveness they might have.

Morris and Buckle (1951–52) have presented an analysis of the dichotomous approaches to punishment as the retributive theory of "deserved" and "just" punishment, on the one hand, and the humanitarian theory of punishment as therapy or treatment, on the other. The retributive approach is seen as an oversimplification of crime causation as a free choice between good and evil. The treatment approach, on the other hand, is seen as attacking the problem realistically. There may be a little blending of both, since punishment for offenses will somehow always be in response to community opinion, but the treatment approach is much more practical in the long run.

OFFICIAL CRIME STATISTICS

Official crime statistics reflect roughly the nature and extent of crime that is reported, as well as the number of persons arrested and successfully prosecuted. Of an estimated 12 million major crimes, probably half might be reported to police; considerably fewer result in arrests—generally between 15 and 30 percent of those reported; over half of the arrests are then brought to court, but generally between 15 and 30 percent of those are convicted as charged, while a few others are convicted on lesser charges. The Federal Bureau of Investigation issues its annual *Uniform Crime Reports* with full knowledge that the law enforcement effort is limited to factors within its control, and the FBI cautions against comparing crime statistics of individual communities against other communities. Variations in crime statistics reflect the density and size of the communities, the composition of the population with respect to age, sex, and race; economic status and mores of the population; stability of the population; climate and seasonal weather conditions; educational, recreational, and religious characteristics of the community; effective strength of the police force; standards of employment to the police force; policies of the prosecuting officials; attitudes and policies of the courts and corrections; relations, leaderships, and attitudes of law enforcement and the community; administrative and investigative efficiency of law enforcement; and organization and cooperation of overlapping police jurisdictions, among other factors. Further, the politicization of crime rate reporting adds a difficult component to measure. Students of crime statistics have found that less than half the crimes actually reported to police get reported in the official crime statistics (Weis and Milakovich, 1974). Several examples can be cited, generally the purpose being to "make the boss look good." A notable example was when President Nixon told Police Commissioner Jerry Wilson of the District of Columbia in December 1969 to reduce the crime rate or he would be replaced (ibid., p. 32). The crime rate was reduced by shaving the statistics, and a celebration party was held at the White House in early 1974 because the crime rate had gone down similarly all over the country (ibid.).

Selective enforcement has also introduced variations in official crime statistics. Prescriptive or idealistic codes, on the one hand, and the practical values and structural organization of society, on the other, result in variations between societies and cultures, within a society, and between preachment and practice. For example, prostitution, gambling, and liquor violations may be against the prescriptive codes but may be permitted and even protected in practice. Variations appear as to who will be affected by law and why. The law does not cover everyone in the same way. Psychological and cultural factors assist in the determination of who is affected by and who will be protected from the legal sanctions (Toch, 1961, p. 9). Review of anthropological studies of crime in different cultures show that many crimes differ from society to society, particularly sex crimes, theft, and vice. The attitude of the people and the economic base of the community affect enforcement policies. The dyssocial offender adjusts well within his own reference group, but violates the law of larger society—an example is the "moonshiner" who makes liquor and sells it at lower cost than taxed whiskey. His service to his immediate society is demonstrated by his income. The prostitute provides a service for which customers will pay large sums in some cases. Gambling meets the emotional needs of many people. All these behaviors, however, are illegal in most jurisdictions in America and are, therefore, criminal. A question arises as to how a service can be defined as criminal, but this question is considered by referring to the traditional beliefs and sentiments or values of the total society, rather than the immediate reference group.

The Soviet system deserves some special attention in this context because the Soviets are convinced that the communistic system will eventually eliminate crime through the development of a perfect social system. A perfect social system would be one in which all phases of the culture meet perfectly all the needs of each of the individual participants within the culture. This can be achieved, according to Soviet criminologists, by eliminating private property and individual need. In such a system, there would be no need for crime.

Plea bargaining is a broad practice in American jurisprudence that really upsets official crime statistics when a social scientist is attempting to study specific crimes. Some estimates are that between 75 and 90 percent of convicted persons have pleaded guilty to a lesser charge in a plea bargaining session. The case of Spiro Agnew is but one of the most visible examples. The National Advisory Commission on Criminal Justice Standards and Goals, released January 14, 1973, recommended retention of plea bargaining because the court system would break down by sheer volume of trials without it. Although plea bargaining has been debated considerably, its opponents generally cite people who have "gotten off" from serious charges to lesser charges, while the proponents point out that if every case had to be *tried,* the court system would break down; further, there would not be enough money available to construct an adequate court system in which everybody could be *tried.* Proponents also argue that plea bargaining permits humanitarian interests to be served. Whatever the merits or demerits of plea bargaining, the fact remains that first-degree murder is frequently reduced to second-degree or manslaughter, grand larceny frequently reduced to petty larceny, felonious assault frequently reduced to assault and battery, breaking and entering frequently reduced to attempted breaking and entering, auto theft frequently reduced to "joyriding," rape sometimes reduced to indecent liberties; there are similar reductions on all serious offenses. The quandary for social scientists comes when they attempt to study people convicted in specific offense categories.

The problems of using official crime statistics in research is that they are a much better measure of public policy than they are of criminal behavior. For example, the homicide rate in Wilmington, Delaware, went up significantly when a professional medical examiner replaced a lay coroner in investigating otherwise unexplained deaths. A pertinent example of probable misinterpretation of statistics can be demonstrated by the experience of two counties adjacent to each other, their names and location understandably remaining anonymous, reporting considerably different rates of juvenile delinquency. Both counties had the same population composition and size, the same socioeconomic base, and were similar in many respects according to the census tracts published by the Bureau of the Census, United States Department of Commerce. Both were small enough so that the probate or county judge handled juvenile cases rather than having separate juvenile court judges. One judge was interested in children and juveniles, went to his county commission and obtained a staff of counselors, hired a retired Ph.D. psychologist, had a special child welfare unit established in his county by the state welfare department, promoted the development of a good visiting teacher group that could provide liaison between the schools and the juvenile court, and brought services to children earlier than had previously been the case. In the next county, however, the judge thought that children did not need this kind of attention. At the end of the year, when the courts' statistics were submitted, the first court had a 6 percent delinquency rate because it included, besides criminal offenses, the juvenile definitions of incorrigibility, truancy, and other problems. The second county reported less than 1 percent of contacts of children with the court. The obvious conclusion would be that the first county had extremely unruly and delinquent children, while the second county had "good" children. This had political implications, and the judge with the good program was hard-pressed to defend his incumbency at election because according to figures, delinquency had risen considerably after the took office. It is generally known that the more professional police departments report more accurately and honestly their crime statistics to the FBI for use in the *Uniform Crime Reports*, while the less professional departments tend to report considerably less— or, perhaps, they "find" less crime. This presents yet another problem to the social scientist attempting to study crime.

Recognizing these limitations, the social scientist is forced to accept the official crime statistics, the official labeling by the court of *legal* guilt as compared with *actual* guilt. The official prison population, the official probation and parole caseloads, and the official juvenile court statistics are the only defensible operational definition of crime.

The same law is applied differently in different areas and cultures. For example, property crimes are traditionally considered more serious in rural areas than in urban areas and receive longer sentences, while crimes against the person tend to receive longer sentences from judges in urban areas than in rural areas. This gives rise to concern about disparity of sentencing when all offenders go to a central prison and compare experiences and sentences. The same law is applied differentially in many rural and urban areas in many respects, frequently depending upon the culture and custom in the area. It is generally assumed that the standards of practice are better in the urban areas because of accessibility to better training and education as well as the presence of more supervision. This principle can be better demonstrated in cases regarding standards of practice in medicine. A Kentucky case in 1933 indicated that "ordinary care and skill" in Louisville was at a different level from that in the rural areas (*Brune* v. *Belinkoff,* 1933). In 1968, a case in Massachusetts extended the area of good standards to an accessible area of fifty miles (*Tanner* v. *Sanders,* 1968). A case in the state of Washington extended the "locality rule" to an accessible area of 110 miles *Pederson* v. *Dumouchel,* 1967). Differential application of law is also subject to the "locality rule." Social scientists have long recognized that there is differential application of law in many areas according to custom and practice, and the courts recognize it in some areas.

Some social scientists have used self-reported statistics on delinquency in order to obtain a more accurate record (Short and Nye, 1958). Accuracy of self-reported behavior, of course, is dependent on controlling several factors, particularly honesty in reporting, guaranteed anonymity, and motivation to report. Many middle-class adolescents and young adults would like to give the image of being worse than they are, while others have values that predispose them to hide delinquent activity. There is no fully accepted confidence that self-reported delinquency is any more reliable than official statistics. At least, arrests and convictions in the official statistics have provided some screening, which is absent in self-reported delinquency. It could be that a combination of both might provide a better index than either individually. As unreliable as they tend to be, the official statistics published by the FBI are the best available and, after comparing them with statistics from other countries and the United Nations Section on Social Defense, it could be concluded that the FBI still has the best statistics on crime ever collected on a national scale.

VICTIMOLOGY

Concern for the victim is as old as crime itself. Compensation to the victim is well enunciated in Exodus 22: 1–9. The criminologists of the Positive School were concerned with the victim, not only in terms of compensation but in terms of his or her contribution to the crime. Lombroso (1896, 1902) considered that passionate criminals sometimes acted under the pressure of victim-provoked emotions. Garofalo (1914, p. 373) similarly called attention to victims who could be regarded as having provoked the offender to action. Tarde (1912, p. 466) called for extenuating circumstances in the law to account for victims' responsibility for some act of the criminal.

The oldest and most persistent concern for the victim, particularly for those who are truly victims rather than participants, is compensation for injury. Schafer (1968) traced the historical development of compensation for the victim from primitive times through the ancient codes and into the Middle Ages, which have been referred to as the golden age of the victim. Criminal procedure is plainly evident in the compensation approaches, particularly in the Germanic common laws, in the Middle Ages (Schafer, 1960, pp. 3–12). In the later Middle Ages, however, the rise of the power of the secular state and ecclesiastical rulers resulted in the decline of compensation for victims as the rulers took over responsibility for protection of individuals and the former victim compensation went to the state or Church in the form of fines. In fact, this marked the beginning of fines paid to the state rather than to the victim.

Compensation to victims of crime in modern society varies with the economic and social system. It is easier to provide compensation to victims of crime on the part of the state using tax funds in a socialistic system that it is in a capitalistic system. The free enterprise system of insurance is sometimes threatened in capitalistic countries. Insurance in America provides policies to cover crimes of almost every type, in jeweler's block, auto theft, fidelity bonds for employees, double indemnity for life policies if the death is by accident or violence, and so on. Crime insurance is included in Title VI of the Housing and Urban Development Act of 1970, primarily providing support for small business.

Compensation has existed in Switzerland since 1937, in New Zealand since 1963, and in the United Kingdom since 1964. This compensation applies where the victim is in need and the offender is insolvent and unable to satisfy the victim's claim for damages. A procedure separate from the courts leads to the state's compensating the victim for the injury or damage caused by the crime.

In 1966, California became the first state in the United States to establish a Victim's Compensation Board, but only $100,000 was appropriated for the entire state. New York became the second state with a victim's compensation board later in 1966, but only $500,000 was appropriated. By 1979 a half-dozen states had this type of group, but activity was quite conservative and limited. A half-dozen states had victim compensation laws of some sort by 1975.

In summary, the American system of compensation for victims of crime has been traditionally in private insurance. There are many types of crime insurance covered by current standard policies, such as burglary insurance, auto insurance including theft, jeweler's block insurance, business interruption insurance as a result of violence and riot, double indemnity life insurance for violent death, fidelity insurance for internal theft by personnel, and homeowners' insurance that includes theft and burglary. The Federal Crime Insurance Program was established under title VI of the Housing and Urban Development Act of 1970, authorizing the federal government to provide crime insurance at an affordable price in any state which, after August 1, 1971, had a critical crime insurance availability problem. By 1983 the Federal Crime Insurance Program included twenty-seven states, the Virgin Islands, Puerto Rico, and the District of Columbia.

Victimology has been seen by a majority of criminologists as a sub-specialty within the field of criminology, while a minority views the concept of victimology as a separate and autonomous science (Mendelsohn, 1963). Hans von Hentig published his *Criminal and His Victim* in 1948, which provided some focus on victimology. It must be noted, however, that the concern about the victim is as old as the concept of personal injury itself, which is much older than the modern concept of crime. At the suggestion of Dr. Paul Cornil, the Dutch-Belgian conferences of December 19–21, 1958, addressed the problem of victimology. Simultaneously, the *Japanese Journal of Legal Medicine and Criminology* published several reports on victimology in 1958. Wolfgang (1958) found that victims in homicides contributed significantly to the offense in at least 26 percent of the cases.

In summary, victimology has emerged as a prominent concern in the legal and political processes in criminal justice. If the state assumes protection of its citizens, then the question arises as to how much responsibility the state should assume when that protection fails. The question of degree of responsibility on the part of the victim for the crime must also be assessed. The triad of the state's responsibility for serving the offender, the victim, and the innocent bystander who might be hurt has become an important legal and political question in modern society.

CRIMINOLOGY IN THE USSR

All contemporary Western theories of crime causation are disclaimed in the USSR (Zeldes, 1981, p. 24). There are three basic general causes of crime in socialistic society (Karpets, 1969, p. 51; also Kuznetsova, 1969, p. 36). First, the historical conditionality of the social phenomena continues. Criminality existed in France before the French Revolution and continued afterward. Second, the objective law of "lagging consciousness" finds expression in vestiges of the remaining mentality of the people who do not reach the high level of socialism. The consciousness of the people is not yet sufficiently developed. Third, the presence and influence of antagonistic socioeconomic systems that exist alongside socialism hinder the development of socialistic thinking, particularly imperialistic propaganda and the subversive activity of subversive governments. When socialism eventually reaches full acceptance, crime will disappear.

CONCLUSIONS

The law is basic to criminal behavior, and the criminal justice system. Without criminal law, there would be no definition of crime. Further, the law determines the rights of individual citizens and the procedure by which society can intervene in their lives, whether for treatment, for punishment, or to isolate them for a number of years. Present-day criminal procedure took a long time to develop; it began with the custom and blood-feud of primitive man, the mores and codes of ancient man, the ritual and social institutions of the Middle Ages and the emergence of law as known in modern times.

The system of law has not been worked out to the satisfaction of all. The law has looked backward for precedence and experience, while the social sciences look forward for prediction and control. Democratic society depends on complaining witnesses for enforcement, which makes it difficult to control many types of crimes, such as white-collar crime, organized crime, and crimes against the morality of the total society, such as prostitution, alcohol, narcotics, and gambling. In the totalitarian state, however, in which the police have a clear mandate to do whatever is necessary to safeguard the welfare of the state, the enforcement of these laws is easier (Berkley, 1969, pp. 1–7). It is generally conceded that the most ardent and active of the enemies of the police come from the political left (ibid., p. 9).

The definitions of crime in a culture reflect the attitudes of that culture toward all affairs of people in that society. The frame of reference, in terms of deviant behavior, established the social structure within which the affairs of people may function in that culture, and the law defines the limits of intolerable deviant behavior. In a speech made after attending a performance of John Galsworthy's play *Justice*, Winston Churchill told the House of Commons in 1910 that "the mood and temper of the public with regard to the treatment of crime and criminals is one of the most unfailing tests of the civilization of any country." (See Ruggles-Brise, 1910.) Politics in a democracy is public policy that reflects the values of the culture.

Crime represents the acting out of disorders of people. The social, economic, and political philosophies of the society determine in part the nature of its definitions of crime and its philosophy of enforcement. Together with its attendant subjects, crime is the meeting place of all facets of culture, central in the observation and consideration of deviant behavior; both individually and collectively, it is represented in the criminal law, which is central to the criminal justice system.

Questions

1. What is meant by the statement that law defines the relationship between the individual and his society?
2. Why is the Code of Justinian important in Western legal history?
3. Why was Beccaria's famous 1764 *Essay on Crimes and Punishments* important in the development of criminal law and criminal justice?
4. Through what three broad phases has law developed?
5. What is a crime?
6. What factors enter into public policy?
7. Evaluate the move toward decriminalization of victimless and other crimes, particularly as it relates to morality.
8. Evaluate official crime statistics.
9. Evaluate self-reported delinquency.
10. Evaluate plea bargaining.

sixteen

CRIMINOLOGY AND CRIMINAL JUSTICE

Criminology is the study of criminal behavior and the justice system. It is the study of law, broken law, and the lawbreaker. The understanding of them requires an understanding of all the social and behavioral sciences, the natural sciences, and the ethical systems and controls embodied in law and religion. Criminology is the meeting place of all the disciplines that focus on the emotional and mental health of the individual and the smooth functioning of society.

Criminal behavior can be explained through sociological, psychological, medical and biological, psychiatric, psychoanalytic, economic, political, cultural, and other social and behavioral approaches. Politics defines the criminal justice system through the promulgation and implementation of public policy in the law and its enforcement. Therefore, criminal behavior and the justice system become central to many disciplines and approaches focusing on the problem of crime in society.

Religion was central to social control until the eighteenth century; since then the state and the law represented by lawyers and the courts have been central to social control. The eighteenth century was pivotal in the history of man, with the Industrial Revolution and the advancement of science bringing about massive changes in philosophy, government, science, industry, economics, and culture. The changes in the criminal justice system resulted in the introduction of prisons (1773 to

1790), probation (1841), parole (1876 with beginnings in 1840 and 1854), and the juvenile court (1899). The modern municipal police department was introduced in London in 1829 and developed in the United States between 1836 and 1850.

There was also a shift in public reaction to crime, from vengeful retaliation to compensation of the victim during ancient and early medieval times. As the feudal system broke down, criminals were frequently exiled to distant lands. England sometimes permitted offenders to return to the homeland after the introduction of the "ticket of leave" by Captain Alexander Macanochie in 1840, but a second offense resulted in life exile. Modern concepts of treatment and rehabilitation began to be developed in 1790 by the Quakers in Pennsylvania and found full expression in the first meeting of the National Congress on Penitentiary and Reformatory Discipline (now the American Correctional Association) in Cincinnati in 1870 (Wines, 1970). The history of public reaction to criminal behavior shows a shift from concern for the community or the protection of society from primitive times to the late eighteenth century. In his famous *Essay on Crimes and Punishments*, Beccaria noted the shifts in social thinking toward a focus on the seriousness of the offense. Lombroso appraised criminality in scientific terms and developed the Positive School of criminology, which focused attention on the individual offender in his *L'uomo delinquente*, published in 1896–1897. When Charles Goring published *The English Convict* in 1913, refuting Lombroso's claim of "born criminals" and biological determinism, the attention of criminologists shifted to social and psychological factors, where they remain today. Nevertheless, vestiges of all previous thinking in regard to deviant behavior and, specifically, criminal behavior and the justice system, have remained to some extent. Protection of society and the welfare of the community remain a prime consideration of law enforcement and remain as part of the considerations, though not the governing one, of the courts and corrections. Differences in focus and general objectives have resulted in some conflict among law enforcement, the courts, and corrections. For this reason, it is important to understand the total criminal justice system and the criminal behavior on the part of individuals it is designed to control.

As former Attorney General Richard Kleindienst testified before the Senate Watergate Investigating Committee in July 1973, the Constitution of the United States is not designed to protect society; rather, it is designed to protect the individual. One of the basic points in the American philosophy of law enforcement is the greater concern for the preservation of individual liberty over the pursuit of justice. The Bill of Rights (the first ten amendments of the Constitution) provides protection for the individual citizen against the tyranny of government. The American system of criminal justice promotes selective enforcement to provide a reasonable amount of law and order as well as a confidence in law. Consequently, the protection of society is a basic element in the criminal justice system, but it is not governing. Any persons working in the criminal justice system who have sworn to uphold the Constitution of the United States must discharge their function with this philosophy in mind.

OVERVIEW OF CRIMINOLOGICAL THEORIES

The Classical School of criminology, symbolized by Beccaria's publication in 1764, emphasized the hedonistic, pleasure-seeking, and pain-avoiding characteristics of man and supported the concept of free will. This set the stage for the emergence of criminal law on the basis of intent between the time of the American and French revolutions and the War of 1812. The Positive School of Criminology was begun by Lombroso in 1896; he drew on his experience as Professor of Psychiatry at Pavia, director of the "lunatic asylum" at Pesaro, and later Professor of Forensic Medicine and Psychiatry at Turin, where he filled the chair of Criminal Anthropology. He focused attention on the individual offender, particularly his biological characteristics. Lombroso considered the criminal to be a "born criminal" and an atavistic "throwback" to savagery. In his later years, Lombroso also accepted social and psychological factors. Lombroso's approach was refuted by Charles Goring in 1913, and the stage was set for the acceptance of social and psychological theories.

The focus on social factors was evident during the first part of the twentieth century, when Parmelee (1922, 1911) pointed out that the majority of research in crime in the early 1900s had been done by sociologists. This interest by sociologists was the reason criminology was included in most sociology departments in American colleges and universities. The rise of intelligence testing also resulted in a focus on psychological factors. Though intelligence scales had been in existence in the late nineteenth century, they were overweighted with sensory tests, particularly the reaction time test; but Alfred Binet and Theophile Simon developed a usable test in Paris in 1905 that was translated into English and brought to the Vineland Training School in New Jersey by Henry Goddard in 1911. (See Anastasi, 1937, p. 19.) Although the early contention by psychologists was that delinquents and criminals were feebleminded, Murchison in 1926 refuted that approach and offenders since that time have been found to be representative of the general population from which they were drawn, as far as intelligence is concerned. The search for causes of crime have tended from that time to focus on social and emotional factors, with some experimentation in conditioning, such as behavior modification, and medical approaches, such as psychosurgery. Legal and procedural difficulties have interfered with behavior modification and psychosurgery, so the social and emotional approaches currently appear to be most useful.

The emergence of the scientific school of criminology as it is viewed today began in approximately 1920 under the leadership of Ernest Burgess of the University of Chicago. Beginning with an ecological approach that emerged into a "delinquent area" thesis, the major early contributions to the understanding of criminology came from this Chicago School. Robert E. Park viewed the community as his unit of investigation and contributed a series of excellent studies in the 1920s and 1930s. Frederic Thrasher's *The Gang*, published in 1927, was a study of 1,313 gangs in Chicago and remains a classic in the field. Thrasher pointed out that gangs are located in the twilight zone of factories and railroads radiating from the central district of the city, with heavy concentration in the geographically and socially interstitial area between the center of the city and the residential districts.

Sheldon and Eleanor Glueck of the Harvard University Law School contributed voluminously to the criminological literature, particularly in the study of criminal careers and comparisons of delinquents with nondelinquents. One of the problems encountered by the Gluecks results from the fact that they essentially ignored the work of others in the field and maintained their own course of study. Consequently, their contributions have not been as well accepted as they probably should have been by many academic criminologists. An example of the conflict regarding the contributions by the Gluecks lies in the Delinquency Prediction Scale (1959), which was used with great success in New York and was simultaneously attacked by researchers for inadequacy in research methods. Despite the controversy, the Gluecks have contributed substantially to the factual information concerning crime and delinquency, even though they did not develop a unitary theory of crime.

Case studies of offenders have been used to understand criminal and delinquent behavior beginning with the work of William Healy, who was primarily concerned with analysis of personalities of juvenile delinquents. Shaw's (1931) study of delinquency was one of the first to use the sociological viewpoint. There have been many case studies and and autobiographies of juvenile and adult offenders since that time.

The first major sociological explanation of criminal behavior was the theory of differential association introduced by Edwin H. Sutherland in 1939. Although this theory was later slightly revised, its primary thesis remains that criminal behavior is learned from associates. Consequently, it is basically a learning theory. Donald R. Cressey, the primary current proponent of this concept, holds that it is not a "bad company" theory but relates it to "definitions favorable to violation of law over definitions unfavorable to violation of law." It is, therefore, concerned with *patterns* of behavior, regardless of who presents them to the individual (Sutherland and Cressey, 1966, p. 85). More research has been done on the theory of differential association than any other theory of criminology in existence. Some scholars have held that reinforcement through punishment and reward is needed for learning criminal behavior; others point out that it does not explain *all* criminal behavior; still others indicate that it is not "association," but "identification," that is important (this is Daniel Glaser's approach). The conceptual forerunners of this theory appear to have been the ideas of moral contamination held by the Quakers when they began the penitentiary movement in 1790 and insisted on solitary confinement to avoid exposure to definitions favorable to criminal behavior and Grabriel Tarde's Law of Imitation in 1912.

Conflict theory, particularly that concerning cultural conflict, has been presented by Thorsten Sellin to explain crime (1938). Conflict of norms exist when divergent rules of conduct govern the specific life situation in which a person functions. Conduct norms in one group of which a person is a member may be different from those of another group of which he or she is also a member. Most easily dramatized is the situation of children of immigrants, who speak one language at home, follow "old country" customs, and then have to participate in school or the workaday world with native American language and customs. Many conflicts thus emerge that have to be resolved. As a consequence of this culture conflict, the proportion of sons of immigrants in prison is significantly higher than the proportion of the native-born white population.

Robert K. Merton (1949, pp. 125–26) has proposed a means-ends theory in which social structures exert pressures on persons to engage in nonconformist as well as conformist conduct (ibid., p. 128). The central hypothesis is that deviant behavior is a symptom of dissociation between culturally prescribed aspiration and socially structured avenues for achieving these goals. The term *anomie* was used to designate the condition in a social system when cultural regulation of behavior is weakened and the respect for certain social norms is reduced by frustration, resulting in normlessness (ibid., pp. 134–46) and a "to hell with it" attitude. Exceptional success or lack of success in this social setting is generally ascribed to "luck" (ibid., pp. 138–39). Sometimes adaptation to cultural goals is rejected, but conformity with institutionalized means is accepted; this occurs when relatively unsuccessful people go along with social institutions and "play it safe." When relatively unsuccessful people retreat, the goals and the institutions are both rejected, and a group "leaves" society through drug abuse, alcohol, vagabond behavior, or other types of alienation. Rebellion occurs when the cultural goals and means are rejected but modification of the social structure is attempted, which could explain university campus "radicals" and Cohen's (1955, p. 34) concept of "delinquent subculture." Miller also supported this viewpoint, indicating that the gang forms a constructive function for adolescents in lower classes, and gang formation is to be expected there (Miller, 1958). Much crime can be explained on the basis of means-end frustration in society or the concept of anomie. Although anomie was originally used by Emile Durkheim to explain suicide in 1897 (Durkheim, 1951, pp. 38–59), Merton applied Durkheim's concept of anomie to criminal behavior.

Cloward and Ohlin (1961) attempted to merge differential association with the anomie or means-end theory in a theory of opportunity in 1961. The general idea was that status deprivation leads to delinquency when youth in a delinquent subculture are deprived of opportunities to achieve their goals. The discrepancy between their aspirations for culturally defined success goals and the actual possibility of gaining these goals by legitimate means results in the use of illegitimate means already accepted by their delinquent subculture. This results in a tendency toward formulation of three types of gangs: (1) criminal, (2) conflict, and (3) retreatist gangs. The criminal gang achieves goals by stealing or other types of crime. The conflict gang is the fighting gang. The retreatist gang may use drugs, alcohol, or other means of alienation from society. It is interesting to note that many of the opportunity programs enacted during the administration of John F. Kennedy received emphasis from Cloward and Ohlin's presentation. Attorney General Robert F. Kennedy was so impressed with it that he shared it with his brother and others, resulting in enactment of the Juvenile Delinquency Control Act of 1961, which he induced Lloyd Ohlin to administer for the first year of its existence. The general emphasis throughout the 1960s was on opportunity programs.

Reckless (1961), who introduced containment theory in 1961, contends that delinquent and criminal behavior is held by outer presures and inner pressures. Outer forces are push-pull environmental influences, while inner containment refers to push-pull forces in favor of and against deviant behavior. Self-concept is seen as the strongest inner containment that prevents delinquent behavior (Reckless et al., 1956).

Neutralization theory was introduced by Sykes and Matza in 1957. The types of neutralization by which a delinquent rationalizes his activity are (1) denial of responsibility, (2) denial of injury, (3) denial of the victim, (4) condemning the condemners, and (5) appealing to higher loyalties, such as protection of friends and other laudable values.

Theories of deviance were introduced in 1964 when Kai Erikson (1964) formulated them, although deviance and labeling had been discussed long before in generalities, such as in Tannenbaum's (1938)"dramatization of evil" idea in 1938. Deviance is not inherent in certain forms of behavior but is a property conferred on these forms by audiences that directly or indirectly witness them; thus it becomes a labeling process. According to Turk (1956), individuals are evaluated unfavorably or favorably because others react to them offensively or inoffensively. Theories of deviance and labeling go together. Labeling is the assigning of a classification such as "delinquent" to an individual; it remains with him. The "self-fulfilling prophecy" as a result of labeling was discussed by Merton (1957, pp. 421–36). Primary deviance is the delinquent act, while secondary deviance is the internalization of the delinquent values obtained from the labeling process, in which the individual's outlook, attitude, and lifestyle become delinquent. Secondary deviance, then, is a "readiness" to be deviant or delinquent.

The concept of drift presented by Matza (1964, chapters 2, 3) occurs when a lower-class youth may find it unnecessary to make a definite commitment to either delinquency or legal conformity and may thus drift in an unidentified area in between. The use of extenuating circumstances can then be used to justify delinquency.

Hirschi (1969, esp. chapter 12) has classified sociological theories into (1) strain theory, (2) cultural deviance theory, and (3) control theory, all of which he considered to be incompatible with one another. Strain theory assumes moral consensus and faith in the individual's own judgment; this is a class theory and is difficult to support with empirical data. These theories deal with values, aspirations, and goals that are difficult to measure, such as Merton's *anomie* and Kingsley Davis's "evil-causes-evil fallacy" proposed in 1938. Cultural deviance theories assume that it is cultures, rather than individuals, who are deviant, and these theories are concerned with delinquent subcultures and socioeconomic class problems. Most people, however, accept the standardized norms of a culture, rather than "subnorms" of a subculture or "class" values. Control theory refers to the group process of socialization. Society's control lies in its ability to "tame" man's animal nature and make him human. Many sociologists can be identified with each of these groups.

THEORIES, CONCEPTS, AND PRACTICE

A brief summary of the theories and approaches, together with the conceptualization and the applications in practice, might be helpful. The theory is the general formulation of system to explain criminal behavior that has greater support than a hypothesis but cannot be considered to be a law. The concept deriving from the theory is in the link between theory and practice and may be used as the unit of measurement for research or evaluation. It is the basic conceptualization that relates to both theory and practice. Practice is the application of theory. For example, the moralistic theory of the Quakers, who established the penitentiary in 1790, was essentially that evil or immoral persons can influence others to be immoral, which in turn causes crime. The concept, then, was moral contamination. All good practice can be guided by good theory, and good theory emerges from good practice. Although many practitioners in the criminal justice system perform their duties without knowledge of the theoretical concerns behind the practice, and on the other hand, many theoretical criminologists fail to follow their theoretical formulations into practice, a genuine understanding of criminal behavior and the criminal justice system necessitates this link between theory and practice. This permits the practitioner to know *why* he or she is proceeding in a certain manner and gives the theoreticians some understandings of the practical application of their theories. The following chart lists theories, concepts, and practices from prehistoric times to the present.

THEORY	CONCEPT	PRACTICE
Theory or approach, significant contributors, and dates.	Link between theory and practice. Basic conceptualization, which may be used as the unit of measurement for research and evaluation. Effectiveness in research ranges from fully objective concepts that can be quantified and used for empirical research to the clinical concepts that are not quantifiable and must be left to expert judgment in evaluation.	Application of theory to practice and the contributions of practice to theoretical understandings.
Development of Spoken Language (100,000-30,000 B.C.). John Stuart Mill (1884) S.I. Hayakawa (1949) (other semanticists before)	Communication with symbols enabling abstract thinking and symbolic interaction.	Language permits abstract thinking which, in turn, permits the development of values, common beliefs and culture, right and wrong, and permits *human* behavior over and above basic animal behavior. Permits theology, philosophy, and other abstract systems.
Beginnings of human behavior, with primitive religion. Funeral rites beginning about 60,000 B.C. Primitive organized religion about 23,000 B.C.	Supernatural Influence. Compassion for others. "Human" behavior refers to values and abstract beliefs.	Favor of the gods. Concern for the welfare of others, keeping handicapped and older people. Concern for deceased relatives and the hereafter. Behavior of people is animal behavior interacting with "human" behavior.

THEORY	CONCEPT	PRACTICE
Demonology Origins lost but probably simultaneous with primitive religion. Continued seriously as late as 1692 in Massachusetts. Still present in some fundamentalistic religions.	Evil or hostile spirit below the rank of god. Originally also included good spirits.	Devils and demons that harass the living. Some definitions include souls and ghosts. Deviant behavior caused by demons' influence.
Fortune telling Practiced as early as 4000 B.C. in Egypt, Babylonia, Chaldea, and China.	Prophecy by religious leaders, oracles, dreams, and the use of many different objects and rituals.	A gifted person can foresee the future of others through psychic powers ranging from magic to extrasensory perception.
Astrology Originated in Mesopotamia about 3500 B.C. Sun's course relative to earth, moon phases, and relative planet movement known accurately by 1000 B.C. Astrology ended as a serious science in the 17th century when the earth was found not to be the center of the universe. Johannes Kepler (1571–1630) studied motions of the planets, then gave up his astrology and horoscope casting.	Signs of the zodiac made by planet positions in relation to sun and earth.	Influence of the universe on human behavior and destiny. Significant influence on ancient and medieval religion and philosophy. Discarded by science when the earth was found not to be the center of the universe, which destroyed the meaning of the planet positions in relation to other systems.
Order in the universe Early Ionian philosophers, 8th and 7th centuries B.C. Pythagoras (c. 530 B.C.) introduced philosophical version of the soul.	Man composed of humors of air, fire, water, and earth, and of pneuma or vital spirit, which later became the soul in some systems.	Man's temperament and, therefore, his readiness to act in certain ways, is dependent upon the proportions of each of these elements that comprise his body.
Philosophy Ancient Greek in origin, probably 8th and 7th centuries. Pre-Socratic era	Attempt to develop ethical systems and some knowledge of order in the universe.	Ideas more important than man himself. Concern for concept of ''justice.'' Acceptance and understanding of the world by reason and logic.

THEORY	CONCEPT	PRACTICE
about 500 B.C. with Parmenides, concerned with theological speculation and nature of reality. Platonic Academy 4th century B.C.		
Theology First theology considered to be Christian interpretations. History in early Greek critical interpretation of classical myths and Hebrew religion founded by Moses around 1215 B.C.	God's will. Monotheistic deity with powers of omniscience, omnipresence, and omnipotence. Soul is vital to life.	Behavior related to the will of God. Theological systems based on attempts to explain existence of evil and sin in the presence of a good and all-powerful God. Acceptance of the world by faith and divine revelation.
Great religious swing and productivity (800 B.C. to 650 A.D.). Prophets of Israel, Zoroaster in Persia, Buddha and Upanishadic peers in India, Confucius and Lao Tzu in China, Jesus in Palestine, Mohammed in Arabia.	Phenomenal outpouring of religious creativity coincided with changes in secular history, development of agriculture, growth of cities, expanded commerce and trade, increased population, great empires.	Introduced ethical systems needed to control expanded economy and civilization where old tribal rituals and myths no longer sufficed. Formed the base for the development of modern criminal law.
Medicine Babylon physicians as early as 3000 B.C. Hippocrates about 400 B.C. considered "father of medicine." Medical school in Alexandria 300 B.C. Galen, Greek physician (c. 130–200 A.D.). considered most distinguished physician in antiquity.	Natural causes for disease and illness.	Diagnosis of causes of disease and deviant behavior and provision of appropriate antidotes or other means for treatment. Understanding of the world by science and natural causes.
Law Primitive law derived from custom and feuds. Present law emerged in ancient Greece with Solon (about 640–570 B.C.) the earliest significant contributor. Canon	Legally prescribed sanctions on individual and group behavior for the welfare of the group or society.	Prescribing in law the essence of ethical systems that promote group living in harmonious manner.

THEORY	CONCEPT	PRACTICE
law or church law about 3rd century A.D. Parliamentary law about 13th century A.D. Criminal law as now known about 1650–1820 A.D.		Present criminal procedure essentially developed in England and America 1776–1812. (England: Jeremy Bentham, Samuel Romilly, William Blackstone. America: Edward Livingston)
Education Education began in Greece during the 5th and 4th centuries B.C., though other cultures, such as Egyptian, Minoan, and Mycenaean, contributed. Aristotle and Plato thought it should be government controlled. In 1642, Massachusetts law provided that parents teach their children reading, law, catechism, and a trade and provided for hiring teachers in towns in 1647. First prison teacher was the chaplain, but the first teacher appointed in prison specifically for the purpose was at Cherry Hill in Pennsylvania in 1844. First full program in a prison was at Elmira Reformatory in New York in 1876.	Skills, both the tools of literacy and a trade. Social and motivational education. Reading and writing, vocational skills, and pro-social attitude. Develop good work and study habits.	Academic school to teach basic reading and writing and to provide a high school diploma, usually on equivalency through the General Education Development (GED) program in the prison, on study release, and NewGate program. Vocational and agricultural schools for trade training. Commercial schools in some prisons.
Psychiatry As the branch of medicine concerned with mental ill health and emotional disturbances, beginning date is not clear. Early Greek physicians left their incantations and used kindness, recreation, and music in treating the mentally ill as early as 860	Mental ill health and emotional disturbance. Defense mechanisms and adjustive techniques.	Treatment by counseling, drugs, psychotherapy, group therapy, and similar approaches.

THEORY	CONCEPT	PRACTICE
B.C. Philippe Pinel (1745–1826) took the chains off the mentally ill at the Bicêtre in Paris in 1795–1797. Jean Charcot (1825–1893) taught Sigmund Freud in clinical neurology. Benjamin Rush (1812) considered to be the "father of American psychiatry." Benjamin Karpman (1939). Voluminous work on criminal behavior. Sutherland and Cressey indicate psychiatric approaches influenced the criminal justice field first around 1905.		
Psychoanalysis Sigmund Freud (1856–1939) developed psychoanalysis while studying hysteria and reported in 1895. First International Congress of Psychoanalysis in 1908.	Subconscious motivation of behavior important. Id, superego, and ego concepts. Defense mechanisms and adjustive techniques.	Emotional catharsis or "ventilating." Free association to get at subconscious repressions and other traumatic conditions.
Classical School of Criminology Beccaria (1738–1794), Montesquieu (1689–1755), Rousseau (1712–1778), Voltaire (1694–1778), Blackstone (1723–1780), Bentham (1748–1832), Romilly (1757–1818). Predecessors in Locke (1632–1704) and Hobbes (1588–1679), the contract writers who promulgated the idea	Free will. Reason. Humanitarian values.	Man is hedonistic and can reason. Seeks pleasure and avoids pain. Laws can be written down describing what is a crime, and the appropriate punishment can be listed. Man can then decide whether or not he wants to commit a crime. The punishment will fit the crime in terms of respective severity. Capital punishment eliminated.

THEORY	CONCEPT	PRACTICE
of government by the consent of the governed.		
Deterrence Cesare Beccaria (1764), Paul Johann Anselm Feuerbach (1813), Gordon Hawkins and Franklin Zimring (1973), Isaac Ehrlich (1972, 1975, 1977)	Punishment and reward determine whether persons will or will not choose to commit crime. Profit and loss regarding crime.	Certainty, swiftness, and severity of punishment determine whether or not "crime pays." Sufficient punishment can deter crime. On the other hand, if the rewards of crime outweigh the punishment, crime will continue to be committed. Is the crime worth it? Cost-benefit analysis of crime and its results.
Phrenology or Craniology Franz Joseph Gall (1758–1828). M. B. Sansom, *Rationale of Crime*, 1846. Emerged from physiognomy, which had been developed by Johann Kasper Lavater (1741–1801) to explain temperament on the basis of outward appearance of the individual. American leader was Johan Gasper Spurzheim (1776–1832). Auguste Comte (1798–1857), sometimes called the "father of sociology," promoted Gall's views.	Bumps on the head	Localization of brain function can be found by determining what areas have been developed by use or by heredity and "reading" the bumps on head. Twenty-seven functions or "instincts" identified.
Positive School of Criminology Cesare Lombroso (1836–1909), Enrico Ferri (1856–1928), Raffaele Garofalo (1852–1934), Arthur MacDonald (1856–1936), Ernest A. Hooton (1939), William H. Sheldon (1940, 1942, 1949).	Biological determinism. Behavior is the function of structure.	The criminal type is biologically determined. Lombroso indicated that he could identify (1) born criminals, (2) insane criminals, (3) criminals by passion, and (4) occasional criminals. Environmental factors were subsequently considered to be of importance.

THEORY	CONCEPT	PRACTICE
Thermic Law Adolphe Quetelet (1796–1874) considered to be the "father of statistics." Mayo-Smith (1907), Kropotkin (1842–1921), Lacasagne (1880)	Climate and temperature.	Crimes against the person are more prevalent in warm climates; crimes against property are more prevalent in cold climates.
Mental Testers Alfred Binet and Theophile Simon (1905). First measurement of individual differences by Maskelyne, astronomer, in 1796. Binet and Henri criticized existing tests in 1895. Binet-Simon scale translated into English and brought to United States by Henry Goddard, Vineland Training School, N.J., in 1911. "Mental test" first employed by James McKeen Cattel in 1890.	Intelligence testing, IQ, aptitude testing, personality testing. Psychologists' interviews and reports.	Individual differences can be measured and used to predict how people will behave in terms of competence, attitude, aptitudes, and general personality structure.
Osteopathy Andrew Taylor Still (1828–1917) founded osteopathy in 1874. Founded American School of Osteopathy at Kirksville, Missouri, in 1892. Now five colleges of osteopathy.	Bones and tissues are basic to health, both physical and mental.	All abnormalities are due to abnormalities in or near joints, bones, and tissue. "Osteopathic lesions" can be produced by strain, injury, infection, from disease elsewhere, and by nervous influences. Lesions reduce the flow of blood and the capability of the body to produce its own antitoxins. Manipulation is the primary treatment approach. Osteopathic psychiatrists are in practice. Rejected by medicine as an oversimplification of complex phenomena. Accepted by Medicare.
Chiropractic D. D. Palmer (1895). Founded Palmer College of Chiropractic,	Nerve system controls all other systems, and its impairment induces disease by reducing the body's resistance. Affects	Manipulation of the spine where the nerves are channeled from the brain to other parts of the body tends to

THEORY	CONCEPT	PRACTICE
Davenport, Iowa. Now four schools in chiropractic in America.	physical and mental health.	open the nerve channels and restore normal nerve functioning. Statistics on successful mental health treatment compare favorably to psychiatry, but some question them. Rejected by medicine as oversimplification of complex phenomena. Originally rejected by Medicare, now approved for "limited services" as of July 1, 1973.
Law of Imitation Gabriel Tarde (1843–1904) Predecessor to Sutherland's theory of differential association.	Influence of others.	Society and behavior can be explained by the influence of mind on mind through the force of imitation. Criminal behavior is spread from person to person in this manner.
Economic Theories William Bonger (1916). Predecessor was Adam Smith (1723–1790), considered to be "father of economics," considered economics a separate study. Karl Marx (1818–1883) and Frederich Engels (1820–1895) wrote *The Communist Manifesto* in 1848 and presented capitalistic system as introducing a division of labor into society that would set up class struggle by blocking opportunity for lower-class workers.	Economic need. Poverty.	Person in economic need who lacks the opportunity to obtain material goods through legitimate means will resort to illegitimate means to obtain them.
Case Study Approach William Healy (1909), Clifford R. Shaw (1930, 1931, 1938), Benjamin Karpman, (1939), Robert Lindner (1944), others.	Biographical data on known offenders.	Study of the lives of offenders helps to understand the dynamics of their emotional and social development. Usable in the treatment process.
Social Work Charles Booth (1903), Jane Addams (1910),	Casework, group work, and community organization.	Provide casework for delinquents and other offenders. Some states require a master's

THEORY	CONCEPT	PRACTICE
Abraham Flexner (1915), Mary Richmond (1917), Virginia Robinson (1930). American Association of Social Workers (now National Association of Social Workers) established in 1921.		degree in social work for employment in the corrections phase of the criminal justice system, such as probation, institutions, and parole for juvenile and adult offenders.
The American School John L. Gillin used this name in 1914 to identify the rise of sociological interest in criminal behavior in America, as compared with the legal, religious, and clinical views prevailing in Europe. Sutherland and Cressey identify 1915 as the beginning of the Sociological School. Frequent conflict between sociological and psychiatric approaches. Maurice Parmelee (1908, 1922)	Social and environmental influences.	People are the product of their environment. Treatment based on changing the environment and helping individuals to perceive their environment differently to reduce their vulnerability to undesirable influences.
Castration Modern castration originated in the United States with the 1907 Indiana law. Supreme Court upheld it in 1927, and twenty states passed laws within ten years, and more states passed laws later until the majority of States had them. Supreme Court held in 1947, however, that criminality was not transmitted genetically, and most states repealed their laws. California probably had the only spe-	Testes secrete androgens, which are directly related to aggression. Also related to sex drive.	Removal of the testes reduces secretion of androgens. Therefore, aggression and sex will both be reduced. Castrated mammals, including man, tend to grow fat and lazy. Some vengeance motives have been suggested, also.

THEORY	CONCEPT	PRACTICE
cific penal castration law; more castrations were done there than in any other state, but the California law was repealed in 1971. Scandinavian countries make greatest use of castration at present.		
Ecology and Gangs— the Chicago School Research and publication at the University of Chicago under Ernest Burgess began heavily around 1927, with Frederic Thrasher, Clifford R. Shaw, Henry D. McKay, Robert Park, Clark Tibbitts, and others.	Delinquency areas and gangs. Delinquency career patterns.	The greatest amount of delinquency and crime comes from the "inner city" or zones of deterioration, whether called slums, ghettos, or Skid Row. Inexpensive and crowded housing characteristic, children "grow up in the streets." Neighborhood and area projects bring in recreational and counseling services to promote prosocial attitudes and behavior.
Sex Reassignment by Surgery The first successful sex change operation was done in Denmark by Niels Hoyer in 1931. The first sex-change operation in the United States was in 1967 at the Gender Clinic at Johns Hopkins Hospital. Literature: Richard Green and John Money (1969), John Money and Ronald Gaskin (1973).	Physiological sex structure should be congruent with the psychological and emotional patterns of the individual in relation to the culturally defined sex roles in society.	Transsexuals who believe that they should belong to the opposite sex from that with which they are identified can have the physiological changes made to fit their psychological and emotional patterns in terms of socially accepted sex roles. Without such change, sex-role confusion interferes with the comfort and mental health of people and can be manifested by deviant behavior.
Psychosurgery First lobotomy done in Lisbon in 1935 by Almeida Lima under the direction of Egas Moniz. Subsequently done in Europe and United States.	Brain considered to be a primary source of aggression. Preventive measures.	Cutting the nerve fibers between the frontal lobes and the thalamus will reduce violence and aggression and make the patient quiet. Too much cutting can make the patient a "vegetable," which has resulted in recent litigation regarding privacy of an individual's person and body.

THEORY	CONCEPT	PRACTICE
Culture Conflict Thorsten Sellin (1938).	Conflict of customs, attitudes, beliefs, and other cultural factors differ in the home or neighborhood from the expected cultural factors in larger society.	Immigrant family problems easiest to portray, but theory includes many other culture conflicts in religion, attitudes toward authority, and many other cultural factors. Children of immigrant parents may be raised in "old country" culture and then have difficulty in adjusting to American culture when they go to school or interact with others in adolescent and adult society.
Theory of Differential Association Edwin H. Sutherland introduced it in 1939, reformulated it slightly in 1947. Forerunners were Gabriel Tarde's law of imitation in 1912 and the Quakers' approach to moral contamination in 1790 (solitary confinement).	Criminal behavior is learned behavior. Depends on intensity and frequency of association with criminal and delinquent patterns of behavior. Moral contamination.	Criminal and delinquent behavior is learned from others. Could be called a "bad companions" theory, but the patterns of behavior could also be learned from parents and others not generally considered to be "companions." Treatment is by introducing new patterns of behavior into the individual's social world and trying to control his or her contacts with undesirable patterns of behavior.
Anomie Robert K. Merton (1949 and 1955). Had considered it as early as 1938. Forerunner was Emile Durkheim, who used the concept in 1897 to explain a type of suicide. Term first appeared in English in 1591 and was used by English theologians in 17th century to mean disregard of divine law.	State of normlessness or lawlessness. Normative standards of conduct weakened or absent. Personal disorientation, anxiety, and social isolation.	Conformity to cultural goals and the institutionalized means of achieving them is the desirable adaptation in society. When the goals are not achievable through accepted means, however, illegitimate means might be used. This occurs frequently when middle-class goals are sought by lower-class youths, who sometimes get "the good things in life" by stealing or other illegitimate means.
Opportunity Theory Richard A. Cloward and Lloyd E. Ohlin (1961).	Legitimate goals combined with illegitimate means produces delinquency in the absence of legitimate opportunity.	When all persons have the opportunity to achieve the legitimate goals they desire, there is no reason to achieve them through illegitimate means. Many of the opportunity programs in the Kennedy and Johnson administrations were based on this theory.

THEORY	CONCEPT	PRACTICE
Alienation Frank Tannenbaum's "dramatization of evil" (1938). Albert K. Cohen (1955), Walter B. Miller (1958).	Gang formation and delinquent subcultures.	When an individual feels frustrated and alienated, he or she seeks support from others similarly alienated. The gang formation provides a new and different world for the individual—one in which the youth is accepted and not alienated.
Identity Emanuel Windholz and Joseph Wheelwright of the Mt. Zion Veterans' Rehabilitation Clinic during World War II (1942–45). Erik Erikson (1963, 1968).	Identity crisis, referring to loss of a sense of personal sameness and historical continuity. William James called it "character."	Potential criminal or delinquent identity by attitude and appearance—for example, "Hell's Angels," with motorcycles and Nazi helmets. Identity confusion in delinquency by severely conflicted youths behaving as confused rebels against society—rebels without a cause. Negative identity in hostile attitudes toward teachers, police, parents, and other authority figures.
Identification Gordon Allport (1954). Erik Erikson (1950).	Imitating the behavior of an ego ideal or an identity one would like to assume. Hero worship.	Making heroes of legendary criminals, including Robin Hood, Jesse James, Billy the Kid, Al Capone, John Dillinger, Ma Barker, and others.
Containment Theory Walter C. Reckless (1961). Predecessor Arthur L. Beeley in 1945.	Inner and outer push-pull forces, which in balance, could produce normal behavior or delinquency.	Outer environment, including associates and temptations, are balanced against inner resistances, with self-concept being the strongest insulator against delinquency.
Prisonization Theory Donald Clemmer (1940, 1965), G. P. Grossner (1958), Lloyd Ohlin and W. C. Lawrence (1959).	Customs and folkways of the prison.	Prisoners associating with each other adopt the "inmate code" for self-protection and gradually accept and inculcate the customs and values of the prison society as opposed to those of normal society outside. Assimilation of the prison culture.
Gang Formation Thrasher (1927), Albert K. Cohen (1955), Walter B. Miller (1955), Cloward and Ohlin (1961), Short and Strodtbeck (1965).	Gang becomes primary group that functionally replaces family in psychosocial development.	The individual who feels the need for acceptance and is dependent upon others for emotional security can find it in a delinquent gang. In turn, he adopts the values and activities of the gang and finds his identification there.

THEORY	CONCEPT	PRACTICE
<u>Behavior Modification</u> B. F. Skinner, 1938, 1953, 1957), John McKee, Kenneth Schwitzgabel.	Punishment and reward as negative and positive reinforcement of behavior.	Consistent reward for desirable behavior and consistent punishment for undesirable behavior. Contingent management as immediate reward and punishment. Token economy as introducing another step of "banking" merits in the reward system. Programmed instruction as presenting information with wrong answers resulting in "leads" to correct answers. Pay for participation in desirable programs.
<u>Social Defense (reaction against Classical and Positive schools)</u> Fellippo Gramatica, president of the Study Center on Social Defense in Genoa (1945). Marc Ancel (1947, 1965). Predecessors in Plato, Thomas More (1516). French Code of 1791 regarding juveniles. Enrico Ferri. United Nations adopted a section on social defense in 1947; name changed in 1972 to Crime Prevention and Criminal Justice Branch because of disagreement about the meaning of social defence. U.N. Social Defence Research Institute headquartered in Rome. C. Ray Jeffery (1971).	Preventive measures.	Scientific method of understanding personality development. Less use of legal fictions like *mens rea* or intent. "In the interests of the child" approach over the "protection of society" as governing principle. Treatment of crime based on sociological principles rather than strictly legal principles. Replace punitive measures in criminal justice system with preventive measures. Crime prevention through environmental design. Humanization of the criminal justice system.
<u>Guided Group Interaction</u> F. Lovell Bixby, Lloyd McCorkle, and Albert Elias (1958). H. A. Weeks (1958). Predecessors at Ft. Knox, Kentucky, dur-	Peer-group responsibility for treatment.	Group treatent program where (1) a social climate is established in which delinquents can examine and experience alternatives relating to a realistic choice between delinquent or conforming behavior; (2) opportunity exists to state

THEORY	CONCEPT	PRACTICE
ing World War II, with Lloyd McCorkle (1943–45). Lamar T. Empey and J. Rabow (1971). Oliver J. Keller and Benedict Alper (1970). Harry Vorrath (1969).		beliefs and values to peers and authority in the form of a group coordinator who is generally present but in the background; (3) a type of social structure that permits examination of the role and legitimacy of authority in the treatment system; and (4) the type of treatment inter-actions that places responsibility on the delinquents themselves through peer-group decision making while granting status to their willingness to involve others in the process. Ex-perience is that delinquents generally arrive at legitimate and conforming decisions after sometimes long debate.
Differential Treatment by Maturity Level Marguerite Warren (1967, 1971). Predecessors in Clyde E. Sullivan, Mar-guerite Grant, and J. Douglas Grant (1957).	Individuals classified on emo-tional maturity level according to their ability to cope with social situations.	Delinquents at maturity level 2 placed in supportive environ-ments and foster homes. Delin-quents at maturity level 3 placed in environments with strong adult support along with group treatment. Delinquents at maturity level 4 placed in family group therapy, individual psychotherapy, or group therapy. Delinquents remain in the home community and, if possible, within their own homes.
Differential Treatment Herbert Quay (1965), Roy Gerard (1969), Loren Karacki (1972). Sullivan, Grant, and Grant (1957) were predecessors to pro-gram currently called I-Level by Marguerite Q. Warren.	Classification in accordance with the needs and security requirements of the individual.	Resident of the institution moves from one stage to a better one or regresses to a poorer one depending upon be-havior. General classification of types of delinquents are (1) un-socialized psychopathic, (2) neurotic-disturbed, (3) in-adequate-immature, and (4) socialized-subcultural. Response to behavior modifica-tion techniques in terms of punishment and reward deter-mines the treatment mode. In use at United States John F. Kennedy Youth Center at Morgantown, West Virginia, since 1968. Also Warren's

THEORY	CONCEPT	PRACTICE
		community treatment project in Sacramento, California
Psychodrama and Sociometrics Jacob L. Moreno (1934 and 1958). Helen Jennings (1943).	Roles and interpersonal bonds. Reciprocal bonds, rejection bonds, and one-way bonds. Tele as the interpersonal bond.	People behave in reaction to other people, which is why roles are part of society. People like each other or dislike each other based on whether the inner tensional maladjustments of the people involved complement or conflict. This is why some people get along right away, and others dislike each other at the beginning of the encounter. Therapy is by role playing in a psychodrama theater before others, including the therapist.
Family Therapy Nathan Ackerman (1958), John Bell (1961).	Treatment of the family as a unit.	Family therapy is complex and deals with the working through of multiple conflicts between individuals or factions within the family group. Neurotic interaction between family members, where one may be "feeding off" another emotionally, can result in deviant behavior on the part of individuals.
White-Collar Crime Edwin H. Sutherland (1945, 1959).	Sharp business practices.	White-collar crime has sharp business practices, "thumb-on-the-scales," "cutting corners" type of behavior that borders on the illegal. Examples: violation of regulations of manufacturing, contracting, commerce, agriculture, and other business occupations.
Control Theory Walter C. Reckless (1961), Travis Hirschi (1969), David Matza (1964). Generic term referring to theories espousing inner controls. John P. Conrad (1965).	People contain themselves.	It is surprising that more crime and delinquency is not committed. Containment and drift activities reach an equilibrium at a rather low level of crime when compared with the opportunities and risks involved.
Strain Theory Classification of theories that includes culture conflict.	Hatred, inequality, discrimination, differences in opportunities.	Society is a battle between the "haves" and "have-nots." Ruling classes are privileged. Lower classes and minorities

THEORY	CONCEPT	PRACTICE
anomie, class structure conflict, and other conflicts and stresses. Tannenbaum (1938), Merton (1949), Cohen (1954), many others.		have to cheat and steal to "equalize" opportunity.
Solidarity Opposition Theory Gresham Sykes and Sheldon Messinger (1960). Named by David Street, Robert Vinter, and C. Perrow (1968). Barry Schwartz (1973).	Inmates respond with solidarity against prison situation and staff.	Inmate suffers from the "pains of imprisonment" (Sykes) and the most crucial element in the response is the inmates' rejection of their rejectors (McCorkle and Korn, 1954). Uniting against the prison administration and staff, inmates are transformed from a group "in itself" to a group "for itself."
Subcultures Albert K. Cohen (1955), Walter B. Miller (1958), David J. Bordua (1961), Lamar T. Empey (1967).	Delinquent subcultures.	In a delinquent subculture, criminal values are normal, so theft and other types of crimes are legitimate means to achieve desirable goals or ends.
Conflict Theory George Simmel (1903–1904), Robert E. Park and Ernest W. Burgess (1924), Clifford R. Shaw and Henry D. McKay (1931), Richard Quinney (1968).	Sociological form of interaction in which groups come into conflict when one overlaps another in areas of interrest and purpose.	Groups must be able to defend themselves and maintain their places in a changing world, whether the groups are criminal, like Capone versus Moran in Chicago during the 1920s, political struggles, or any other form of conflict. The individual identified with the group is accepted based on his loyalty to the group and whether or not the group can "depend on" him.
Labeling Theory Howard S. Becker (1963). Predecessors in Frank Tannenbaum's "dramatization of evil" (1938) and Edwin M. Lemert (1951). Lemert discussed "secondary deviation" in 1967. Stanton Wheeler and Leonard S. Cottrell (1966).	Social definitions of crime and deviance create crime and deviance. When a person is identified and officially labeled as a criminal or delinquent, it is difficult to reverse.	Self-fulfilling prophecy (Merton, 1957)—persons who are labeled tend to accept the label and to play the expected role that derives from it.

THEORY	CONCEPT	PRACTICE
Theory of Deviance Edwin M. Lemert (1951). Associated with labeling theory.	Primary deviance is the act of crime or delinquency that is labeled by society. Secondary deviance is the attitudes and "readiness" to act again in a criminal manner or the acceptance of deviant values. Deviant behavior used as defense, attack, or adjustment in society, called secondary deviation.	The first act of primary deviation is followed by social penalties, with police, courts, and correctional programs involved. Further primary deviation follows, and stronger official penalties result. Hostility develops in the individual and he reaches a crisis in the tolerance level expressed by official reaction, and the deviant conduct is strengthened and deviate roles with deviant social status accepted by the person as his identity.
Theory of Neutralization Gresham Sykes and David Matza (1957).	Neutralization of sanctions against delinquent behavior by rationalizing oneself out of the moral bind between parental teachings and delinquent behavior.	Neutralizes blame and guilt by (1) denial of responsiblity, (2) denial of injury, (3) feeling that victim deserved it, (4) condemnation of the condemners who are worse than he is, and (5) appeal to higher loyalties, such as helping a friend, not "squealing" on associates.
Drift David Matza (1964).	Lower-class boy "drifts" into delinquency.	Lower-class boy drifts in an unidentified area between delinquency or conformity without making a commitment to either. Criminal laws are not rigidly and uniformly enforced, so the delinquent may extend the legal boundaries to extenuating circumstances to fit his own situation, so he can justify it. Question should be why people do not commit more crime, rather than why they do commit it.
Reference Group Theory Daniel Glaser (1958), Martin R. Haskell (1961), Muzafer Sherif (1953).	Reference group is the group whose attitude and perspective constitutes the frame of reference of the individual. Could be called an identification group.	The criminal gang may serve to reflect the attitudes and perspective of the individual member without having "taught" him those attitudes and perspectives, though they may be mutually reinforcing. Most important, the gang does serve as his frame of reference in his outlook on social values.

THEORY	CONCEPT	PRACTICE
Operant Conditioning B. F. Skinner (1938, 1953, 1957), Ferster and Skinner (1957), J. L. Michael (1970) A phase of behavior modification.	Conditioning based on experiments of reward and punishment in psychological laboratories.	Learning procedures in social situations involve (1) operant strengthening, or reinforcement through changes in environment or stimuli that increase the probability of behavior change; (2) operant weakening or punishment that changes environment to reduce continuation of present behavior; (3) extinction of behavior, which is a function of its occurrence without reinforcement or punishment; (4) ambient stimulus relevance, which occurs when reinforcement or punishment can be a change superimposed on conditions similar to those during previous reinforcement or punishment, which strengthens the effect; (5) conditioned reinforcement or punishment, which occurs when these stimulus conditions of reinforcement or punishment existing prior to the event become, themselves, reinforcers or punishers; and (6) motivation, which consists of environmental operations that alter the effectiveness of particular classes of reinforcers or punishers, influencing the probability of the occurrence of behavior previously under control of these stimulus contingencies. This is a laboratory approach to behavior modification.
Reality Therapy William Glasser (1965).	Face reality on a ''here-and-now'' basis. Not interested in ''causes.'' Ask what—not why.	Patient is placed in a position in which he or she is made to face reality by the therapist, who takes no ''excuses.'' After facing reality, the patient is put into a decision-making posture in which he or she must decide whether or not he or she wishes to take the ''responsible path.'' All anyone can do

THEORY	CONCEPT	PRACTICE
		is to be responsible by doing right and accept the pleasure or pain that is the consequence of his or her actions. Concept of mental illness not acceptable.
Gestalt Therapy Frederick S. Perls, Joan Fagan, and Irma Lee Shepherd (1970), Robert Resnick (1969). Predecessors were Max Wertheimer (1912) and earlier writings of Kurt Kof-fka, Wolfgang Kohler, and Kurt Lewin (1951).	Whole is greater than the sum of the parts, so context is most important. Perception of "the big picture," rather than atomized living.	Emphasize positive directions and constructive goals of living. Motivation most important. Neurosis is (1) phony, where people play games; (2) phobic, where we relate to fears; (3) an impasse, where people are caught and lose environmental support, becoming "loners;" (4) implosive, where people despair, grieve, and loathe themselves in feelings of unworthiness; and (5) explosive, where previously unused energies are freed and used in an impactive way. Self-growth can be achieved by meditation, introspection, and listening to oneself.
Transactional Analysis Eric Berne (1961, 1964, 1972). Thomas A. Harris (1967).	Roles of parent, adult, and child.	People function in the roles of parent, adult, and child, with a tendency to emphasize one type of role over the others. When two people confront each other, six ego states are involved. When the roles are complementary, for example, one a parent and the other a child, communication is facilitated. On the other hand, cross-transactions reduce communication and multiple cross-transactions produce confusion. Technique is used in some prisons and correctional institutions, such as the Illinois State Penitentiary at Vienna.
Learning Disabilities Samuel A. Kirk (1952) (special education), Lester Tarwopol (1970), Bruce Lane (1980) (delinquency)	*Dyslexia, minimal cerebral dysfunction, specific learning difficulties* are terms relating to learning difficulties in delinquents.	Relationship between learning disabilities and delinquency has been demonstrated as being significant. While police pick them and "normals" up at about the same rate, learning disabled youths are adjudicated

THEORY	CONCEPT	PRACTICE
		delinquent more frequently. Wide diversity in traits and etiology. Heredity more important, with emotional problems and attitudes secondary. Some have called learning disability a "political invention" to direct resources to otherwise unclassified groups, rather than a clinical classification clearly defined.
Biodynamics J. H. Masserman (1955), David Abrahamsen (1960)	Interaction between organism and its environment, resulting in harmony or frustration, stress, and anxiety.	Organisms actuated by physiological need; react to their milieus in terms of individual needs, capacities, and experience; when goal-oriented activities are frustrated, techniques change to reach the goal; and when two or more motivations conflict, anxiety produces neurotic behavior, or the organism becomes disorganized, regressive, and symbolic or psychotic.
Physical Growth Abnormalities I. S. Wile (1947), Roy C. Wunderlich (1975).	Criminals and children both biologically and emotionally immature.	Habits of wrong living and wrong thinking have hardened the criminal over the years so he does not respond to "sociopolitical" treatment—counseling.
Nutrition and Diet Elizabeth L. Rees (1975), Irwin Stone (1972), Abram Hoffer (1962), W. Kaufman (1943), H. J. Rinkel (1951 and 1962), Alexander Schauss (1979, 1980).	Many chronic degenerative diseases, both physical and mental, derive from malnutrition. "Affluent starvation" exists in many progressive societies where food is rich in calories and food artifacts but lacks nutritional value.	Food without nutritional value has resulted in many psychiatric and physical diseases from hypoglycemia and functional hyperinsulinism to saccharine diseases to psychiatric diseases and other conditions that require orthomolecular nutrition. Nutritional problems contributing to crime include imbalances in mineral content, excessive quantities of one food (including milk), and many other shortages.
Metabolism Franz Alexander (1950), Roy C. Wunderlich (1970), O. Fenichel (1954).	Problems of stress, hyper-or hypoactivity, irritability, reduced attention span, alcoholism and drug use, and other conditions are related to metabolic imbalance.	Offenders should be subjected to routine urinalysis, blood count, insulin, and tuberculin tests, tests for kidney, liver, and other organ dysfunction, and other imbalances that

THEORY	CONCEPT	PRACTICE
		cause abnormal reaction to "normal" stimuli. Glucose test can identify hypoglycemia as a cause of fainting, sweating, irritability, and other problems that interfere with social functioning.
Biofeedback Barbara Brown (1974), Gary Mills and Leslie Solomon (1974). Predecessor was Fr. William Graham Sumner, Ph.D., who invented the polygraph (erroneously called a lie detector) about 1900.	Immediate and continuous signals of such biological functions as skin temperature, blood pressure, galvanic reflex (transmission of electric impulse over skin), EEG, EMG (electromyography), heartbeat, and other biological functions.	Can be used to facilitate relaxation and detoxification from drugs. Used in many hospital settings in treatment of emotional problems, stress management, pain control, and other assistance in relief of human potential. Sometimes substituted for hypnosis. Polygraph based on galvanic reflex, pulse, and breathing to detect involuntary reaction to stress while answering questions. Suggestion with biofeedback measures (relaxation).
Biosocial Approaches C. R. Jeffrey (1977), Sarnoff Mednick (1977), Leonard Hippchen (1978), H. J. Eysenck (1977), Seymour Halleck (1975).	$P_v = G_v \times E_v$ ←P_v = variation in phenotype G_v = variation in genetic structure X = interaction E_v = variation in environment ←$S \times E \times O = B$ S = stimulus X = interaction E = environment O = organism B = behavior	Humans adapt to their environment by behavior that includes an interacting and combined response by the organism to the environment. Patterns of behavior are triggered by certain biological and cultural interactions that recall the chemically coded message of memory and past experiences with present stimuli. There can be no learning without a biological base that is really bioenvironmental or biosocial.
The "New Criminology" Ian Taylor, Paul Walton, Jock Young (1973).	Marxist interpretation of class struggle that makes the criminal justice system a tool of the ruling class to keep the lower classes subjugated.	Criminal justice system is used by the ruling middle- and upper-class whites to keep the poor and the minorities oppressed.
Conflict Austin Turk (1969), William Chambliss, Robert Seidman (1971, 1976).	Study the present system without changing it.	Legalistic definitions of crime have prompted neglect of some serious offenses committed by the dominant group while poor people and minorities are arrested.
Critical Richard Quinney (1973, 1975, 1977),	Identify with present system while changing it from within.	Everything that has been done must be redone. Inquiry into how normative content of

THEORY	CONCEPT	PRACTICE
William Chambliss (after 1976), Taylor, Walton, and Young (1973).		criminal law is internalized by various segments of society.
Radical Herman and Julia Schwendinger (1974, 1977), Anthony Platt (1974), Paul Takagi (1977), Barry Krisberg (1975), Steven Spitzer (1976).	Destroy the present system and replace it.	Criminal justice system has to be replaced with a more equitable system. Criticism no longer an end in itself but a weapon to destroy the system and change the present practice—a praxis. Subordinate theory to practice.
The Criminal Personality Samuel Yochelsen and Stanton E. Samenow (1976, 1977).	Crime is caused by the "criminal mind" rather than by disadvantageous socioeconomic surroundings and circumstances.	53 errors in thinking, primarily lying, cheating, fearfulness, anger, zero state or worthlessness, superoptimism that he will not be caught, "criminal pride," and other errors in thinking.
Criminology in the USSR I. I. Karpets (1969, 1977), N. F. Kuznetsova (1969), B. S. Nikiforov (1972), Ilya Zeldes (1981), Peter Solomon (1978).	Inculcation of socialistic thinking and behavior.	Crime is caused by (1) historical conditioning of social phenomena, (2) "lagging consciousness" of people that slows the inculcation of socialistic thinking and behavior, and (3) the influence of antagonistic systems existing alongside socialism that includes imperialistic propaganda and the subversive activity of imperialistic governments.

THE APPLICATION OF THEORY TO PRACTICE

Crime is so complex that a single theory or small constellation of theories is difficult to operationalize and evaluate through controlled research. There is disagreement between the research and the clinical viewpoints, most graphically demonstrated by the demand for solid research by sociologists and experimental psychologists, on the one hand, and the more pragmatic clinical viewpoint held by psychiatrists, clinical psychologists, and social workers on the other. The differences can be illustrated by statements made by two outstanding persons in their respective fields, one a sociologist and the other a psychiatrist. A young sociologist contends that "treatment without research is quackery."[1] At

---

[1]Comment by Ronald Akers, sociologist, while chairing a section of the Southern Conference on Corrections, Tallahassee, Florida, February 28, 1974.

the other extreme, DeHart Krans, a psychiatrist who has specialized in electroconvulsive therapy replied in this way to a query from this writer in 1974 as to what electroshock really did: "We do not know what it does. All we know is that it works. Maybe, the research boys will tell us what it does a hundred years from now. In the meantime, we will get a lot of good out of it."

This difference in viewpoint underlies many of the disagreements in the field of criminal justice. A notable previously mentioned example is the Glueck Delinquency Prediction Scale, which the researchers attack as being based on faulty methodology, but which the New York City Youth Board contends works in the field of practice. It is apparent that this problem will continue, with research-oriented scholars wanting empirical evidence and clinically oriented practitioners searching for "what works," sometimes almost on a trial-and-error basis. These disparate viewpoints will probably never become congruent. It is apparent that both are needed. The history of innovation and progress has been that the clinicians or practitioners initiate new programs, and the researchers evaluate them.

Ferracuti and Wolfgang (1964) attempted to find a way to integrate the clinical and the sociological approaches and found it difficult to accomplish. A summary of the clinical approach to evaluation as compared to the concept of statistical prediction still leaves many problems (Meehl, 1956). Statistical evaluations are always easier when the data are available, but human behavior leaves so many variables uncontrolled that statistics simply are not adequate, as official crime statistics so well demonstrate. On the other hand, clinical judgments must rely on the competence of the persons doing the judging, and experience suggests that they are not universally reliable (Thorne, 1970, p. 332). Further, the programs in the control and treatment of crime have broad implications that are not suited to single theories. The following models of these understandings, theories, and programs, previously discussed in chapter 2, were suggested by the President's Commission on Law Enforcement and Administration of Justice.

1. The regulatory model—sees the goals of corrections primarily as control—detection of crime, apprehension, trial, and punishment.

2. The psychogenic (or "patient") model—believes offenders are emotionally maladjusted and in need of individual therapy.

3. The sociogenic model—considers sociological factors, such as social disorganization, cultural conflict, cultural lag, individual disorganization, and social alienation as complex variables in the patterns of crime and criminal behavior. An important premise of the approach is that certain crimes and forms of delinquency are symptoms of failure and disorganization of the community, especially in cases where the offenders are those who have been deprived of the very bases for law-

abiding conduct, such as adequate educational and vocational training and employment opportunities. [*Task Force Report*, 1967, p. 7]

Most theories fit one model or another. In addition to restraint,
behavior modification, reality therapy, peer pressure, and similar approaches relate to the control model of regulatory model. The medical,
therapy, casework, and counseling approaches relate to the psychogenic
model. Opportunity programs, urban renewal, environmental design,
and welfare programs relate to the sociogenic model. The traditionally
oriented sociologist focuses on a specific set of variables in the study
of crime, such as urban-rural crime rates, delinquency areas, crime
rates, race, socioeconomic class and conditions, age, sex, nativity, family
status, juvenile gang processes, and other social and demographic factors. It becomes obvious that a combination of approaches is needed
in the understanding, control, and treatment of crime.

Criminality is not a medical condition subject to medical definitions, white coats, rubber gloves, cleanliness, and morality. Neither is
it a "here-and-now" isolated phenomenon devoid of background in social
and emotional problems. Criminality is a lifestyle in which deviation
from expected social behavior damages society or offends the sensitivities and behavioral standards of others. This behavior ranges from borderline criminality, in which the individual occasionally and perhaps
accidentally "tests the limits" of tolerable behavior, to the extreme of
the "dangerous offender" who spends a lifetime killing and robbing people. No single discipline has the answer or the explanation, though most
have made significant contributions. The accrued knowledge can be
brought to bear on the problem of criminality, which is defined so by
social and ethical expectations and implemented by sanctions provided
by the political leaders in the law. This sociopolitical event known as
crime, then, cannot be completely explained in medical, sociological,
psychoanalytic, psychological, or any other single approach. Psychedelic, kaleidoscopic, erotic, and mystical thinking do not attack the
realistic problem of crime.

Sociology has been seen as having an overwhelming ethnocentric
character. Clinard (1960) criticized American sociology in the area of
criminological theory because it limited itself to a series of events in
only one society—American. Several academic criminologists have
reacted to the domination of the single discipline of sociology over
theoretical criminology, indicating that social work, psychology, psychiatry, law, and education, among other disciplines, have a significant
contribution to make to the interdisciplinary study and practice of criminology (Jeffery, 1971, p. 261).

Further, different theories and approaches have been seen as con-
fusing and actually impeding treatment. Ex-offenders tend to see the

reasons for their difficulties as immediate events and factors related to their offenses, while theoreticians tend to see crime in terms of the broad predisposing causes, and sometimes there is little communication. One ex-offender who had completed three sentences in major Midwestern prisons for a total of sixteen years and came to the university to study criminology commented that those theories are "funnier than the Sunday comics!"

A clinician who directs the treatment center at the Massachusetts Correctional Institution has written that some of the terminology used by theoreticians "strikes me as a specious, glib generalization, which is as superficial as it is inaccurate. . . . It is hard enough to labor in the vineyard without having to undo the danger of pretentious _____."[2] The most effective worker in the criminal justice system appears to be a socially oriented person who can relate to others in a consistent manner. Knowledge of human behavior and social problems can enhance effectiveness. Matching clients and workers is an important part of the treatment process (Palmer, 1967). Long clinical experience has indicated that few workers relate equally well with all types of other people, and the range of treatment styles needed for a wide variety of offenders can hardly be acquired by a single person.

There is danger that practitioners may become wedded to one theory or one approach, forsaking all others, which gives them a single parameter or continuum as a frame of reference. This will make them effective with a few who respond to this one approach, but they will miss the majority of cases. Human behavior, including criminal behavior, is motivated not by a single influence or force but by a multiplicity of influences and forces that can be patterned in a variety of ways. Although there may be a patterning tendency in similar circumstances, the emotional dynamics that motivate people's behavior results in a situation where each constellation of problems is unique to the individual involved.

It is obvious that no single discipline—sociology, psychology, psychiatry, theology, economics—has any all-encompassing theory that will explain crime and deviant behavior on the part of individuals or groups. As the discipline that has contributed most to criminological research, sociology would seem to have the logical function of bringing together the contributions of many disciplines for purposes of better understanding through research of this serious social problem. As the primary agents of social control, the lawyers and the courts, aided by the clergy, would be in the best position to find the balance between the individual and society with a minimum of conflict and irritation and in a

---

[2] Letter to this writer from Harry L. Kozol, psychiatrist and director, the Treatment Center at Massachusetts Correctional Institution, Bridgewater, Mass., dated June 7, 1973.

logical manner. As the discipline that has contributed most to understanding of individual deviant behavior, psychiatry and its compatriots, clinical psychology and social work, still have the responsibility of contributing much more in terms of education and increasing the understanding of the police, the correctional officer, and others who work with people in trouble.

The situation was described well by Professor Gerhard O. W. Mueller (1969), when he stated:

> For have we not learned, above all else, that this social animal called man can survive in concert, even if every individual member alone could not? A blind man, a deaf man, and a dumb man stand a good chance of surviving—if they stand together. A blind criminal justice, a deaf forensic psychiatry and a dumb sociological criminology stand a good chance not only of survival—if they stand together—but also of bettering humanity's plight. [p. 199]

CONCLUSIONS

Crime is a by-product of civilization. Most civilized members of society obey authority and conform to the norms prevailing in their culture. Their obedience and compliance may vary in degree, but law-abiding citizens remain within the limits of tolerance. It is when people deviate beyond the level of social tolerance that their organs of justice in society label the deviant behavior as a crime or delinquency or, for that matter, as insanity and incompetence. Crime, then, is a sociopolitical event subject to the definitions of the society in which it occurs.

The social response to crime in terms of treatment of offenders is dependent upon the advance of the civilization and the affluence of the society. Public policy is always a blend of economics and humanitarian values. In fact, humanitarian values become important when society becomes sufficiently affluent to afford them. The per capita GNP (gross national product) is one measurable index of the advance of a society according to its economic development, with the average being about $1,000 a year, such as in Venezuela, as compared with five times that for the United States and West Germany (Benoit, 1974, p. 16). Because crime is a by-product of civilization, the larger and more complex societies have both higher crime rates and more sophisticated methods of social control. The per capita GNP correlates with higher crime rates, higher educational levels, and higher welfare programs.

Public policy is made by the political leadership in Congress and state legislatures on the basis of what the people need and want in terms of social programs and what the society can afford to finance. Many of the humanitarian values come from the religious backgrounds and social orientation of the politicians, who are most frequently reflections of the values of the constituencies that voted them into office. Research and theory seldom get into public policy, except when an expert witness uses research findings to support his or her testimony before a committee that has confidence in the witness. It is important for the researcher and theoretician to combine with the practitioner to convert research findings and sophistication into public policy through constructive political activity, but they need to be able to communicate with each other before trying to communicate with political leaders who make policy and appropriate funds with which to finance programs.

There are many practitioners well accepted by most political leaders who are trying to get good ideas into public policy. August Vollmer (1964), who initiated police education at the University of California when he was chief of police at Berkeley, has called attention to the futility of simply employing repressive methods in enforcement:

> I have spent my life enforcing laws. It is a stupid procedure and has not, nor will it ever solve the problem unless it is supplemented by preventive measures. [p. 32]

In full agreement, Karl Menninger (1968) said:

> Could not a better way be found for dealing with despair and ignominy and poverty and frustration and bitterness than to let pressures mount until they result in social aggression and irreversible tragedy?
>
> We must find ways of preventing personality and social disorganization in hundreds of thousands of patients for whom we do not even have a good diagnostic prescription at the present time. [pp. 20, 189]

It is the understanding of crime and deviant behavior that can lead society to more productive action. It is the theory of crime and delinquency that contributes to the knowledge of the total problem that can help bring cohesiveness to the criminal justice system. The common goal is the protection of society. The more immediate objective of law enforcement is to apprehend the criminal and get him off the streets. The court system remains aloof, attempting to "referee" a fair and impartial trial, trying not to get into it on either side. The interest of the correctional component of the "system" is in rehabilitation and successful release of the citizen-offender as a self-respecting, wage-earning, tax-paying member of the society. The immediate objectives of each component of the "system" are mutually exclusive and are frequently at odds with one another. An understanding of the problem and its components can assist in helping all forces pull together for the common goal of the protection of society. When the understanding of why the total system exists and how mutual support can unify the present "nonsystem" in criminal justice is known, then many of the communication problems between segments of this fragmented system can be solved for the benefit of all society. It has been fragmented by attempts at over-simplification. It is obvious that criminology, criminal behavior, and the justice system are too complex, too intertwined with all of society to be the province of a single approach or discipline. The five blind men were describing their versions of the elephant correctly. The blind criminal justice practitioner, the deaf forensic psychiatrist, and the dumb sociological criminologist can stand together and help solve humanity's plight. A more comprehensive understanding of the viewpoints of all who are positively and constructively attempting to work together in this field of criminal behavior and justice can bring deviant behavior into tolerable limits for the benefit of all civilization.

Questions

1. When and why did the Church relinquish its role as the primary agent of social control and the national state and lawyers assume greater responsibility for social control?

2. Give a brief overview of criminological theories.

3. What was the immediate impetus for the Juvenile Delinquency Control Act of 1961 and subsequent governmental "opportunity" programs?

4. What are the relationships between theories, concepts, and practices in the field of corrections?

5. What is the difference between primary deviance and secondary deviance?

6. Evaluate the conflict between research sociologists, who deal in statistics and empirical evidence, on the one hand, and the psychiatrists and other clinicians working in the field, who use clinical judgment and opinion, on the other, in assessing the effectiveness of correctional programs.

7. What three modalities or approaches are used to explain crime and delinquency and to control it?

8. Evaluate the "medical model" in corrections.

9. What are the disadvantages of selecting a single approach while rejecting others, in theory and/or practice, when dealing with offenders in the criminal justice system?

10. Why does conflict emerge between the three components of the criminal justice system—the police, the courts, and corrections—and how can that conflict be replaced with mutual understanding and support?

BIBLIOGRAPHY

ABRAHAMSEN, DAVID. *Crime and the Human Mind.* New York: Columbia University Press, 1944.

_____. "Family Tension, Basic Cause of Criminal Behavior," *Journal of Criminal Law and Criminology* 20 (September–October 1949), 330–43.

_____. *The Road to Emotional Maturity.* Englewood Cliffs, N.J.: Prentice-Hall, 1958.

_____. *The Psychology of Crime.* New York: Columbia University Press, 1960.

ACKERMAN, NATHAN W. *The Psychodynamics of Family Life: Diagnosis and Treatment of Family Relationships.* New York: Basic Books, 1958.

_____. "Family Therapy," in Silvano Arieti, ed., *American Handbook of Psychiatry,* vol. III. New York: Basic Books, 1966.

ADAMS, L.R. "An Experimental Evaluation of the Adequacy of Differential Association Theory and a Theoretical Formulation of a Learning Theory of Criminal Behavior," unpublished Ph.D. dissertation, Florida State University, Tallahassee, 1971.

_____. "Differential Association and Learning Principles Revisited," *Social Problems* 20 (Spring 1973), 458–69.

AICHORN, AUGUST. *Wayward Youth.* New York: Viking, 1935; originally published in Vienna, 1925.

AKERS, RONALD. *Deviant Behavior: A Social Learning Approach.* Belmont, Calif.: Wadsworth, 1973.

ALEXANDER, FRANZ. "The Development of Fundamental Concepts of Psychoanalysis," in F. Alexander and H. Ross, eds., *Dynamic Psychiatry.* Chicago: University of Chicago Press, 1952.

————, AND WILLIAM HEALY. *The Roots of Crime.* New York: Knopf, 1935.

————, AND HELEN ROSS, eds. *Dynamic Psychiatry.* Chicago: University of Chicago Press, 1952.

ALLISON, JOEL. "Religious Conversion: Regression and Progression in an Adolescent Experience," *Journal for the Scientific Study of Religion* 8 (Spring 1965), 23–38.

ALLPORT, GORDON W. *The Nature of Prejudice.* Cambridge, Mass.: Addison-Wesley, 1954.

ALPERT, G. P. In *Criminal Justice Review* 2 (Fall 1977), 137–39.

AMERICAN FRIENDS SERVICE COMMITTEE. *Struggle for Justice.* New York: Hill & Wang, 1971.

AMERICAN INSTITUTE OF BIOLOGICAL SCIENCES, BIOLOGICAL SCIENCE CURRICULUM STUDY. *Biological Science, Molecules to Men.* Boston: Houghton Mifflin, 1963.

AMERICAN PSYCHIATRIC ASSOCIATION. *Diagnostic and Statistical Manual of Mental Disorders,* Washington, D.C.: American Psychiatric Association, 1980.

ANASTASI, ANNE. *Differential Psychology.* New York: Macmillan, 1937.

ANCEL, MARC. *La Défence sociale nouvelle.* Paris: Cujas, 1954.

————. *Social Defense: A Modern Approach to Criminal Problems.* New York: Schocken, 1966.

ANDERSON, WALT. "The Strange Powers of Alternative Medicine," *Human Behavior* 3 (May 1974), 24–29.

ANTHONY, E. J. "The History of Group Psychotherapy," in H. I. Kaplan and B. J. Sadock, eds., *Comprehensive Group Psychotherapy.* Baltimore: Williams & Wilkins, 1971.

ARIETI, SILVANO, ed. *American Handbook of Psychiatry.* New York: Basic Books, vols. I and II, 1959; vol. III, 1966.

ARMSTRONG, K. G. "The Retributivist Hits Back," *Mind* 70 (1961), 486–87.

ASCH, S. E. *Social Psychology.* Englewood Cliffs, N.J.: Prentice-Hall, 1952.

ASH, PHILIP. "Convicted Felons' Attitudes toward Theft," *Criminal Justice and Behavior: An International Journal of Correctional Psychology* 1 (March 1974), 21–29.

BALES, ROBERT F. *Interaction Process Analysis.* Cambridge, Mass.: Addison-Wesley, 1950.

————. "The Equilibrium of Small Groups," in A. P. Hare, E. F. Borgatta, and R. F. Bales, eds., *Small Groups: Studies in Social Interaction.* New York: Knopf, 1955.

BALL, R. A. "Neutralization as a Self Factor in Delinquency Risk," from *A Report to the Ohio Youth Commission and Columbus Public Schools,* based on a Ph.D. dissertation, Ohio State University, Columbus, 1965.

BANAY, RALPH S. "Physical Disfigurement as the Factor in Delinquency and Crime," *Federal Probation* 7 (January–March 1943), 20–24.

BARNES, G. E. "The Alcoholic Personality: A Reanalysis of the Literature," *Journal of Studies on Alcohol*, 40, no. 7 (1979), 571–634.

BARNES, HARRY E. *The Evolution of Penology in Pennsylvania*. Indianapolis: Bobbs-Merrill, 1927.

_____, AND NEGLEY K. TEETERS. *New Horizons in Criminology*, 3rd ed. Englewood Cliffs, N.J.: Prentice-Hall, 1959.

BARRON, MILTON L. *The Juvenile in Delinquent Society*. New York: Knopf, 1964.

BARTON, ROY F. *Half-Way Son*. New York: Harcourt, Brace, 1930.

BEASLEY, R. W., AND GEORGE ANTUNES. "The Etiology of Urban Crime," *Criminology: An Interdisciplinary Journal* 11 (February 1974).

BEATTY, JACKSON. "Similar Effects of Feedback Signals and Instructional Information," in David Shapiro et al., *Biofeedback and Self-Control–1972*. Chicago: Aldine, 1973.

BECKER, HOWARD S. *The Outsiders: Studies in the Sociology of Deviance*. New York: Free Press of Glencoe, 1963.

_____. "Deviance and Deviates," in David Boroff, ed., *The State of the Nation*. Englewood Cliffs, N.J.: Prentice-Hall, 1965.

_____, AND I. L. HOROWITZ. "The Culture of Civility," *Trans-Action* 7 (1970).

BEDAU, HUGO ADAM. *The Death Penalty in America: An Anthology*. Garden City, N.Y.: Doubleday/Anchor, 1967.

BEELEY, A.L. "A Socio-psychological Theory of Crime and Delinquency: A Contribution to Etiology," *Journal of Criminal Law, Criminology and Police Science* 45 (December 1945), 394–96.

BENDER, LAURETTA. "Organic Brain Conditions Producing Behavior Disturbances: A Clinical Survey of Encephalitis, Burn Encephalopathy, and the Traumatic States," in N. D. C. Lewis and B. Pacella, eds., *Modern Trends in Child Psychiatry*. New York: International Universities Press, 1945.

BENEDEK, THERESE. "Personality Development," in Franz Alexander and Helen Ross, eds., *Dynamic Psychiatry*. Chicago: University of Chicago Press, 1952.

BENJAMIN, HARRY, AND R. E. L. MASTERS. *Prostitution and Morality*. New York: Julian Press, 1964.

BENOIT, EMILE. "Comment: A Survivalist Manifesto," *Society* 12 (March–April 1974).

BERGIN, ALLEN E., AND SOL L. GARFIELD, eds. *Handbook of Psychotherapy and Behavior Change: An Empirical Analysis*. New York: Wiley, 1971.

BERKLEY, GEORGE E. *The Democratic Policeman*. Boston: Beacon, 1969.

BERNE, ERIC. *Transactional Analysis in Psychotherapy*. New York: Grove, 1961.

_____. *Games People Play*. New York: Random House, 1964.

_____. *What Do You Say After You Say Hello?* New York: Grove, 1972.

BISHOP, CHARLES H., JR., AND EDWARD B. BLANCHARD. *Behavior Therapy: A Guide to Correctional Administration and Programming.* Athens: University of Georgia Institute of Government, November 1971.

BLATTY, WILLIAM PETER. *The Exorcist.* New York: Bantam Books, 1971.

BOLTON, T. L. "The Growth of Memory in Schoolchildren," *American Journal of Psychology* 4 (1891–92), 362–80.

BONGER, WILLIAM A. *Criminality and Economic Conditions.* Boston: Little, Brown, 1916.

BONNET, PHILIP. "Diagnosis of Biochemical Disorders," in L. Hippchen, ed., *Holistic Approaches to Offender Rehabilitation.* Springfield, Ill.: Thomas, 1982, pp. 110–33.

The Book of Common Prayer—and Administration of the Sacraments and Other Rites and Ceremonies of the Church. New York: Church Pension Fund, Protestant Episcopal Church in the United States, 1945.

BOOTH, CHARLES. *Life and Labor of the People of London: Final Volume, Notes on Social Influences and Conditions.* London: Macmillan, 1903.

BORDUA, D. J. "Delinquent Sub-cultures: Sociological Interpretations of Gang Delinquency," *Annals of the American Academy of Political and Social Science* 338 (November 1961), 116–36.

BORKIN, JOSEPH. Review of *The Criminal Personality. Federal Bar Journal* 35 (Summer–Fall 1976), 237–41.

BOTTING, DOUGLAS. *The Pirates.* Alexandria, Va.: Time-Life Books, 1978.

BOTTOMS, A. E. "Methodological Aspects of Classification in Criminology," *Methodological Aspects of Classification in Criminology,* in the series *Collected Studies in Criminological Research,* vol. X. Strasbourg: Council of Europe, 1973.

BOWER, ELI. *Early Identification of Emotionally Handicapped Children in School.* Springfield, Ill.: Thomas, 1960.

BOWLBY, JOHN. *Separation: Anxiety and Anger—Attachment and Loss,* vol. II. New York: Basic Books, 1973.

BOYER, PAUL, AND STEPHEN NISSENBAUM. *Salem Possessed: The Social Origins of Witchcraft.* Cambridge, Mass.: Harvard University Press, 1974.

BRACE, CHARLES LORING. *The Dangerous Classes of New York, & Twenty Years' Work Among Them.* New York: Wynkoop & Hallenbeck, Publishers, 1872. Reprinted by Washington, D.C.: National Association of Social Workers, 1973.

BRANDT, RICHARD B. *Ethical Theory: The Problems of Normative and Critical Ethics.* Englewood Cliffs, N.J.: Prentice-Hall, 1959.

BRANHAM, VERNON C., AND SAMUEL B. KUTASH, eds. *Encyclopedia of Criminology.* New York: Philosophical Library, 1949.

BREIHAM, W. H. *The Complete and Authentic Life of Jesse James.* New York: Fell, 1953.

BRENNER, C. *An Elementary Textbook of Psychoanalysis.* New York: International Universities Press, 1955.

BRODSKY, STANLEY, ed. *Psychologists in the Criminal Justice System.* Carbondale, Ill.: American Association of Correctional Psychologists and ADMARK, 1972.

BRODY, E. B. "Psychiatry and Prejudice," chap. 39 in Silvano Arieti, *American Handbook of Psychiatry.* New York: Basic Books, 1966.

BRODY, SYLVIA. *Patterns of Mothering.* New York: International Universities Press, 1956.

BROMBERG, WALTER. *Crime and the Mind.* Philadelphia: Lippincott, 1948.

_____, AND TERRY C. ROGERS. "Authority in the Treatment of Delinquents," *American Journal of Orthopsychiatry* 16 (1946).

BROWN, BARBARA B. *New Mind, New Body: Bio-feedback: New Directions for the Mind.* New York: Harper & Row, 1974.

BROWN, CLAUDE. *Manchild in the Promised Land.* New York: Macmillan, 1965.

BROWN, F. A., AND Y. H. PARK. "Synodic Monthly Modulation of the Diurnal Rhythm of Hamsters," *Proceedings of the Society of Experimental Biological Medicine* 125 (1967), 712–15.

BUGENAL, J. F. T. "Five Paradigms for Group Psychotherapy," *Psychological Reports* 10 (1962), 607–10.

BURGESS, R. L., AND R. L. AKERS. "A Differential Association-Reinforcement Theory of Criminal Behavior," *Social Problems* 14 (1966), 128–47.

BURKS, B. S., D. W. JENSEN, AND L. M. TERMAN. *Genetic Studies of Genius,* 3, *The Promise of Youth: Follow-Up Studies of a Thousand Gifted Children.* Stanford, Calif.: Stanford University Press, 1930.

BURNS, ROBERT E. *I Am a Fugitive from a Georgia Chain Gang.* New York: Vanguard, 1932.

BUROS, OSCAR KRISEN, ed. *The Seventh Mental Measurements Yearbook (1972).* Highland Park, N.J.: Gryphon, 1972.

BURT, CYRIL. *The Young Delinquents.* New York: Appleton, 1925.

CALDWELL, MORRIS G. "Group Dynamics in the Prison Community," *Journal of Criminal Law, Criminology and Police Science* 46 (January–February 1956), 648–57.

CALDWELL, ROBERT. *Criminology.* New York: Ronald Press, 1956.

CARNEGIE, DALE. *How to Win Friends and Influence People.* New York: Simon and Schuster, 1939; subsequently published by Pocket Books, division of Simon and Schuster.

CARPENTER, MARY. *Juvenile Delinquency.* London: Cash, 1853.

CARROL, DENIS, AND JEAN PINATEL. *The University Teaching of Social Sciences.* Paris: UNESCO, 1957.

CARTWRIGHT, DARWIN, AND ALVIN ZANDER, eds. *Group Dynamics: Research and Theory,* 2nd ed. Evanston, Ill.: Row Peterson, 1960.

Case Histories of Mental Illness under Chiropractic. Davenport, Iowa: Clear View Sanitarium and Palmer School of Chiropractic, 1953.

CAVAN, RUTH SHONLE. *Juvenile Delinquency*. Philadelphia: Lippincott, 1962a.

———. *Criminology*, 3rd ed. New York: Crowell, 1962b. *Census of Population: 1980*, vol. II, *Persons in Institutions and Other Group Quarters*, Washington, D.C.: U.S. Bureau of the Census, 1981.

CHANG, DAC H., AND WARREN B. ARMSTRONG, eds. *The Prison: Voices from the Inside*. Cambridge, Mass.: Schenkman, 1972.

CLARK, KENNETH. *Dark Ghetto—Dilemmas of Social Power*. New York: Harper & Row, 1965.

CLECKLEY, HERVEY M. *The Mask of Sanity*. St. Louis: Mosby, 1955.

CLEMMER, DONALD. *The Prison Community*. New York: Rinehart, 1958; originally published Boston: Christopher Press, 1940.

CLINARD, MARSHALL. "Criminological Theories of Violations of Wartime Regulations," *American Sociological Review* 11 (June 1946), 258–70.

———. "Criminological Research," in R. K. Merton et al., eds. *Sociology Today*. New York: Basic Books, 1959, pp. 510–13.

———. "The Relation of Urbanization and Urbanism to Criminal Behavior," *American Sociological Review* 25 (April 1960), 253–57.

———, AND RICHARD QUINNEY. *Criminal Behavior Systems: A Typology*. New York: Holt, Rinehart and Winston, 1967.

CLOWARD, RICHARD A., AND LLOYD E. OHLIN. *Delinquency and Opportunity: A Theory of Delinquent Gangs*. New York: Free Press, 1961.

COHEN, ALBERT K. *Delinquent Boys: The Culture of the Gang*. Glencoe: Free Press, 1955.

———. "The Sociology of the Deviant Act: Anomie Theory and Beyond," in Donald R. Cressey and David A. Ward, eds. *Delinquency, Crime and Social Progress*. New York: Harper & Row, 1969.

———, ALFRED LINDESMITH, AND KARL SCHUESSLER. *The Sutherland Papers*. Bloomington, Ind.: Indiana University Press, 1956.

COHEN, LAWRENCE D., JAMES R. KLUEGEL, AND KENNETH C. LAND. "Social Inequality and Predatory Criminal Victimization: An Exposition and Test of a Formal Theory," *American Sociological Review* 46 (October 1981), 505–24.

COLEMAN, JAMES C. *Abnormal Psychology and Modern Life*, 3rd ed. Glenview, Ill.: Scott, Foresman, 1964.

COLVIN, BILL D. "Computer Crime Investigators: A New Training Field," *FBI Law Enforcement Bulletin* 28 (July 1979) 9–12.

COMMITTEE ON CHILD PSYCHIATRY OF THE GROUP FOR THE ADVANCEMENT OF PSYCHIATRY, *Psychopathological Disorders in Childhood: Theoretical Considerations and a Proposed Classification*. New York: Aronson, 1966 and 1974.

Congressional Record, Proceedings and Debates of the 96th Congress, 1st sess., vol. 125, no. 7, January 25, 1979.

CONKLIN, JOHN E., ed. *The Crime Establishment: Organized Crime and American Society*. Englewood Cliffs, N.J.: Prentice-Hall, 1973.

CONRAD, JOHN P. *Crime and Its Correction.* Berkeley: University of California Press, 1965.

COOKE, JAMES. "The Invisible Enterprise," *Forbes,* September 29, 1980, 60–71.

COOLEY, CHARLES HORTON. *Social Organization.* New York: Scribner's, 1909.

CORMIER, MIRIAM KENNEDY, JADWIGA SANGOWICA, AND MICHEL TROTTIER. "The Problem of Recidivism and Treatment of the Latecomer to Crime," *Canadian Journal of Corrections* 3 (1961), 51–65.

COTLOW, LEWIS. *The Twilight of the Primitive.* New York: Macmillan, 1971.

CRESSEY, D. B. "Application and Verification of the Differential Association Theory," *Journal of Criminal Law and Criminology* 43 (May–June 1952), 51–52.

CRESSEY, DONALD R., AND DAVID A. WARD. *Delinquency, Crime, and Social Process.* New York: Harper & Row, 1969.

Crime and Seasonality. Washington, D.C.: Bureau of Justice Statistics, May, 1980.

Crime in the United States—1980: Uniform Crime Reports. Washington, D.C.: Federal Bureau of Investigation, released September 10, 1981.

Criminology—A Bibliography: Research and Theory in the United States 1945-1972. Philadelphia: Center for Studies in Criminology and Criminal Law, University of Pennsylvania, 1974.

CROMBIE, A. C. *Medieval and Early Modern Science.* New York: Doubleday, 1972.

CROY, HOMER. *Jesse James Was My Neighbor.* New York: Duell, Sloan, and Pierce, 1949.

D'ASARO, B., C. GROSBECK, AND C. NIGRO. "Diet-Vitamin Program for Jail Inmates," *Journal of Orthopsychiatry* 5 (1975).

DAVENPORT, C. B. *The Nam Family.* Lancaster, Pa.: New Era, 1912.

DAVID, DEBORAH. "March for Independence in Africa and Abroad," *The Burning Spear, African People's Socialist Party* 3 (May 15–June 15, 1974).

DAVIS, ALAN J. "Sexual Assaults in the Philadelphia Prison System," *Trans-Action* 6 (December 1968), 8–16.

DE BEAUMONT, GUSTAV, AND ALEXIS DE TOCQUEVILLE. *On the Penitentiary System in the United States and Its Application in France.* Carbondale, Ill.: Southern Illinois University Press, Arcturus Books edition, 1979; first published in 1833.

DE QUIROS, C. B. "Enrico Ferri," in *Encyclopedia of the Social Sciences,* vol. IV. New York: Macmillan, 1931.

DEWEY, JOHN. *Human Nature and Conduct.* New York: Holt, 1922.

Diagnostic and Statistical Manual of Mental Disorders, 3rd ed., Washington, D.C.: American Psychiatric Association, 1980.

DIAZ, CARMEN. "A Study of the Ability of 11th Grade Girls to Apply the Principles of Moral Law to Actual and Hypothetical Life Situations," unpublished Ph.D. dissertation, Fordham University, 1952.

DIDATO, SALVATOR V. "Delinquents in Group Therapy: Some New Techniques," in C. J. Sager and H. S. Kaplan, eds., *Progress in Group and Family Therapy.* New York: Brunner/Mazel, 1972.

DOMINIC, M. "Religion and the Juvenile Delinquent," *American Catholic Sociological Review* 15 (October 1954), 256–64.

DUGDALE, RICHARD. *The Jukes*. New York: Putnam, 1877.

DUNCAN, J. T., AND MARC CAPLAN, comp. *White-Collar Crime: A Selected Bibliography*. Washington, D.C.: National Criminal Justice Reference Service, U.S. Dept. of Justice, September 1980.

DURKHEIM, EMILE. *Suicide*. New York: Free Press, 1951; originally published in 1897 as translated by John A. Spaulding and George Simpson.

_____. *The Rules of the Sociological Method*. Glencoe, Ill.: Glencoe Press, 1959; originally published in 1894.

DYMOND, ROSALIND F. "A Scale for the Measurement of Empathic Ability," *Journal of Consulting Psychology* 13 (1949), 127–33.

EISSLER, K. R., ed. *Searchlights on Delinquency: New Psychoanalytic Studies*. New York: International Universities Press, 1949.

ELLIS, J. W. "Classification as the Basis for Rehabilitation of Prisoners," *New Bulletin*, National Society of Penal Information 2 (February 1931).

EMPEY, LaMar T. "Delinquent Theory and Recent Research," *Journal of Research in Crime and Delinquency* 4 (January 1967) 32–42.

_____, AND JEROME RABOW. "The Provo Experiment in Delinquency Prevention," *American Sociological Review* 26 (October 1961), 679–95.

ERICKSON, E. H. *Childhood and Society*. New York: Norton, 1950.

ERICKSON, M. L. "Group Violations, Socioeconomic Status and Official Delinquency," *Social Forces* 52 (September 1962), 41–52.

ERNST, JOHN L. "An Analysis of Religious and Ethical Habits of a Group of Convicts," *University of Pittsburgh Bulletin* 27 (November 15, 1930), 47–53.

EYNON, T. G., AND W. C. RECKLESS. "Companionship at Delinquency Onset," *British Journal of Criminology* 12 (October 1961), 162–70.

EYSENCK, S. B. G., AND H. J. EYSENCK. "Crime and Personality: An Empirical Study of the Three-Factor Theory," *British Journal of Criminology* 10 (1970), 225–39.

EZORSKY, GERTRUDE. *Philosophical Perspectives on Punishment*. Albany, N.Y.: State University of New York Press, 1972.

FAGAN, JOAN, AND IRMA LEE SHEPHERD, eds. *Gestalt Therapy Now*. New York: Harper & Row, 1970.

FALEK, ARTHUR, RAY CRADDICK, AND JULIUS COLLUM. "An Attempt to Identify Prisoners with an XYY Chromosome Complement by Psychiatric and Psychological Means," *Journal of Nervous and Mental Disease* 150 (1970), 165–70.

FARRIS, E. J., E. H. YEAKEL, AND H. S. MEDOFF. "Development of Hypertension in Emotional Gray Norway Rats after Air Blasting," *American Journal of Physiology* 144 (1945), 331–33.

FATTAH, EZZAT A. "A Critique of Deterrence Research with Particular Reference to the Economic Approach," *Canadian Journal of Criminology* 25 (January 1983).

FBI Law Enforcement Bulletin, vol. 28, no. 7, July 1979.

FENTON, NORMAN, ERNEST G. REIMER, AND HARRY A. WILMER. *The Correctional Community: An Introduction and Guide.* Berkeley: University of California Press, 1967.

FERDINAND, THEODORE N. *Typologies of Delinquency: A Critical Analysis.* New York: Random House, 1966.

FERRACUTI, FRANCO, AND MARVIN E. WOLFGANG. "Clinical vs. Sociological Criminology: Separation or Integration?" *Excerpta Criminologica*, July –August 1964, 407–10.

Final Report of the Grand Jury, Miami. Circuit Court of Florida in and for the County of Dade, fall term, 1981.

FINCHER, JACK. "The Terman Study Is 50 Years Old," *Human Behavior* 2 (March 1973), 8–15.

FINLEY, K. THOMAS. *Mental Dynamics: Power Thinking for Personal Success.* Englewood Cliffs, N.J.: Prentice-Hall, 1966.

FISCHER, C. S. "On Urban Alienations and Anomie: Powerlessness and Social Isolation," *American Sociological Review* 38 (June 1973), 311–26.

FISHER, SEYMOUR. *The Female Orgasm.* New York: Basic Books, 1973.

FITZGERALD, R. V. *Conjoint Marital Therapy.* New York: Aronson, 1973.

FOX, R. G. "The XYY Offender: A Modern Myth?" *Journal of Criminal Law, Criminology and Police Science* 62 (March 1971), 59–73.

FOX, VERNON. "The Effect of Juvenile Institutionalization on Adjustment in Prison," unpublished master's thesis, Michigan State University, 1943.

_____. "The Effect of Counseling on Adjustment in Prison," *Social Forces* 32 (March 1954).

_____. *The Florida Prisoner: A Base Line Study of the Characteristics of the Prison Population of Florida with Special Reference to Mental Ill-Health.* Jacksonville: Florida Council on Mental Health Training and Research, 1961.

_____. "What Is a Crime?" *University of Florida Law Review* 16 (Fall 1963), 143–62.

_____. *Handbook for Volunteers in Juvenile Court.* Reno, Nev.: National Council of Juvenile Court Judges, 1973.

_____. *Violence behind Bars.* Westpoint, Conn.: Greenwood, 1974; originally published in New York, 1956.

FRANKLIN, S. D. *Measurement of the Comprehension of the Precepts and Parables of Jesus.* Iowa City: University of Iowa Press, 1929.

FRANKS, CYRIL M., AND G. TERENCE WILSON, eds. *Annual Review of Behavior Therapy Theory and Practice.* New York: Brunner/Mazel, 1973.

FREEMAN, WALTER. "Psychosurgery," in Silvano Arieti, ed., *American Handbook of Psychiatry*, vol. II. New York: Basic Books, 1959.

FREUD, SIGMUND. *Civilization and Its Discontents.* London: Hogarth, 1953; originally published in 1930 as translated by Joan Riviere.

————. *Group Psychology and the Analysis of the Ego.* London: Hogarth, 1922.

FRIEDLANDER, KATE. *The Psychoanalytic Approach to Juvenile Delinquency.* London: International Universities Press, 1949.

FRIEDRICHS, ROBERT W. "The Potential Impact of B. F. Skinner upon American Sociology," *American Sociologist* 9 (February 1974).

FROMM, ERICH. *Escape from Freedom.* New York: Rinehart, 1941.

FRY, HENRY P. *The Modern Ku Klux Klan.* New York: Negro University Press, 1969; originally published by Sinall Maynard, Boston, 1922.

GADDIS, THOMAS E. *The Birdman of Alcatraz.* New York: New American Library, 1956.

————, AND JAMES O. LONG. *Killer: A Journal of Murder.* New York: Macmillan, 1970.

GAGNÉ, DENIS. "Dans les concepts de la déviance et de la délinquance des mineurs," in Denis Szabo et al., *L'Adolescent et la société.* Brussels: Dessart, 1972.

GALL, FRANZ JOSEPH. *Origins of the Moral Qualities and Intellectual Facilities of Men, and the Conditions of Their Manifestations,* trans. by W. Lewis, Jr. Boston: Marsh, Kapen and Lyon, 1835.

GALLIHER, J. F., AND J. A. CAIN. "Citation Support for the Mafia Myth in Criminology Textbooks," *American Sociologist* 9 (May 1974), 68–74.

GARMON, WILLIAM S. *Who Are the Criminals?* Nashville: Broadman, 1968.

GAROFALO, RAFFAELE. *Criminology,* trans. by Robert W. Millar. Boston: Little, Brown, 1914.

GARRETT, HENRY E. *Great Experiments in Psychology.* New York: Appleton-Century, 1941.

GEIS, GILBERT. *Not the Law's Business?: An Examination of Homosexuality, Abortion, Prostitution, Narcotics, and Gambling in the United States.* Washington, D.C.: National Institute of Health, 1972.

Gender Identity Clinics and Private Surgeons. Baton Rouge, La.: Erickson Educational Foundation, Apri 26, 1972.

GEORGIA, FLORITA. "Inquiry into the Causes of Crime," *Journal of Criminal Law, Criminology and Police Science* 44 (May–June 1953), 1–16.

GERARD, ROY. "Institutional Innovations in Juvenile Corrections," *Federal Probation* 34 (December 1970), 37–44.

GIBBONS, DON C. *Changing the Law Breaker: The Treatment of Delinquents and Criminals.* Englewood Cliffs, N.J.: Prentice-Hall, 1965.

————. *Society, Crime, and Criminal Careers.* Englewood Cliffs, N.J.: Prentice-Hall, 1968.

————, AND DONALD L. GARRITY. "Some Suggestions for the Development of Etiological and Treatment Theory of Criminology," *Social Forces* 38 (October 1963), 51–58.

GIBRAN, KAHLIL. *The Prophet,* New York: Alfred A. Knopf, 1973. Originally published 1923.

GILBERT, J. A. "Researches on Mental and Physical Development of School Children," *Studies of the Yale Psychological Laboratory* 2 (1894), 40–100.

GILCH, K. R. "Parolee House," *Youth Authority Quarterly* 24 (Winter 1972), 3–12.

GILL, H. B. "An Operational View of Criminology," *Archives of Criminal Psychodynamics* 49 (October 1957).

GILLILAND, A. R. "The Attitude of College Students toward God and the Church," *Journal of Social Psychology* 11 (1940), 11–18.

GILLIN, JOHN L. *Criminology and Penology*. New York: Appleton-Century-Crofts, 1945.

_____. *The Wisconsin Prisoner*. Madison: University of Wisconsin Press, 1946.

GINSBURG, BENSON E. "The Violent Brain: Is It Everyone's Brain?" in C. R. Jeffery, ed., *Biology and Crime*. Beverly Hills, Calif.: Sage, 1979, pp. 47–64.

GIULIANI, RUDOLPH. "Insanity Defense: Abolish in All But a Few Cases," *Justice Assistance News* 3 (October 1982).

GLASER, B., AND A. STRAUSS. *The Discovery of Grounded Theory*. London: Weidenfeld and Nicholson, 1968.

GLASER, DANIEL. "Review of Principles of Criminology," *Federal Probation* 20 (December 1956), 66–67.

_____. "The Sociological Approach to Crime and Corrections," *Law and Contemporary Problems* 23 (Autumn 1958), 681–702.

_____. *The Effectiveness of a Prison and Parole System*. Indianapolis: Bobbs-Merrill, 1964.

_____, ed. *Crime in the City*. New York: Harper & Row, 1970.

_____. "Politicalization of Prisoners: A New Challenge to American Penology," *American Journal of Corrections* 33 (November–December 1971), 6–9.

_____. *Adult Crime and Social Policy*. Englewood Cliffs, N.J.: Prentice-Hall, 1972.

_____, ed. *Handbook of Criminology*. Chicago: Rand McNally, 1974.

GLASS, JUSTINE. *They Foresaw the Future: The Fascinating Story of 6,000 Years of Fulfilled Prophecy*. New York: Putnam's 1969.

GLASSER, WILLIAM. *Reality Therapy*. New York: Harper & Row, 1965.

_____. *Schools without Failure*. New York: Harper & Row, 1969.

GLICK, RON. In *Victimology: An International Journal* 4 (1979), 403–407.

GLUECK, SHELDON. "Theory and Fact in Criminology," *British Journal of Delinquency* 7 (October 1956).

_____. *The Problem of Delinquency*. Boston: Houghton Mifflin, 1957.

_____, AND ELEANOR GLUECK. *Five Hundred Criminal Careers*. New York: Knopf, 1930.

_____, AND ELEANOR GLUECK. *Five Hundred Delinquent Women*. New York: Knopf, 1934a.

_____, AND ELEANOR GLUECK. *One Thousand Juvenile Delinquents*. Cambridge, Mass.: Harvard University Press, 1934b.

———, AND ELEANOR GLUECK. *Later Criminal Careers*. New York: Commonwealth Fund, 1937.

———, AND ELEANOR GLUECK. *Physique and Delinquency*. New York: Harper, 1956.

———, AND ELEANOR GLUECK. *Predicting Delinquency and Crime*. Cambridge, Mass.: Harvard University Press, 1959.

———, AND ELEANOR GLUECK. *Unraveling Juvenile Delinquency*. Cambridge, Mass.: Harvard University Press, 1966.

GODDARD, H. H. *Feeblemindedness: Its Causes and Consequences*. New York: Macmillan, 1914.

GODDARD, H. N. *The Kallikak Family*. New York: Macmillan, 1912.

GOFFMAN, ERVING. "The Moral Career of the Mental Patient," *Psychiatry* 22 (1959), 123–42.

GOITEIN, P. L. "Character Assay in Delinquency," in Robert M. Lindner and Robert V. Seliger, *Handbook of Correctional Psychology*. New York: Philosophical Library, 1947.

GOLDBERG, N. "Jews in the Police Records of Los Angeles, 1933–1947," *Yivo Annual of Jewish Social Science* 5 (1950), 266–91.

GOODMAN, LINDA. *Sun Signs*. New York: Taplinger, 1968.

GOODMAN, MORRIS. *Modern Numerology*. New York: Fleet, 1967.

GORDON, R. A., J. F. SHORT, JR., D. S. CARTWRIGHT, AND F. L. STRODTBECK. "Values and Gang Delinquency: A Study of Street-Corner Groups," *American Journal of Sociology* 69 (September 1963), 109–28.

GORING, CHARLES. *The English Convict: A Statistical Study*. London: His Majesty's Stationery Office, 1913.

GOULD, JULIUS, AND W. L. KOLB, eds. *A Dictionary of the Social Sciences*. New York: Free Press of Glencoe, 1964.

GOULDNER, A. W. *The Coming Crisis of Western Sociology*. New York: Avon, 1970.

GRAMATICA, FILLIPPO. *Principes de defense sociale*. Paris: Cujas, 1963.

The Great Ideas: A Syntopicon of Great Books of the Western World. Chicago: Encyclopedia Britannica, 1952.

GREEN, HANNAH. *I Never Promised You a Rose Garden*. New York: Signet, 1964.

GREEN, RICHARD, AND JOHN MONEY, eds. *Transsexualism and Sex Reassignment*. Baltimore: Johns Hopkins Press, 1969.

GREEN, WAYNE E. "Swinging Pendulum: Burger Court Rulings Please Police, and More of Same Are Likely," *Wall Street Journal*, February 14, 1974.

GREER, SCOTT. *The Emerging City: Myth and Reality*. New York: Free Press, 1962.

GRISWOLD, H. JACK, MIKE MISENHEIMER, ART POWERS, AND ED TROMANHAUSER. *An Eye for an Eye*. New York: Pocket Books, 1972.

GRUPP, STANLEY E., ed. *Theories of Punishment.* Bloomington: Indiana University Press, 1971.

GUHL, F. A. M. "The Social Order of Chickens," *Scientific American,* February 1956, 42–46.

HAHN, PAUL H. *The Juvenile Offender and the Law.* Cincinnati: Anderson, 1971.

HALL, C. A. "A Comparative Psychologist's Approach to Problems in Abnormal Psychology," *Journal of Abnormal and Social Psychology* 28 (1933), 1–5.

HALLECK, SEYMOUR. *Psychiatry and the Dilemmas of Crime.* New York: Hoeber Medical Books, 1967.

HALLETT, ROBIN. *Africa to 1875.* Ann Arbor: University of Michigan Press, 1970.

Handbook of Case Work in Classification Methods for Offenders. New York: American Prison Association, 1934.

Handbook of Correctional Psychiatry, vol. I. Washington, D.C.: United States Bureau of Prisons, 1968.

HANEY, BILL, AND MARTIN GOLD. "The Juvenile Delinquent Nobody Knows," *Psychology Today,* September 1973, 49–52.

HARDMAN, DALE G. "The Constructive Use of Authority," *NPPA Journal* 6 (July 1960).

HARNO, BRUCE, E. W. BURGESS, AND JOHN LANDESCO. *Parole and the Indeterminate Sentence.* Springfield, Ill.: State of Illinois, 1928.

HARRIS, THOMAS. *I'm OK—You're OK.* New York: Harper & Row, 1967.

HARTSHORNE, HUGH. *Studies in Deceit.* New York: Macmillan, 1928.

_____, and M. A. MAY. "Recent Improvements in Devices for Rating Character," *Journal of Social Psychology* 1 (1930), 66–77.

HASKELL, M. R. "Toward a Reference Group Theory," *Social Problems* 8 (Winter 1960–61) 220–30.

HASLAM, PHYLLIS. *The Woman Offender.* Toronto: John Howard Association of Ontario, 1973.

HASSLER, ALFRED. *The Diary of a Self-Made Convict.* Chicago: Regnery, 1954.

HAVIGHURST, ROBERT J., AND HILDA TABA. *Adolescent Character and Personality.* New York: Wiley, 1949.

HAWKINS, GORDON, AND FRANKLIN ZIMRING. *Deterrence.* Chicago: University of Chicago Press, 1973.

HAYS, D. G., AND R. R. BUSH. "A Study of Group Actions," *American Sociological Review* 19 (1954), 693–701.

HEALY, WILLIAM. *The Individual Delinquent.* Boston: Little, Brown, 1915.

_____, AND AUGUSTA BRONNER. *Delinquents and Criminals: Their Making and Unmaking.* New York: Macmillan, 1926.

_____, AND AUGUSTA BRONNER. *New Light on Delinquency and Its Treatment.* New Haven, Conn.: Yale University Press, 1936.

HEATH, JAMES. *Eighteenth Century Penal Theory*. New York: Oxford University Press, 1963.

HEFFERLINE, R. F., AND LOUIS J. J. BRUNO, "The Psychophysiology of Private Events," in David Shapiro et al., eds., *BioFeedback and Self-Control—1972*. Chicago: Aldine, 1973.

HELLINE, QUENTIN. "The Recruitment for Community Involvement," *American Correctional Congress of Correction Proceedings—1971*. College Park, Md.: American Correctional Association, 1972.

HENDERSON, D. K. *Psychopathic States*. New York: Philosophical Library, 1939.

HERRNSTEIN, R. J. "I.Q.: Measurement of Race and Class?" *Society* 10 (May–June 1973), 5.

HEWITT, L. E., AND R. L. JENKINS. *Fundamental Patterns of Maladjustment: The Dynamics of Their Origins*. Springfield, Ill.: State of Illinois, 1946.

HILL, NAPOLEON, AND W. CLEMENT STONE. *Success through Positive Mental Attitude*. Englewood Cliffs, N.J.: Prentice-Hall, 1960.

HINDELANG, M. J. "The Commitment of Delinquents to Their Misdeeds: Do Delinquents Drift?" *Social Problems* 14 (1970), 502–9.

———. "A Learning Theory Analysis of the Correctional Process," *Issues in Criminology* 5 (Winter 1970).

HINSIE, L. E., AND ROBERT J. CAMPBELL. *Psychiatric Dictionary*, 4th ed. New York: Oxford University Press, 1970.

HIPPCHEN, LEONARD J., ed. *Ecologic-Biochemical Approaches to Treatment of Delinquents and Criminals*. New York: Van Nostrand, 1978.

HIPPLER, ARTHUR E., AND STEPHEN CONN. *Northern Eskimo Laws and Their Relationship to Contemporary Problems of "Bush Justice."* Fairbanks: University of Alaska Institute of Social, Economic and Government Research, 1973.

HIRSCHI, TRAVIS. *Causes of Delinquency*. Berkeley: University of California Press, 1969.

HOFFER, ABRAM. "Crime, Punishment, and Treatment," *Journal of Orthopsychiatry* 3 (1979).

———. "Nutritional Therapy," in L. J. Hippchen, ed., *Holistic Approaches to Offender Rehabilitation*. Springfield, Ill.: Thomas, 1982, pp. 207–36.

HOFFER, ERIC. "New Roles for Retirees," *Modern Maturity* 16 (June–July 1973).

HOFFMAN-BUSTAMANTE, DALE. "The Nature of Female Criminality," *Issues in Criminology* 8 (Fall 1973), 117–36.

HOLLAND, BERNARD C., AND RICHARD S. WARD. "Homeostasis and Psychosomatic Medicine," chap. 23 in Silvano Arieti, ed., *American Handbook of Psychiatry*. New York: Basic Books.

HOLLIS, FLORENCE. *Casework: Psychosocial Therapy*. New York: Random House, 1964.

HOLMES, OLIVER WENDELL. *Collected Legal Papers*. Gloucester, Mass.: Peter Smith Publications, 1920.

HOMANS, GEORGE C. *The Human Group*. New York: Harcourt, Brace, 1950.

_____. "Commentary," in Herman Turk and Richard L. Simpson, eds., *Institutions and Social Exchange: The Sociologies of Talcott Parsons and George C. Homans.* Indianapolis: Bobbs-Merrill, 1971.

HOMER, F. D. *Guns and Garlic: Myths and Realities of Organized Crime.* West Lafayette, Ind.: Purdue University Studies, 1974.

HOOTEN, EARNEST. *Crime and the Man.* Cambridge, Mass.: Harvard University Press, 1939.

HOSKINS, R. G. *Endocrinology.* New York: Norton, 1941.

HOYER, NIELS. *Man into Woman: An Authentic Record of a Change of Sex.* New York: Dutton, 1933.

HUFFMAN, ARTHUR V. In the *1969 Annual Report of the Department of Public Safety.* Springfield: State of Illinois, 1970.

HUIE, WILLIAM BRADFORD. *Ruby McCollum: Woman in the Suwannee Jail.* New York: Dutton, 1956.

HULL, C. *An Introduction to Behavior Theory Concerning the Individual Organism.* New Haven, Conn.: Yale University Press, 1952.

HUMPHREYS, LAUD. *Tearoom Trade.* Chicago: Aldine, 1970.

IANNI, FRANCIS A. J. "New Mafia: Black, Hispanic and Italian Styles," *Society* 11 (March–April 1974), 26–39.

Information on Transsexualism for Law Enforcement Officers. Baton Rouge, La.: Erickson Educational Foundation, August 1973.

JACOBS, PATRICIA A., MURIEL BRUTON, AND MARIE MELVILLE. "Aggressive Behavior, Mental Subnormality and the XYY Male," *Nature* 208 (December 25, 1965).

JAFFE, A. J., AND S. D. ALINSKY. "A Comparison of Jewish and Non-Jewish Convicts," *Jewish Social Studies* 1 (1939), 359–66.

JAMES, PRESTON E. *An Outline of Geography.* New York: Ginn, 1935.

JAMES, WILLIAM. *The Varieties of Religious Experience: A Study of Human Nature.* New York: Modern Library, 1936; originally published New York: Longmans, Green, 1902.

JEFFERY, C. R. "An Integrated Theory of Crime and Criminal Behavior," *Journal of Criminal Law, Criminology and Police Science* 49 (March–April 1959) 533–52.

_____. *Crime Prevention through Environment Design.* Beverly Hills, Calif.: Sage, 1971.

_____, ed. *Biology and Crime.* Beverly Hills, Calif: Sage, 1979.

JENNINGS, HELEN H. *Leadership and Isolation.* New York: Longmans, Green, 1943.

JESNESS, C. F. "Preston Typology Study: Final Report." Sacramento, Calif.: Institute for the Study of Crime and Delinquency in collaboration with the California Youth Authority, 1968 (mimeographed).

JOHNASEN, C. P. "A Re-Evaluation and Critique of the Logic and Some Methods of Shaw and McKay," *American Sociological Review* 14 (October 1949), 608–17.

JOHNSON, A. M. "Juvenile Delinquency," in Silvano Arieti, ed., *American Handbook of Psychiatry*, vol. I. New York: Basic Books, 1959.

JOHNSON, ELMER HUBERT. *Crime, Correction, and Society.* Homewood, Ill.: Dorsey, 1964 and 1968.

JOHNSON, T. F. "Treating the Juvenile Offender and His Family," *Juvenile Justice* 24 (November 1973), 41–45.

JONES, KATHRYN MILLER. *A Bibliography on Personal Violence: An Index for Understanding and Prevention, 1950–1971.* Houston: University of Texas at Houston, 1971.

JONES, LeROI (IMAMU AMEER BARAKA). "The Legacy of Malcolm X, and the Coming of the Black Nation," in Raymond F. Betts, ed., *The Ideology of Blackness.* Lexington, Mass.: Heath, 1971.

KAHN, EUGENE. *Psychopathic Personalities.* New Haven, Conn.: Yale University Press, 1931.

KALMER, LEO, AND ELIGIUS WEIR. *Crime and Religion.* Chicago: Franciscan Herald Press, 1936.

KANN, JAMES. "Social Scientists' Role in Selection of Juries Sparks Legal Debate," *Wall Street Journal*, August 12, 1974.

KARACK, LOREN, AND ROBERT R. LEVINSON. "A Token Economy in a Correctional Institution for Youthful Offenders," *Howard Journal of Penology and Crime Prevention* 13 (1970).

KARPMAN, BENJAMIN. *Case Studies in the Psychopathology of Crime*, 4 vols. Washington, D.C.: Medical Sciences Press, 1939.

_____. *The Hangover: A Critical Study of the Psychodynamics of Alcoholism.* Springfield, Ill.: Thomas, 1957.

KELLER, OLIVER J., AND BENEDICT ALPER. *Halfway Houses.* Boston: Heath, 1970.

KELLER, R. "A Sociological Analysis of the Conflict and Critical Criminologies," Ann Arbor: University Microfilms; unpublished Ph.D. Dissertation, University of Montana, 1976.

KINSEY, W. E., AND ROBERT J. CAMPBELL. *Psychiatric Dictionary*, 4th ed. New York: Oxford University Press, 1970.

KITTRIE, NICHOLAS N. *The Right to Be Different: Deviance and Enforced Therapy.* Baltimore: Johns Hopkins Press, 1971.

KLEIN, MELANIE. In *International Journal of Psychoanalysis* 39 (1958), 84–90.

KLUCKHOHN, CLYDE, AND HENRY A. MURREY, eds. *Personality in Nature, Society, and Culture.* New York: Knopf, 1953.

KNIGHT, R. P. "Evaluation of the Results of Psychoanalytic Therapy," *American Journal of Psychiatry* 98 (1941), 434–46.

KOBLER, JOHN. *Capone: The Life and World of Al Capone.* New York: Putnam, 1971.

KOBRIN, SOLOMON. "The Conflict of Values in Delinquency Areas," *American Sociological Review* 16 (October 1951), 653–62.

KORN, RICHARD R., AND LLOYD W. McCORKLE. *Criminology and Penology*. New York: Holt, 1959.

KOZOL, HARRY L. "Provisional Guidelines for Diagnostic Identification of the Dangerous Person" (mimeographed).

_____, R. J. BOUCHER, AND R. R. GAROFALO. "The Diagnosis and Treatment of Dangerousness," *Crime and Delinquency* 18 (October 1972), 371–92.

KRAFT, I. A. "Child and Adolescent Group Psychotherapy," in H. I. Kaplan and B. J. Saddock, eds., *Comprehensive Group Psychotherapy*. Baltimore: Williams & Wilkins Company, 1971.

KRILL, D. F. "Existential Psychotherapy and the Problem of Anomie," *Social Work* 14 (1969), 33–49.

KROTH, J. A., AND MARVIN S. FORREST, "Effects of Posture and Anxiety Level on Effectiveness of Free Association," *Psychological Reports* 25 (1969).

KUHLMAN, H. R. *Biennial Report*. St. Paul: Minnesota State Board of Control, 1925–26.

KVARACEUS, W. C. "Delinquent Behavior and Church Attendance," *Sociology and Social Research* 28 (March 1944), 284–89.

_____. "Juvenile Delinquency and Social Class," *Journal of Educational Sociology* 18 (September 1944), 51–54.

_____. *Juvenile Delinquency and the School*. Yonkers, N.Y.: World Book, 1945.

_____. "Forecasting Juvenile Delinquency," *Journal of Education* 138 (April 1956), 1–43.

_____, AND W. B. MILLER. *Delinquent Behavior, Culture and the Individual*. Washington, D.C.: National Education Association, 1959.

LAITINEN, LAURI V., AND KENNETH E. LIVINGSTON, eds. *Surgical Approaches in Psychiatry*. Baltimore: University Park Press, 1973.

LANDIS, J. R., SIMON DINITZ, AND W. C. RECKLESS. "Implementing Two Theories of Delinquency: Value Orientation and Awareness of Limited Opportunity," *Sociology and Social Research* 47 (July 1963), 408–16.

LANG, KURT. "Alienation," in Julius Gould and William L. Kolb, eds., *A Dictionary of the Social Sciences*. New York: Free Press, 1964.

LANGS, ROBERT, ed. *The Technique of Psychoanalytic Psychotherapy*, vol. I. New York: Aronson, 1973.

LAROCHE, ERNEST, AND LOUIS TILLEY. "Weather and Crime in Tallahassee," *Journal of Criminal Law and Criminology* 47 (July–August 1956), 218–19.

LARSEN, RICHARD W. *Theodore Bundy: The Deliberate Strangler*. Englewood Cliffs, N.J.: Prentice-Hall, 1980.

LAUNE, FERRIS F. *Predicting Criminality*. Evanston, Ill.: Northwestern University Press, 1936.

LAVATER, J. K. *Essays on Physiognomy; For the Promotion of the Knowledge and the Love of Mankind*, trans. by P. Holcroft. London: G. G. and J. Robinson, 1789.

LEDERMAN, J. *Anger and the Rocking Chair: Gestalt Awareness with Children.* New York: McGraw-Hill, 1969.

LEE, HENRY. "The 10 Most Wanted Criminals of the Past 50 Years (1972)," *Liberty* 1 (Fall 1972).

LEIBOLD, PAUL F. "Catholic Doctrine and Philosophy of Correction," *American Correctional Association Centennial Congress of Correction Proceedings—1970.* College Park, Md.: American Correctional Association, 1971.

LEMERT, EDWIN. *Social Pathology.* New York: McGraw-Hill, 1951.

_____. *Human Deviance, Social Problems, and Social Control.* Englewood Cliffs, N.J.: Prentice-Hall, 1965.

LEMKAU, PAUL V. "Mental Hygiene," in Silvano Arieti, ed., *American Handbook of Psychiatry*, vol. II. New York: Basic Books, 1959.

LENTZ, W. P. "Rural-Urban Differentials in Juvenile Delinquency," *Journal of Criminal Law and Criminology* 47 (September–October 1956), 311–39.

LETKEMANN, PETER. *Crime as Work.* Englewood Cliffs, N.J.: Prentice-Hall, 1973.

LEWIN, KURT. *Field Theory in Social Science.* New York: Harper, 1951.

LIEBER, ARNOLD L. *The Lunar Effect: Biological Tides and Human Emotions,* Garden City, N.Y.: Anchor/Doubleday, 1978.

_____, AND CAROLYN R. SHERIN. "Homicides and the Lunar Cycle: Toward a Theory of Lunar Influence in Human Emotional Disturbance," *American Journal of Psychiatry* 129 (June 1972), 69–74.

LIGATO, JOHN, AND JAMES DEWEY. "Behavior Modification Principles—Now in an Institutional Setting," *American Journal of Correction* 36 (March–April 1974), 37–41.

LINDESMITH, ALFRED R., AND H. WARREN DUNHAM. "Some Principles of Criminal Typology," *Social Forces* 19 (March 1941), 307–14.

LINDNER, ROBERT. *Rebel without a Cause.* New York: Grune & Stratton, 1944.

_____, AND ROBERT V. SELIGER, eds. *Handbook of Correctional Psychology.* New York: Philosophical Library, 1947.

"Link between XYY Syndrome and Criminality Not Clear," *Public Health Reports* 89 (October 1969).

LISKA, A. E. "Interpreting the Causal Structure of Differential Association Theory," *Social Problems* 16 (1966), 485–92.

LOGAN, GUY B. H. *Masters of Crime.* London: Stanky Co., 1928.

LOMBROSO, CESARE. *L'uomo delinquente,* 5th ed. Torino: Fratelli Bocca, 1896.

_____. *Delitti vecahi e delitti nuovi.* Torino: Fratelli Bocca, 1902.

LONG, JEAN. "A Symbiotic Taxonomy for Corrections," *American Journal of Correction* 27 (November–December 1965), 4–7.

LONG, SHARON K., AND ANN D. WITTE. "Current Economic Trends: Implications for Crime and Criminal Justice," in D. N. Wright, ed., *Crime and Justice in a Declining Economy.* Cambridge, Mass.: Oelgeschlager, Gunn & Hain, 1981.

LOTTIER, STUART. "Distribution of Criminal Offenses in Metropolitan Regions," *Journal of Criminal Law and Criminology* 29 (1938–39), 39–43.

LOVE, ROBERTUS. *The Rise and Fall of Jesse James.* New York: Putnam, 1926.

LUNDEN, WALTER A. "Pioneers in Criminology—Emile Durkheim (1858–1917)." *Journal of Criminal Law, Criminology and Police Science* 49 (May–June 1958), 2–9.

LYFORD, GEORGE J. "Boat Theft," *FBI Law Enforcement Bulletin* 49 (October 1980).

McCANN, R. V. "The Self-Image and Delinquency," *Federal Probation* 20 (September 1956), 14–23.

McCORKLE, LLOYD W., ALBERT ELIAS, AND F. LOVELL BIXBY. *The Highfields Story.* New York: Holt, 1958.

McCOY, C. B., AND D. H. GONZALEZ. "Florida's Foreign-Born Population: A Growing Influence on Our Economy," *Dimensions* III (1982).

McKINNEY, JOHN C. *Constructed Typology and Social Theory.* New York: Appleton-Century-Crofts, 1966.

McLANE, E. D., M. A. O'BRIEN, AND S. A. WEMPLE. "A Comparison of the Effectiveness of the Teaching-Learning Process in Groups Participating and Not Participating in the Character Research Project," *Union College Student Character Research* 1 (1954) 63–78.

McWILLIAMS, CAREY. *Ill Fares The Land: Migrants and Migratory Labor in the United States.* Boston: Little, Brown and Company, 1942.

MACLEAN, DON. *Pictorial History of the Mafia.* New York: Myriad, 1974.

MacCORQUODALE, K., P. MEEHL, AND EDWARD C. TOLMAN. In A. T. Poffenberger, ed., *Modern Learning Theories.* New York: Appleton-Century-Crofts, 1954.

MAHRER, ALVIN R., AND LEONARD PEARSON, eds. *Creative Developments in Psychotherapy.* New York: Aronson, 1973.

MAIER, N. R. F., N. M. GLASER, AND J. B. KLEE. "Studies in Abnormal Behavior in the Rat, III. The Development of Behavior Fixation through Frustration," *Journal of Experimental Psychology* 26 (1940), 521–46.

MAKARIUS, LAURA. "The Crime of Manabozo," *American Anthropologist* 75 (June 1973), 633–75.

MANNHEIM, HERMANN, ed. *Pioneers in Criminology*, 2nd ed. Montclair, N.J.: Patterson Smith, 1973.

MANNLE, H. W. "An Empirical Exploration and Interpretation of Neutralization Theory Predicated upon Sexual Differences in The Socialization Process," unpublished Ph.D. dissertation, Florida State University, 1972.

_____, AND J. DAVID HIRSCHEL. *Fundamentals of Criminology.* Albany, New York: Delmar Publishers, 1982.

MARCUSE, H. *Eros and Civilization.* Boston: Beacon, 1955.

MARK, VERNON H., AND FRANK R. ERVIN. *Violence and the Brain.* New York: Harper & Row, 1970.

MARMOR, J. In *Archives of General Psychiatry* 3 (1960).

MARX, KARL. *Critique of Political Economy, 1859*. English trans. New York: International Library, 1904.

_____, AND FRIEDRICH ENGELS. *The Communist Manifesto*. London: J. E. Burhard, 1848. Current edition published New York: Washington Square Books, a division of Simon & Schuster, 1964. Also, current edition published Baltimore: Penguin, 1967.

MARYLAND DIVISION OF CORRECTION, "Penitentiary Gets Mental Health Clinic," *Newsletter* 4 (1973).

MASSERMAN, J. B. *The Practice of Dynamic Psychiatry*. Philadelphia: Saunders, 1955.

MASURE, R. H., AND W. C. ALLEE. "Flock Organization and Shell Parakeet *Melopsittaucus Undulatus Shaw*," *Ecology* 15 (1934a), 388–98.

_____, AND W. C. ALLEE. "The Social Order in Flocks in the Common Chicken and Pigeon," *Auk* 51 (1934b), 306–27.

MATZA, DAVID. *Delinquency and Drift*. New York: Wiley, 1964.

MAYO-SMITH, RICHMOND. *Statistics and Sociology*. Cambridge: Cambridge University Press, 1907.

MEAD, G. H. "The Sociology of Impunity Justice," *American Journal of Sociology* 23 (March 1918), 577–602.

MEARS, D. A. "Mental Disease and Cervical Spine Distortions," *ACA Journal of Chiropractic*, September 1965.

MEDNICK, SARNOFF, AND KARL O. CHRISTIANSEN, eds. *Biosocial Bases of Criminal Behavior*. New York: Gardner, 1977.

MEEHL, PAUL E. *Clinical vs. Statistical Prediction*. Minneapolis: University of Minnesota Press, 1954; 7th printing, 1973.

MEGARGEE, EDWIN I. *The Psychology of Violence and Aggression*. Morristown, N.J.: General Learning Press, 1972.

MENNINGER, KARL. *The Crime of Punishment*. New York: Viking, 1968.

Mental Disorders: Glossary and Guide to Their Classification in Accordance with the Ninth Revision of the International Classification of Diseases. Geneva: World Health Organization, 1978.

MERTON, R. K. "Social Structure and Anomie," *American Sociological Review* 3 (October 1938), 672–82.

_____. *Social Theory and Social Structure*. Glencoe, Ill.: Free Press, 1957.

_____, AND ASHLEY MONTAGU. "Crime and the Anthropologist," *American Anthropologist* 42 (July–September 1940).

METRO-DADE POLICE DEPARTMENT. *County Totals Offense Data—1980 Annual Report*, Miami, Fla.

MIDDLETON, WARREN C., AND PAUL J. FAY. "Attitudes of Delinquent and Non-Delinquent Girls towards Sunday Observances, the Bible and War," *Journal of Educational Psychology* 32 (October 1941), 555–58.

MILLER, CANDY. "Group Methods at Criswell House," unpublished manuscript, Florida State University School of Criminology, Tallahassee, 1971.

MILLER, N. "Extensions of Liberalized S-R Theory," in S. Koch, ed., *Psychology: A Study of Science, II.* New York: McGraw-Hill, 1959.

MILLER, WALTER B. "Lower-Class Culture as a Generating Milieu of Gang Delinquency," *Journal of Social Issues* 14 (1958), 5–19.

_____. "Implications of Urban Lower-Class Culture for Social Work," *Social Service Review* 33 (September 1959), 219–36.

MILLS, CLARENCE A. *Climate Makes the Man.* New York: Harper, 1942.

MINOR, JOHN R. "Church Membership and Commitment to Prisons," *Human Biology* 3 (September 1931), 429–36.

MINUCHIN, SALVADOR, BRAULIO MONTALVO, BERNARD G. GUERNEY, JR., BERNICE L. ROSMAN, AND FLORENCE SCHUMER. *Families of the Slums: An Exploration of Their Structure and Treatment.* New York: Basic Books, 1967.

MONAGHAN, WILLIAM J. "HEW Report on Chiropractic," in *The Best of Law and Medicine, 1968–70.* Chicago: American Medical Association, 1970.

MONEY, JOHN, AND ANKE A. ERHARDT. *Man and Woman, Boy and Girl.* Baltimore: Johns Hopkins University Press, 1973.

MONTAGU, ASHLEY. "The Biologist Looks at Crime," *The Annals* 217 (September 1941).

_____. "Chromosomes and Crime," *Psychology Today* 2 (October 1968), 43–49.

MONTGOMERY, RANDAL. "The Outlaw Motorcycle Subculture," *Canadian Journal of Criminology and Corrections* 19 (October 1977), 356–61.

MOORE, T. V. *The Driving Forces of Human Nature and Their Adjustment: An Introduction to the Psychology and Psychopathology of Emotional Behavior and Volitional Control.* New York: Grune & Stratton, 1948.

MORENO, JACOB L. *Who Shall Survive?: Foundations of Sociometry, Group Sociotherapy, and Sociodrama.* New York: Beacon, 1953; first ed.: *Who Shall Survive?* Nervous and Mental Diseases Publishing Co., Washington, D.C., 1934.

MORLEY, JACKSON, ed. *Crimes and Punishment,* vol. I. New York: Symphonette, 1973.

MORRIS, ALBERT. In *Harvard Law Review* 70 (February 1957), 753–58.

_____. "The Comprehensive Classification of Adult Offenders," *Journal of Criminal Law, Criminology and Police Science* 56 (June 1967), 197–202.

MORRIS, NORVAL, AND DONALD BUCKLE. "The Humanitarian Theory of Punishment: A Reply to C. S. Lewis," *20th Century* 6 (Summer 1962), 20–26.

_____, AND GORDON HAWKINS. *The Honest Politician's Guide to Crime Control.* Chicago: University of Chicago Press, 1970.

MORRIS, TERENCE. *The Criminal Area.* London: Routledge & Kegan Paul, 1958.

MPITSOS, C. J., AND W. J. DAVIS. "Learning: Classical and Avoidance Conditioning on the Mollusk Pleurobranchaea," *Science* 180 (April 20, 1973), 317–20.

MUDGE, E. L. *Our Pupils: Psychology for Church School Teachers*. New York: Methodists Books, 1930.

MUELLER, GERHARD O. W. *Crime, Law and the Scholars*. Seattle: University of Washington Press, 1969.

MURCHISON, CARL. "American White Criminal Intelligence," *Journal of Criminal Law and Criminology* 15 (August 1924), 154–57.

_____. *Criminal Intelligence*. Worcester, Mass.: Clark University Press, 1926.

NÁDVORNIK, P., J. POGÁDY, AND M. SRAMKA. "The Results of Stereotactic Treatment of the Aggressive Syndrome," in L. V. Laitinen and K. E. Livingston, eds., *Surgical Approaches in Psychiatry*. Baltimore: University Park Press, 1973.

NASH, IRWIN. "American Migrant Workers," *Society* 11 (March–April 1974).

NASH, JAY ROBERT. *Bloodletters and Badmen: A Narrative Encyclopedia of American Criminals from the Pilgrims to the Present*. New York: Evans and Co., distributed in association with Lippincott, 1973.

NATIONAL ACADEMY OF SCIENCES. *Deterrence and Incapacitation*. Washington, D.C., 1978.

NATIONAL INSTITUTE OF MENTAL HEALTH, ALCOHOL, DRUG ABUSE, AND MENTAL HEALTH ADMINISTRATION. *How You Can Handle Pressure*. Rockville, Md.: NIMH, April 1973.

NEBELKOPF, ETHAN. "Holistic Programs for the Drug Addict and Alcoholic," in L. J. Hippchen, ed., *Holistic Approaches to Offender Rehabilitation*. Springfield, Ill.: Thomas, 1982.

NEIL, ANDREW. "Dateline: Miami, April 15, 1992," *The Economist* (London), Vol. 285, No. 7259, October 16, 1982, After p. 66, pp. 1-26.

NELSON, VICTOR F. *Prison Days and Nights*. Boston: Little, Brown, 1932.

NETTLER, GWYNN. *Explaining Crime*. New York: McGraw-Hill, 1974.

NEWCOMB, T. M. *Social Psychology*. New York: Dryden, 1950.

NEWMAN, GRAEME. *The Punishment Response*. New York: Lippincott, 1978.

NEWMAN, H. H. *Multiple Human Births: Twins, Triplets, Quadruplets, and Quintuplets*. New York: Doubleday, 1940.

NIDEFFER, R. M. "Alpha and the Development of Human Potential," in David Shapiro et al., eds., *Biofeedback and Self-Control—1972*. Chicago: Aldine, 1973.

NOLAN, WILLIAM A. *Healing: A Doctor in Search of a Miracle*. New York: Random House, 1974.

NOVEY, SAMUEL. *The Second Look: The Reconstruction of Personal History in Psychiatry and Psychoanalysis*. Baltimore: Johns Hopkins Press, 1968.

OESTERREICH, TRAUGOTT K. *Possession and Exorcism*, trans. by D. Ibberson. New York: Causeway Books, 1974.

OHLIN, LLOYD E. *Selection for Parole*. New York: Russell Sage Foundation, 1951.

OPP, K. D. "Problems of Classification in Criminology," in *Methodological As-*

pects of Classification in Criminology, in the series *Collected Studies in Criminological Research*, vol. X. Strasbourg: Council of Europe, 1973.

ORSAGH, THOMAS, AND ANN D. WITTE. "Economic Status and Law: Implications for Offender Rehabilitation," *Journal of Criminal Law and Criminology* 72 (July–August 1981), 1055–1071.

OSTOW, MORTIMER, AND BEN-AMI SCHARFSTEIN. *The Need to Believe: The Psychology of Religion.* New York: International Universities Press, 1954.

OVERHOLSER, WINFRED. "Isaac Ray," in Hermann Mannheim, ed., *Pioneers in Criminology*, 2nd ed. Monclair, N.J.: Patterson Smith, 1973.

PABON, EDWARD. *The Relationship between Youth Crime and Employment—An Assessment of Impact.* New York: Community Service Society, 1981.

PALM, ROSE, AND DAVID ABRAHAMSEN. "A Rorschach Study of the Wives of Sex Offenders," *The Journal of Mental and Nervous Diseases*, 119 (February 1954), 167–72.

PALMER, T. B. *Personality Characteristics and Professional Orientations of Five Groups of Community-Treatment-Project Workers: A Preliminary Report on Differences among Treaters.* Sacramento, Calif.: Community-Treatment-Project Report Series No. 1, 1967.

PANKEN, SHIRLEY. *The Joy of Suffering.* New York: Aronson, 1973.

PAR, R. E., AND E. W. BURGESS. *Introduction to Science of Sociology.* Chicago: University of Chicago Press, 1924.

PARKER, D. B. "Step-by-Step Approach to Computer Security," *Security World* 16 (September 1979).

PARMELEE, MAURICE F. *The Principles of Anthropology and Sociology in Their Relations to Criminal Procedure.* New York: Macmillan, 1908.

_____. *Criminology.* New York: Macmillan, 1922 and 1924.

PARSONS, TALCOTT. "Illness and the Role of the Physician: A Sociological Perspective," *American Journal of Orthopsychiatry* 21, (1951a).

_____. *The Social System.* New York: Free Press, 1951b.

PAUL, JULIUS. "Return of Punitive Sterilization Proposals," *Law and Society Review* 3 (1968).

PEALE, NORMAN VINCENT. *The Power of Positive Thinking.* Englewood Cliffs, N.J.: Prentice-Hall, 1952 and 1956; subsequently reprinted several times by Fawcett Publications.

PELFREY, WILLIAM V. "The Influence of the New Criminology on the Study of Crime," unpublished Ph.D. dissertation, Florida State University, Tallahassee, 1978.

PERLS, FREDERICK S. "Four Lectures," in Joan Fagan and Irma Lee Shepherd, eds., *Gestalt Therapy Now.* New York: Harper & Row, 1970.

PETERSON, R., H. C. QUAY, AND G. R. CAMERON. "Personality and Background Factors in Juvenile Delinquency as Inferred from Questionnaire Responses," *Journal of Consulting Psychology* 23 (1959), 305–9.

PHELPS, H. A. *Principles and Laws of Sociology.* New York, 1936.

PLATT, ANTHONY. "Prospects for a Radical Criminology in the United States," *Crime and Social Justice* 1 (Spring–Summer 1974), 2–10.

POLLAK, OTTO. *The Criminality of Women*. Philadelphia: University of Pennsylvania Press, 1950.

POLSTER, E., AND M. POLSTER. *Gestalt Therapy Integrated*. New York: Brunner/Mazel, 1973.

PORTER, MARGARET E., AND IRENE R. KIERNAN. "A Study of Behavior Disorder Correlations between Parents and Children," *American Journal of Orthopsychiatry* 33 (April 1963).

POSPISIL, LEOPOLD. *Anthropology of Law: A Comparative Theory*. New York: Harper, 1971.

POUND, ROSCOE. *Criminal Justice in America*. New York: Holt, 1930.

POWELL, J. C. *The American Siberia: Or Fourteen Years' Experience in a Southern Convict Camp*. Montclair, N.J.: Patterson Smith, 1970; originally published in Chicago, 1891.

PRATT, J. H. "The Tuberculosis Class: An Experiment in Home Treatment," *Proceedings of the New York Conference on Hospital Social Service* IV (1917), 49–68.

PRICE, BARBARA RAFFEL, AND NATALIE J. SOKOLOFF, eds. *The Criminal Justice System and Women: Women Offenders - Victims - Workers*. New York: Clark Boardman Company, Ltd., 1982.

PRICE, THELMA, AND WHATMORE, P. B. "Behavior Disorders and Patterns of Crime among XYY Males Identified at a Maximum Security Hospital," *British Medical Journal*, March 4, 1967, 533–36.

PRICHARD, J. C. *A Treatise on Insanity and Other Disorders Affecting the Mind*. London: Sherwood, Gilbert & Piper, 1835.

QUAGLIANO, JAMES V. *Chemistry*. Englewood Cliffs, N.J.: Prentice-Hall, 1958.

QUAY, H. C. "Personality Dimensions in Delinquent Males as Inferred from Factor Analysis of Behavior Ratings," *Journal of Research in Crime and Delinquency* 1 (1964), 33–37.

_____. *Juvenile Delinquency: Research and Theory*. New York: Van Nostrand, 1965.

QUETELET, ADOLPH. *Sur l'Homme et le developpement de ses facultes: Saessai de physique sociale*. Paris: Bachelier, 1835.

QUINNEY, RICHARD, AND JOHN WILDEMAN. *The Problem of Crime: A Critical Introduction to Criminology*, 2nd ed., New York: Harper & Row, 1977.

RADKE, MARIAN, HELEN G. TRAEGER, AND HADASSAH DAVIS. "Social Perception and Attitudes of Children," *Genetic Psychology Monographs* 40 (1949), 327–447.

RADZINOWICZ, LEON. "Variability in the Sex Ratio of Criminality," *Sociological Review* 29 (January 1937), 76–102.

RAWLS, JOHN. "Rule Utilitarianism," in G. Ezorsky, ed., *Philosophical Perspectives on Punishment*. Albany: State University of New York Press, 1972.

RECKLESS, WALTER C. "An Experimental Basis for Revision of Correctional Programs," *Federal Probation* 6 (January–March 1942), 24–26.

_____. "A New Theory of Criminal Behavior," *Federal Probation* 25 (December 1961a), 42–46.

_____. "A New Theory of Delinquency and Crime," *Federal Probation* 25 (December 1961b), 42–46.

_____. *The Crime Problem*, 5th ed. New York: Appleton-Century-Crofts, 1973; first published 1950.

_____, SIMON DINITZ, AND ELLEN MURRAY, "Self-Concept as an Insulator against Delinquency," *American Sociological Review* 21 (December 1956), 744–46.

REES, ELIZABETH LODGE. "Aluminum Toxicity As Indicated by Hair Analysis," *Journal of Orthomolecular Psychiatry* 1 (1979), 37–43.

_____. "Diagnosis of Growth-Developmental Malfunctioning," in Leonard J. Hippchen, ed., *Holistic Approaches to Offender Rehabilitation*. Springfield, Ill.: Thomas, 1982, pp. 134–54.

REID, J. E. *The Reid Report*. Chicago: Reid, 1967.

REID, SUE TITUS. *Crime and Criminology*, 2nd ed. New York: Holt, Rinehart and Winston, 1979.

REIK, THEODOR. "The Unknown Murderer," in Harold Greenwald, ed., *Great Cases in Psychoanalysis*. New York: Aronson, 1973.

REISS, ALBERT J., JR. "Delinquency as the Failure of Personal and Social Controls," *American Sociological Review* 16 (1955).

_____, AND A. L. RHODES. "Status Deprivation and Delinquent Behavior," *Sociological Quarterly* 4 (Spring 1963), 136–49.

RHINE, LOUISA E. *Hidden Channels of the Mind*. New York: Morrow, 1961.

RIBTON-TURNER, C. J. *A History of Vagrants and Vagrancy and Beggars and Begging*. Monclair, N.J.: Patterson Smith, 1972; originally published London: Chapman and Hall, 1887.

RIESMAN, DAVID, RAUEL DENNEY, AND NATHAN GLASER. *The Lonely Crowd*. New Haven, Conn.: Yale University Press, 1950.

ROCHE, PHILIP Q. *The Criminal Mind*. New York: Grove, 1959.

ROCHMAN, S., AND J. TEASDALE. *Aversion Therapy and Behavior Disorders: An Analysis*. Coral Gables, Fla.: University of Miami Press, 1969.

ROEBUCK, JULIAN B. *Criminal Typology: The Legalistic, Physical, Constitutional, Hereditary, and Sociological Approaches*. Springfield, Ill.: Thomas, 1967.

_____, AND R. H. ATLAS. "Chromosomes and the Criminal," *Corrective Psychiatry and Journal of Social Therapy* 15 (1969).

_____, AND MERVYN L. CADWALLADER. "The Negro Armed Robber as a Criminal Type: The Construction and Application of a Typology," *Pacific Sociological Review* (Spring 1961).

ROGERS, CARL. "Client-Centered Therapy," in Silvano Arieti, ed., *American Handbook of Psychiatry*, vol. III. New York: Basic Books, 1966.

ROSANOFF, A. J., ET AL. "Criminality and Delinquency in Twins," *Journal of Criminal Law and Criminology* 24 (January–February 1934), 923–34.

ROSENBERG, BERNARD, AND HARRY SILVERSTEIN. *The Varieties of Delinquent Experience.* Waltham, Mass.: Blaisdell, 1969.

ROSENQUIST, CARL M., AND EDWIN I. MEGARGEE. *Delinquency in Three Cultures.* Austin: University of Texas Press, 1969.

ROSSI, PETER H., EMILY WAITE, CHRISTINE E. BOSSE, AND RICHARD E. BERK. "The Seriousness of Crimes: Normative Structure and Individual Differences," *American Sociological Review* 39 (April 1974), 224–237.

ROTHGEB, CARRIE LEE, ed. *Abstracts of the Standard Edition of the Complete Psychological Works of Sigmund Freud.* New York: Aronson, 1973.

ROTHMAN, DAVID. *The Discovery of the Asylum: Social Order and Disorder in the New Republic.* Boston: Little, Brown, 1971.

ROUKE, F. L. "Recent Contributions of Psychology to the Study of Criminal Justice," *Journal of Criminal Law and Criminology* 41 (November–December 1950), 446–55.

ROUSSEAU, JEAN JACQUES. *Emile*, trans. and ed. by W. H. Payne. New York: Appleton, 1892.

RUBENSTEIN, RICHARD L. "Age of Agony," *Research in Review* 75 (September 1982) 3–12. (Florida State University bulletin.)

RUDOFF, A. "The Soaring Crime Rate: An Etiological View," *Journal of Criminal Law, Criminology and Police Science* 62 (December 1971).

RUGGLES-BRISE, EVELYN. *The English Prison System.* London: Macmillan, 1910.

RULE, ANN. *The Stranger beside Me.* New York: Norton, 1980.

RUNYON, TOM. *In for Life.* New York: Norton, 1953.

———. "Prison Shocks," in Robert G. Caldwell, *Criminology.* New York: Ronald, 1956.

RUSHING, W. A. *Deviant Behavior and Social Progress.* Chicago: Rand McNalley, 1973.

SALERNO, RALPH, AND J. S. TOMPKINS. *The Crime Confederation: Cosa Nostra and Allied Operations in Organized Crime.* Garden City, N.Y.: Doubleday, 1969.

SARBIN. T. R. In *Crime & Delinquency* 25 (July 1979), 392–96.

SARGENT, WILLIAM. *The Mind Possessed.* Philadelphia: Lippincott, 1974.

SATCHELL, MICHAEL. "Bent, But Not Broken," *Parade*, October 10, 1982, pp. 6–7.

SATIR, VIRGINIA. *Conjoint Family Therapy.* Palo Alto, Calif.: Science and Behavior Books, 1974.

SAUL, LEON J. *Emotional Maturity.* Philadelphia: Lippincott, 1947.

SAXON, M. *White-Collar Crime—The Problem and the Federal Response.* Library of Congress Congressional Research Service, 1978.

SCHAFER, STEPHEN. *Restitution to Victims of Crime.* Chicago: Quadrangle, 1960.

———. *The Victim and His Criminal.* New York: Random House, 1968.

_____. *Theories in Criminology.* New York: Random House, 1969.

SCHANCHE, DON A. *The Panther Paradox: A Liberal's Dilemma.* New York: David McKay, 1970.

SCHAUSS, A., AND C. E. SIMONSEN. "A Critical Analysis of the Diets of Chronic Juvenile Offenders," *Journal of Orthopsychiatry* 8 (1975).

SCHEVERISH, PAUL G. "The Labeling Perspective: Its Bias and Potential in the Study of Political Deviance," *American Sociologist* 8 (May 1973).

SCHLAPP, M. G. "Behavior and Gland Disease," *Journal of Heredity* 15 (1924), 11.

_____, AND E. H. SMITH, *The New Criminology.* New York: Liveright, 1928.

SCHMID, C. F. "Urban Crime Areas: Part II," *American Sociological Review* 25 (October 1960).

SCHMIDEBERG, MELITTA. "Treating the Unwilling Patient," *British Journal of Delinquency* IX (October 1958), 117–21.

SCHRAG, CLARENCE. *Crime and Justice—American Style.* Washington, D.C.: U.S. Government Printing Office, 1971.

SCHUR, EDWIN M. "Deviance and Public Policy," in D. R. Cressey and D. A. Ward, eds., *Delinquency, Crime, and Social Process.* New York: Harper & Row, 1969.

SCHWARTZ, HERMAN S., ed. *Mental Health & Chiropractic: A Multidisciplinary Approach.* New York: Sessions, 1973.

SCHWARTZ, R. D., AND J. H. SKOLNICK, "Two Studies of Legal Stigma," *Social Problems* 10 (April 1962), 133–42.

SCHWENDINGER, HERMAN. "Editorial," *Crime and Social Justice* 1 (Spring-Summer 1974).

SCHWITZGEBEL, KENNETH L. *Development and Legal Regulation of Coercive Behavior Modification Techniques with Offenders.* Chevy Chase, Md.: National Institute of Mental Health Center for Studies of Crime and Delinquency, February 1971.

SEAGLE, WILLIAM. *The History of Law.* New York: Tudor, 1946.

SELCHRIST, ELSEI. *Dreams: Your Magic Mirror.* New York: Cowles, 1968.

SELLIN, THORSTEN. *Culture Conflict in Crime.* New York: Social Science Research Council, 1938.

_____. *Slavery and the Penal System.* New York: Elsevier, 1976.

SELZNICK, PHILIP. "The Sociology of Law," in Robert K. Merton, Leonard Broom, and Leonard S. Cottrell, Jr., eds., *Sociology Today: Problems and Prospects.* New York: Basic Books, 1959.

SHAPIRO, DAVID, T. X. BARBER, LEO V. DiCARA, JOE KAMIYA, NEAL E. MILLER, AND JOHANN STOYVA, eds. *Biofeedback and Self-Control—1972: An Aldine Annual on the Regulation of Bodily Processes and Consciousness.* Chicago: Aldine, 1973.

SHAW, CLIFFORD R. *The Jack-Roller.* Chicago: University of Chicago Press, 1930.

_____. *Brothers in Crime.* Chicago: University of Chicago Press, 1938.

————, AND HENRY D. McKAY, "Social Factors in Juvenile Delinquency," *Report on the Causes of Crime,* June 26, 1931.

————, AND HENRY D. McKAY. *Juvenile Delinquency and Urban Areas.* Chicago: University of Chicago Press, 1942 and 1969.

————, IN COLLABORATION WITH M. E. MOORE. *The Natural History of a Delinquent Career.* Chicago: University of Chicago Press, 1931.

SHAW, GEORGE BERNARD. *The Crime of Imprisonment.* New York: Philosophical Library, 1946.

SHEERER, M. "Cognitive Theory," in G. Lindzey, ed., *Handbook of Social Psychology.* Cambridge, Mass.: Addison-Wesley, 1954.

SHELDON, WILLIAM H. *Varieties of Temperament.* New York: Harper, 1942.

————. *Varieties of Delinquent Youth: An Introduction to Constitutional Psychiatry.* New York: Harper, 1949.

————, S. S. STEVENS, AND W. B. TUCKER. *Varieties of Human Physique.* New York: Harper, 1940.

————, EMIL M. HARTL, AND EUGENE McDERMOTT. *Varieties of Delinquent Youth.* New York: Harper, 1949.

SHIBUTANI, TAMOTSU. "Reference Groups as Perspectives," *American Journal of Sociology* 60 (May 1955), 562–69.

SHORT, JAMES F., JR. "Street Corner Group and Patterns of Delinquency: A Progress Report," *American Catholic Sociological Review* 24 (Spring 1963), 13-32.

————, AND F. IVAN NYE. "Extent of Unrecorded Juvenile Delinquency, Tentative Conclusions," *Journal of Criminal Law, Criminology and Police Science* 49 (1958), 296–302.

————, RAY A. TENNYSON, AND KENNETH I. HOWARD. "Behavior Dimensions of Gang Delinquency," *American Sociological Review* 28 (June 1963), 13–32.

SIMMEL, GEORG. "The Persistence of Social Groups," *American Journal of Sociology* 3 (1898), 662–98; 4, 35–40.

————. *Soziologie,* partially trans. by Albion W. Small, "The Sociology of Conflict," *American Journal of Sociology* 9 (1903–4), 490–501.

SIMPSON, R. L., AND H. M. MILLER. "Social Status and Anomia," *Social Problems* 10 (1936).

SINGER, RICHARD. "The Coming Right to Rehabilitation," in Michele G. Hermann and Marilyn G. Haft, eds., *Prisoners' Rights Sourcebook.* New York: Clark Boardman, 1973.

SKINNER, B. F. *Walden Two.* New York: Macmillan, 1948.

————. *Science and Human Behavior.* New York: Macmillan, 1953.

SMITH, PHILIP M. "Organized Religion and Criminal Behavior," *Sociology and Social Research* 33 (May 1949), 362–67.

SOBE, S. "Training School in Northern Nigeria," *Canadian Journal of Corrections* 4 (1962).

"Social Factors Affecting the Volume of Crime," in *Physical Basis of Crime: A*

Symposium. Easton, Pa.: American Academy of Medicine, 1914, pp. 53–67.

SOLOMON, PETER H. *Soviet Criminologists and Criminal Policy: Specialists in Policy-Making.* London: Macmillan, 1978.

SOROKIN, PITIRIM A. *Contemporary Sociological Theories.* New York: Harper, 1928.

_____. *Social and Cultural Dynamics.* New York: American Book, 1937.

SPARLING, JOHN. "Jury Selection," in Henry Wade, Prosecution Course. Dallas County District Attorney's Office with assistance from the Texas Criminal Justice Council, 1974.

SPENCER, HERBERT. *Sociology.* New York: Appleton, 1892.

_____. *Principles of Sociology.* New York: Appleton, 1897.

_____. *Shakespeare and the Nature of Man,* 2nd ed. New York: Macmillan, 1949.

SROLE, LEO. "Social Integration and Certain Corollaries," *American Sociological Review* 21 (December 1956), 709–16.

STAFFORD-CLARK, DAVID. *Crimes of Violence: The Report of a Conference on Crime Sponsored by the University of Colorado, August 15–18, 1949, on the Boulder Campus.* Boulder: University of Colorado Press, 1950.

STAINBROOK, E. "Experimentally Induced Conclusive Reactions of Laboratory Rats," *Journal of Comparative Psychology* 39 (1946), 243–64.

STARBUCK, E. D. "Contributions to the Psychology of Religion," *Journal of Psychology* 8 (1897).

_____. *Child Mind and Child Religion.* Chicago: University of Chicago Press, 1908.

Statistical Abstracts of the United States—1972. "No. 385. Farm Wage Workers—Characteristics and Earnings: 1969 and 1970." Washington, D.C.: Bureau of the Census, 1973.

Statistical Abstract of the United States—1982-83. "No. 78. Population in Institutions and Other Group Quarters, by Race, Type of Quarters, and Sex: 1960 and 1980." Washington, D.C.: Bureau of the Census, 1983.

STEARNS, A. W. "Unfit Personalities for the Military Services," In J. McV. Hunt, ed., *Personality and the Behavior Disorders,* vol. 2. New York: Ronald Press, 1944.

STERN, GARY S., C. ROBERT MILLER, HARWOOD W. EWY, AND PAMELA S. GRANT. "Perceived Control: Bogus Pulse Rate Feedback and Reported Symptom Reduction for Individuals with Accumulated Stressful Life Events," *Biofeedback & Self Regulation* 15 (March 1980), 37–49.

STITT, SONIA S. "Overt Masturbation in the Classroom," *American Journal of Orthopsychiatry* 10 (1940), 801–4.

STOCK, R. W. "XYY and the Criminal," *New York Times Magazine,* October 20, 1938.

STONE, CALVIN P. "A Comparative Study of the Intelligence of Three-Hundred-Fifty Men of the United States," *Journal of Criminal Law and Criminology* 12 (1921), 238–57.

STONE, W. CLEMENT. *The Success System That Never Fails.* Englewood Cliffs, N.J.: Prentice-Hall, 1962.

STRAHL, MARGARET O., AND NOLAN D. C. LEWIS, eds. *Differential Diagnosis in Clinical Psychiatry: The Lectures of Paul H. Hoch.* New York: Science House, 1972.

STRATTON, J. R. "Differential Identification and Attitudes toward the Law," *Social Forces* 46 (1967), 256–62.

STRUPP, HANS H. "The Outcome Problem in Psychotherapy Revisited," in Alvin R. Mahrer and Leonard Pearson, eds., *Creative Developments in Psychotherapy.* New York: Aronson, 1973.

Study of Criminological Course Offerings, questionnaire. Del Mar, Calif.: CRM Books, 1974.

STÜRUP, GEORG K. *Treating the "Untreatable": Chronic Criminals at Herstedvester.* Baltimore: Johns Hopkins Press, 1968a.

———. *Treatment of Sexual Offenders in Herstedvester, Denmark: The Rapist.* Copenhagen: Munksgaard, 1968b.

SUMPHAUZER, J. S. *Behavior Modification with Juvenile Delinquents: A Critical Review* 1 (Tallahassee: Federal Correctional Institution, 1970).

SUTHERLAND, E. H. "Is 'White-Collar Crime' Crime?" *American Sociological Review* 10 (April 1945), 132–39.

———. *White Collar Crime.* New York: Dryden, 1949.

———, AND DONALD R. CRESSEY. *Principles of Criminology,* 7th ed. Philadelphia and New York: Lippincott, 1966.

———, AND DONALD R. CRESSEY. *Criminology,* 10th ed. New York and Philadelphia: Lippincott, 1978.

SYKES, GRESHAM M. "Men, Merchants, and Toughs: A Study of Reactions to Imprisonment," *Social Forces* 4 (1956), 130–38.

———. "The Pains of Imprisonment," in *The Society of Captives, a Study of Maximum Security Prison.* Princeton, N.J.: Princeton University Press, 1958.

———. "The Rise of Critical Criminology," *Journal of Criminal Law and Criminology* 65 (June 1974), 206–213.

———. *Criminology.* New York: Harcourt Brace Jovanovich, 1978.

———, AND DAVID MATZA. "Techniques of Neutralization: A Theory of Delinquency," *American Sociological Review* 22 (1957), 664–70.

SZASZ, THOMAS S. "The Myth of Mental Illness," *American Psychologist* 15 (1960), 113–18.

———. *The Myth of Mental Illness.* New York: Hoeber Medical Books, 1962.

———. *The Manufacture of Madness.* New York: Harper & Row, 1970.

———. "Crime, Punishment, and Psychiatry," in Abraham S. Blumberg, ed., *Current Perspectives in Criminal Behavior.* New York: Knopf, 1974.

TAFT, DONALD R., AND RALPH W. ENGLAND, JR. *Criminology,* 4th ed. New York: Macmillan, 1964.

TANNENBAUM, FRANK. *Crime and the Community.* New York: Columbia University Press, 1936.

TARDE, GABRIEL. *Les lois de l'imitation.* Paris: Alcan, 1890; English trans. by E. C. Parsons. New York: Holt, 1903.

———. *Penal Philosophy*, trans. by R. Howell. Boston: Little, Brown, 1912.

TARTER, D. E. "Heeding Skinner's Call: Toward the Development of a Social Technology," *American Sociologist* 8 (November 1973), 153–58.

Task Force Report: Organized Crime. Washington, D.C.: President's Commission on Law Enforcement and Administration of Justice, 1967.

TAYLOR, IAN, PAUL WALTON, AND JOCK YOUNG. *The New Criminology.* London: Routledge & Kegan Paul, 1973, and New York: Harper & Row, 1973.

"Terrorism in California." Sacramento, Calif. Dept. of Corrections, 1974. Summarized in *Criminal Justice Digest* 2 (July 1974), 1–8.

THOMAS, DOROTHY SWAINE. *Social Aspects of the Business Cycle.* London: Routledge & Kegan Paul, 1925.

THOMAS, W. I. *The Unadjusted Girl.* Boston: Little, Brown, 1923 and 1937.

THORNBERRY, TERENCE P., AND JOSEPH E. JOCOBY. *The Criminally Insane: A Community Follow-up of Mentally Ill Offenders.* Chicago: The University of Chicago Press, 1979.

THORNDIKE, H. L. *Animal Intelligence.* New York: Macmillan, 1911.

THORNE, FREDERICK C. "Diagnostic Implications of Integrative Psychology," in Alvin R. Mahrer, ed., *New Approaches to Personality Classification.* New York: Columbia University Press, 1970.

THRASHER, FREDERIC M. *The Gang.* Chicago: University of Chicago Press, 1927.

TIBBITTS, CLARK. "Reliability of Factors Used in Predicting Success or Failure on Parole," *Journal of Criminal Law and Criminology* 22 (1932), 855–84.

TIMASHEFF, NICHOLAS S. *Sociological Theory: Its Nature and Growth*, 3rd ed. New York: Random House, 1955.

TOBY, JACKSON. "The Differential Impact of Family Disorganization," *American Sociological Review* 22 (October 1957), 505–12.

TOCH, HANS. "Introduction to Legal Psychology," in Hans Toch, ed., *Legal and Criminal Psychology.* New York: Holt, Rinehart and Winston, 1961.

———, ed. *Legal and Criminal Psychology.* New York: Holt, Rinehart and Winston, 1961.

TOLAND, JOHN. *The Dillinger Days.* New York: Random House, 1963.

TRUAX, C. B., AND K. M. MITCHELL. "Research on Certain Therapist Interpersonal Skills in Relation to Process and Outcome," in Allen E. Bergin and Sol L. Garfield, eds., *Handbook of Psychotherapy and Behavior Change.* New York: Wiley, 1971.

TULCHIN, SIMON H. *Intelligence and Crime.* Chicago: University of Chicago Press, 1939.

TURK, AUSTIN. "Conflict and Criminality," *American Sociological Review* 31 (June 1956), 338–52.

———. *Criminality and Legal Order.* Chicago: Rand McNally, 1969.

TURK, AUSTIN T., *Political Criminality: The Defiance and Defense of Authority.* Beverly Hills: Sage Publications, 1982.

TURNER, R. H. "The Role Taking, Role Standpoint, and Reference Group Behavior," *American Journal of Sociology* 61 (January 1956), 316–28.

TYLER, GUS, ed. *Organized Crime in America: A Book of Readings.* Ann Arbor: University of Michigan Press, 1962.

U.S. CONGRESS, House Committee on Internal Security, Black Panther Party, 91st Cong., 2nd sess., 1970; also *Staff Study—The Black Panther Party. Its Origin and Development as Reflected in Its Official Weekly Newspaper, The Black Panther, Black Community News.* Washington, D.C.: House of Representatives, 1970.

U.S. Department of Transportation, Office of Civil Aviation Security, Federal Aviation Administration, *Aircraft Hijackings and Other Criminal Acts Against Civil Aviation, Statistical and Narrative Reports–Updated to January 1, 1983.* Washington, D.C. (May 1983) 1.

VAN SERTIMA, IVAN. *They Came before Columbus,* New York: Random House, 1976.

VETTER, HAROLD J., AND JACK WRIGHT. *Introduction to Criminology.* Springfield, Ill.: Thomas, 1974.

———, AND IRA J. SILVERMAN. *The Nature of Crime.* Philadelphia: Saunders, 1978.

"Violent Crime and the E.E.G.," *British Medical Journal* 2 (1970).

VOLD, GEORGE B. *Theoretical Criminology.* New York: Oxford University Press, 1958.

VOLLMER, AUGUST. "Community Coordination," in V. A. Leonard, ed., *Police Organization and Management.* Brooklyn, N.Y.: Foundation Press, 1964.

VORRATH, HARRY. *Guided Group Interaction.* Red Wing, Minn.: Minnesota State Training School, 1969.

———, AND LARRY K. BRENDTRO. *Positive Peer Culture.* Chicago: Aldine, 1974.

WALLACE, R. K., AND H. BENSON. "The Physiology of Meditation," *Scientific American,* February 1972, 85–90.

WARD, DAVID A., AND GENE G. KASSEBAUM. "Homosexuality: A Mode of Adaptation in a Prison for Women," *Social Problems* 12 (Fall 1964), 159–77.

———, AND GENE G. KASSEBAUM. *Women's Prisons.* Chicago: Aldine, 1965.

WARNER, SAM B. "Factors Determining Parole from the Massachusetts Reformatory," *Journal of Criminal Law and Criminology* 14 (1923), 5–14.

WARREN, M. Q. "The Case for Differential Treatment of Delinquents," *Annals of the American Academy of Political and Social Science* 381 (January 1969), 47–59.

———. "Differential Treatment," in *Inscape* (Fall 1971), 23–26.

———. *Correctional Treatment in the Community Setting: A Report of Current Research.* Washington, D.C.: National Institute of Mental Health, 1972.

WATTENBERG, W. W. "Church Attendance and Juvenile Misconduct," *Sociology and Social Research* 34 (January 1950), 195–202.

WECHSLER, HERBERT. "The Challenge of a Modern Penal Code," *Harvard Law Review* 65 (1952), 1105–30.

WEINER, SAUL, GRANT SUTHERLAND, ALLAN A. BARTHOLOMEW, AND BRYAN HUDSON. "XYY Males in a Melbourne Prison," *Lancet*, January 20, 1938, 150.

WEISINGER, MORT. "Is Astrology a $100 Million Hoax?" *Parade*, June 3, 1973, 5.

WENDT, HERBERT. *From Ape to Adam: The Search for the Ancestry of Man.* Indianapolis: Bobbs-Merrill, 1972.

WEXLER, DAVID B. "Token and Taboo: Behavior Modification, Token Economies, and the Law," *California Law Review* 61 (1973), 81–109.

WHEELER, STANTON. "Socialization in Correctional Communities," *American Sociological Review* 26 (October 1961).

_____, AND LEONARD S. COTTRELL, JR. "The Labeling Process," in *Juvenile Delinquency: Its Prevention and Control.* New York: Russell Sage Foundation, 1966.

WHIPPLE, G. C. *Vital Statistics.* New York: Wiley, 1923.

WHITE, R. C. "A Study of Residence and Place of Offense of Felons in Indianapolis," *Social Forces* 10 (May 1932).

WHYTE, WILLIAM F. "Small Groups and Large Organizations," in J. H. Rohrer and M. Sherif, eds., *Social Psychology of the Cross Roads.* New York: Harper, 1951.

_____. *Street Corner Society.* Chicago: University of Chicago Press, 1955.

WICKS, NORMAN. "Reality Therapy—Socialization: New Model, Old Make?" *Proceedings of the Ninth Annual Research Meeting* 2 (April 1969), 135–38. State of Washington: Department of Institutions Research Report.

WICKS, R. J. *Applied Psychology for Law Enforcement and Correction Officers.* New York: McGraw-Hill, 1974a.

_____. *Correction Psychology: Themes and Problems in Correcting the Offender.* San Francisco: Canfield, 1974b.

WILKERSON, D. R., WITH JOHN AND ELIZABETH SHERRILL. *The Cross and the Switchblade.* New York: Geis, 1963.

WILKINSON, J. E., D. P. MULLEN, AND R. B. MORTON. "Sensitivity Training for Individual Growth—Team Training for Organization Development?" *Training and Development Journal* 22 (1968), 47–53.

WILLIAMS, HENRI. "Politics of Venereal Disease," *The Burning Spear, African People's Socialist Party* 3 (May 15–June 15, 1974).

WILLIAMS, R. M., JR. *American Society.* New York: Knopf, 1951.

WILSON, CICERO, KENNETH J. LENIHAN, AND GAIL A. GOOLKASIAN. *Employment Services for Ex-offenders: Program Models.* Washington, D.C.: U.S. National Institute of Justice, by Abt Associates, 1981.

WILSON, MARGARET S. "Pioneers in Criminology—Gabriel Tarde," *Journal of*

Criminal Law, Criminology and Police Science 45 (May—June 1954), 3–11.

WILSON, ROB. "Who Will Care for the 'Mad and Bad?' " *Corrections Magazine,* February 1980.

WINES, ENOCH C., ed. *Transactions of the National Congress on Penitentiary and Reformatory Discipline Held at Cincinnati, Ohio, October 12–18, 1870.* Reprint. College Park, Md.: American Correctional Association, 1970.

WINN, STEVEN, AND DAVID MERRILL. *Ted Bundy: The Killer Next Door.* New York: Bantam, 1980.

WIRTH, LOUIS. "Urbanism as a Way of Life," *American Journal of Sociology* 44 (July 1938), 3–24.

WITTMER, H. L., AND RUTH KOTINSKY, eds. *New Perspectives for Research on Juvenile Delinquency.* Washington, D.C.: U.S. Department of Health, Education and Welfare, 1955.

WOLFGANG, MARVIN. *Patterns in Criminal Homicide.* Philadelphia: University of Pennsylvania Press, 1958.

YABLONSKY, LEWIS. *The Violent Gang.* New York: Macmillan, 1962.

YOCHELSON, SAMUEL, AND STANTON E. SAMENOW. *The Criminal Personality,* vol. I, *A Profile for Change.* New York: Aronson, 1976.

———, AND STANTON E. SAMENOW. *The Criminal Personality,* vol. II, *The Change Process.* New York: Aronson, 1977.

ZELANY, L. D. "Feeblemindedness and Criminal Conduct," *American Journal of Sociology* 38 (January 1933), 564–76.

ZELDES, ILYA. *The Problems of Crime in the U.S.S.R.* Springfield, Ill.: Thomas, 1981.

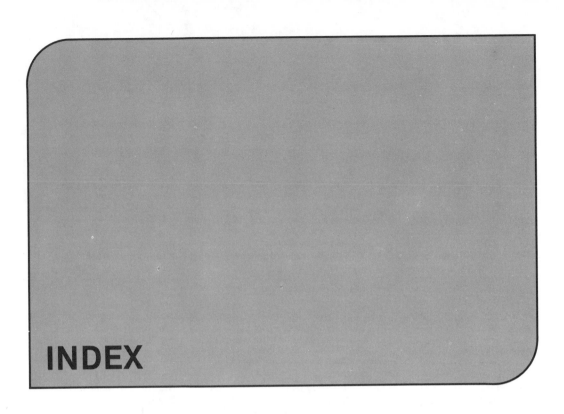

INDEX